Stratification and Inequality Series
The Center for the Study of Social Stratification and Inequality,
Tohoku University, Japan
Volume 5

Social Justice in Japan

Stratification and Inequality Series

The Center for the Study of Social Stratification and Inequality,
Tohoku University, Japan

Inequality amid Affluence: Social Stratification in Japan
Junsuke Hara and Kazuo Seiyama

Intentional Social Change: A Rational Choice Theory
Yoshimichi Sato

Constructing Civil Society in Japan: Voices of Environmental Movements
Koichi Hasegawa

Deciphering Stratification and Inequality: Japan and beyond
Yoshimichi Sato

Social Justice in Japan: Concepts, Theories and Paradigms
Ken-ichi Ohbuchi

Stratification and Inequality Series
The Center for the Study of Social Stratification and Inequality,
Tohoku University, Japan
Volume 5

Social Justice in Japan

Concepts, Theories and Paradigms

Edited by

Ken-ichi Ohbuchi

Translated by
Leonie R. Stickland

This English edition first published in 2007 by
Trans Pacific Press, PO Box 120, Rosanna, Melbourne, Victoria 3084, Australia
Telephone: +61 (0)3-9459-3021 Fax: +61 (0)3-9457-5923
Email: info@transpacificpress.com
Web: http://www.transpacificpress.com

Copyright © Trans Pacific Press 2007

Designed and set by digital environs, Melbourne. http://www.digitalenvirons.com

Printed by BPA Print Group, Burwood, Victoria, Australia

Distributors

Australia and New Zealand
UNIREPS
University of New South Wales
Sydney, NSW 2052
Australia
Telephone: +61(0)2-9664-0999
Fax: +61(0)2-9664-5420
Email: info.press@unsw.edu.au
Web: http://www.unireps.com.au

USA and Canada
International Specialized Book Services (ISBS)
920 NE 58th Avenue, Suite 300
Portland, Oregon 97213-3786
USA
Telephone: (800) 944-6190
Fax: (503) 280-8832
Email: orders@isbs.com
Web: http://www.isbs.com

Asia and the Pacific
Kinokuniya Company Ltd.

Head office:
Shin-Mizonokuchi Bldg. 2F
5-7 Hisamoto 3-chome
Takatsu-ku, Kawasaki 213-8506
Japan
Telephone: +81(0)44-874-9642
Fax: +81(0)44-829-1025
Email: bkimp@kinokuniya.co.jp
Web: www.kinokuniya.co.jp

Asia-Pacific office:
Kinokuniya Book Stores of Singapore Pte., Ltd.
391B Orchard Road #13-06/07/08
Ngee Ann City Tower B
Singapore 238874
Telephone: +65-6276-5558
Fax: +65-6276-5570
Email: SSO@kinokuniya.co.jp

All rights reserved. No production of any part of this book may take place without the written permission of Trans Pacific Press.

ISBN 978-1-876843-78-6 (Hardback)
ISBN 978-1-876843-84-7 (Paperback)

Contents

Figures	vi
Tables	viii
Preface *Ken-ichi Ohbuchi*	ix
Acknowledgements	xviii
List of contributors	xix

Part I: The Sense of Justice and Fairness and its Outcomes
1 The Social Bonds of Justice: Theory and Research
    Ken-ichi Ohbuchi 3
2 A Sense of Unfairness as Stratum Consciousness in
    Contemporary Japan *Michio Umino* 34
3 Distributive Fairness and Procedural Fairness in Ultimatum
    Bargaining *Mitsuteru Fukuno* 55
4 The Structure of Justice: Theoretical Considerations
    Ken-ichi Ohbuchi 72
5 Procedural Justification in Egalitarian Resource Allocation
    Shinobu Kitani 93

Part II: Justice and Fairness in Social Relations
6 Forgiveness and Justice: Victim Psychology in Conflict
    Resolution *Naomi Takada* and *Ken-ichi Ohbuchi* 107
7 Justified Discrimination *Tōru Tamura* 127
8 Self-recognition in Japanese Culture: Discrimination and
    Assimilation *Toshitake Takata* 149
9 Intra-group Fairness, Group Identification and Inter-group
    Aggression *Tomohiro Kumagai* 171
10 Is Fairness Useful for Stress Management in Organisations?
    Yōichirō Hayashi and *Naotaka Watanabe* 192

Part III: Justice and Fairness and Social Problem-Solving
11 Consensus-building in Public Development: Fairness
    Theory and the Creation of a New Field of Research
    Toshiaki Aoki 211
12 Sociological Perspectives on Environmental Justice: The
    Case of a German Residents' Movement *Sōko Aoki* 239
13 The Procedural Fairness of Public Participation in
    Environmental Planning: The Karlsruhe Project
    Yukio Hirose 264

Notes	291
Bibliography	295
Index	330

Figures

1.1	The justice-bond hypothesis	5
1.2	Group values and group-orientation	8
1.3	Evaluation of organs of state, perceptions of social justice, and attitudes towards the state	15
1.4	Assessment of attitudes towards the state by age	17
1.5	Justice bonds vis-à-vis the state and distributive/procedural justice	18
1.6	Influence of perceptions of multi-level fairness on life satisfaction and attitudes toward the state	20
1.7	Perceived social fairness and protest action	23
1.8	The relationship between perceived fairness, immutability belief and normative protest	23
1.9	Two theoretical models relating to litigant responses	26
1.10	The influence of self-interest and procedural fairness upon the responses of civil litigants	27
1.11	Attitudes to the company organisation and fairness evaluation	31
3.1	The effect upon the social utility function of the relationship between parties in conflict	57
3.2	Fairness evaluation of role-assignment procedures	63
3.3	Path diagram relating to offer/proposal acceptability	65
3.4	Evaluation of allocator neutrality in the offer process	66
4.1	The conceptual relationship between justice and fairness	85
5.1	Feasible advantage area	97
5.2	The Nash bargaining solution	97
5.3	The Kalai-Smorodinsky solution	99
6.1	The content of third-party utterances and forgiving behaviour	125
7.1	Path analysis of the effect exerted by dehumanising labels and the aggression of the other upon aggressive behaviour	146
8.1	Intercultural disparity in the self-devaluative tendency	151
8.2	Disparity in self-devaluation/self-enhancement due to presence or absence of competition	157
8.3	Self/other status and emotional experience	159

8.4	Self/other status and self-devaluative or self-enhancing tendencies	160
8.5	Basic modes of self-recognition and related theories	167
9.1	The dual group-identification model	183
9.2	Average scores by condition in items on acceptance and group identification	187
9.3	Results of path analysis on group identification due to voice and acceptance	188
9.4	Results of ANOVA by voice and victim in relation to intensity of aggression	189
10.1.	Correlated uniqueness model	202
10.2	Hypothesis (Full Mediation): a model to which alternative model paths have been added	204
11.1	Classification of consensus-building studies relating to public development	215
11.2	Procedural fairness and participatory behaviour	220
11.3	The relationship between fairness and place-attachment/ community pride	221
11.4	The framework of general fairness studies	225
11.5	The theoretical structure of the attitude-formation mechanism	228
11.6	Attitude-formation when there is inadequate presentation of information (low self-relevance group)	229
11.7	Attitude-formation when there is adequate presentation of information (low self-relevance group)	230
11.8	Comparison between a superficial conformity group and an internal conformity group (ratings)	235
11.9	The route of influence of peer pressure	236
12.1	The geographical location of Wackersdorf, Germany	249
12.2	Structural outline of the confrontation (prior to site occupation)	258
12.3	Structural outline of the confrontation (after site occupation)	260
13.1	Procedures of citizen participation in Karlsruhe	271
13.2	Structural model of public acceptance of the plan	286

Tables

1.1	Protest items and their factor analysis	22
2.1	Stratum consciousness relating to social evaluation	36
2.2	Prescribed factors for a sense of unfairness in general	45
2.3	The correlation between a sense of unfairness and life satisfaction	47
2.4	The correlation between a sense of unfairness and life satisfaction (when statistically controlled by a sense of satisfaction with society)	47
2.5	The relationship between recognition of the 'principle of ideal social-resource allocation' and the 'principle of actual social-resource allocation'	52
4.1	The meanings of *seigi*, *kōsei* and *kōhei* in Japanese	74
4.2	Notions of justice/fairness in the history of Western thought	83
4.3	Fairness criteria and social principles	89
5.1	The calculation of egalitarian equivalents	99
6.1	Motivations for forgiveness	113
6.2	Correlations between motives for forgiveness and forgiving behaviour	114
6.3	Correlations between 14 strategies and forgiveness	115
6.4	The benefits and costs of forgiveness and retribution	118
7.1	Effect of dehumanising labels: means and standard deviations of social concerns, perception of hostility and aggressive behaviour	145
10.1.	Mean values, standard deviations and correlation coefficients	200
10.2	Results of confirmatory factor analysis of organisational justice	202
10.3	Fit index of examined models	204
11.1	Results of binominal logistic regression analysis	234
12.1	Events related to the nuclear reprocessing plant in Wackersdorf	253

Preface
Ken-ichi Ohbuchi

Among Western scholars, the Japanese have been seen as having a feeble sense of justice, and fairness as being disregarded in Japanese society (Kidder and Muller, 1991; Triandis, 1995). The rationale for this view was that Japanese people had a weak awareness of individual rights, and that their judgements were made according to tradition and social custom. In actual fact, a values survey conducted with Japanese participants some fifteen years ago shows that values such as affluence and efficiency occupied the top ranks, with fairness only figuring in seventeenth place. If a similar survey were to be conducted now, however, justice/fairness would probably rank among the top three.

There have been numerous phenomena in recent years which suggest a heightened concern for fairness among the Japanese. In elections, there are growing numbers of cases in which candidates who appeal to civic sensibilities make a good showing at the polls, the conventional form of organisational election which emphasises the dispensation of favours no longer being accepted. Candidates emphasise the dispensation of favours because they assume that electors are only interested in their own profit and loss, but the values of the electorate actually have already changed. Even more than personal profit and loss, might not the majority of Japanese citizens be eager to see this country in which they live being run in a just manner? A values-gap has opened up between politicians who think light of fairness and citizens who attach weight to it, and this might also be considered a fundamental cause of the public distrust of politics of recent years.

As such, fairness has steadily emerged as an important pivotal point of evaluation among the Japanese when examining social issues. In the second chapter of this volume, Michio Umino ventures to attribute this to Japanese people's loss of their previous ability to believe simplistically in future happiness, due both to the dampening of rapid economic growth, and to their becoming able to survey their surroundings and compare themselves with others. Until now, however, there was insufficient investigation into issues relating to the Japanese view of justice, such as the criteria the Japanese use to judge fairness, for example, or the cognitive processes of fairness-judgement, or, moreover, how evaluating a certain social event as fair or unfair alters people's responses to that event.

This book is a compilation of papers by Japanese scholars who are grappling with these very issues. The authors are researchers from the fields of social psychology and sociology, and they approach the question of the Japanese view of fairness through diverse methods, including theoretical analysis, mathematical analysis, laboratory experimentation, survey research, field studies, and so on. It is not easy to discuss these in an integrated manner, nor is it claimed that these papers clarify every aspect of the Japanese view of fairness. Even so, each chapter, in its own way, incorporates meaningful and productive research which imparts a sense of future development potential. The chapters are introduced below.

The composition of this volume

The first section is made up of five papers which theoretically and empirically examine the mechanism of fairness judgement, using Japanese participants. Psychological researchers into justice hitherto have mainly studied the behaviour of people who have been treated unjustly, but Chapter One, written by Ken-ichi Ohbuchi, focuses not upon that aspect, but upon what happens in people who have been treated justly, and, especially, the long-term effects of the latter treatment. The author has investigated the Japanese perception of justice by targeting the state and the government, the judicial courts and the legal system, and corporate organisations, finding that, in relation to any of these social organisations, such positive attitudes as pride and attachment were strengthened and cooperative behaviour towards the institutions increased among people who perceived them to be just. The author's findings demonstrate that, for the Japanese, justice fulfils the role of a bond which binds individuals to groups. Of particularly deep interest is research which examines the links among perceptions of fairness, immutability beliefs in the state and protest action, the author having elucidated the characteristics of social movements in Japan, based on his findings that, while the majority of Japanese people harbours an 'immutability belief in the state' – a belief that the basic structure of Japanese society will remain fundamentally unchanged, regardless of any change of government – it is those who believe that the society is capable of change, even while perceiving Japanese society to be unfair, who most eagerly engage in protest action.

In Chapter Two, Michio Umino has utilised data from the Social Stratification and Mobility Surveys (SSM Surveys) which have been repeatedly implemented in Japan to examine how people's perception of fairness vis-à-vis the allocation of social resources differs among various strata (according to educational background, occupational position and income). Sixty per cent of Japanese people harboured feelings of unfairness towards society, the principal reason being differences in social achievement due to educational background. As the main status-achievement route in Japanese society is taken as being 'high educational background → high-stratum occupation → high income' (Tominaga, 1979), it was predicted that people with a superior educational background, or those engaged in occupations gained through higher education, such as professional or managerial occupations, would have a lower sense of unfairness, but the survey results indicated the opposite. Umino offers a relative deprivation interpretation, arguing that though such people think that they, personally, with their high educational qualifications and high-level occupations, are entitled to receive high incomes, they actually feel that 'just because they have obtained high educational qualifications, it does not necessarily follow that they are advantaged in terms of income,' and the gap between their expectations and reality gives rise to a sense of unfairness. In addition, while most Japanese consider that it is fair for resource allocation to be carried out according to the principle of 'effort,' in actual practice, they recognise that, on the contrary, resource allocation is conducted in accordance with the 'achievement' principle, and regard this, also, as one of the reasons for the pervasive sense of unfairness.

Conflict of interest is inevitable among people who engage in social life. It can occur not only in the workplace, but also in local communities, schools, or even in families. Negotiation is a standard means employed by people in times of conflict. If the parties involved are preoccupied only with self-interest, then it will be difficult to achieve consensus, so it is necessary to strive for resolution from a more social perspective which transcends self-interest. In such instances, what people are interested in is fairness. The paper by Mitsuteru Fukuno, comprising Chapter Three, uses the experimental paradigm called ultimatum bargaining to examine how people respond to the rivalry between the maximisation of self-interest and the attainment of fairness – the fundamental motivations of negotiating parties. The behaviour exhibited by participants in those situations is not consistent with the maximisation of self-interest, and the author interprets this as proof of people's behaviour being regulated not merely by self-interest, but also by fairness concern. Fukuno's paper additionally focuses upon individual divergence in fairness concern.

The fact that justice and fairness are polysemic concepts has contributed to the confusion in understanding which has arisen in relation to this issue. In Chapter Four, Ohbuchi takes up this challenge, proposing new theory relating to the links between justice and fairness. Unlike other scholars of fairness, Ohbuchi regards justice and fairness as different things. He sees justice (*seigi*) as the goal for which certain social groups aim, or social ideals (such as freedom and equality, democracy, social welfare, and industrial nation-building, or state order, religious doctrine, and the like). Fairness (*kōsei*), on the other hand, is defined according to a 'Treatment/Deservedness' formula. 'Deservedness' refers to individuals' qualifications, entitlements and rights, while 'Treatment' means things of positive or negative value which individuals receive, such as compensation, rewards, penalties, and so on. The major point in Ohbuchi's theory is that deservedness in the fairness formula is governed by justice. In a society which has freedom and equality as its social ideal, for example, individual achievement is seen to be deservedness in judgements of fairness. Conversely, contribution to the state, in a society with the maintenance of state order as its social ideal, or faith and devotion, in a society with religious doctrine as its social ideal, will probably be what constitutes deservedness, which itself regulates fair resource-allocation. In this way, in his paper, Ohbuchi has proposed a new theory of the structure of fairness which regards deservedness – one of the elements of fairness judgements – as being something which is founded upon justice.

Shinobu Kitani's paper, comprising Chapter Five, is also a theoretical one, but, unlike Ohbuchi's in the previous chapter, it strives to clarify the meaning of fairness from a perspective of rationality like that of game theory. When people acknowledge only the freedom to pursue individual advantage, without making equality or efficiency the rule, as this also results in similar egalitarian allocations, the author asserts that equality and fairness are not a priori propositions, but are the consequence of individuals' rational choice. That which is deemed in this analysis to be the advantage which people pursue is not an objective good such as mere money or property. What A. Sen calls 'capability' is a kind of broad-ranging convenience, a right to live in affluence which is brought about by objective goods, and Kitani replaces this with the notion of 'priority,' a favourite term employed by G.A. Cohen and others. This point, too, reflects the author's endeavours to discard the narrow hypotheses which were common in conventional game theory and mathematical analysis, and to zero in upon the more realistic behavioural mechanism which people adopt.

Part Two is made up of five papers which examine the role played by fairness in the occurrence and resolution of social conflict. In order to resolve social conflicts where there is a clash of self-interest among the parties involved, it is necessary to appeal to a principle with a more highly public nature, one which transcends individual profit and loss – in other words, the principle of justice and fairness. Nevertheless, as can be seen in situations such as ethnic conflict, this principle often incurs the reward of vengeance, and sometimes exacerbates conflict rather than dampening it. For this reason, forgiveness is sought from the parties involved, but forgiveness and justice/fairness seem at first glance to be contradictory principles. This is because forgiveness includes the relinquishment of the legitimate exercise of right. Might there be a way of avoiding the contradiction between forgiveness and justice, and reconciling the two? In Chapter Six, Naomi Takada and Ken-ichi Ohbuchi grapple both theoretically and empirically with this difficult challenge. According to Ohbuchi, who has defined justice as a social ideal, justice is not a single entity. The one among its elements which stands in opposition to forgiveness is a view of justice which takes respect for individual rights as its social ideal. Conversely, if a view of justice which has social harmony as its social ideal is emphasised, then this will probably promote forgiveness, instead. The authors cite examples of empirical research, suggesting that a departure from a narrow view of justice would enable the harmonisation of justice and forgiveness.

The most serious form of social injustice is discrimination of various types. This means the unjustifiably unfair treatment of people from certain groups, behind which lie bias and stereotypes referring to minorities, foreigners, and believers in other religions. The vital psychological factor necessary for escaping such warped social cognition and treating the people it targets fairly is empathy – in other words, perceiving the targets without distortion, as fellow human beings. In actuality, however, this is difficult, because numerous systems and stimuli which facilitate distorted social cognition exist in the social environment. In Chapter Seven, Tōru Tamura discusses such systems and stimuli as these, later focusing upon dehumanising labels, the effects of which he has attempted to verify experimentally. Dehumanising labelling refers to derogatory terms such as 'Axis of Evil' or 'devils and beasts (*kichiku*)' which are used to indicate certain specific individuals or groups, and which demean their targets, emphasising the latter's low value. It is clear from analysis of wartime mass media and case studies of bullying, as well, that such labelling has fuelled people's enmity and aggression, and has played a part in the aggravation of social conflict and discrimination. In this chapter, the author uses experimental methods to attempt an analysis of the effect and social psychological mechanism of dehumanising labelling.

Chapter Eight, by Toshitake Takata, is a discussion of the dynamics of Japanese people's self-recognition from the viewpoint of cultural psychology. Though a tendency towards self-enhancement is common among Westerners, the Japanese, conversely, show a self-deprecating bent. In relation to this, there is a view which attributes this to a Japanese motivation for self-betterment which constantly strives to direct individuals' attention to their own faults, and to rectify them. Takata, however, has made it clear that the situation is not as simple as that, asserting that Japanese self-recognition changes depending upon group circumstances. He cites two types: self-other distinction by means of downward comparison, and self-other assimilation, which emphasises similarity – while the Japanese are fundamentally self-other assimilatory, underlining their similarity with other members of their in-group, they make self-other distinctions vis-à-vis others belonging to out-groups, meaning that downward comparison intensifies. In consequence, there is an underlying modality of self-recognition in Japanese culture in both tendencies, whether of self-enhancement or self-devaluation, and Takata concludes that their manifestation differs according to group circumstances.

Chapter Nine, by Tomohiro Kumagai, is a paper which aims to elucidate the mechanism of the escalation of group conflict typically seen in inter-ethnic struggles. Here, the author concentrates upon the role of fairness. People who perceive that they have been treated fairly within their group strengthen their identification with the group, and cooperative behaviour also increases (Chapter One of this volume). Kumagai theoretically examines the factors in group identification, positing that fair treatment gives rise to group attraction in terms of a sense of assurance and self-definition, and, on this assumption, he empirically investigates its influence upon group conflict. One of the causes of the escalation of inter-group conflict is the aggressive intervention of third parties other than the immediate victims. Through experimental research, the author has proven his hypothesis that, if a third party observes how members of his/her in-group are harmed, that third party will interpret this as his/her own group having been attacked, and thus will be motivated towards retaliatory action. Moreover, the stronger the group identification, the greater will be the possibility of aggressive intervention. There are points worth noting in the study by this author who asserts that, in groups of Japanese people, intra-group fair treatment has the negative effect of intensifying inter-group conflict.

Fairness in the workplace is also an important theme, and the fact that Japanese employees who perceive that they are being treated fairly further cement their bond with their company has also been discussed by Ohbuchi in the first chapter. In Chapter Ten, Yōichirō Hayashi and Naotaka Watanabe focus upon organisational fairness from the viewpoint of employee well-being and welfare, including stress management and mental health. There are many stresses in the workplace, but the authors have postulated that the response to these is moderated by trust in the organisation. Using Japanese company employees as their research participants, Hayashi and Watanabe tested their hypothesis which says that the stress response would be weak in employees who, though experiencing stress, perceived the fairness of the organisation, and had a strong sense of trust in it. SEM (Structural Equation Modelling) analysis supported their hypothesis, and, based on its results, the authors have proposed that, in these times of increasing fluidity in the labour market, Japanese firms should also make positive efforts to improve the level of perceived fairness among their employees.

Part Three comprises papers which discuss issues concerning the environment – a point of social controversy in Japan in recent years – from the viewpoint of fairness. Chapter Eleven is a paper by Toshiaki Aoki which focuses upon public development in Japan. During its period of rapid economic growth, Japanese society saw an advance in infrastructure development, and today, in a quantitative sense, the necessity for public development has decreased. At the same time, however, it is mainly the qualitative aspects of projects, such as environmental conservation, improvement of the urban landscape, development processes, and the like, which have come under scrutiny, and the question of how to enable social consensus-building among parties directly and indirectly involved in developments, and how to gain those parties' cooperation, have become today's challenge. In his review of studies carried out in Japan, the author divides consensus-building research into theoretical studies – which, in actual and hypothetical settings, empirically examine the theories of social science and the predictions deduced from them – and field studies, which analyse actual examples of development. In the former field, which includes studies by the author himself, procedural fairness is confirmed as promoting cooperative behaviour by local community residents towards public development, but it is emphasised that this is mediated by justice bonds. Toshiaki Aoki proposes a model of positive/negative attitude-formation whose five causal factors are distributive fairness (micro distributive fairness and macro distributive fairness), procedural fairness, trustworthiness and prototypes, and he examines the validity of this model.

In the United States in the 1980s, environmental justice theory arose in response to damage from environmental contamination having occurred in a concentrated manner in areas occupied by people of colour and low-income earners. In Chapter Twelve, Sōko Aoki classifies environmental justice into four categories, namely, 'environmental justice in the community,' 'utilitarian environmental justice,' 'environmental justice as distributive justice' and 'environmental justice as a remedy to passive environmental injustice,' and presents 'participatory-democracy-oriented environmental justice,' which strives to conquer the elitism of contemporary society, as a new perspective. This is a view which makes clear the unjust distribution of harm relating to the outbreak and impact of environmental problems, and makes the standpoint of the parties involved and the egalitarian allocation of opportunities for participation the axis for countermeasures. The author takes up a protest movement against a nuclear power plant in the German village of Wackersdorf, and elucidates the route by which environmental justice is achieved as she follows in detail that movement's process of expansion. This movement initially had a strongly closed nature, but, in the process of devising an oppositional stance vis-à-vis state power, it steadily grew more open, ultimately transcending local interests and arriving at a kind of environmental justice with a highly public nature which demanded 'legitimate policy' from the government. Japanese residents' movements tend to become exclusivist, and, for that reason, often are criticised as being 'regional egotism,' but the author's case-study analysis offers a key to overcoming this problem.

Chapter Thirteen, by Yukio Hirose, is also a paper which explores ways to implement social consensus-building aimed at the resolution of environmental issues. These days, social benefits and provision of information are considered insufficient for securing public acceptance for environmental planning in which opinions are divided, and it is considered necessary to establish diverse opportunities for public participation in the plan-drafting process. The object of the author's focus for examination of this issue is the participatory conference model tried out in the Germany city of Karlsruhe to determine how to introduce a new public transport system in order to alleviate traffic congestion in the inner city area. Participatory conferences can take the form of stakeholder conferences, in which stakeholders and experts engage in debate, or citizens' panel conferences, in which ordinary citizens who do not have a vested interest receive information provided by the parties involved and conduct debate. In the Karlsruhe case, however, a hybrid form which combined the two types was adopted. After having carried out a detailed analysis of this case study, the author implemented a social survey by means of interviews targeting Karlsruhe citizens, and makes it clear that this conference rated highly on procedural fairness in terms of representativeness, disclosure of information and opportunity for expression of opinion, and that this culminated in public acceptance of the planning proposal. There are increasing numbers of cases in Japan, too, of citizens' participation in environment-related planning, and the author suggests that a method such as that used in the Karlsruhe Project might be effective, especially when there is a great division of opinion among citizens.

As outlined above, this volume is made up of thirteen papers which directly or indirectly discuss Japanese views of fairness. These include ones which attempt theoretical or mathematical analysis relating to the mechanism of fairness judgement, ones which attempt empirical investigation by testing hypotheses to do with the causes and effects of perceptions of fairness, as well as ones which analyse cases relating to social consensus-building. The majority of fairness theories cited in these papers are ones proposed by Western scholars, and no uniquely Japanese fairness theory makes an appearance. In that sense, it probably must be said that study of the Japanese view of fairness has only just begun. We look forward to the further expansion of much of the research introduced in this volume, and hope that the publication of this book will spur the emergence of more original fairness studies in Japan.

Acknowledgements

This volume is a collection of the fruit of research activities at the Division of Fairness, the Center for the Study of Social Stratification and Inequality (CSSI) at Tohoku University. The CSSI was established in the summer of 2003 to break through limitations concerning the study of social stratification and inequality in Japan.

The publication of this volume was made possible by a grant offered by the CSSI, whose financial support is gratefully acknowledged. I also thank Airin Izumi, Hiroshi Endō and Hiroaki Ozaki for their excellent secretarial work at the CSSI. The contributors of this volume are grateful to Dr Leonie Stickland for her excellent translation of their Japanese texts into English. Last, but not least, I genuinely appreciate the editorial support of Professor Yoshio Sugimoto of La Trobe University, Director of Trans Pacific Press. His professional skills as editor of academic books made the publication process of this volume go smoothly.

Ken-ichi Ohbuchi
22 January 2007

List of contributors

Ken-ichi Ohbuchi
Professor, Department of Psychology, Graduate School of Arts and Letters, Tohoku University

Michio Umino
Professor, Department of Behavioural Science, Graduate School of Arts and Letters, Tohoku University

Mitsuteru Fukuno
Associate Professor, Department of Management Information, Faculty of Business Administration, Hokkai-Gakuen University

Shinobu Kitani
Associate Professor, Department of Resource and Environmental Economics, Graduate School of Agricultural Science, Tohoku University

Naomi Takada
Graduate student, Department of Psychology, Graduate School of Arts and Letters, Tohoku University

Tōru Tamura
Graduate student, Department of Psychology, Graduate School of Arts and Letters, Tohoku University

Toshitake Takata
Professor, Department of Cultural Studies, Miyagi Gakuin Women's University

Tomohiro Kumagai
Postdoctoral Research Fellow, The Center for the Study of Social Stratification and Inequality (CSSI), Tohoku University

Yōichirō Hayashi
Research Fellow, Japan Society for the Promotion of Science

Naotaka Watanabe
Professor, Graduate School of Administrative Science, Keio University

Toshiaki Aoki
Associate Professor, Department of Civil Engineering, Tohoku Institute of Technology

Sōko Aoki
Graduate student, Department of Sociology, Graduate School of Arts and Letters, Tohoku University

Yukio Hirose
Professor, Department of Environmental Policies, School of Environmental Studies, Nagoya University

Part I
The Sense of Justice and Fairness and its Outcomes

1 The Social Bonds of Justice: Theory and Research

Ken-ichi Ohbuchi

Responses to fairness and unfairness

In the domain of psychological studies on fairness, the focus has long been directed at the mechanism for judging fairness. Through investigations of what means people use in judging a particular decision to be fair, or the necessary conditions for people to judge it fair, the criteria for distributive justice and the contributing factors to procedural justice have been made clear. In recent years, another issue to draw attention has been the impact of fairness and unfairness – in other words, what kind of changes occur in people when they have been treated fairly or unfairly.

Responses to unfairness

According to Tyler, Boeckman, Smith and Huo (1997), many studies have shown that people who have been treated unfairly harbour dissatisfaction and that they act to try to rectify the situation and restore it to a fair state. People who believe that their wages are unreasonably low, for example, try to reduce the amount of work they do and to confine their activity to a level comparable to their low remuneration, while people who have suffered at the hands of another try to punish the perpetrator and to restore balance, in a negative sense. Interestingly, the motivation for the restoration of fairness arises even in the case of people who gain unjust benefit, as the work of Greenberg (1988) and others has shown. People who have been paid unreasonably large remuneration attempt to accomplish a commensurate amount of work.

People who have been treated unfairly do not, however, necessarily initiate action aimed at the restoration of fairness. It sometimes happens that people simply put up with the unjust situation, in reluctant resignation, while in other cases they reinterpret the situation as actually not being unfair, and try to convince themselves of this. The latter is called 'psychological fairness restoration,' and the aggrieved party often employs a mental strategy called 'justification' in attempting to carry it out. There are various reasons for this: the cost of realistic equity restoration is high (such as in cases where conflict with the other party is predicted); recognition of the self as victim wounds self-esteem; and so on. Moreover, people who have a Just World Belief (JWB) have a tendency to judge that they have suffered injury because there was some wrongdoing on their part, also (Tyler et al., 1997).

For almost the same reasons, justification can also occur in people who have unreasonably benefited (Tyler et al., 1997), because, in this case, attempting to restore realistic fairness damages their self-interest, and recognising that they have unjustly benefited injures their self-esteem. There is also a tendency for people with a strong JWB to give this a self-interested interpretation, namely, that their having benefited to that extent means that they deserve it. It thus often happens that both victims and victimisers reinterpret an unfair state of affairs as actually being fair, and do not initiate action to restore realistic fairness.

Responses to fairness: justice bonds

On the other hand, what might happen to people who have been treated fairly? For example, according to studies in the workplace, it is found that people who have been paid an adequate wage have the greatest level of satisfaction towards their work and have the strongest work ethic, in comparison to people paid unreasonably low wages, of course, but also to those whose remuneration is unjustly high (Prichard, Dunnette and Jorgenson, 1972). This indicates that fairness is something more important to people than mere profit and loss. People place special value on things being fair, and have a strong desire that fairness be attained. At times, it is also something strong enough to transcend individual interest.

There are various ways of thinking as to why people have such a strong interest in fairness, and from what that interest derives. There are different kinds of researchers – Thibaut and Walker (1975), for example, take the utilitarian view that it can ultimately be reduced to self-interest, while Lerner (1982) asserts that a tendency towards fairness is human nature. Setting aside the question of the origin of this interest in fairness, we can see that one important result generated

Figure 1.1: The Justice-bond hypothesis

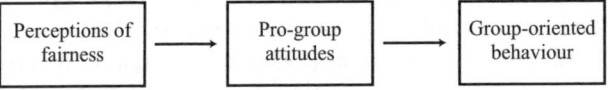

Source: Ohbuchi, 2003, 2004a

by the experience of fairness is the impact it has upon the relationship between the individual and society or the group. It is known that employees who feel that they are being treated fairly by their company intensify their pride and attachment towards the company (Tyler and Blader, 2000). In addition, they work hard for the company's sake, and come to behave so as to demonstrate their loyalty (Moorman, 1991).

The various studies which have investigated responses to fair treatment have found that the short-term effect of fairness is the heightening of individuals' sense of satisfaction with their treatment, while long-term effects include the stimulation of commitment (a pro-group attitude) toward the affiliated group, and group-oriented behaviour. The latter effect, namely, the phenomenon of the strengthening of positive attitudes and behaviour towards the affiliated group, is of particularly deep interest, and we call the various theories dealing with this phenomenon 'justice-bond hypotheses' (Ohbuchi, 2003, 2004a). The view of justice-bond hypotheses, as shown in Figure 1.1, is that perceived fairness fortifies pro-group attitudes, and this, in turn, stimulates group-oriented behaviour. In other words, by this hypothesis, we predict that people who have received just treatment will redouble their positive attitudes towards the group (attachment, group identification, pride, et cetera), and, as a result, will increase their group-oriented behaviour (contributions to the group).

The evolution of justice-bond studies

Relational concerns in procedural justice

Research into justice bonds developed from procedural justice studies. Procedural justice studies emphasise that people have an interest not only in the outcomes of social decisions, but also in the decision-making process. Thibaut and Walker (1975) introduced the concept of control to this field, but their theory was one which was based on an instrumental model. This meant that people's interest in procedure was something which proceeded from self-interest, and procedural justice signified that self-interested activity would be guaranteed. This way of thinking is also shared by procedural justice theorists such as Vidmar and Miller (1980) and Leventhal (1980).

By contrast, Lind and Tyler (1988) have sought to depart from an instrumental model by asserting that procedural justice reflects not only self-interest, but also people's social interest. Their justice theory has been expanded through that work, its aspect as a general theory dealing with the connection between the individual and the group rather than with a specific social phenomenon such as conflict resolution gathering strength, and an investigation into the bond hypothesis has also been attempted.

In Thibaut and Walker's instrumental model, procedural justice is assessed from the degree of control, but Tyler and Lind (1992) focus upon the quality of treatment by authority figures. When people feel that they have received treatment from authorities which is commensurate with their rights and qualifications as members of a group, then their perception of procedural justice is heightened, but, in the opposite situation, when they feel that they have received unfair treatment, a perception of procedural unfairness is generated. Putting these ideas into concrete form, Tyler and Lind have postulated that there are three types of social variable regulating the perception of procedural justice. These they called the relational concerns of procedural justice: trust, neutrality and status recognition.

These relational factors were the product of a preceding series of studies on fairness by Tyler and Lind. Initially, they were focusing upon the 'voice' effect as a factor in procedural justice. In the instrumental model, voice was seen as process control, and the feeling that this had an influence upon the decision-making process was thought to produce a perception of fairness. However, Tyler, Rasinski and Spodick (1985), who found that voice enhanced the perception of procedural justice even in circumstances where it was understood that voice would have no impact upon the decision, the effect of the expression of opinion, in itself – in other words, its expressive value – was considered to be the source of perceived fairness, while the instrumental function of voice came to be considered as inessential to a perception of fairness. Later, Tyler (1988) obtained research results indicating that the voicing of opinion, by itself, was insufficient to produce a sense of procedural justice, and that a feeling that one's voice had been taken seriously by decision-makers, and given due consideration, was important. Through such research (Tyler, 1990; Tyler and Griffin, 1991), Tyler and Lind arrived at the opinion that interpersonal perception of authority figures and leaders – that is to say, conjecture as to their attitudes and motivation – is an essential factor in judgments of procedural fairness, and from this was generated the notion of relational factors.

Relational factors, as the name suggests, are things which express the quality of the relationship between individuals and groups. Their being contributing factors in procedural justice shows that procedural justice is something closely linked with social bonds. In other words, recognising that one's own group is procedurally fair thus includes feeling that the relationship between oneself and the group is an appropriate one.

Group values and group-orientation

Procedural justice and group values

Empirical examination of the justice-bond hypothesis has been pursued by Tyler and his colleagues (De Cremer and Tyler, 2005, for example). According to Tyler's hypothesis, fair treatment – and procedural justice which is spawned by relational factors, in particular – enhances individuals' status within their groups. As relational factors suggest, perceiving that one is respected by the group produces the feeling that the individual is valued by the group, and, through this, pro-group attitudes are strengthened. This is what Tyler calls 'group value.' This is an individual's positive attitude towards the group, something which is made up of affirmative cognition and convictions (group unity, and so on), as well as positive emotions (group commitment such as loyalty, attachment, and pride).

Tyler, Degoey and Smith's research (1996) measured group value, with the aim of confirming that this mediated such group-oriented behaviour as allegiance. Figure 1.2 illustrates the theoretical model employed in that study. In this model, group value is composed of two variables: one is group pride, in which members feel that the group to which they belong is being run fairly, and have a sense of pride in their group; the other is intragroup respect, in which individual self-esteem is fortified by members' feeling that they each are respected by authority figures as full members of their group. Tyler and his co-researchers predicted that positive feelings towards authority figures, i.e., relational variables, would strengthen the perception of fairness, and that these mediated two types of group value, thus promoting group-oriented behaviour. They measured assessment of authority figures (instrumental factors, relational factors, fairness evaluations),

Figure 1.2: Group values and group-orientation

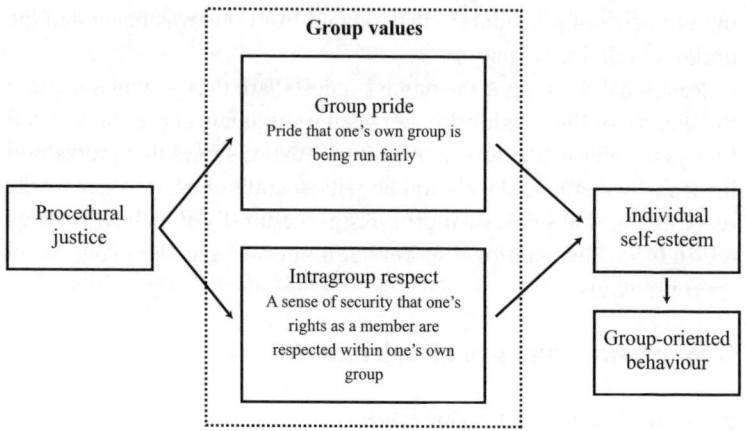

Source: Tyler et al., 1996

group value (group pride and intragroup respect), group-oriented behaviour, and so on, in relation to the members of four types of group, including family, school, workplace, and society in general. In the family case, participants were university students, the authority figures being their parents. With schools, these were university students and teaching staff, respectively; in the workplace case, these were university academic staff and their superiors; and with society in general, these were citizens and courts of law. Surveys were conducted using a questionnaire, except in the case of citizens, who were surveyed by telephone. The moderating function of group value was largely confirmed in all groups as a result of regression analysis. In other words, the relational factors included in positive perceptions towards authority figures enhanced pride in the group and a sense of intragroup respect and, through this, group-oriented behaviour was motivated. By contrast, instrumental factors including large reward or advantageous treatment had almost no connection with group value or group-oriented behaviour. These research findings confirmed anew that group-oriented behaviour arose not from utilitarian interest, but from positive, intragroup relationships and pro-group attitudes.

Trust in authority

Among relational variables, Tyler and Degoey (1995) focused especially upon trust in authority. From the instrumental standpoint, trust means 'risk calculation,' namely, the likelihood, in terms of probability, of the other party behaving in a way advantageous to oneself (Williamson, 1991). As this prediction is based upon the other party's past action, it is natural, from the point of view of instrumental motivation, for the individual to obey authority figures that are 'trustworthy,' obedience previously having led to a favourable outcome. For this reason, from an instrumental standpoint, the advantageousness of the outcome can be expected to be a facilitating factor in allegiance. In opposition to this, in the group-value theory, trust is seen as an attribute of the goodwill of authority figures. As one relational factor, this is predicted to strengthen individuals' pro-group attitudes, this then promoting allegiance.

Tyler and colleagues reviewed six relevant studies to investigate the influence on compliance (group-oriented behaviour) towards authority figures of instrumental factors vis-à-vis authority (the favourableness of outcome, control) and relational factors (trust, neutrality, status respect). Authority figures meant parents, company superiors, administrative institutions, police, legislatures, law courts, and so on. In any analysis of these, the favourableness of outcome among instrumental factors, and trust in authority among relational factors, were vital decisive factors in compliance. In addition, this research makes it clear, from an analysis of workplace data, that trust is emphasised when individuals are concerned with the maintenance of relationships with authorities, or when group identity is strongly developed, and these facts also illustrate the relational aspect of trust.

Though 'treatment by the group' is mentioned, because groups themselves are obscure, what people actually experience is the words and deeds of authority figures such as parents, superiors or managers. As authorities are recognised as representing groups, it is considered natural for trust in them to become an important regulating factor in positive attitudes towards those groups.

Procedural justice and distributive justice

In the research of Tyler and others, the effects of procedural justice and of relational factors, in particular, have been emphasised in the strengthening of social bonds. This is because, in line with what has already been stated, relational factors are things which suggest the quality of the relationship between the group and the individual, and therefore facilitate the strengthening of social bonds. I wonder, however, whether no other contributing factors in fairness, especially factors to do with distributive justice (including equity, equality, necessity, and so on) make any contribution to social bonds. As we see from subsequent studies, this is not necessarily so, because, even from the perspective of resource allocation, the feeling that one is being treated fairly increases one's trust in one's own group. Nevertheless, the appropriateness of procedures is behind the appropriateness of distribution, and is more often regarded as a fundamental indicator expressing the appropriateness of a group's system and its management. For example, employees who feel that their pay this month was adequate in terms of the amount of work they did will probably have a sense of satisfaction with their work, and increase their faith in the company which affords them proper treatment, but if a rational wage system is in place, and employees recognise that appropriate distribution is implemented by that system, then their trust will probably grow even stauncher in future. It is also pointed out in the work of Tyler et al. (1996) that, for this reason, procedural justice is seen by researchers to be a more potent morphogenetic factor in social bonding than distributive justice.

Justice bonds: two standpoints

The justice-bond hypothesis asserts that perceptions of fairness tie individuals and groups together. Why, then, might perceiving that one's own group was being run fairly strengthen affinitive attitudes towards the group, and increase group-oriented behaviour? Researchers have attempted to explain this principally from two standpoints – the utilitarian standpoint and the group-value standpoint.

The utilitarian standpoint
The utilitarian standpoint relating to justice bonds means something which focuses attention upon the utilitarian function provided by fairness. People remain members of a certain group for a long time because they anticipate the benefits they can obtain by belonging to that group. However, if the running of the group seems haphazard, then they are unlikely to gain the assurance that they will obtain benefits commensurate with their own rights. For example, if company executives look as though they are deciding employees' promotions on the basis of personal preferences, then the majority of employees will harbour a sense of insecurity that even if they do work for that company, they perhaps will not be able to obtain adequate

remuneration befitting their performances, and will probably move to another company if the opportunity arises. On the other hand, if a group is being managed fairly, then, as members can anticipate that they will be able to obtain reward commensurate with their respective qualifications and rights, as a long term prospect, then they will probably remain in that group for a long time, and become willing to make efforts for the sake of the group. Thus, according to the justice-bond hypothesis seen from the utilitarian standpoint, a perception of fairness vis-à-vis a group fulfils the role of a heuristic indicating that proper distribution of reward in the group can be anticipated, and this can be considered to promote members' positive attitudes towards the group and group-oriented behaviour.

Studies which investigated justice bonds from the utilitarian standpoint can be seen mainly in the field of industrial organization (Moorman, 1991; Organ, 1988). Moorman (1991), for one, dealt with organisational citizenship behaviour (OCB) as group-oriented behaviour, and examined its links with fairness perception. OCB signifies positive, cooperative behaviour towards an organisation. Moorman ventured the hypothesis that perceptions of fairness towards the group and job satisfaction probably promoted OCB, and conducted questionnaire surveys targeting the employees of two companies. As a result, it was found that a perception of fairness towards the organisation facilitated OCB more strongly than did job satisfaction. In Moorman's interpretation, employees who recognised that the organisation was being operated fairly thought that a long-term exchange relation with the organisation would produce ample benefit, and were motivated by OCB to strive to maintain or expand the organisation.

Groups provide various kinds of reward to their members. In the case of companies, this mainly constitutes economic reward, but groups also offer different types of reward such as a sense of security, information, evaluation and endorsement. Within such sustained social relationships, fairness probably works as a heuristic which spawns the anticipation of appropriate distribution of social rewards, also.

The standpoint of group-value theory

Theories which focus upon an aspect of the connection between individuals and groups apart from reward allocation are social identity theory and group-value theory. The key concept in these theories is self-esteem. According to Tajfel and Turner's (1979) social identity theory, individuals cherish the desire to improve the status and value of their own groups, with which they identify. This psychological process emerges independently of the presence or absence of any reward provided by the group. The reason for the generation of such desire is that an individual's self-esteem depends, at least in part, upon the group. We delight in seeing our own country's athletes participate in the Olympics because we feel that those athletes' performance raises the status of our own group (state, ethnic group, et cetera). Similarly, our feeling miserable if the company for which we work causes some trouble and is criticised in the mass media is caused by our inkling that, due to the lowering of the company's social status, our own pride will deteriorate, we being a member of that group. This kind of thing happens because individual self-esteem depends on the status of the group. Just as people make efforts because of their wish to maintain or enhance their individual self-esteem, they have a similar desire to enhance the status and value of their group. There are several ways to do this, but one is to confirm the relative superiority of one's own group in comparison with other groups. Another way is a bias mechanism which seeks to find proof that one's own group is superior to other groups; or tries to heighten the position of one's own group by distorting reality and showing contempt for other groups. 'In-group bias,' which gives a favourable evaluation to fellow members of one's own group, also arises from this mentality.

The status of one's own group is not necessarily based solely upon comparison with other groups. It can also be enhanced by finding an outstanding feature in one's group, and using this to satisfy group self-esteem. Fairness is one example of such an excellent social value. Fairness is part of the moral code, and, moreover, is a moral virtue placed in the upper ranks of moral standards. Thinking that one's own group is being run fairly thus increases pride in the group, and one's own pride as a member of that group probably also is heightened. This is the factor which Tyler et al. (1996) called 'group pride' in their group-value research. A perception of fairness is thus considered to enhance individuals' attachment and positive attitudes towards the group by strengthening group pride and individual self-esteem, while a bonding process emerges – one which promotes group-oriented behaviour. The fairness of one's own group raises the status of the group from the perspective of moral values, and activates social bonds, but this is a socio-psychological process different in nature from social bonds which arise due to benefits that the group bestows.

The above discussion shows that there are two views on justice bonds: the utilitarian viewpoint and the group-value viewpoint. I do not claim that only one of these two standpoints is correct – both have validity. Our research, which I shall discuss below, indicates that there are two types of social justice bond, in other words, that social justice bonds are strengthened by two separate paths. These, it goes without saying, are the utilitarian path and the group-value path.

Justice-bond studies in Japan

In Japanese society, struggling to recover since the collapse of the so-called 'Bubble' Economy, structural reform has been tried in various spheres, but this has not been progressing smoothly. Given such circumstances, we foresee that 'fairness' might be an important keyword in the quest for future direction in Japan.

Historically, in Japan, to discuss justice or fairness has been said to be 'wet behind the ears,' and for an adult to do so has been seen as immature. Even among Western scholars, there is the view that the notion of fairness is disdained in Japan (Triandis, 1995). However, in light of Japanese social behaviour of recent years, fairness can be considered to exert an influence upon people's judgments, as a subject of great interest. There are increasing numbers of cases in which conventional organisational elections emphasising influence-peddling no longer have currency, and in which candidates who appeal to civic sensibilities are putting up a good fight. The candidates, surmising that the constituency is likely to be interested only in personal profit and loss, lay emphasis on influence-peddling, but, in actual fact, the constituency's set of values has already changed. While personal profit and loss is all very well, would not the majority of citizens rather see their country of residence run fairly? A gulf has opened between politicians who have contempt for fairness and citizens who have high regard for it, and this could be considered the root cause of the distrust of politics in recent years.

In this manner, fairness has gradually emerged as an important evaluative axis when investigating social issues among the Japanese. Nevertheless, sufficient investigation has not been carried out in relation to such essential questions as by what means the Japanese judge something as fair; how a judgement of fairness is structured; and how the assessment of a certain social phenomenon as fair or unfair alters Japanese people's responses to that phenomenon. With such concerns in mind, we have endeavoured for several years to conduct empirical research in order to elucidate the Japanese sense of fairness.

As I have previously stated, according to the justice-bond hypothesis, fairness generates a perception that the individual is being recognised as a full member by the group, and is being respected by authority. The core of this hypothesis is the idea that people's loyalty towards organisations or groups is not something spontaneous, but is something born of the recognition that they are being fairly treated by those bodies, and respected by them. Fairness thus functions as a 'bond' which ties individuals to society. This perception of fairness, however, in which individuals' loyalty can be understood to change according to the treatment they receive, has a heavily individualistic peculiarity. Might fairness perform the function of a 'bond' which ties groups and individuals together even among the Japanese, who are assumed to have a collectivist culture?

Perceived fairness and attitudes to the state

People's attitudes towards the state are varied. While some Japanese have pride in their country of Japan and wish to contribute to its advancement, if possible, there are others who dislike their own country and desire to escape to another land, if they have the chance. This divergence in attitudes towards the state is thought to arise due to individuals' differing social experience, beliefs and philosophies, but we have postulated that perceived fairness in relation to the state is a probable contributing factor. According to the justice-bond idea, as I will explain later as a hypothesis, people who judge that the Japanese state is being run fairly are likely to have correspondingly strong positive attitudes towards that state.

Evaluation of the state and the perceptions of justice

In 1996, we conducted a mail survey of three thousand adults randomly chosen from fifteen cities and towns all over Japan, in order to examine the association between perceived fairness and attitudes to the state (Ohbuchi and Imazai, 1999). The outcome of our analysis of data from the 993 respondents (representing a return rate of 33.1 per cent) is shown in Figure 1.3. In this study, we measured two types of attitude towards the state: emotional commitment, showing the strength of emotional ties including pride in, and loyalty towards, the state; and utilitarian commitment, based on the anticipation that

Figure 1.3: Evaluation of organs of state, perceptions of social justice, and attitudes towards the state

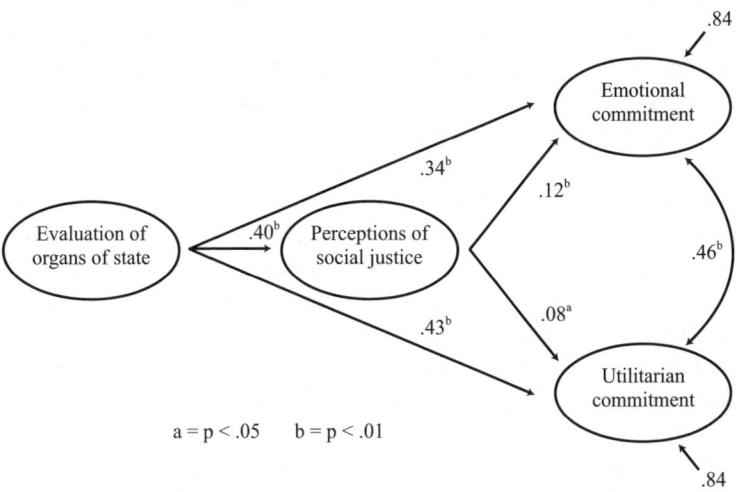

Source: Ohbuchi and Imazai, 1999

citizenship would bring forth future reward. A 'perception of social justice' means a response to the question of whether the participant thinks that Japanese society is fair.

We set up a hypothesis like the following between perceived fairness and commitment vis-à-vis the state. Firstly, in line with the group-value-bond hypothesis, people who feel that the state is being run fairly are likely to have pride in their own country, and feel attachment to the state, as citizens (emotional commitment). Secondly, in line with the utilitarian bond hypothesis, people who feel that their own country is being run fairly are likely to anticipate that they will be able to receive adequate allocation of resources, commensurate with their rights as citizens (utilitarian commitment).

In this study, we also focused on functional evaluation of the state as a factor influencing a perception of social justice. As this amounts to a factor in procedural justice, this asks whether people think that various organs of state are being run appropriately. When deciding whether the state is fair, people probably focus their attention on whether the various organs (administrative authorities, et cetera) which the state operates are functioning appropriately in their decision-making and their handling of problems. Specifically, we had respondents evaluate the functionality of the state from such perspectives as information-disclosure, information-gathering (the accuracy of information), citizens' opportunity for voice, and representation.

The path coefficients in Figure 1.3 are the outcome of multiple regression analysis. We can see that, as predicted, functional evaluation of state organs intensified a perception of social justice, and a perception of social justice strengthened two kinds of commitment, namely, positive attitudes towards the state. These results show that the more people feel that Japanese society is fair, the more likely they are to feel a strong engagement with the state, and that the justice-bond hypothesis is also appropriate in relation to Japanese attitudes to the state. In addition, the fact that functional evaluation of the state increased the perception of fairness suggests that procedural justice is significant as a bond factor, as Tyler and others have asserted.

This figure further indicates that functional evaluation of the state impacts directly upon attitudes to the state without going through any perception of fairness. However, as I have explained above, because functional evaluation is situated as a contributing factor in procedural justice, its direct impact can also be interpreted as a bond effect. In fact, as the word '*kōsei* (fair/just)' has multiple meanings for the Japanese, presumably there would have been quite a few people having trouble deciding if directly asked the question: 'Is Japanese society *kōsei*?' This is probably why this variable did not show as strong a relevance to other variables as we had expected.

Figure 1.4, incidentally, is one which shows perceptions of social justice, attitudes to the state, and functional evaluation of the state, by age-group. An examination of this shows us that the perception of social justice is low in all age-groups (the middle point on the scale being 4), and Japanese people overall see their own country as not very fair. By looking at attitudes to the state, however, we can see that the older the respondent, the more positive the attitude becomes. As younger people in general are critical of society, this might reflect a universal phenomenon, but there might also be some special reason for this trend in Japanese society. The older people are those who worked as active participants in the industrial field during Japan's post-war period of rapid economic growth. These are people who experienced the state having grown more prosperous by the year, and the standard of living having soared. They are people who, along with that fortunate life experience, also have the self-conceit to believe that they are the ones who made the country prosper. This is why they are thought to have especially strong pride and attachment (emotional

Figure 1.4: Assessment of attitudes towards the state by age

[Figure: Line graph showing attitudes towards the state by age group (20-29, 30-39, 40-49, 50-59, 60-69) with four lines: Utilitarian commitment (highest, ranging ~4.3-5), Emotional commitment (rising from ~3.5 to ~5), Functional evaluation (~3 to ~3.3), Perception of fairness (~2.5-2.9). Y-axis from 2 to 5.5.]

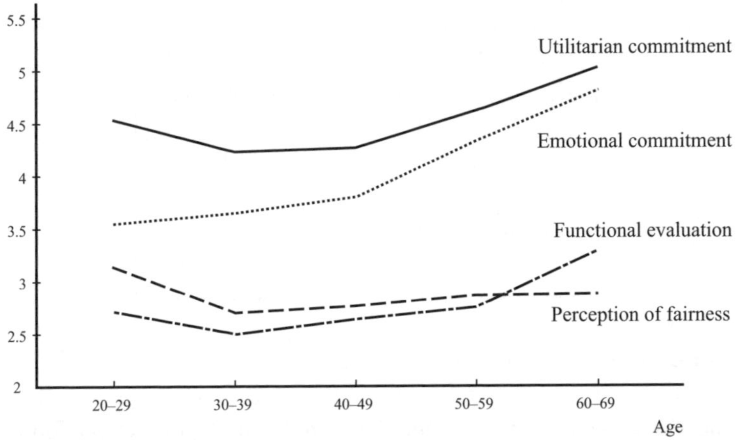

Source: Ohbuchi and Imazai, 1999

commitment) towards, as well as faith (utilitarian commitment) in, the Japanese state (Ohbuchi, 2004b).

Social justice and attitudes to the state at multiple levels

In the research of Ohbuchi and Imazai (1999), Japanese people's perception of fairness vis-à-vis the state was low, overall. However, according to the standpoint from which the data is considered, it can also be assumed that their judgement of fairness differs. People spend their social lives as members of diverse groups. When judging from the standpoint of a parent, they probably pay attention to state measures regarding education, welfare, and so on, yet when making a judgement as a member of a company, they are likely to shift their focus towards systems and policies in such fields as economics or industry. Because their judgement of fairness will change along with their standpoint, we can posit that people have a multi-dimensional perception of fairness in relation to Japanese society. We then measured Japanese people's perception of social justice by means of three levels: macro-level; occupational; and regional – and investigated the link between these and attitudes to the state (Ohbuchi 2004b). We had the various participants make judgements about the fairness of Japanese society, with the 'macro-level' meaning from the standpoint of a citizen; the 'occupational level' being from an occupational standpoint (including housewives

Figure 1.5: Justice bonds vis-à-vis the state and distributive/procedural justice

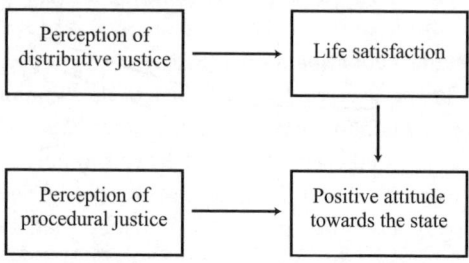

Source: Ohbuchi and Fukuno, 2003

and students); and the 'regional level' meaning from the standpoint of a resident living in a particular area.

In this study, we measured perceptions of fairness, dividing them into distributive justice and procedural justice. Theoretically, and also from empirical findings, it is thought that though short-term effects such as a sense of satisfaction are pronounced in distributive justice, long-term effects such as social bonds are weak, in comparison to procedural justice. Based on our ability to postulate this, we framed a hypothesis between perceived fairness and attitudes to the state, as in Figure 1.5. A perception of distributive justice has the short-term effect of increasing people's life satisfaction, and, through this, indirectly strengthens their positive attitudes to the state, but, on the other hand, we predicted that a perception of procedural justice, as posited in the group-value theory of Tyler and others, would directly intensify positive attitudes towards the state.

Furthermore, in this study, for the reason explained in the previous section, we avoided directly quizzing respondents about the intensity of their perception of fairness, and decided instead to measure fairness factors, and deal with perceived fairness as a latent variable existing behind those factors. Over the three standards – macro-level, occupational, and regional – we measured equity, equality and need as factors in distributive justice, and opportunities for voice (process control) and respect (relational factor) as factors in procedural justice, respectively.

In this survey, in 2001, we posted survey sheets to 3,000 adult ordinary citizens randomly selected from sixteen cities and towns all over Japan, and received 862 responses (a return rate of 28.7 per cent).

In this survey, we asked respondents what opinions they held about Japanese society, the state, and the government, and had them evaluate items which measured such things as fairness factors, life satisfaction, and attitude to the state. When we analysed their responses using the structural equation model (SEM), on the regional level, the perception of fairness exerted no influence of its own upon either life satisfaction or attitude to the state. On the other hand, as is shown in Figure 1.6, the predicted effect was observed in perceived fairness on both the macro-level and occupational standards. On macro-level and occupational standards, therefore, distributive justice increased life satisfaction and, in the process, indirectly reinforced positive attitudes towards the state. By contrast, on macro-level and occupational level, procedural justice directly strengthened positive attitudes towards the state. As such, this research found that, by measuring two types of perceived fairness by multiple levels, a sense of social justice strengthens people's ties with the state, and reconfirmed the fact that justice bonds are at work in Japanese people's relationship with the state.

This study showed that when people are making judgements as citizens, their perception of social justice is not necessarily the same as when they are making judgements as members of an occupational group. This suggests that people have a multi-dimensional cognition of the relationship between themselves and the nation, shifting their axis of attention according to the group to which they belong. It should also be emphasised that, as has been the case with Western research results, procedural justice has exhibited a stronger bonding effect than distributive justice in research targeting Japanese, too.

Protest action and immutability beliefs relating to the state
In the justice-bond hypothesis, perceptions of fairness cause the formation of pro-group attitudes, and it is predicted that group-oriented behaviour will be promoted by this. What, then, might group-oriented behaviour towards the state be like? Behaviour based on patriotism, community service and so on fits this definition, and it can be surmised that people who perceive the state to be fair will often engage in such behaviour. In the opposite situation, according to the justice-bond hypothesis, it can be predicted that the behaviour of people who perceive the state to be unfair will often include being hostile to or critical of state authority, or disregarding state regulations. We thus attempted an investigation of this hypothesis (Ohbuchi, 2004c).

Figure 1.6: Influence of perceptions of multi-level fairness on life satisfaction and attitudes toward the state

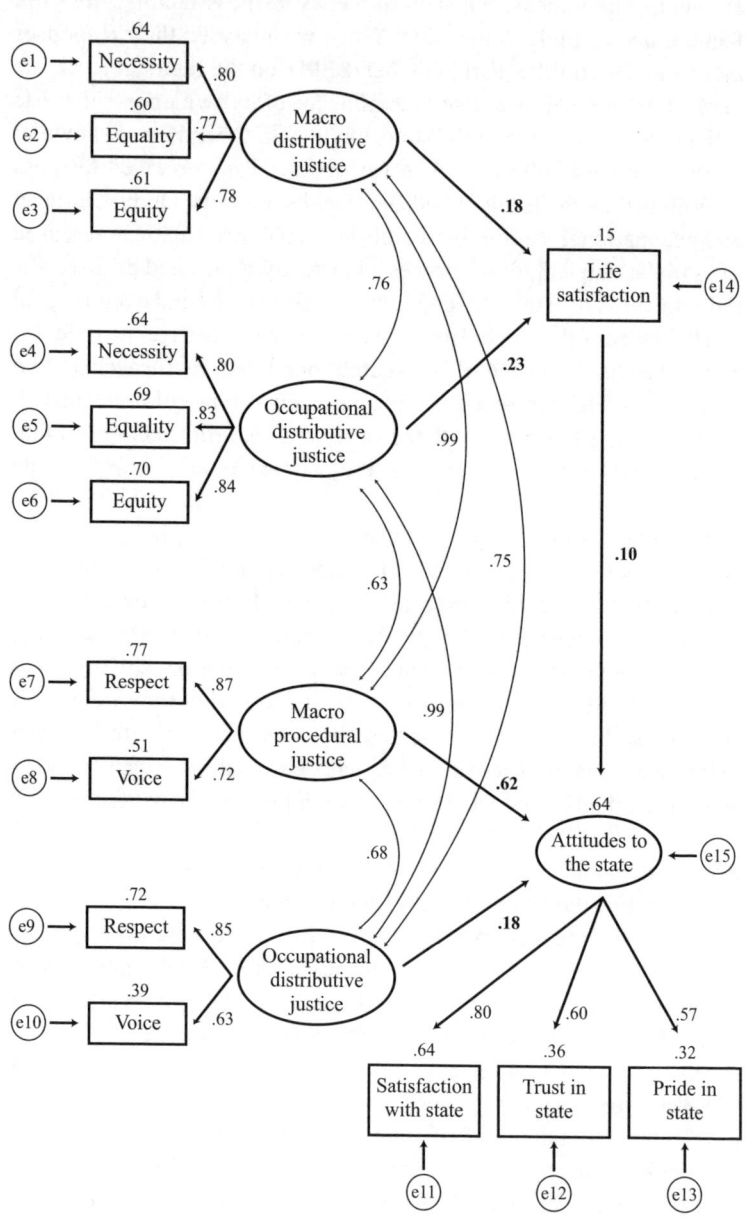

Source: Ohbuchi et al., 2005

In this study, we introduced one more variable. In research relating to Japanese political awareness, it is often suggested that the majority of Japanese people have the belief that though the government may change, the structure of the Japanese state fundamentally will not alter (Ohbuchi, Fukuno and Imazai, 2003). This immutability belief has two types. One is a view that has an affirmative regard for the unchanging structure of Japanese society – there are some people, especially among those who are conservative-leaning, who see Japanese society as a familistic community bound together by mutual aid and trust, within which each member is given appropriate treatment, and naively believe in the fairness of Japanese society (Sakuta, 1985). This is what perhaps should be called the Japanese version of JWB.

On the other hand, there are also some people who have a negative immutability belief. They cynically remark that whoever becomes Prime Minister, or whichever party holds office, ultimately Japan will not change. They stubbornly believe that Japanese society has an unfair structure which benefits only one portion of the population, and feel a political impotence, namely that reform would be difficult to accomplish (Yamada, 1994). An immutability belief in the state, in either a positive or negative sense, is a belief that Japanese society has a unique structure and mechanism in which Japanese people's value system and behaviour are deeply rooted, and that all efforts by certain political leaders to try to force a change would be fruitless.

By combining perceptions of fairness and immutability beliefs, we set up two further hypotheses. The group which thinks that the state is both unfair and immutable believes that it would still be impossible to change social injustice even if protest action were mounted, and so little protest action is expected of its members. However, as people who regard the state as unfair but not immutable think that they can change social injustice through protest action, they will thus probably engage frequently in protest.

For the three years from 2000 to 2002, we employed the postal method to request surveys from 9,600 adults randomly selected from all over the country, and received responses from 2,564 (a return rate of 26.7 per cent). The survey sheets included question items asking about the perception of fairness vis-à-vis the state, immutability belief, and protest action. We separated the respondents into high-group or low-group in accordance with their perception of fairness and immutability belief. We measured protest action in the sixth question, but factor analysis showed that this was composed of the two dimensions of 'normative protest' and 'anti-normative protest' (Table

Table 1.1: Protest items and their factor analysis

Category and item	Factor 1	Factor 2
Normative protest		
I support and/or participate in the activities of a group which petitions and makes demands to the government and administrative system	0.811	0.025
I directly convey my thoughts and demands to the government and administrative system	0.695	0.213
I vote in elections for candidates who are critical of the government and administrative system	0.625	0.067
Anti-normative protest		
Even if there is an election, I do not vote	−0.044	0.821
I am disinclined to observe social rules, such as traffic rules	0.150	0.789
As far as possible, I make efforts to legally avoid paying tax	0.364	0.508
Contribution	1.690	1.606

Note: Principal component analysis and varimax rotation. The cumulative contribution ratio of the two factors is 58.71%.

Source: Ohbuchi, 2004c.

1.1). Subsequently, we investigated the two dimensions of protest by analysis of variance.

Firstly, Figure 1.7 shows a comparison of the two types of protest in high- and low-ranking people in terms of perceived fairness. As we predicted on the basis of the justice-bond hypothesis, protest action increases along with a perception of the Japanese state as unfair, and this was the same with both normative and anti-normative types. Figure 1.8 compares normative protest, with respondents divided into four groups by perception of fairness and immutability belief. Among these four groups, people who believed that the state could be changed, even while feeling that Japanese society was unfair, showed the greatest propensity for protest. As we predicted, even among people who have a perception of social injustice, those who think that this can be changed display a stronger tendency to initiate protest action than people who think that it cannot be changed.

In this chapter, I have already discussed the reason for people not actually carrying out such protest, they having striven for rationalisation, even while sensing injustice, but the results of our research show that people who have a feeling of efficacy tend to engage in action which aims to rectify that injustice. Moreover, no

Figure 1.7: Perceived social fairness and protest action

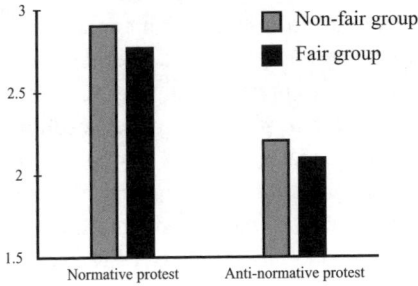

Source: Ohbuchi, 2004c

Figure 1.8: The relationship between perceived fairness, immutability belief and normative protest

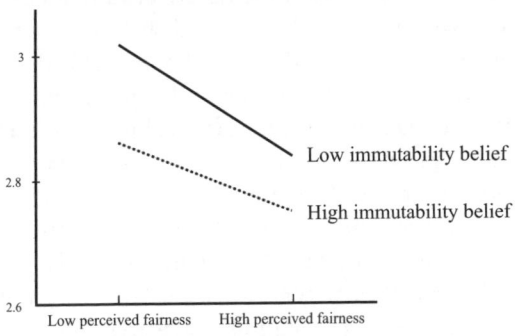

Source: Ohbuchi, 2004c

influence of immutability belief in regard to anti-normative protest was seen.

Citizens' perception of fairness and trust in civil proceedings

In whatever domain – home, school, workplace, or region – conflict and struggle are an inalienable part of social life. People's ability to resolve these constructively determines their standard of social adjustment and well-being. When settlement cannot be reached by the parties involved, people often seek the help of a third party to solve the problem, and there are social institutions which assist conflict resolution. One of the foremost is civil proceedings.

In order to prevent situations in which social conflict becomes complicated and strong antagonism arises between people, or escalates into violence, or to prevent this from threatening the social order, most countries have in place a conflict resolution institution called the court system. Legal specialists design this institution, and are charged with the responsibility of running it so that it functions properly. The job of justices, as the title suggests, is to resolve social conflict in a just and fair manner. However, the question of how the users of this institution evaluate legal proceedings is a different matter. As losing parties sometimes denounce the proceedings for having resulted in an 'unreasonable decision,' it can be appreciated that users do not necessarily see lawsuits as fair.

Litigants' assessment of the fairness of legal proceedings: two standpoints
There are two ways of looking at the nature of fairness judgements made by concerned parties in relation to litigation (Ohbuchi, 2004d). One is the self-interest perspective, which postulates that litigants' sole interest is self-interest. According to this perspective, litigants really are not interested in whether the proceedings are fair. Declaring that it had been a 'fair decision' if they won, but an 'unfair decision' if they lost, served to justify their self-interest. Underlying this hypothesis is the premise that ordinary citizens care little or nothing about fairness, self-interest clearly taking priority. Thus, if we are to go along with this hypothesis, then we can consider their responses to litigation to be regulated almost entirely by interest.

The other perspective is the procedural justice perspective. According to this hypothesis, people have an essential interest in whether the legal judgement they receive is fair (Lind et al., 1990). Trials always involve victory or defeat, and it is natural for litigants to experience feelings of pleasure if they win, but of displeasure if they lose. However, according to this perspective, it can be supposed that even if litigants win, if they consider that the hearing was insufficient or unfair, then they cannot completely rejoice, and, on the other hand, even if they lose, if they can feel that all sides received a full hearing, then their sense of dissatisfaction will be mitigated. Findings that support this supposition can be found in Western research (Lind and Tyler, 1988).

Could an interest in procedural justice also be found among Japanese litigants? Or might their response be regulated solely by self-interest? To investigate this matter, we conducted interview surveys of users of Japanese civil proceedings (Ohbuchi, Sugawara, Teshigahara and Imazai, 2005).

Justice bonds: faith in the judicial system

In this study, as well as litigants' responses to legal proceedings, we also examined attitudes towards the judicial system. If we follow the justice-bond hypothesis, it can be predicted that, in the case of litigants who have felt that the proceedings they experienced were fair, not only will they be satisfied with the outcome of the proceedings (a short-term effect), but they will also increase their confidence in the state's judicial system itself which underlies those proceedings (a long-term effect). In line with the two perspectives discussed above, we set up theoretical models relating to the impact exerted by the merits and demerits (advantageousness) of legal proceedings and perceptions of fairness vis-à-vis case hearings upon feelings of satisfaction with the outcome of litigation and confidence in the judicial system. Figure 1.9(a) illustrates the self-interest perspective.

According to this hypothesis, parties whose case outcome was favourable are expected to be satisfied with that result, and to strengthen their faith in the judicial system which provided an outcome to their advantage. This emphasises the action of utilitarian bonds. Figure 1.9(b) shows the procedural justice perspective. This predicts that, while it is natural for the reaction of the parties concerned to be influenced by interest, litigants who perceived that the deliberation process was fair also further increased their sense of satisfaction (or decreased their dissatisfaction) with the case outcome, and redoubled their faith in the judicial system, as a result of that perception. We posited that such faith was something that arose through a different mental process from that of interest, and that it contains the action of group-value bonds.

This study is a reanalysis of data from the 'Survey of Civil Litigants (*Minji soshō riyōsha chōsa*)' conducted in 2000 by the Japanese government's Justice System Reform Council Committee (Shihō seido kaikaku shingikai, 2001). In the survey, requests for participation were mailed to 1612 parties involved (as plaintiffs or as respondents) in civil cases which had concluded at the first hearing by reason of judgement, settlement, or withdrawal; structured interviews were conducted with those who consented; and, ultimately, 591 responses were obtained. The survey questions were wide-ranging, but we subjected to SEM analysis those responses relating to the favourableness of the outcome and degree of satisfaction; the

Figure 1.9: Two theoretical models relating to litigant responses

(a) Self-interest hypothesis

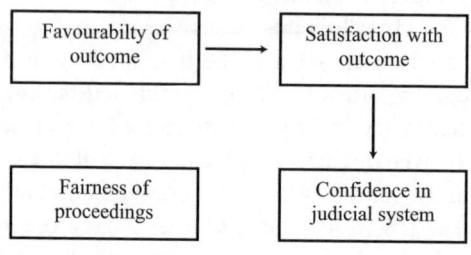

(b) Procedural justice hypothesis

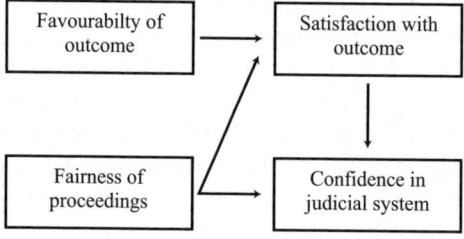

Source: Ohbuchi et al., 2005

fairness of the hearing and its contributing factors; and faith in the judicial system.

Figure 1.10 shows the outcome of the analysis. It can be seen that the favourableness of the outcome strongly regulates the degree of satisfaction, and, it goes without saying, the more favourable the outcome, the more satisfied litigants were with the result. On the other hand, procedural justice fortified confidence in the judicial system along with enhancing the level of satisfaction. However, the favourableness of the outcome intensified procedural justice factors (process control) and relational factors, and indirectly contributed to procedural justice. This indicates that litigants obtaining a favourable outcome tend to evaluate the deliberation in their case as having been appropriate. Seen from this point, this research result can be assumed to support the self-interest perspective, as it is a distortion

Figure 1.10: The influence of self-interest and procedural fairness upon the responses of civil litigants

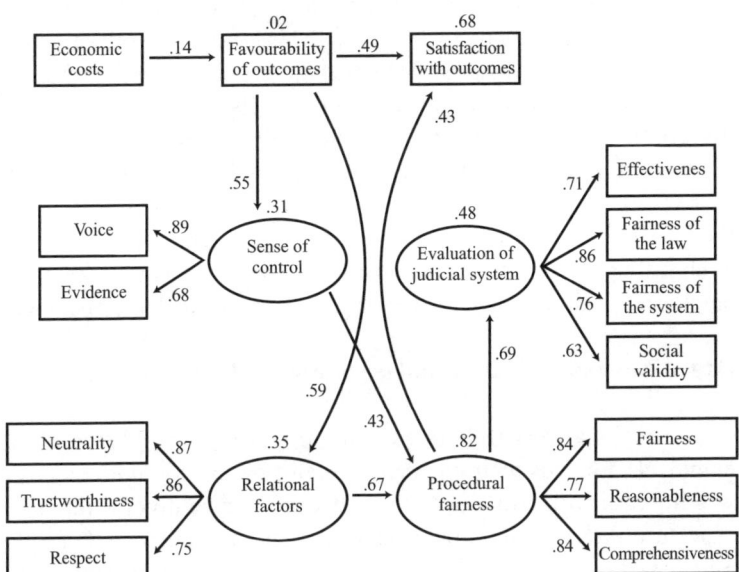

Source: Ohbuchi et al., 2005

by self-interest of the evaluation of fairness. This is because the favourableness of the outcome directly and indirectly influences all reactions to legal proceedings and the judicial system, as can be read from Figure 1.10.

However, when we tested the magnitude of the effect, it was confirmed that evaluations of procedural justice contain a unique component that cannot be fully explained by the favourableness of the outcomes (Ohbuchi et al., 2005). By the same analysis, it was also found that in terms of confidence in the judicial system, procedural justice had greater effect than the favourableness of outcomes.

Such analysis results show that litigants have an interest in the procedural justice of proceedings, independently of whether the outcome was good or bad, and that a judgement of fairness intensifies trust in the judicial system. In this way, in overview, the results of this research suggest that the impact of litigants' interest is indeed strong in terms of their reaction to proceedings, but that justice bonds are in operation even among the Japanese.

Fairness and group-orientation in corporate structures

People who work for companies are almost always interested in whether they are being treated properly. This is why the work situation became the root of fairness studies. There are many people who are dissatisfied with their low pay, but there are also some who are more dissatisfied with their unfair treatment. Even among doctors and pilots, who, in the eyes of society, are regarded as being highly-paid, there are probably quite a few who feel dissatisfied, thinking that they are unreasonably lowly-valued in comparison with their peers. Such feelings of dissatisfaction probably have a strong influence upon employees' attitudes towards the organisation to which they belong.

Organisational evaluation and organisational commitment

Organisational researchers call the pro-group attitudes held by employees towards their company 'organisational commitment.' As was the case with attitudes to the state, this can be divided into two aspects: utilitarian commitment and emotional commitment (O'Reilly and Chatman, 1986; Hayashi, 2004). Utilitarian commitment expresses a stance of willingness to remain with the organisation, in the anticipation of future reward such as promotion or higher pay, while emotional commitment, by contrast, is an affirmative attitude consisting of feelings of unity, attachment, pride, and so on towards the group.

The strength of such group commitment depends on how employees view their own company organisation. We were able to postulate that group evaluation comprises the two aspects of rewardability and fairness (Hayashi and Ohbuchi, 1999). This resembles the self-interest and interest in procedural justice in the case of litigants. The rewardability of the organisation does not mean merely an economic issue such as pay, though it does indicate whether employees perceive that they are receiving sufficient remuneration in that company. Social compensation such as acceptance by peers and support from bosses is also included.

The second factor regulating employees' attitudes to the organisation is the perception of fairness. Studies in the West have illustrated that the more fairly employees feel that their organisation is being run, the stronger their commitment will be to that organisation (Masterson, Lewis, Goldman and Taylor, 2000; Tyler and Lind, 1992). The correlation between a perception of fairness and utilitarian commitment can be explained from the perspective of the utilitarian bond hypothesis. In other words, if the organisation is being run fairly, then employees can anticipate that in future, also, they will be able to receive reward commensurate with their performance. On the other hand, emotional commitment is understood from the viewpoint of the group-value bond hypothesis. According to the group-value theory of Tyler and others, employees who feel that they are being treated fairly will feel that they are being respected by the organisation, their self-esteem will be enhanced (intra-group respect), and they will come to have pride in their group, regarding a fair organisation as a superior one (group pride). Will the association between perceived fairness and pro-group attitudes posited in Western research also be discovered among Japanese company employees, I wonder? We attempted an empirical investigation in regard to this question (Hayashi and Ohbuchi, 1999).

Group orientation and OCB

In the justice-bond hypothesis, pro-group attitudes formed through fair treatment promote co-operational behaviour towards the group – in other words, it proposes that they fortify group-orientation. In my research on protest responses to the state (Ohbuchi, 2004c; Ohbuchi et al., 2003), discussed above, findings suggesting this were made, but how might the situation be in organisational studies?

Organisational psychologists have focused their attention on Organisational Citizenship Behaviour (OCB) as being group-oriented behaviour. This is defined as 'spontaneous actions that go beyond the call of duty or job requirements' (Hayashi, 2004). Employees of Western corporations are hired upon the exchange of employment contracts, setting out their job descriptions in minute detail, with their companies. Consequently, employees have no obligations apart from those stipulated in these contracts. However, a firm will be unable to sustain its business performance unless it makes its decisions as the occasion demands within an economic environment which changes minute by minute, or it expands its corporate activities in a flexible manner. For this reason, smooth organisational management is difficult unless there are employees who will do other tasks, too, if asked, or who will help a colleague in need, or teach a new employee who is not very familiar with the situation, or who will think of the organisation as a whole, and voluntarily perform tasks that, strictly speaking, are not their own responsibility. This is why employees' OCB has come to be stressed as group-orientation in Western corporations since the 1990s, and, with the idea that perceived fairness vis-à-vis the organisation is what promotes this, research emphasising justice bonds has begun to be conducted (Moorman, 1991).

In Japanese firms, on the other hand, the outline of each employee's job stipulating what his or her duties are has never been made very clear, and so engagement in OCB out of consideration for the group as a whole has been regarded as a natural thing. However, as this has remained an unspoken rule, there are individual differences in reactions to it, and while there are some Japanese employees who do only their own work, there are also those who actively take on tasks that are outside their usual roles. It is our hypothesis that, in the case of Japanese employees, also, difference lies in perceived fairness and pro-group attitudes vis-à-vis the company.

Organisational fairness and its effect

Organisational researchers often make a further distinction apart from distributive and procedural justice, namely, interpersonal justice. Conceptually, this corresponds roughly to the relational factors within procedural justice. The wage system, assessment system, decision-making system, complaints-management system and suchlike become the targets in procedural justice evaluations relating to an organisation, and the question of how fairly are intra-group systems designed and are functioning becomes the issue. Even within procedural justice, these are evaluations which focus upon the organisational system and structural aspects. In this connection, interpersonal aspects such as whether bosses' attitude and stance in dealing with subordinates are fair are also included in procedural justice evaluations, and this component is called 'interpersonal justice.' The former are structural aspects of procedural justice, while the latter can be situated as an operational aspect (Hayashi, 2004).

Based on the justice-bond hypothesis, we predicted that a connection like that shown in Figure 1.11 would exist among organisational evaluation, a pro-group attitude (organisational commitment), and group-orientation (OCB). In 1997, we distributed survey sheets to 300 Japanese company employees and requested their participation. Of that number, we received responses from 154 (a return rate of 51.3 per cent). On these survey sheets, we sought evaluations regarding the company organisation for which they worked, from the viewpoint of rewardability and fairness (distributive, procedural,

Figure 1.11: Attitudes to the company organisation and fairness evaluation

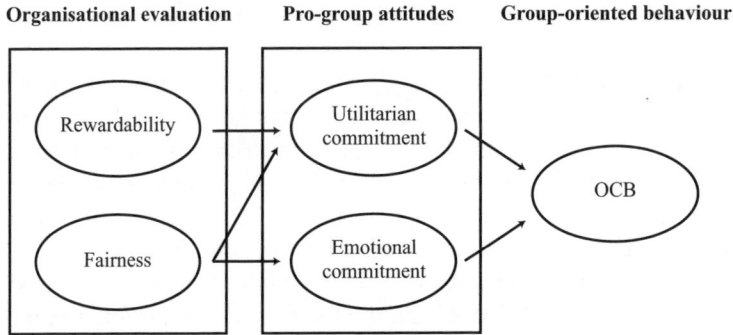

Source: Hayashi and Ohbuchi, 1999.

and interpersonal), and also requested answers to questions relating to attitudes to the company (utilitarian and emotional commitment) and group-oriented behaviour (OCB). As we used other variables in the survey than these, the results of path analysis were complex, but when we extracted only the relevant parts, the associations which we had postulated in Figure 1.11 were found. In other words, the level of reward strengthened employees' utilitarian commitment, and this stimulated group-oriented behaviour (OCB). On the other hand, with employees who perceived the organisation as fair, both utilitarian and emotional commitment grew in unison, resulting in the promotion of group-oriented behaviour. This is why we can conclude that the operation of justice bonds, which include utility and group-value, was identified in this survey targeting Japanese corporate employees.

Remaining issues

In this chapter, we focused upon the phenomenon called social bonds, as an outcome of fairness, tracked the evolution of theories dealing with this issue, and, furthermore, considered several empirical studies based on the justice-bond hypothesis which we had conducted with Japanese people as participants.

As a result, justice bonds were identified in each case – in attitudes of ordinary citizens towards the state, responses by litigants to legal proceedings, and organisational evaluations by company employees – and this showed that fairness performs the role of combining people with social groups. In the research process, a number of new topics for investigation have emerged. At the end of this chapter, I would like to take up some of them for discussion.

Dimensions of fairness in self-interest evaluations

In reactions of litigants to legal proceedings, the favourableness of the outcome had an impact upon the judgement of fairness (Ohbuchi et al., 2005). Furthermore, though I did not touch upon it in this chapter, a correlation was seen between reward levels and judgements relating to distributive justice in employees' organisational evaluations (Hayashi and Ohbuchi, 1999). The strong interlocking of interest judgements and perceptions of fairness in this manner is widely seen in fairness studies (Hayashi, 2004). Could it be that this fact, as noted in the self-interest hypothesis, shows that a concern for fairness is actually nothing more than a polite fiction to rationalise interests, or that fairness judgements are being distorted by self-interest?

We suspect that the very opposite might be true. When we had company employees evaluate their organisation's rewardability, we asked them if they were receiving adequate remuneration, but from what viewpoint did the respondents answer, I wonder? Supposedly, the majority would have tried to make an assessment by comparing their remuneration with that of people in a similar position to themselves (colleagues, people of the same status in other companies, school classmates, et cetera). Without such a standard for comparison, would not they have been unable to answer as to what constituted appropriate treatment, and what was sufficient pay? In our interpretation, people most likely establish their own capacity through social comparison, and compare this with the actual treatment they receive. If rewardability evaluation in itself already includes a judgement of fairness, then we could assume there to be a strong association between the two. As studies of relative deprivation (Olson, Roese, Meen and Robertson, 1994) indicate, it is hard for us to make evaluations without having any criteria for comparison with our own interest and treatment. In that sense, in society and within the group, fairness can be considered to be an essential dimension used when individuals judge the quality of the treatment they receive.

Procedural justice as resource allocation

The second remaining question concerns the connection between distributive and procedural justice. This distinction is a fundamental one in this field, but the difference is not always obvious. Tyler et al. (1997) state that the object of distributive justice judgments is not material resources alone, as social resources such as respect, appraisal, love, and so on, also are included. If this be so, then how might these social resources differ from what Tyler called 'relational factors' in procedural justice?

We suspect that, in fact, procedural justice also might make an issue of resource allocation. Through their studies of legal proceedings, Thibaut and Walker (1975) saw control – in other words, the thing which influences judgments – as a factor in procedural justice. Concretely, this means whether opportunities for voice and the assertion of opinions are to be given. When conflicting parties are given an equal voice, they feel that they have been fairly treated. In another instance, even if would-be entrants to a particular school cannot pass the entrance examination, if those aspirants have been given a chance to take the examination, then this is regarded as procedurally fair treatment. Thus, one can view the distribution of such opportunities as self-expression, self-assertion, or voice as being one factor contributing to the rise of procedural fairness.

Another type, as I have already noted, is relational factors, namely, the allocation of social resources. Having one's existence acknowledged by people (especially authority figures); being respected; or being given sympathy, empathy, and aid – these all involve interpersonal justice, which has been emphasised in organisational studies. When considered in this light, it can be seen that there is no essential difference between procedural justice and distributive justice, merely one stemming from a difference in allocated resources.

In Chapter Four, we propose that fairness generally can be expressed with a 'treatment/deservedness' formula, but if we also regard procedural justice as resource allocation, then it is easy to apply this formula to the judgment of procedural fairness. If we follow this formula, procedural justice can be seen as the giving to individuals (within a certain social relationship or group) of resources of opportunity and social resources commensurate with their qualifications (as litigants, employees, students, family members, or the like). There are still numerous questions remaining, however, such as the connection between entitlement and justice in procedural fairness, or whether there are sufficient types of distributed resources – each being a topic worthy of further consideration.

2 A Sense of Unfairness as Stratum Consciousness in Contemporary Japan
Michio Umino

Society is full of issues of fairness and unfairness. If one takes a glance around, one notices that countless distributions are being carried out – the 'distribution of remuneration for work' seen in the wage system; the 'distribution of civic duties' seen in the tax system; the distribution of the 'right to life,' such as in organ-transplants from the brain-dead; and so on – and that within each lurks the question of fairness. Fairness encompasses the issues of what kind of distribution to implement (distributive justice), and by what method distribution is to proceed (procedural justice), and without the resolution of these problems, society is not viable. Of these two, this chapter will deal with the issue of 'distributive justice.' The chapter will focus particularly upon the distribution of social resources such as income, educational background and occupational status. As the allocation of social resources is the subject of research in stratification studies, the task of this chapter will be to provide an overview of research on the sense of unfairness (especially studies on the sense of unfairness based on statistical social surveys) from the stratification studies viewpoint.

A sense of unfairness as stratum consciousness[1]

The subject of stratification studies is social stratification, in other words, the unequal distribution of social resources. When we try to approach this topic from the aspect of social consciousness, a sense of unfairness is a typical indicator, because the evaluation given to the distribution of 'social resources' – the collective designation given to the material assets, relational assets, cultural assets, et cetera, which form the 'source for the satisfaction of individual needs' (Tominaga, 1979, p. 3) – can be considered to be a sense of unfairness as social consciousness.[2]

Previous factors which have been studied as constituting stratum consciousness include (a) perceived image of stratification; (b) occupational prestige score; and (c) stratum identification. These respectively indicate (a') the image that people hold of society's stratification structure; (b') the evaluation of the social status of individuals who constitute the various strata; and (c') the situation of self in society.

Relative to this, the second aspect of stratum consciousness is 'all types of social consciousness understood in terms of their link with strata' (Hara, 1990). Once the stratification structure is conceptualised by means of an unequal distribution of social resources, this becomes an evaluation of the distribution of social resources.

An evaluation of the distribution of social resources (hereafter referred to as 'social evaluation,' in its narrow sense) is further composed of two aspects: (1) the 'sense of satisfaction' which is an affective evaluation of the standards of distributed resources (the affluence of the society); and (2) the 'sense of unfairness' which is a cognitive evaluation of the allocation of distributed resources.[3] Of these, as the principal focus of attention in stratification issues is more towards the allocation, rather than the standards, of resource distribution, this chapter will focus its interest mainly on a 'sense of unfairness,' rather than on a 'sense of satisfaction.'

In order for a social evaluation in the form of a 'sense of unfairness' to arise, there must first be cognition of the object. The object of cognition for a sense of unfairness is the circumstances of distribution of social resources in the pertinent society. The unequal distribution of social resources causes the genesis of social stratification, and recognition of that fact constitutes the aforementioned 'perceived image of stratification.' In order for a 'perceived image of stratification' to be a cognition tied to a sense of fairness, the conditions of resource allocation must be acknowledged. However, recognition of the conditions of resource allocation alone will not generate an evaluation of fairness or unfairness. When that allocation is compared with the 'ideal situation' and the discrepancy is large, people feel that it was 'unfair.' Here, the 'ideal situation' becomes the evaluation benchmark because it is something that arises by means of an 'ideal allocation principle' based on a 'perception of social justice' in the mind of the evaluator. Consequently, even under identical circumstances of resource allocation, if the evaluators' 'perception of social justice' is different, then their 'ideal allocation principle' and 'ideal situation' will also differ, and, as a result, neither will their 'sense of unfairness' as a social evaluation be the same.

Table 2.1: Stratum consciousness relating to social evaluation

Aspects of consciousness	Object standards	
	Micro-standards	Macro-standards
Cognitive	Stratum-identification consciousness	Perceived stratum image
	Occupational prestige	
Affective evaluation	Life satisfaction	Social satisfaction
Cognitive evaluation	Sense of having experienced unfairness	Sense of unfairness
Behavioural	Lifestyle	Political orientation

Note: Micro-standards: awareness which has the self (or others) as its object. Macro-standards: awareness which has the whole of society as its object. Political orientation: how one intends to engage with politics.

Source: Umino, 2000b.

Incidentally, in similar manner to other dimensions of social evaluation, there are two standards in a sense of fairness: micro-standards and macro-standards. The former is an evaluation of whether the self (or another particular individual) is receiving unfair treatment (a perception of unfair experience); while the latter is an evaluation as to whether the society in question (this does not have to be the society in which the self lives) is distributing resources unfairly. These two are interrelated. If unfairness exists on macro-standards, then the probability of unfair experience on micro-standards is likely to rise. Conversely, if one has an unfair experience on micro-standards, then a projection mechanism operates and one might come to think that other people also are having an unfair experience. This probably means evaluating society itself as unfair.

If we build upon the conceptual argument above, we can classify stratum consciousness relating to social evaluation as in Table 2.1.

Unfairness Issues Exposed

Our daily life is brimming with problems of unfairness. However, they do not necessarily come to light. As far as we know, the first time that a sense of unfairness was asked about in Japanese public-opinion polls was in the survey conducted by the Prime Minister's Office in December 1975. In 1979, the *Mainichi Shimbun*, one of Japan's nationwide newspapers, began to insert questions about a sense of unfairness in its public-opinion poll. In short, until the late 1970s, neither the government nor the mass media showed any interest in the issue of unfairness (Mabuchi, 2000).

Two conditions can be thought to have played a vital role in the social emergence of unfairness issues. The first is the economic slowdown which pivoted upon the 1973 Oil Crisis. The second is the sharpening of people's sense of entitlement, due to various incidents which occurred in the late 1960s.

As a result of the first condition, 'economic slowdown,' people became unable naively to imagine a bright future for themselves. Until then, people had been able to affirm their own lives by comparing their past and future selves. However, when this became difficult, people's eye then began to be concentrated upon comparison with others. Yet, if we question whether this immediately tied to the appearance of fairness issues, we find that this was not the case. Admittedly, though an actual judgement of fairness is swayed by egocentric bias, a judgement of fairness is fundamentally a public judgement which is also open to others. In other words, this means that I think that what I judge as fair ought also to be judged by others as fair. This is an attribute of the sense of fairness which is definitively different from a sense of satisfaction or mere preference. This is because it is necessary for a shared value which is convincing not only to one personally, but also to others, to exist behind fair distribution. In this way, a judgement of fairness is always accompanied by a judgement of what constitutes proper conditions. It is probably no wonder that an awakening of an awareness of rights which accompanied the social problematisation of such issues as the Vietnam War, Civil Rights Movement, student protests of the late 1960s and environmental pollution has exerted an influence in the emergence of such judgements as social judgements.

In this way, in the 1970s, the issue of a sense of fairness became a central question in social evaluation. Since 1973, the *Asahi Shimbun* has been reporting the results of its public-opinion poll conducted at the year-end as a New Year's special feature article. The poll's question about respondents' 'image of society' has respondents choose words to describe society from a list of various descriptors such as 'free,' 'prosperous,' 'stable,' 'confused,' 'lonely,' and so on, and 'unfair' always ranks in the top three. In people's image, 'unfair' is thus one of the most natural words to describe society (Mabuchi, 2000).

The structure and evolution of the sense of unfairness

Research on the 'sense of unfairness' in SSM Surveys

There is one social survey which Japanese sociology can boast to the world. This survey, the 'Social Stratification and Mobility Survey,' known as the 'SSM Survey,' is a statistical social survey now targeting adult males and females throughout Japan (males only until 1975), which has been planned and implemented every ten years since 1955 with the cooperation of many social scientists, principally sociologists. At the time of writing, preparations for the 2005 survey are in progress. Through this survey, such basic structures of society as occupational structure and inequality have been clarified.[4] In this chapter, I shall introduce findings gained from studies on the sense of unfairness, based on social surveys, centring upon research based on this series of SSM Surveys, but, prior to that, I shall reflect upon the SSM Surveys up until and including the 1995 Survey (the fifth survey), while focusing my attention upon the 'sense of unfairness.'

Interest in class consciousness – the 1950s

The First Nationwide SSM Survey, which was conducted in 1955, was a survey begun in a form concordant with stratification studies originally done mainly in the West, but, at the same time, 'strong interest was shown in the issue of class consciousness, reflecting the influence of Marxism, which characterised intellectual life in post-war Japan, and of Centers, whose work was widely read in the early 1950s' (Tominaga, 1979, p. 16). For that reason, various questions relating not only to stratum identification and class identification, but also to stratum consciousness, were included. In fact, in the first survey, such opinions as: 'If one works hard, one's life will become easier'; and, 'It is society's fault that there are some people whose lives will not become easier even though they do work hard' were called into question (Nihon Shakai Gakkai Chōsa Iinkai (Japanese Sociological Society SSM Research Committee), 1958). This question, while being one which reflects an age in which 'an easy life' (affluence, liberation from poverty) were sought, was at the same time also a question relating to social evaluation. Let us note the fact that at this point, questions relating to a sense of fairness ('Are workers treated fairly?'), questions about the discrepancy between male and female wages (about differentiating between the wages of males and females 'doing the same work at the same workplace'), and so on, were already being asked.

Openness and success in life – the 1960s

In the 1960s, Japan plunged into a period of rapid economic growth, and the material affluence which people pursued steadily became a reality. However, in the late 1960s, the strains of rapid economic growth became apparent in the guise of the pollution issue and student protests. In 1967, the 'Basic Law for Environmental Pollution Control' was formulated, manifesting governmental accountability for environmental conservation.

Nevertheless, this still did not yet impact upon the Second SSM Survey in 1965. In his analysis of this survey, Yasuda (1971) devotes a considerable number of pages to social consciousness, though his research interest was in 'social mobility' and 'success in life,' and there is hardly any analysis from the viewpoint of 'how people evaluate society.' Yasuda (1973) also conducts analysis of 'consciousness about strata' (the number of classes; presence or absence of continuity; presence or absence of polarity, et cetera), but the viewpoint of social evaluation does not exist.

Stratification structure and status-attainment process – the 1970s

Advanced industrial economies passed through the era of social movements in the 1960s and met the Oil Crisis in 1973. Sakamoto (2005), building on an analysis of the 'Nationwide Survey on Japanese National Character,' a continuing survey conducted eleven times, once every five years, from 1953 to the present, calls this period 'the greatest turning point in the post-war history of Japanese people's consciousness.'

The Third SSM Survey, implemented in 1975, was planned and carried out in such a period, but that turning point is not reflected in the survey contents. This third survey, comprising a 'Social Stratum and Mobility' survey and an 'Occupational Ranking and Evaluation' survey, was one which 'attempted to situate Japan as one of the advanced industrial societies, and reveal that the stratification structure shared by industrial societies also exists in Japan' (Hara, 1998), and high-level analysis relating to the stratification structure and status attainment process was undertaken (Tominaga, Ed., 1979).

In relation to consciousness, also, aspiration towards education and occupation was analysed as being something which mediates the status attainment process. Stratum identification, occupational prestige and occupational attractiveness were minutely analysed. In the criteria for question items, 'a sense of satisfaction' made its appearance. This suggests that a 'social evaluation' viewpoint had started to appear, linked with research on social indicators which was flourishing in that era.

The emergence of perceptions of fairness – the 1980s

In the 1980s, the kinds of challenges we still face today began to surface. According to a report entitled: *Japan in 2000*, published in 1982 by the Long-Term Outlook Committee of the Economic Council, the challenges our nation faces comprise the following three: (1) responses to the internationalisation of economic society and various issues of a global scale; (2) efforts aiming to make society a comfortable one in which to live, in preparation for the escalating ageing of the population; and (3) the maintenance of vitality in economic society, along with the achievement of its maturity.

Under such conditions, the major feature of the Fourth Survey, conducted in 1985, was the addition of women to the respondents (sampled population). A significant role was also anticipated in relation to stratum consciousness, and class/stratum identification was sought multilaterally. From the fourth survey onwards, items concerning a sense of unfairness (a sense of unfairness in general, and a sense of unfairness due to a specific attribute) were inserted. Though similar items to do with a sense of unfairness had been surveyed by a government agency (the Prime Minister's Office) and the mass media (the *Mainichi Shimbun*), this was the first time that these had been included in an academic survey. In this way, the SSM Survey did provide questions that evaluated stratification structure, albeit insufficiently.[5]

Inquiry into the social evaluation mechanism – the 1990s

With the advent of the Fifth Survey in 1995, questions on a sense of satisfaction and a sense of fairness came to be seen as fundamental issues, along with traditional questions such as those on stratum identification, occupational prestige, political party support, and so on. In relation to the sense of fairness, various questions connected with evaluation of Japanese society, including the 'ideal reward-allocation principle' and 'actual reward-allocation principle,' et cetera, were introduced, joining those introduced in 1985 on 'a sense of unfairness in general' and 'a sense of unfairness due to a specific attribute.' The aims, through these questions, were a theoretical analysis of the sense of fairness and an elucidation of its mechanism. The majority of the results are contained in Miyano (1998), and the main portion has been published in Umino (2000a).[6]

Above, we have simply reviewed the history of stratum consciousness studies in post-war Japan, while focusing upon the sense of unfairness. Upon such reflection on the research history, it can be seen that there has been a consistent quest for basic stratum consciousness, such as stratum identification. In addition, it can be inferred that the frames of reference of social evaluation and the sense of fairness had not been made issues in the period during which society was developing in a stable manner, but had been made issues in times when society was in chaos and was groping for direction.

Measurement of a sense of unfairness in SSM Surveys

As we have seen, research based on statistical social surveys into the sense of unfairness began from the 1985 SSM Survey. The question that forms its nucleus, which is a modified version of the wording of the opinion polls conducted by the *Mainichi Shimbun*, straightforwardly asked whether respondents thought that Japanese society was fair.

On a sense of unfairness in general:

Question: Generally speaking, how fair do you think Japanese society today is? Which of the expressions in the list is closest to how you feel?
   1) Fair;
   2) Quite fair;
   3) Not very fair;
   4) Unfair

The distribution of responses to this question was as follows: Fair (4 per cent); Quite fair (34 per cent); Not very fair (40 per cent); Unfair (20 per cent); Unclear/No response (2 per cent) (1985 Survey, nationwide, adult males only). This means that approximately 60 per cent of respondents answered that Japanese society was unfair.

In the 1985 SSM Survey, the question about the sense of unfairness in general was followed by a question similar to that below:
On a sense of unfairness due to specific attribute:

Question: Besides the overall evaluation that you have just given me, do you think the following kinds of unfairness exist? Please indicate all the kinds of unfairness that you see as existing.
1) Unfairness due to gender;
2) Unfairness due to age;
3) Unfairness due to education;
4) Unfairness due to occupation;
5) Unfairness due to wealth or poverty;
6) Unfairness due to family background;
7) Unfairness due to the region in which one lives or one was born;
8) Unfairness due to political or religious beliefs.

When the responses to this question are ranked according to an unfairness indication ratio, unfairness due to 3) 'educational background' ranked highest at 64 per cent, followed by 5) 'rich/poor' (57 per cent); 4) 'occupation' (51 per cent); 1) 'gender' (40 per cent); 6) 'family background' (36 per cent); 7) 'region' (35 per cent); 2) 'age' (28 per cent); and 8) 'ideology' (24 per cent). The main status-achievement route in Japanese society is assumed to be 'high educational background → high-stratum occupation → high income' (Tominaga, 1979), but I wish to draw attention to the fact that unfairness due to 'educational background,' 'occupation' and 'income (rich/poor),' which feature in this route, is frequently indicated.

Both the sense of unfairness in general and sense of unfairness due to a specific attribute change with the times. In actual fact, there are also some theses which follow those changes (Mabuchi, 2000; Hichibe, 2002; Umino, 2005). The direction of change cannot be said to be invariable, however, nor is the scale of the fluctuation notable. For this reason, in spite of various efforts, no unified results have been obtained in relation to the causes of variation. In this chapter, therefore, my discussion will concentrate more upon studies employing cross-sectional analysis, rather than time-series analysis.

Disparities in a sense of unfairness by attribute

Although 1985 SSM Survey targeted not only adult males but also adult females, it is impossible to clarify the difference in a sense of unfairness between the genders, as the survey actually consisted of three kinds of independent surveys, only one of which, whose respondents were adult males, contained questions on a sense of unfairness. In consequence, in the 1985 survey, into which questions on a sense of unfairness were introduced for the first time, a comparison by gender on the sense of unfairness could not be done. In the 1995 survey, however, the target population was expanded to include adult females, and a comparison by gender became possible. According to that comparison, a higher proportion of women than men indicated a sense of unfairness in general. Moreover, the older the respondent, and the higher the educational background, the lower was the tendency to indicate a sense of unfairness. In relation to occupation, apart from there being an outstanding low sense of unfairness due to managerial occupation, no great difference can be seen (Oda and Abe, 2000).

Umino et al. conducted intermittent awareness surveys (in 1986, 1994, 1999 and 2003) targeting senior high school students and their parents in the Sendai metropolitan area. According to these surveys, in relation to a sense of unfairness in general, a consistent tendency for male high school students, female high school students and mothers to be at a similar level, but for fathers' sense of unfairness to be one step lower, can be seen. On the reason for this, Umino (2005) proposes a 'commitment hypothesis' (the stronger a person's commitment to society, the less their tendency to harbour a sense of unfairness towards that society. Fathers generally commit to society more greatly than mothers or senior high school students, and so it is harder for them to have a sense of unfairness) and has reached a positive conclusion as a result of statistical analysis of survey data.

Might the manifestation ratio of a sense of unfairness due to a specific attribute vary with different attributes? According to Oda and Abe (2000), who analysed the 1995 SSM Survey, there are some attributes which manifest a clear difference by gender, and some which hardly differ. In other words, on unfairness by 'age,' 'family background,' et cetera, women's sense of unfairness is higher than men's, but with the other attributes, scarcely any difference between the sexes can be observed. When the data is examined in terms of age, there is a frequent tendency for a sense of unfairness to diminish in inverse proportion with age, similarly to a sense of unfairness in general. However, under examination in terms of educational background, in contrast to the sense of unfairness in general, in all cases of a sense of unfairness due to a specific attribute, the higher the level of education, the higher was a sense of unfairness. Finally, when data by occupation is examined, we see that the respondents who point out the existence of unfairness in society over all the various domains are those engaged in managerial and professional occupations, and white-collar workers in large companies. Though people in managerial occupations, in particular, show an extremely low sense of unfairness in general, they have a high tendency to show a sense of unfairness due to a specific attribute.

The characteristics of a sense of unfairness

From this, it has become clear that, when we take attributes as our point of reference, the senses of unfairness in general and unfairness due to a specific attribute indicate different behaviour. How, then, might these two be related? To answer this question, Umino and Saitō (1990) applied factor analysis to the responses regarding a sense of unfairness due to the eight specific attributes and those concerning a sense of unfairness in general, and arranged the respective senses of unfairness in the factor space. If a sense of unfairness in general were the synthesis of the senses of unfairness due to the eight specific attributes, then the sense of unfairness in general would be situated amid the senses of unfairness due to the eight specific attributes, in the factor space. However, in reality, the senses of unfairness due to the eight specific attributes are divided roughly into two groups, and the sense of unfairness in general lay not amid these two groups, but on their margin. This suggests that there exists some other potent element apart from a sense of unfairness due to a specific attribute, as a constituent element of a sense of unfairness in general. In other words, a 'sense of unfairness in general' is not simply the synthesis of the separate senses of unfairness due to specific attributes previously mentioned. Moreover, it was also found that a sense of unfairness in general had scant connection to a sense of unfairness due to a specific attribute by ascribed status such as gender, age, or the like, but was strongly linked to a sense of unfairness due to a specific attribute by achieved status such as educational background and occupation.

If a sense of unfairness in general is to be taken as not being merely a synthesis of the senses of unfairness due to specific attributes, then what other kinds of elements might influence the formation of a sense of unfairness in general? The hypothesis that the person's social status has an impact is refuted by data analysis, as no great influence is exerted by status variables such as the edu-

Table 2.2: *Prescribed factors for a sense of unfairness in general*[a]

Meaning and direction of attitudinal variables	Strength of influence[b]
Dislikes Liberal-Democratic Party (LDP)	0.177
Has 'unfairness due to occupation'	0.202
Dissatisfaction with income	−0.152
Agrees that 'even with effort, politics will not improve'	−0.165
Has 'unfairness due to wealth/poverty'	0.132
Has low stratum identification	0.128
Dislikes Democratic Socialist Party (DSP)	0.091
Disagrees that 'people in authority should be respected'	0.069
Disagrees that 'it is better to put more effort into one's own work than into politics'	0.071
Multiple correlation coefficient 0.520	Determination coefficient 0.271

Notes:
a = Multiple regression analysis by STEP method.
b = Standardised partial regression coefficient.
Data: 1985 SSM Survey.
Source: Umino and Saitō (1990).

cational background, occupational status and income of the person in question and his/her parents.

Therefore, after removing status variables from the variables obtained in the surveys, and making all the remaining sixty-one attitudinal variables candidates for explanatory variables, I have chosen those attitudinal variables which impact upon a sense of unfairness in general, by means of multiple regression analysis.

From scrutiny of these results, it can be read that being unfavourably disposed towards the political establishment as it was in 1985 ('Dislikes the Liberal-Democratic Party: LDP,' and 'Dislikes the Democratic Socialist Party: DSP'); having a sense of unfairness due to specific attributes ('occupation' and 'wealth/poverty'); giving a low evaluation to one's own stratum status; being dissatisfied with one's income; having a low sense of political validity (a strong sense of powerlessness); and not being authoritarian contribute to the intensification of a sense of unfairness in general. From this outcome, it can be considered that a sense of unfairness in general in contemporary Japan is regulated by the two elements: one's degree of liking towards the social system; and the recognition and evaluation of one's status, focusing on one's occupation (Umino and Saitō, 1990).

Oda and Abe (2000) conducted follow-up tests using data analysis of the 1995 survey, and confirm the same tendency. A sense of unfairness thus is not something which simply reflects people's dissatisfaction or interest as it stands.

The sense of unfairness and sense of satisfaction[7]

As I have already stated, approximately six out of every ten people harboured a sense of unfairness vis-à-vis society. However, it does not follow that people who harbour a sense of unfairness towards society simultaneously feel dissatisfaction with life. When asked how satisfied they were with 'life in general' (in the 1985 survey, nationwide adult males only), sixty-four per cent of respondents replied that they were 'satisfied with life.' When we consider these two figures together, it turns out that at least two out of every ten people are still satisfied with life, even while thinking that society is unfair. How, then, might a sense of unfairness (in general) and a sense of satisfaction (with life) be related, in actuality?

As can be seen in Table 2.3, there is a correlation between a sense of unfairness and a sense of satisfaction with life; the more satisfied people thought they were, the more likely they were to give a 'fair' response. However, it can also be seen that even among people who reported satisfaction with life, more than half their number replied that society was unfair.

What kind of causal relationship could there be, then, between a sense of unfairness and a sense of satisfaction with life? Is satisfaction high when a sense of fairness is high, or, conversely, does the sense of fairness rise when satisfaction is high? Or is there some cause common to both which heightens both a sense of fairness and a sense of satisfaction?

As a key to estimating causality from the correlation, I shall employ elaboration.[8] Here, in order to find the causal relationship between a sense of fairness and life satisfaction, I shall introduce a third variable, namely, a sense of satisfaction with society. However, as social satisfaction was not measured in the SSM Survey, here I shall conduct my examination using data (from a survey conducted by the author and a colleague, targeting residents of Sendai City) which includes all three of these variables. The tabulation results are shown in Table 2.4.

As it can be seen from this table, if the sense of satisfaction with society is equal, then irrespective of whether respondents think that

Table 2.3: The correlation between a sense of unfairness and life satisfaction (%)

Life satisfaction	Sense of unfairness		Total	(Actual count)
	Fair	Unfair		
Satisfied	44.0	56.0	100.0	(741)
Neither satisfied nor dissatisfied	29.7	70.3	100.0	(293)
Dissatisfied	29.6	70.4	100.0	(162)
Total	38.6	61.4	100.0	(1196)

Data: 1985 SSM Survey.
Source: Umino and Saitō, 1990.

Table 2.4: The correlation between a sense of unfairness and life satisfaction (when statistically controlled by a sense of satisfaction with society)

Life satisfaction	Satisfaction with society		Dissatisfaction with society	
	Fair	Unfair	Fair	Unfair
Satisfied with life (%)	88.3	82.8	45.9	36.8
(Radix of %)	(137)	(93)	(85)	(424)

Data: SPIKE Survey.
Source: Umino and Saitō, 1990.

society is fair or unfair, their sense of satisfaction hardly changes. If we focus attention on this fact, we find that the possible causality is one of the following three: [1] sense of fairness → sense of satisfaction with society → sense of satisfaction with life; [2] sense of fairness ← sense of satisfaction with society → sense of satisfaction with life; or [3] sense of fairness ← sense of satisfaction with society ← sense of satisfaction with life. However, with a perfunctory statistical argument alone, it is not possible to understand which of these constitutes the real causal relationship. It is necessary to mobilise substantial knowledge relating to the problem. With this issue, if we consider the following two points together – (1) social satisfaction and a sense of fairness are both macro-standard judgements; and (2) people generally start from micro-cognition in their surroundings, and tend to expand and generalise from this – then, out of the three candidates noted above, we can judge that the causal process [3] in the above schema which has life satisfaction, a micro-standard, as its starting point, is the one which arises. There is thus no direct causal relationship between a sense of fairness and life satisfaction.

The paradox of a sense of unfairness by educational background[9]

The 'sense of unfairness due to a specific attribute' which was investigated in the 1985 survey was also employed in the 1995 survey, with some slight alteration in the wording. In the 1995 survey, respondents were asked: 'Apart from a general evaluation, do you think that any of the following kinds of unfairness exists in Japanese society today?,' and in relation to each of eight criteria (attributes) including gender, age, educational background, and so on, they were required to choose one of three responses: 'There is a lot'; 'There is a little'; or 'There is none.' When attributes were ranked in descending order according to the proportion of people whose answer to this question on unfairness was affirmative (the total of 'a lot' and 'a little'), the result was: 'educational background,' 88 per cent; 'income,' 84 per cent; 'gender,' 83 per cent; 'occupation,' 82 per cent; 'assets,' 78 per cent; 'race, ethnicity, or nationality,' 77 per cent; 'age,' 75 per cent; and 'family background, 69 per cent (1995 survey, nationwide adult males and females). The type of unfairness felt this time by the greatest proportion of people was, in the same way as in 1985 survey, 'unfairness due to educational background.' With the other attributes, also, there is almost the same tendency.

Naturally, this result might not be particularly startling. This is because the awareness that contemporary Japanese society is an 'education-conscious society' (in other words, that a superior educational background is necessary in order to gain high social status and high income) is one shared by society as a whole. In an education-conscious society, people with low educational qualifications are placed in a socially-disadvantaged position. This is due to the relative difficulty of acquiring things which are considered socially desirable (social resources), such as high social status and high income. Consequently, people with low educational qualifications have no alternative but to content themselves with low social status and low wages, and, without doubt, feel unfairness due to educational background.

From this line of thought, we could venture the following predictions: 1) the better a person's educational background, the lower his/her sense of 'unfairness due to educational background' is likely to be; and 2) people in occupations such as professional or managerial occupations, which are obtained through high educational qualifications, are all the more likely to have a low sense of 'unfairness due to educational background.'

However, the tendencies that actually exist are the opposite of these. Among people in the high-education stratum when examined by educational background, and people in professional or managerial occupations when examined by occupation, the sense of 'unfairness due to educational background' is high. In reality, the proportions of people who answered that 'unfairness due to educational background' exists in contemporary Japanese society were: junior-high-school graduates (85 per cent); senior-high-school graduates (90 per cent); graduates of specialised technical high schools and junior colleges (95 per cent); and university graduates (93 per cent) (The tendency is not rectilinear; the high ratio in specialised technical high schools and junior colleges is thought to be due to the social position peculiar to specialised vocational schools, and to the large number of females among junior college graduates). In addition, people in professional occupations (94 per cent) or managerial occupations (95 per cent) have a higher sense of unfairness due to educational background than people engaged in blue-collar work in medium- to small-scale enterprises (89 per cent), or in agriculture, forestry and fishing (84 per cent). Why could this be?

One hypothesis that could be considered is the 'enlightenment effect hypothesis.' According to this hypothesis, people with high educational qualifications have gained the ability to objectify their own position by means of intellectual training and contact with all kinds of value judgements within the educational process. Therefore, they are aware that their being in a high position in real society is the result of their high level of education having worked to their advantage (not only because of their own efforts and ability). In other words, they may be thought to acknowledge their own present status as being due to the very existence of 'unfairness due to educational background.'

Now, let us examine whether this hypothesis is correct. In the same survey, there was a question such as the following. This asked whether the respondent agreed with the opinion that 'just because one has obtained high educational qualifications, it does not necessarily follow that one will be advantaged in terms of income.' If the 'enlightenment effect hypothesis' were valid, then, among respondents with a superior educational background, the ratio of people who believe in the existence of unfairness due to educational background would be higher among the people who disagreed (those who thought that high educational qualifications were tied to high income) than those who agreed (those who did not think that high educational qualifications automatically led to high income).

The converse is true, however. Among the people with high educational qualifications, the proportion of people who said that there was 'unfairness due to educational background' is 52 per cent among those who agreed with the statement (meaning they did not think that high educational qualifications automatically led to high income), while the proportion is 35 per cent among those who disagreed (meaning they considered that high educational qualifications were tied to high income).

Now, how might we explain the tendency described above, which cannot be explained by the 'enlightenment effect'? If there be a mechanism such as the following, then the tendency noted above should be generated; people with a superior educational background tend to think that 'when it comes to the distribution of social resources such as status and income, a premium should be set on educational background,' whereby they can justify their own high status and income. This means that, for people who think thus, the more they consider that high educational credentials are connected with high income, the lower their tendency will be to report a 'sense of unfairness due to educational background,' as it seems natural to them for high educational attainment to be tied to high income. I shall call such a way of thinking a 'self-justification hypothesis.'

If this self-justification hypothesis were taken as correct, then how could we explain the fact that a high proportion of people with a superior educational background and an occupation gained as a result of higher education (professional or managerial occupations) report a 'sense of unfairness due to educational background?' They think that they themselves, as people with high educational qualifications and a high-level occupation, deserve to receive a high income. However, in today's Japan, 'just because one has obtained high educational qualifications, it does not necessarily follow that one will be advantaged in terms of income.' As for people who answered in the affirmative to this statement (the total of those who said either that they 'agreed,' or 'somewhat agreed'), though the ratio among those with educational backgrounds limited to graduation from senior high school, junior college or specialised vocational high school was between sixty-eight and sixty-nine per cent, it reached seventy-three per cent among university graduates. Irrespective of their opinion that they deserved to receive a high income, they replied that there was 'unfairness due to educational background' in society, because, in actual fact, 'it does not necessarily follow that [someone with a superior education] will be advantaged in terms of income.'[10]

Principles of social-resource allocation: ideal and actual

In the 1995 SSM Survey, questions relating to principles of allocation were added to those about a sense of unfairness in general and a sense of unfairness due to a specific attribute.

On the principle of ideal social-resource allocation:

Question: There are various views, such as the ones below, about what kind of people deserve to obtain high status or economic affluence. Please choose the one which most closely matches your opinion.
 1) Preferably, the greater people's achievement is, the more they should obtain;
 2) Preferably, the more effort people put in, the more they should obtain;
 3) Preferably, people in need should obtain as much as they need;
 4) Preferably, everyone should obtain about the same amount.

On the principle of actual social-resource allocation:

Question: Now, which of the following four statements do you think most closely matches the actual situation in Japanese society today?
 1) The greater people's achievement, the more they obtain;
 2) The more effort people put in, the more they obtain;
 3) People in need obtain as much as they need;
 4) Everyone obtains about the same amount.

As for the outcome, though the preferences of the respondents themselves (as to the allocation principles operating in Japanese society) were: 'achievement,' 23 per cent; 'effort,' 57 per cent; 'need,' 9 per cent; 'equality,' 6 per cent and 'Don't know'/No response, 4 per cent, whereas per centages in terms of respondents' recognition of the present situation were: 'achievement,' 53 per cent; 'effort,' 19 per cent; 'need,' 11 per cent; 'equality,' 3 per cent; and 'Don't know'/No response, 15 per cent. While there were many people who thought that social resources ought ideally to be allocated by a principle of 'effort,' in actuality, the majority of people acknowledged that they were allocated by the 'achievement' principle.

Among the criteria listed here, in contrast to 'achievement,' which is considered something which is swayed by inborn ability because everyone is thought equally capable of 'effort,' allocation of social resources according to this criterion is probably considered fair. In

Table 2.5: The relationship between recognition of the 'principle of ideal social-resource allocation' and the 'principle of actual social-resource allocation' (%)

Principle of ideal allocation	Principle of actual allocation					
	Achievement	Effort	Need	Equality	DK; N/A	Total
Achievement	14.1	2.5	2.3	0.9	3.1	22.9
Effort	29.2	13.4	6.7	0.7	7.2	57.1
Need	5.4	1.4	1.2	0.4	0.9	9.4
Equality	3.3	1.1	0.6	0.4	1.0	6.4
DK; N/A	0.6	0.3	0.1	0.1	3.1	4.1
Total	52.6	18.8	10.8	2.6	15.2	100.0

Data: 1995 SSM Survey. N=2704.
Source: Miyano, 2000.

short, the effort principle can be considered an equitable principle seen from the perspective of the individual, and the achievement principle an equitable principle seen from the perspective of society and groups which are the recipients of the achievement.

Saitō and Yamagishi (2000) interpret observational outcomes such as these in the following manner: Japanese people have a strong tendency to find value in the very fact that effort has been made. Here, the effort principle refers to a philosophy that says 'individuals should be evaluated by effort itself, and allocation decided accordingly.' However, the effort principle is a criterion with low visibility. There is no instrument that can measure the amount of effort in a short time. This is probably because, in order to conduct an evaluation in terms of effort, the evaluator needs to observe how the evaluatee 'does her/his job,' and to that end, the evaluator needs to 'spend time together' with the evaluatee. When attention is directed at such points, the effort principle can be seen to have fostered long-term affiliations among people, and, as a result, has been supported by a system which inhibits translocation.

As I have previously noted, a judgement of fairness ideally must be something that transcends individual interest. In other words, there needs to be 'neutrality' vis-à-vis the individual interest of the judge. When we examine the relationship among this 'neutrality,' the 'principle of ideal allocation' and the 'principle of actual allocation,' there is a tendency for people whose neutrality is high to prefer 'achievement' and a tendency for people with low neutrality to favour 'effort.' This connection is not logical, but nonetheless it is affinitive. As a process by which such links are generated, Saitō and Yamagishi (2000) have speculated as follows: namely, that the effectiveness of the effort principle is facilitated in the daily lives of people who have comparatively stable social relationships in which there exists a clear-cut boundary with out-groups. Additionally, people who have such social relationships have diminished opportunities for exposure to different points of view and interests, and neutrality is hard to acquire. They contend that the mutual relation between neutrality and a preference for the effort principle is a spurious correlation arising due to the common cause of social relationships. They also have conducted analysis of the GSS (General Social Survey) carried out in the United States of America, discovering and adding their own considerations as to a tendency for respondents with low neutrality to prefer the achievement principle, which is opposite to the Japanese case.

Conclusion

In the above discussion, I have principally consolidated findings obtained in connection to the sense of unfairness, based on the results of the SSM Survey (Nationwide Survey of Social Strata and Social Mobility). However, due to the constraints of space, there were numerous findings to which I could not allude. Please refer to Umino (2000a) for more detail. In addition to this, there also exist two comprehensive survey studies which deal with the sense of unfairness: the '1991 Perceptions of Social Justice Survey'; and the 'Japanese Social Justice Project 1997 (JSJP97),' both projects being led by Miyano. The former was conducted as part of an international comparative study, ISJP, which stands for International Social Justice Project (Kluegel et al., 1995), and its results are contained in Chūō Daigaku Shakai Kagaku Kenkyūjo, Ed. (1996) and Miyano, Ed. (1996). The JSJP97 project was planned and executed mainly by members who had been in charge of the 'sense of unfairness' section in the SSM95 Survey project, and their outcomes are published in an English report (Miyano, Ed. 2000). Hichibe (2002) is a well-organised review concerning the survey studies on the sense of unfairness which have been conducted in Japan.

Though the study of the sense of unfairness, especially research based on social surveys, has a history of nearly twenty years, this leaves many issues worthy of elucidation. The elucidation of a sense of unfairness as social evaluation is an important, basic task, both to spur the autonomy of each individual citizen and to realise a just society. Even greater promotion is surely necessary.

3 Distributive Fairness and Procedural Fairness in Ultimatum Bargaining
Mitsuteru Fukuno

Self-interest and fairness concern in ultimatum bargaining

Though the causes for divergence of interests in negotiation are diverse, in this chapter I shall limit my discussion to adjustment of interests, which makes economic resources its major issue, and I shall examine the role of self-interest and fairness concern – the fundamental motivations which arise in bargaining situations. While specifically discussing fairness concern in ultimatum bargaining from the two perspectives of distributive fairness and procedural fairness, I shall demonstrate that perceptions of procedural fairness are determined by three factors, namely: formal procedure, interactional fairness, and the allocator's competitive orientation.

In bargaining over economic resources, the first proposed motivation is the maximisation of economic self-interest (e.g., Neale and Bazerman, 1991), by which the bargainer is thought to aspire to choose the most appropriate behaviour for resource acquisition. Attempts to understand the negotiation process by thus assuming people's economic rationality have been made in economic negotiation studies based on game theory (Roth, 1995, for example).

Bargainers, on the other hand, have a strong concern for the fairness of allocation outcomes (Messick, 1993; Schelling, 1960). The importance of fairness in resource allocation has been pointed out by many scholars (Blount, Bazerman and Neale, 1995; Cohen, 1991; Deutsch, 1975; Tripp, Sondak and Bies, 1995). According to research relating to resource bargaining, gaining a more favourable outcome than one's opponent does not necessarily maximise utility (Bazerman, Loewenstein and White, 1992; Loewenstein, Thompson and Bazerman, 1989). Loewenstein et al. (1989) examined what kind of payoff allocation most greatly enhanced their American experimental participants' satisfaction in an imagined situation where each participant, having developed a product with a friend and attempted to apply for a patent, received notice from a company which had already secured a patent for a similar product, to the effect that the company would like to purchase the rights to a portion of the product design for $3000, an offer which the two of them accepted.

Using an eleven-point scale ranging from –5 (extremely dissatisfied) to +5 (extremely satisfied), participants evaluated their level of satisfaction with seven allocation outcomes – when their friend's payoff was $300 (or $200 or $100) greater than their own; when both had equal payoffs; and when their own payoff was $300 (or $200 or $100) greater than their friend's. As a result, the allocation outcome which most greatly enhanced people's degree of satisfaction was equal allocation, in which there was no disparity between the proportions each obtained (Figure 3.1).[1] This result suggests that, in resolving conflict of interest to do with economic resources, bargainers' judgment and behaviour are governed by concern for the attainment of a fair outcome, which differs from the motivation of the pursuit of self-interest.

It is further perceived that, due to an orientation towards fair outcomes, even decisions which seem rational from an economic point of view are sometimes perceived as unfair. Through a telephone interview survey of Toronto citizens, Kahneman, Knetsch and Thaler (1986) illustrated that people judge the raising of a certain product's price by sellers, in response to a rise in demand for that product, to be unfair. This result shows that, even in circumstances where economic rationality which says that product price will be determined by supply and demand is in effect, individuals' own subjective standards of fairness will strongly influence their decision-making in economic transactions.

In this manner, people are motivated by concern for fairness as well as concern for self-interest in adjustment of interests relating to economic resources. What kind of influence, then, might these concerns have upon negotiation outcomes? In this chapter, I survey the results of Western and Japanese research using the paradigm called ultimatum bargaining, which is appropriate for examination of the roles of these two concerns.

Ultimatum bargaining is carried out in the following way: two experimental participants are asked to divide up a given resource: S. That resource does not constitute a reward for some kind of input. No prior power differential is assumed between the two players, they being in a mutually equal relationship, and they are usually meeting for the first time. For the purposes of allocation, one player is assigned the role of

Figure 3.1: The effect upon the social utility function of the relationship between parties in conflict

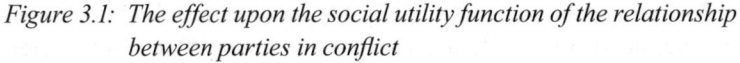

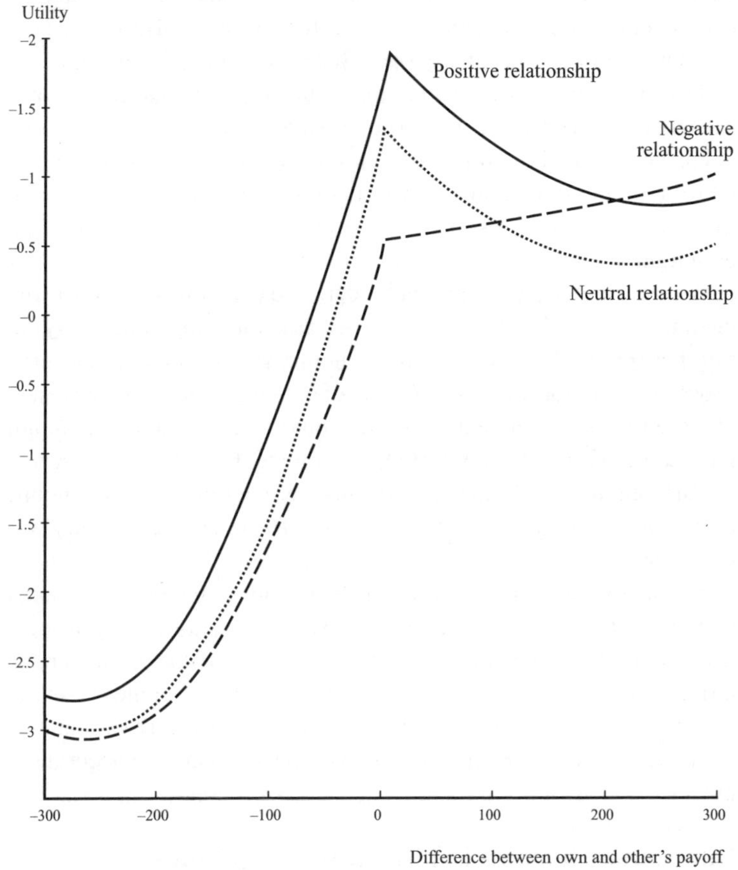

allocator, and the other that of recipient. The allocator freely decides a, representing his or her own share of S, and offers the recipient a share consisting of $S - a$. Here, the recipient decides whether to accept or reject that offer. If the recipient accepts the offer, the bargain is struck and each player can take her or his share of the resource in line with the allocator's offer. If the recipient rejects the offer, however, negotiations are broken off and neither party gets anything.

If the economic hypothesis of the maximisation of self-interest held true, then the allocator in ultimatum bargaining would be expected to offer as small a share as possible, and the recipient to accept any offer greater than 0. In other words, in this situation, both participants can choose the most rational strategy if they behave according to the sole motivation of wanting to maximise their own individual advantage. However, in actual practice, allocators tend to make offers which are close to equal allocation, and recipients tend to reject offers which are too small (Güth, Schmittberger and Schwarze, 1982, for example).

The first researchers to conduct empirical investigation into ultimatum bargaining were the German game theorists, Güth, Schmittberger and Schwarze (1982). As reviewed by Camerer (2003), there have since been many reports of Western studies employing this paradigm. The results of most studies which have used this paradigm, including those conducted in Japan (see Fukuno, 1999, for one), consistently show a similar tendency to that described above, the median value of the allocator's offered amount being about forty- to fifty per cent of the total allocation amount, and the mean value being about thirty- to forty per cent. Offers of one- to ten per cent and offers of more than fifty per cent are seldom observed.[2] In addition, though it is rare for recipients to reject offers of forty- to fifty per cent, when the offered amount falls below twenty per cent of the total amount, there is a stronger tendency to reject the offer, in one out of every two participants.

In the next section, I examine the behaviour of recipients vis-à-vis unequal offers. If we see bargaining as a decision-making process which extends to the agreement stage, then it becomes necessary to consider also whether the bargain is struck. It thus becomes essential to consider not only the offering behaviour of the allocator, but also the behaviour of the recipient, which directly affects the negotiation outcome.

Distributive fairness in ultimatum bargaining

As already stated, the most influential explanation pertaining to recipients' behaviour in rejecting unequal offers which mean small payoffs is one which emphasises recipients' fairness concerns (Thaler, 1988; Murnighan and Pillutla, 1995). It has been demonstrated by many scholars that, in social situations of resource allocation and suchlike, people evaluate or react to other people's behaviour or the outcomes of that behaviour from the viewpoint of fairness (Tyler, Boeckmann, Smith and Huo, 1997). If recipients perceive an unequal offer from an allocator to be unfair, then they are motivated to repair that inequity. Rejection of an unequal offer means zero benefit for both parties, but it is possible to rectify the inequity in payoffs. From this, it is natural to infer that a recipient's reaction of rejection towards an unequal offer involves fairness concern.

The question of how a recipient's perception of unfairness is aroused by unequal offers has been examined from the two perspectives of distributive fairness and procedural fairness. The former is based on the absolute or relative size of the offer to the recipient, while the latter says that unjust treatment towards the recipient gives rise to a perception of unfairness.

As there is no input from the parties concerned prior to resource allocation in ultimatum bargaining, it is impossible to conduct a fairness evaluation with input and outcome as criteria for comparison. However, if we think that 'because the input of the parties involved is 0 in both cases, then their input will be equal,' there will therefore be a high probability that making the outcome equal – in short, equal allocation – will be judged to be fair. Based on such a judgement, the recipient in ultimatum bargaining is thought to expect equal allocation, and to reject an offer that seems all too unfair from the perspective of distributive fairness. In this case, the recipient is assumed to make a judgement on distributive fairness by focusing upon the relative difference between the amount which he or she is offered and that of the other player (Bolton and Ockenfels, 2000). In other words, as recipients make the proportion which they will take from the whole amount their criterion for judgement of fairness, and offers of fifty per cent of the total are seldom rejected, this seems valid. From a similar angle, Fehr and Schmidt (1999) offer a model called inequality-aversion, but in this model, it is assumed that the recipient makes a fairness judgement focusing on the absolute discrepancy between her or his payoff and that of the other player. Even if the relative payoffs out of the total amount are equal, it is taken that the recipient's envy will increase as the absolute discrepancy between the two payoffs widens.

Using students at the University of Zurich and the Swiss Federal Institute of Technology in Zurich (ETHZ) as participants, Falk, Fehr and Fischbacher (2003) conducted experiments which examined the validity of these two explanations. In an ultimatum bargaining condition in which 10 points were to be divided, the allocator made an offer of 8 to him- or herself, and 2 to the recipient. If the recipient accepted this offer, he or she obtained an amount of cash in line with those proportions. In this experiment, however, even if the recipient rejected the offer, both players were able to get ten per cent of the respective offers. In other words, in this situation, when the offer was accepted, the payoff was (8, 2), but when it was rejected, the payoff became (.8, .2), meaning that the relative payoff obtained by the recipient was the same, irrespective of whether she or he accepted or rejected the offer. If, as Bolton and Ockenfels (2000) assert, recipients are concerned only about the relative proportions of the payoffs, then, as long as the payoff ratio remains equal, all recipients can be expected to accept an offer of (8, 2) because it will be considered desirable to obtain a larger amount of the resource – in other words, no rejections will be expected to occur. If, on the other hand, Fehr and Schmidt's (1999) assertion is correct, then it will be expected that an offer of (8, 2), where the difference between each player's payoff is greater than in an offer of (.8, .2), will sometimes be rejected. The results of the experiments did not support the prediction of Bolton and Ockenfels (2000) that all recipients would accept an offer of (8, 2), but did support the assertion of Fehr and Schmidt (1999).[3] This shows that when a recipient makes a judgement of distributive fairness, she or he focuses not only upon the relative proportions of the payoffs to each player, but also on the absolute value of the difference between the respective payoffs. In other words, the recipient's judgement of distributive fairness can be considered to be carried out not by comparing the proportion that his or her own payoff represents in terms of the entire pie – that is, by comparing that payoff with the total amount – but by comparing his or her payoff with that of the other player. Moreover, if we take it that the recipient concentrates upon the absolute size of each player's payoff, then the size of the whole pie itself might also be capable of influencing distributive fairness judgements.

Both of these explanations are based on comparison between players' payoffs, but, on the other hand, the recipient could also be understood to have rejected the offer simply because she or he was dissatisfied with the absolute value of the offered amount. It is possible that the recipient's behaviour was regulated not by a judgement of fairness by means of comparison with the other player's payoff, but due to the minimal nature of the offer itself. If this interpretation holds true, then it can be thought that the recipient will reject an unequal offer, regardless of whether he or she knows the total amount which is to be divided. However, Straub and Murnighan (1995) have reported that experimental participants who knew the total amount to be divided were more likely to reject unequal offers than were those who did not have that knowledge, in experiments with American participants. In Japan, I also conducted similar investigations using scenario experiments (Fukuno, 1999), and have reported that both the acceptance ratio and the incidence of fair judgements vis-à-vis unequal offers consisting of minimal amounts fall further when there is information given about the size of the total pie than when there is no such information (Fairness judgement $M = 4.18$ vs. 2.31; Acceptance ratio 50.0 per cent vs. 14.5 per cent).[4] From this, it can be seen that it is more a question of the relative evaluation of the value of an offer rather than its absolute evaluation that governs a recipient's behaviour.

Procedural fairness in ultimatum bargaining

Procedural fairness means not the fairness of outcomes, but the fairness of the decision-making procedure relating to the allocation of outcomes. Lind and Tyler (1988) asserted that people's concern for procedure was not something which always arose out of self-interest, but also reflected the quality of the treatment they received from the decision-makers or authority figures. When people feel that they have received treatment which is appropriate to their own rights and qualifications from decision-makers, their sense of procedural fairness is enhanced, while a sense of procedural unfairness arises if they feel that they have received unjust treatment. In recent years, scholars of social fairness have argued that procedural fairness is divided into two categories: evaluation of formal procedure, and interactional fairness (see, for example, Folger and Cropanzano, 1998; Greenberg, 1990; Niehoff and Moorman, 1993). 'Formal procedure' means the objective evaluation of fairness relating to the procedures employed in instances of resource-allocation and decision-making. Examples which could be cited include the questions of whether a particular procedure is one which is always consistently applied to all members involved in that allocation system (i.e., there is consistency), or whether the decision-makers have made their decision from a neutral standpoint, without incorporating their individual interest (i.e., there is bias-suppression) (Leventhal, 1980; Leventhal, Kruza and Fry, 1980).

Yet another aspect of procedural fairness is the evaluation of interactional fairness. 'Interactional fairness' means that decision-makers put themselves into the shoes of the accepters of their decision when making a decision by means of a particular procedure (Bies, 1987; Bies and Moag, 1986; Tyler and Bies, 1990). In other words, the way in which decision-makers implement decision-making procedures, or how the decision-makers respond to the accepters of the decision, affects perceptions of interactional fairness. In concrete terms, points such as a careful response to the rights and dignity of the accepters of the decision and ample explanation referring to the decision form the keys for such judgement. Ultimatum bargaining studies which can be organised from the perspective of procedural fairness mainly can be classified according to these two ideas.

The effect of formal procedure: role-assignment procedure

One type of formal procedure which should be examined in ultimatum bargaining situations is probably role-assignment procedure, in which experimenters generally decide who will take the roles of allocator and recipient. Participants in ultimatum bargaining are more likely to perceive that resource-control lies in the hands of the one acting as the allocator, rather than the one playing the role of the recipient (Murnighan and Pillutla, 1995). Because of this, a person who has been assigned the role of recipient might feel that his or her right to take the allocator's role has been unilaterally denied by the experimenters, and feel it is unfair for that reason.

In the West, Hoffman, McCabe, Shachat and Smith (1994), for example, have added to their investigation a condition that participants be made to win the right to the allocator's role on the basis of their score in a general-knowledge quiz, when the roles in ultimatum bargaining are being decided. The results showed that the American participants in the experiment who won the role of allocator were more likely to make offers favourable to themselves than participants who had been assigned the allocator's role by the experimenters. Recipients, moreover, did not reject the unequal offers produced by such a method. Recipients are thought to have tolerated being dealt with in an unjust manner because they perceived the exercise of power by an opponent who had won the role of allocator to be just.

In Japan, we (Fukuno and Ohbuchi, 2003) examined the influence upon Japanese recipients' behaviour of the arbitrariness of procedure, as another aspect to formal procedure in ultimatum bargaining, by manipulating that arbitrariness by means of instructions when deciding the roles of allocator or recipient. We told one half of the participants who had been assigned the recipient's role that the experimenters had decided the roles arbitrarily, while telling the remaining half that a student unconnected with the experiment had chosen the roles by drawing lots, thus emphasising the low arbitrariness of the role-assignment.

Figure 3.2: Fairness evaluation of role-assignment procedures

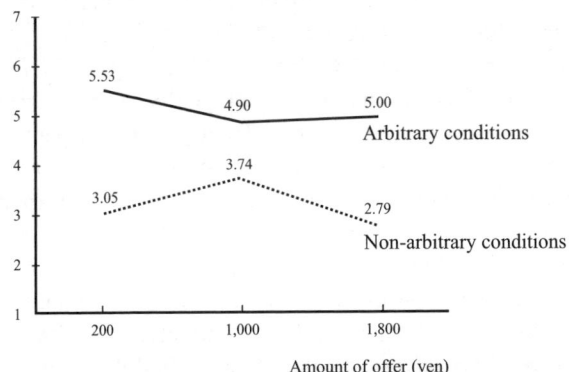

The experiment resulted in the participants in non-arbitrary condition giving a higher fairness evaluation to the role-assignment procedure (M = 5.19, as in Figure 3.2) than the participants in arbitrary condition (M = 3.19). Moreover, path analysis resulted in the arbitrariness of role-assignment procedure being shown to be linked with formal procedure evaluation. There was no link, however, between the arbitrariness of role-assignment procedure and the acceptance of unequal offers. This suggests that experimental participants made a distinction between control by the allocators in terms of the allocators allocating resources – yet another formal procedure in ultimatum bargaining – and control by the experimenters in terms of role-assignment.

Effect of interactional fairness: distributive intent of allocator

As interactional fairness is governed by the quality of the treatment given out by decision-makers, interactional fairness in ultimatum bargaining has an intimate connection with allocators' behaviour. The behavioural intent of the allocator during the offering process, especially, is thought to strongly influence the recipient's evaluation of interactional fairness. Using American students in an MBA programme, Kramer, Shah and Woerner (1995) investigated the influence exerted upon recipients' reactions by allocators' negative intent. The experimenters told the experimental participants that the ultimate offer would be decided by the following procedure: first, the allocator would decide upon an offer; next, the experimenters would add a certain per centage to that offer and determine the ultimate amount to be offered to the recipient. Participants were told that the proportion to be added would be decided by lottery, the range being between −100 per cent and +100 per cent. As a result of the experiment, participants reacted more in accordance with the equality of the offer initially decided by the allocators than with the equality of the ultimate offer. In other words, there was a greater tendency for a participant to accept an offer in the condition where the allocator had initially offered half the total amount, even if the ultimate offer were lower, than in the condition where the allocator had initially made a small offer, even if the ultimate offers were equal. This result indicates that the recipient has a strong concern towards the intentionality of the allocator.

Falk, Fehr and Fischbacher (2003) conducted experiments using Zurich university students, employing a method different from that of Kramer et al. (1995), and have demonstrated the effect of the distributive intent of the allocator. Choosing from a pair of offers, the allocator made one offer (8, 2), but the alternative offer, which was not chosen, was either (5, 5), (2, 8) or (10, 0). In this case, the allocator's intent in relation to the (8, 2) offer would change according to which alternative offer was the one not chosen. If (8, 2) is the offer made in a condition where an offer of either (8, 2) or (5, 5) is possible, then the recipient will probably judge this offer to be unfair, and perceive that the allocator is selfish. If the allocator offers (8, 2) when the alternative is (10, 0), then he or she will be judged to have consideration towards the recipient's payoff. If the allocator offers (8, 2) instead of (2, 8), she or he will probably be judged not so much as having been selfish as having avoided incurring a personal loss in relation to a choice in which there was an inevitable disparity in payoffs. In the experimental results, while the offers made to recipients were (8, 2) in all conditions, their rejection rates differed according to which of the alternative offers was not chosen. The offer-rejection rate was forty-four per cent when the unchosen offer was (5, 5), while it dropped to twenty-seven per cent when (2, 8) was unchosen, and to nine per cent when (10, 0) was the unchosen offer. Irrespective of the fact that the range of shrinkage in the recipient's payoff was greater when the unchosen offer was (2, 8) rather than (5, 5), the rejection rate was higher when the unchosen offer was (5, 5). It was shown from this that the recipient evaluated the allocator's intent to offer by focusing not simply upon whether the allocator had tried to make the recipient's payoff smaller, but upon whether, for example, the allocator had tried to deviate from distributive fairness, even if the amount of change to his or her payoff were small.

Further to this, Blount (1995) in the United States reports that when procedure was altered so that offers were stochastically determined using a computer programme, the recipient more readily accepted unequal offers generated stochastically by computer. As there was an identical possibility of an unequal offer being made by the stochastic method in both cases, it can be understood that it was easily seen as being fair. It as shown that, even with the same unequal offer, that made by a allocator her- or himself tended to be perceived as being procedurally unfair in as much as there still remained some intention of self-serving behaviour.

In Japan, Fukuno and Ohbuchi (2003), using a similar paradigm to Blount (1995), have investigated the effect of allocator intentionality by having ninety-nine university students carry out ultimatum bargaining. The results showed that recipients to whom an unequal offer (¥200) was made by the personal decision of allocators assigned a lower evaluation to the neutrality of those allocators than did recipients whose unequal offer was decided by roulette (M = 1.95 vs. 4.23; see Figure 3.3).

Moreover, as can be appreciated from Figure 3.3, even among unequal offers, the evaluation of allocator neutrality fell further when the offer to the recipient was ¥200 out of a total pie of ¥2000

Figure 3.3: Path diagram relating to offer/proposal acceptability

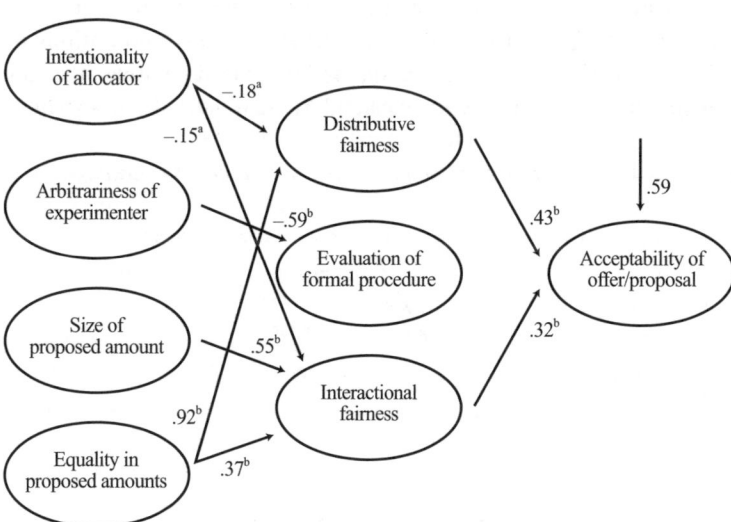

a = p < .05; b = p < .01.

than when it was ¥1800. Even though both offers were unequal in distributive terms, why, I wonder, was procedural fairness in the case of the ¥1800 offer evaluated as being about the same level as when the offers were equal? In ultimatum bargaining, it is the allocator who decides what to offer the recipient, and the allocator can decide the size of the respective shares without being subjected to limitation by any other person. For this reason, even if the allocator offers ¥1800 out of a total of ¥2000 to the recipient, this does not mean that the allocator's behaviour was unjustly subject to limitation, it arguably being a result obtained with the endorsement of the allocator. As long as the allocator's rights have not been eroded, the recipient can be thought not to have perceived the process of offering ¥1800 as procedurally unfair.

Furthermore, as shown in Figure 3.4, we can also elicit a number of considerations from the results of path analysis conducted in order to explore the relational structure among the situational factors in ultimatum bargaining (arbitrariness, allocators' intentionality, equality of offers and size of offers), fairness evaluations by recipients (evaluations of the fairness of role-assignment procedure, and interactional and distributive fairness, respectively), as well as offer acceptability. The first consideration is the fact that not only distributive fairness, but also interactional fairness – one aspect of procedural fairness – stipulated recipients' reactions. Scholars of organisational fairness have found that appropriate treatment by employees' superiors nurtured the employees' perceptions of fairness towards their organisation, and increased positive attitudes towards it (Greenberg, 1990; Bies and Moag, 1986). Tyler and Lind

Figure 3.4: Evaluation of allocator neutrality in the offer process

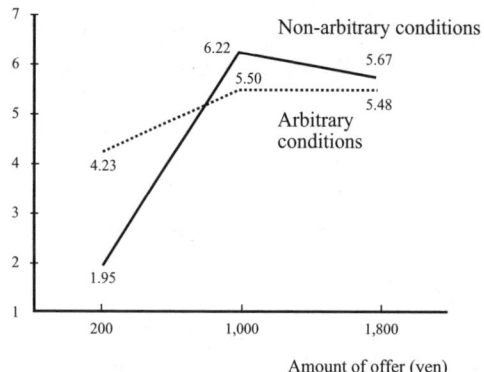

(1992), moreover, asserted that the most important prescriptive factors in procedural fairness are relational factors, the perceived nature of authority being of particular significance. In comparatively simple negotiation situations like ultimatum bargaining, the people concerned have a strong social psychological interest such as this, which motivates their reaction.

The second consideration I could cite is the fact that while distributive fairness relied strongly upon the equality of the offers, interactional fairness reflected both the equality and the size of offers. Experimental participants were more likely to accept an offer of ¥1800 than one of ¥200, even though both represented unequal offers. This result is consistent with the findings of Loewenstein et al. (1989). In addition, Diekmann, Samuels, Ross and Bazerman (1997) have elucidated the fact that people are more likely to evaluate an offer as fair if it is advantageous rather than disadvantageous to them. Researchers have hitherto interpreted such results as indicating that fairness evaluation was distorted due to the influence of self-interest (e.g., Messick and Sentis, 1993). These results mean, however, not that the fairness evaluation is distorted, but rather that it reflects a valid judgement called interactional fairness. When there is distortion of fairness evaluations, such cases can mostly be interpreted from the perspective of distributive fairness. Indeed, deciding that a result advantageous to oneself was fairer than a disadvantageous one, in circumstances where there was ambiguity in the criteria relating to fair allocation, would probably be understood from a distributive viewpoint as meaning that self-interested cognitive justification had been implemented. However, Fukuno and Ohbuchi (2003) suggest the possibility that fairness evaluation in this instance is being carried out not from a distributive perspective, but from a perspective of interactional fairness. Offers which are advantageous to the recipient can be thought simultaneously to convey the message that the allocator respects the self-esteem and identity of the recipient, while the recipient also carries out a fairness evaluation from an interactional viewpoint, using the interpersonal consideration shown by the recipient as a key. For the recipient in ultimatum bargaining, the interactional aspect of fairness might be more vital than its distributive aspect. For that very reason, perhaps the size of an offer did not so much directly promote its acceptance as indirectly stimulate it, mediated also by perceptions of interactional fairness.

Thirdly, it should also be emphasised that interactional fairness was affected by various aspects of the offers, including their size, equality, intentionality, and so on. From the simple experience of receiving an offer of a certain sum of money, the recipient seeks a multidimensional understanding of all aspects of that experience, and it can be inferred that he or she is carrying out a fairness evaluation through such complex social cognition. The fact that the allocator's intentionality enhanced interactional unfairness judgements suggests that it is not the lowness of offers alone that constitutes the source of a threat to identity. In other words, judgements of interactional fairness are influenced by the allocator's intentions, namely, how the allocator intends to treat the recipient, independently of the size of the offer, or offer equality. This means that judgements of interactional fairness in ultimatum bargaining are strongly regulated by whether allocators in the offer process have intended to effect equal offers, irrespective of whether the resulting offers turn out to be equal. As it can also be appreciated from the fact that low offers decided by allocators were more likely to be rejected than low offers determined by roulette, threats to identity can be considered to stem not so much from unfair treatment itself, but to be brought about by the intention of a allocator who deliberately attempts to treat another unfairly.

From the investigations in this section, it was strongly suggested that the recipient in ultimatum bargaining evaluates the allocator's offer not only from the perspective of distributive fairness, but also from that of procedural fairness. It should especially be noted that procedural fairness evaluations had a stronger connection with offer acceptance than did distributive fairness evaluations. For example, though recipients were more likely to reject offers of ¥200 than offers of ¥1800, there was no significant difference between these in evaluations of the distributive fairness of the offer amounts, and a disparity equating to rejection was detected only in evaluations of procedural fairness. This suggests that it is the fairness of the offer process, rather than the fairness of the offer itself, that needs to be afforded greater importance for understanding the recipient's reaction. Falk et al. (2003) have illustrated the limitations of attempts to comprehend recipients' evaluations of offers from the sole perspective of distributive fairness. The recipients in their experiments using Swiss university students were each given unequal offers of (8, 2), and, if they accepted, were able to obtain an outcome commensurate with that allocation. If they rejected that offer, however, they were placed in a situation where the offers became (6, 0). If one judges this purely from the viewpoint of distributive fairness, it will be expected that an offer of (8, 2) will not be rejected, because if the recipient focuses upon what she or he will receive in terms of relative proportions (Bolton and Ockenfels, 2000), then that per centage will be smaller when the offer changes to (6, 0), though if the recipient pays more attention to the disparity between his or her payoff and that of the allocator (Fehr and Schmidt, 1999), then the discrepancy between the offers to each party will be equivalent in each pair, it being −6 in either case. However, in actual practice, nineteen per cent of participants rejected an (8, 2) offer, and the prediction that offers of (8, 2) would never be rejected was not supported. As neither of the theoretical projections relating to distributive fairness evaluations was supported, there still is a limit to how far one can seek to apprehend the evaluation of recipients' offers from the aspect of distributive fairness.

Individual difference factors: social value orientation

From the preceding discussion, it has been shown that allocators' intentionality in making offers greatly influences recipients' fairness evaluations and decision-making. In this section, I examine competitive orientation – yet another aspect of allocator intentionality in ultimatum bargaining which constitutes a vital key to the judgement of procedural fairness. Studies of responsibility-attribution in aggressive situations have pinpointed the justice of intentionality and motivation as a cognitive factor which governs victims' reactions to intentional aggression (e.g., Ferguson and Rule, 1983). Victims first judge intentionality, in terms of whether the harm was inflicted deliberately. If harmful intent is attributed, then, next, the motivation behind that intentional harm is judged. From this, allocators' intentions in ultimatum bargaining arguably could be judged from the two viewpoints of (a) whether the allocator deliberately carried out unequal allocation; and (b) what the motivation behind that unequal allocation was. However, as I have already discussed intentionality in a previous section, here I will consider the justice of the motivation.

The actor's orientation itself does not constitute intention, but knowing actors' will and orientation provides an important clue for judging their behavioural intent. Social value orientation (e.g., Van Lange, 1999) is one concept which expresses actors' orientation. This refers to preference vis-à-vis the self-other outcome patterns in mutual interdependence, and can be roughly classified into co-operational orientation, which aims for the maximisation of harmony between self-other advantage or the reduction of disparity in advantage; individualistic orientation, which aims for the maximisation of self-interest without concern for the advantage of other parties; and competitive orientation, which aims for the magnification of disparity in self-other advantage. In ultimatum bargaining, as the amount of resources to be allocated is fixed, it is theoretically impossible to discern whether the social value orientation of allocators who make unequal offers is individualistic or competitive. Generally, however, as recipients who are offered unequal payoffs perceive a threat to their identity (Fukuno and Ohbuchi, 2001), recipients are considered more likely to perceive the orientation of allocators making unequal offers as being aimed at the amplification of the allocators' own advantage by slighting recipients' advantage, than as simply aiming to expand the allocators' own advantage.

While most research relating to social value orientation has been conducted in the West, elucidating the social value orientation of negotiators, as well as the connection between negotiating behaviour and the results of negotiation (De Dreu and Van Lange, 1995; De Dreu, Weingart and Kwon, 2000; Olekalns, Smith and Kibby, 1996), Fukuno and Ohbuchi (2005) have carried out studies in Japan from the perspective of how the behaviour of negotiators is governed by their perception of their opponents' social value orientation. Fukuno and Ohbuchi (2005) focused upon how recipients' behaviour is affected by the way in which they perceive the intentions of allocators in ultimatum bargaining, from the perspective of social value orientation. In this research, ultimatum bargaining was carried out by a method in which each allocator chose one out of three alternatives which showed both players' payoffs, and made that offer to the recipient. In all cases, the recipients received an unequal offer in which the allocator was to get ¥1800 and the recipient ¥200, but, under a competitive orientation condition, both players' payoffs in the other alternatives were manipulated so that this particular offer would be the most competitive choice out of the three. Under a condition of individualistic orientation, on the other hand, payoffs were manipulated so that an offer of ¥1800 to the allocator and ¥200 to the recipient would represent the most individualistic choice of the three alternatives. These experiments resulted in the acceptance ratio for the competitive offer being lower than that for the individualistic offer (33.3 per cent *vs.* 60.0 per cent), even though the offered amounts were the same. This suggests that the negative reaction of recipients often seen vis-à-vis unequal offers is linked with a perception of allocators' competitive motivation. In other words, recipients can be considered to have reacted sensitively to allocators' concern for the maximisation of difference rather than to allocators' concern for the maximisation of the latter's self-interest. Conventional game-theoretical projections relating to recipients' acceptance of offers are mostly thought to have been made from an individualistic perspective (for example, that recipients will accept any offer, however low, because of the feeling that 'something is better than nothing'), but one could argue that the results of Fukuno and Ohbuchi (2005) prompt a redefinition of the very premise upon which game-theoretical predictions are based.

4 The Structure of Justice: Theoretical Considerations

Ken-ichi Ohbuchi

For the past decade or so, we have conducted social psychological research into fairness, using Japanese people as participants. This has mainly comprised studies relating to procedural fairness and the influence it exerts upon the social relationships of individuals (Ohbuchi, 2004a, 2006a). In those papers, we repeatedly considered the essential qualities of justice and fairness, but, in this chapter, I wish theoretically to examine the conceptual structure of justice and discuss the association between justice and fairness criteria, in particular.

What do we mean by 'fairness'?

We Japanese often use the words *kōsei* and *kōhei* to mean 'fairness,' but many of us would probably be hard-pressed for an answer if challenged anew to define those terms. Fairness is a multi-faceted concept which has a number of meanings. It is the aim of this chapter to analyse what kind of structure it has, but first, I will conduct a preliminary consideration of the notion of fairness, as a basis for the discussion to follow.

Social behaviour and fairness

If we think about when people use the words for fairness, *kōsei* and *kōhei*, we can glimpse the essence of the ideas behind those terms. If a mother were to turn to her family and say, 'I have decided to go jogging for thirty minutes every morning, to lose weight,' what might her family say in response? It would probably be simple – they might agree, by saying something like: 'That's a good idea. You should definitely give it a go,' or venture a cautious opinion such as: 'Exercise is all very well, but you'd better not overdo it.' Such responses leave no room for notions of fairness (*kōsei* or *kōhei*). Why might that be? It is because the mother's utterance expresses a purely individual action. However, what might happen if, following this utterance, the mother had said: '...so, from now on, I won't be able to get your breakfast ready, so all of you get your own breakfast before you go, won't you?'[1] This time, might not there be some disgruntled reactions from members of the family, such as: 'That'll be a nuisance,' or 'I've never heard of such a thing!' To exaggerate, this family's dissatisfaction might be expressed as: 'That's unjustifiable,' or 'That's not fair!'

Why, I wonder, does the concept of fairness make its appearance in the latter responses? It is because the mother's second utterance expresses social behaviour. Social behaviour signifies a situation in which a certain person's decision or action has an impact upon someone else. As a general rule, fairness is not applicable to totally individual behaviour and individual decision-making which has no effect upon others. However, once a certain person's decision or act exerts an influence upon another, then that becomes a target for the application of fairness. Consequently, we can say that fairness is one criterion for evaluating whether social behaviour is appropriate. When a parent hands out sweets to a number of children, the children conscientiously scrutinise the conditions of distribution, and if there is even a hint of bias, there are cries of 'Not fair!' or accusations of favouritism. Even small children have a sense of fairness and unfairness. For people living in society, therefore, fairness is developed from early on as an extremely important evaluation criterion, and functions as something for assessing the behaviour of the self and others, and for guiding the same.

Justice and fairness in Japanese: *kōsei*, *kōhei* and *seigi*

The Japanese language has several terms which can be translated into English as 'fairness' or 'justice' – *kōsei*, *kōhei* and *seigi*, but each of these is used with a slightly different nuance among Japanese people. Moreover, those differences can be considered an important key to understanding the meaning and structure of 'fairness.'

Kōhei is the word closest in meaning to the English term, 'fairness.' The Japanese commonly employ it in the sense of 'equal(ity).' Generally, it is a concept indicating the appropriate distribution of benefit and cost among the people involved, or the principle behind such distribution. In concrete terms, this means 'giving equal rights, opportunities and treatment to the parties involved,' while it might be described in the abstract as 'respect for individual rights.'

By contrast, *kōsei* indicates conformity to group rules or contracts, and can also be used interchangeably with *gōhōsei* (legality/

Table 4.1: The meanings of seigi, kōsei and kōhei in Japanese

Seigi	Kōsei	Kōhei
• Universal values which transcend the ages (morality, ethics, thought) • Social ideals (social objectives) which ought to be achieved	• Conformity to the rules and contracts of society and groups (legality) • Appropriate resolution of social issues • Legitimacy of procedure leading to outcomes	• Appropriate distribution among parties involved (adjustment of interest) • Giving the parties involved equal rights, opportunities and treatment • Legitimacy of outcomes

legitimacy), but it is a notion which emphasises formalistic rather than substantial aspects. If we compare *kōhei* and *kōsei*, we find that *kōhei* expresses the legitimacy of a particular distributive situation, or the substantial appropriateness of a certain decision, while *kōsei* is a concept emphasising the process and procedure of distribution and decision-making. In either case, both *kōhei* and *kōsei* are regarded as criteria for assessing the appropriateness of a certain social act or social decision.

Seigi, on the other hand, refers to a universal value which transcends rules and laws, and is seen as one vital aspect of morality, ethics and philosophy. To put it more succinctly, *seigi* is an idea which expresses a social principle whose attainment is desirable, that is to say, 'that society should be like this.' This also could be rephrased as 'a social goal which guides people.' In that sense, *seigi* is morality and ethics, but also incorporates a strong social orientation which is not composed totally of individual values. The social orientation seen in *seigi* is, naturally, also something which is seen in *kōsei* and *kōhei*, meaning that these terms all are evaluation criteria for social behaviour.

The Japanese words *kōhei*, *kōsei* and *seigi* are thus each used in a slightly different sense. All of them, moreover, express a certain part of the idea of justice and fairness. How, then, should we think about defining the concept of justice and fairness, the meaning of which is so complex and multi-faceted?

Notions of justice and fairness in Western thought

Japanese people are said to believe that the terms 'justice' and 'fairness' are things imported from the West. However, though this might be true of the words themselves, it does not follow that Japan lacked the ideas or concepts they express. Words such as *gi* (justice/ morality/rectitude), *michi* (way/path) and *rinri* (ethics) are thought at least partially to have included the meanings of justice and fairness. However, considering the accumulation of debate relating to *seigi* and *kōsei*, we can probably rightly say that Western thought has provided many theories and dissertations upon which to draw. In this chapter, then, I will briefly survey the history of Western thought from the perspective of justice theory, and, through that process, ponder the meanings of justice and fairness.

Ancient Greek philosophy: Plato's discourse on the state

Plato's discourse on the 'state' discusses the form of an ideal state or *politeia*, but in that discussion, the notion of fairness (*seigi*) is afforded a core position (Tanaka, 1978; Fujikawa, 1984). Seen from the international situation at that time (meaning the regional situation in Greece's proximity), people were strongly dependent upon the *polis* (city-state). If their own state were to be conquered by another country or ethnic group, and their state were annihilated, then its individuals would not be able to survive, either. It was only by their belonging to their own state, and that state being peaceful and secure, that the existence of the individual and the family could be assured. Such a notion that 'the individual owes his/her very existence to the state' is something which was widely and universally seen in ancient times, not in Greece alone.

In a society where the individual depends entirely upon the state, the maintenance and prosperity of the state becomes that society's objective. Plato considered what kind of state system and administration would be necessary in such circumstances, and advocated the theory of a 'state ruled by philosophers' as his ideal state. According to this theory, the ideal state is made up of three parties: the philosopher-rulers (politicians), the guardians (the military) and the producers (ordinary citizens), which separately embody the three virtues of wisdom, courage and moderation. If all parties endeavour to fulfil their duty in the respective positions in which they are situated, then the state will grow strong, be preserved and flourish. Meanwhile, the state distributes resources to reward the contribution of such individuals. To the politicians, it gives power; to the soldiers, honour; and to the citizens, wealth. According to Plato, justice meant that society was run in such a way as to bring about such harmonious mutual interdependence between the state and the individual. Seen from the perspective of the state, this justice constituted the preservation of social order, while from the individual viewpoint, it meant receiving decent treatment. However, in ancient society, in which the individual owed his/her existence to the state, the very preservation of the state was the greatest goal, and herein lies the principle of justice. For that reason, individual reward itself was not the thing for which people aimed, but was an additional gain which accompanied the prosperity of the state, and was nothing other than a flow-on grant from the state.

Still, it is the mission of philosophers who are worthy rulers to design the state system so that it complies with justice, and to run the state so as to implement fair distribution. This is because the survival of the state rests upon the shoulders of these philosophers. The reason why this vital role is given to philosophers is that wise and knowledgeable philosophers are the only ones who recognise what justice is, and can use it to administer the state. Soldiers and citizens do not have the ability to recognise what justice is. The only people to have it are those extremely rare philosophers who have exceptional ability.

From the above, Plato's notions of justice can be condensed into two points. The first is that justice is a norm that aims for a harmonious relationship between the state and the individual, but that goal lies in the maintenance and prosperity of the state. The second is that justice is something which is understood and debated by certain elite members of society who possess special qualities, and is not something in which ordinary citizens can be involved.

Medieval Christian thought: Patristic philosophy

Medieval Europe was situated in an age in which the influence of Christianity extended to all domains of society. Thanks to the endorsement of the Pope of Rome, the rulers of every country in Europe were able to gain justification for the political power they exerted over their respective countries. Moreover, through its churches located in every corner of each country, Christianity controlled not only spiritual aspects such as morality and values, but every single dimension of people's lives, including rituals and customs.

Christian doctrine also encompasses discourse relating to justice, as seen in the Patristic philosophy exemplified by St Augustine, for example (Fujikawa, 1984; Yamada, 1968). According to this, the notion of justice is a matter appertaining to God, and is an issue which surpasses human reason. God created the world according to a sublime plan, and effects justice in all realms in which it should be implemented. However, that is a work which transcends human understanding, humans being able solely to submit to what God has ordained, to the will of God – that will itself being the only justice, as far as humans are concerned.

Who, though, can know the will of God? Only the clergy, comprising bishops, priests, and so on. They alone can hear the voice of God and know God's will. That is why the sole route for conveying the meaning of justice to the mundane world is through the priesthood, and both the people and the policy-makers come to accept the Church's directions as manifesting God's will, and are obliged to obey it.

The legitimacy of 'earthly realms' such as states was endorsed by their swearing allegiance to God, and by their promising to support the Church and its enterprises (God's works). Actual states contained many elements far removed from justice, such as war, discrimination and repression, but their existence was justified by their support of the Church. Order in the 'Kingdom of God,' mediated by the Church, thus provided the foundation for the justification of the feudal order in 'earthly realms,' and this deemed the feudal order, which included slavery, as being the 'natural order' based on the will of God (Fujikawa, 1984).

Transcendent justice and the justice elite

In relation to the concept of justice, a similar salient feature can be perceived in both Patristic philosophy and Plato's discourse on the state, namely the point that they both regarded justice as being something outside the realm of ordinary people's cognition. 'What is justice?' was deemed a question to which only a very small proportion of the population could know the answer – those who had special qualifications, or had undergone special ascetic training – in other words, a chosen justice elite. In the sense that it was beyond the pale of the experience and knowledge of the general populace, the justice discussed in Patristic philosophy is also stereotypically transcendent justice, and the clergy in medieval society were afforded a special position due to their having the specific ability to appreciate this.

From social contract discourse to modern philosophy

It was only after the dawn of the age of social contract theory that the notion of justice, which hitherto only an elite section of the population had been allowed to discuss, at last fell into the hands of ordinary citizens. Justice arguably came into its own in both name and reality within the philosophy of social contract theory. However, as social contract theory shows quite different modalities in its early and late periods, here let us look at the concept of justice and the relationship between the individual and the state, focusing upon Hobbes, who falls in the early period, and Rousseau, who belongs to the later.

Enlightenment philosophy and human justice
Social contract discourse is the view that autonomous individuals enter into mutual contracts and form a state. Underlying this is the idea of enlightenment, in which complete trust is placed in individual reason and rationality (Brumfitt, 1972). In ages prior to that, judgement as to what kind of social mechanism would be desirable, or what was good or evil, for example, was deemed to belong to God's domain, and mortals needed only to obey God's teachings. With the people-focused artistic revival movement of the Renaissance as a turning point, there was a new emphasis on the image of humans as escaping from reliance upon God, and thinking and acting independently, and philosophical theories and ideas which placed their trust in individual reason and powers of judgement began to be developed within this flow. As in Kant's Critique of Pure Reason, the notion of justice was taken as something that also could be perceived and discerned by human reason, with the result that the concept of justice, hitherto seen as transcendent, became the object of human thought and judgement. Social contract discourse, too, is a philosophy born from the midst of such a current.

Hobbes' theory of absolute sovereignty
There is one premise common to every hypothesis in social contract theory: the presumption of a state of nature and natural rights. In the age of feudalism, there was a great disparity in people's rights according to their social class, and that was regarded by the social system of the time as a rightful thing. Social contract theorists, however, asserted that human beings have been given as their birthright an equal right to freedom, without being bound by their place or family of origin. As this right exists prior to the state, and is something inherent which has not been granted artificially by a state or social system, it was called a natural right.

The state of nature refers to the situation when human beings with such natural rights gather together. This is a condition predating the emergence of structured societies such as the state, but is something that did not actually exist historically, it being a logical assumption for the purpose of considering the establishment mechanism of the state – in short, a thought experiment that imagines 'What if...?' Hobbes viewed such a state of nature as an extremely bleak condition. People all have a selfish desire for wealth, fame and power, and, moreover, have an equal measure of freedom to pursue these as their natural right. Given such a state of nature, struggle and conflict are thus inevitable (Boucher and Kelley, 1994). Hobbes argued that the unlimited exercise of natural rights would lead to ruination. Human beings yearn to break away from this insecure and frightening state of nature, and their desire for peaceful coexistence grows. As a result, they mutually limit their 'natural rights' by contract, aiming instead for the establishment of a more stable rational order. This leads to the birth of laws and states.

Even though contracts which delegate individuals' rights are entered into, there still needs to be strong public authority to guarantee their implementation. A sovereign state is established by the handing over to a particular sovereign of that public authority which guarantees the implementation of the people's contract, with the people's consent. Once they have entrusted their rights by means of a contract to the sovereign, the people, as subjects, must absolutely obey their ruler. In this way, Hobbes justified the absolute monarchy system which had begun to hold sway in the countries of Europe at that time, as being based on a social contract.

In Hobbes' theory, justice means the fulfilment of a contract. While the state strives for social order and stability through a right of governance which involves coercion, the individual, on the other hand, submits to the state in accordance with the contract. This constitutes justice (Fujikawa, 1984). While taking the basic rights of human beings as its starting point, Hobbes' social contract theory places more emphasis on the preservation of order in society as a whole, even if this means its repression, and so his justice principle, which should be the guideline for action for people and society, is fundamentally no different from that of the age of medieval feudalism.

Rousseau's doctrine of popular sovereignty
Unlike Hobbes, Rousseau's thinking refined and developed social contract theory into a democratic social contract theory of popular sovereignty, without allowing it to end in a compromise with the monarchy. Rousseau also assumed a state of nature, but it was considerably different from that described by Hobbes. Rousseau presumed

that human beings had not merely self-interest, but also an essential empathetic interest and sympathy for others, and, though in a state of nature, people still respected each other's rights, and created a simple but friendly and peaceful paradise. His 'natural man' has neither the notion of good and evil, nor evil thoughts and passions, neither does 'he' engage in conflict due to excessive desire for possession. Rousseau asserts, however, that the advancement of industrial technology brought about the expansion of private ownership rights, and this caused the goodness of natural beings in the state of nature to be lost, and a range of inequalities arose due to a struggle for power (Fujikawa, 1984). Rousseau's theory included criticism of modern civilisation, saying that those things which brought about inequalities in human society – the emergence of ownership rights, the advent of role differentiation and policymakers, the centralisation of power, and so on — were man-made systems (Rousseau, 1985).

In order to inhibit excessive competition and resolve inequalities, people use contracts to form legitimate control structures – that is to say, states. However, Rousseau and Hobbes' views also differ in regard to the scope of power which such states can wield. According to Rousseau, even if they have created a state by means of a contract, individuals do not yield all of their freedom to the policymakers. Individuals retain equal rights to enjoy their own freedom. The power which is given to policymakers by contract is something which should be used for the maximum realisation of people's rights. In consequence, Rousseau decided, if the policymakers were to breach that contract, then people could dismiss those policymakers and choose new ones.

Rousseau argued that a state which fulfilled such conditions could only take the form of a republic in which sovereignty rested with the people, and his ideas became the foundation of present-day Western European democracy. What, then, was justice, in Rousseau's eyes? It was the realisation of the freedom and equality which human beings have had as a natural right all along. The aim of society will inevitably be the achievement of that principle. Accordingly, all social systems and laws must be designed and implemented in order to serve this principle of justice. It is probably true to say that the view which equates human rights with justice – one widely embraced in contemporary Western societies – was established by Rousseau.

Contemporary theories of justice: Rawls' justice theory
In the present day, justice is debated from a variety of standpoints, but the one which is most widely accepted is Rawls' theory of justice. In

the current age of advancing globalisation, there is great incidence of conflict arising between peoples and groups with disparate religions, beliefs or cultures, and its resolution is often extremely difficult. If there does exist a principle of universal and rational justice which all people accept, then this is likely to become the principle that will replace the exercise of force or suchlike as the way to resolve all conflict. Rawls attempted to explore the principle of justice by focusing upon the question of how to distribute as fairly as possible the benefits comprising the fruits of social cooperation (Rawls, 1971).

Traditional contract theory presupposes a state of nature, and pursues the argument that people will actively construct a society self-ruled by the consent of each individual, but, in Rawls' case, he hypothesises an original position freed from all interests. This, referring to individuals placed in a position in which they have absolutely no knowledge of their own class, status, qualifications, assets, ability, talent, history, character, inclinations, or whether their natural or social situation is fortunate or unfortunate, determines what kind of method of distribution would be accepted, given such a position. This was the assumption under which Rawls formulated several principles of justice, through his so-called 'veil-of-ignorance' experiments.

The first of these principles is called the liberty principle, and is one which states: 'each person is to have an equal right to the most extensive basic liberty compatible with a similar liberty for others' (Rawls, 1971, p. 24). This is what individualistic justice principles since Rousseau had driven home, and assumes that, before individual dignity, nothing can impinge upon this, neither for the national interest nor for social welfare. It asserts that the individual has the liberty to do whatever she or he likes, as long as this does not encroach on others' rights.

The second principle, called the difference principle, states: 'social and economic inequalities are to be arranged so that: a) offices and positions must be open to everyone under conditions of fair equality of opportunity; b) they are to be of the greatest benefit to the least-advantaged members of society' (Rawls, 1971, p. 303). Many kinds of inequalities exist in actual society, however, and it is not necessarily a good thing for there to be no inequalities. For example, there are some super-elite sportspeople whose annual earnings are astronomical, but, just because that is unequal, would it be better for them to be paid the same as unknown sportspeople? People not only accept certain inequalities, but sometimes even advocate them. What kinds of inequalities, then, would accord with justice?

As expressed in the above difference principle, Rawls regarded increasing the amount distributed to all people involved to the maximum possible as fitting the criterion for justice. For example, say there is a company which pays only one portion of its employees highly: if it is anticipated that advantage to the company as a whole will rise through the work of that one portion of employees, meaning distribution to the other employees will also increase, and, in addition, if it is guaranteed that any employee could attain that well-remunerated position by working hard, then that will be seen as a fair thing. However, if the highly-paid employees are not making a significant contribution to the performance of the company as a whole, or if high pay is limited to one particular clan, then that would constitute unfairness.

In Rawls' view, overall advantage is not the sole consideration. For example, even though it might be for the benefit of the whole, it is not acceptable for individual benefit to be sacrificed. In Rawls' theory of justice, the natural rights of the individual (liberty and equality) take priority over the benefit of the whole, and it is not permissible for the latter to lead to the erosion of individual rights.

Notions of justice: past and present

We have looked at typical notions of justice seen in the history of Western thought, and Table 4.2 draws together their various key points. In ancient Greece, as argued in Plato's *Republic*, the state was something that was supported and maintained by the wisdom of the philosopher-rulers, the courage of the military and the hard work of the citizens. In that age in which the individual was fully reliant upon the state, the survival of the state was the social goal which was given priority over everything. That is why preserving the state and making it prosper were construed as justice in those times. Moreover, under such a social ethos, it was considered fair social administration to allocate reward (power, status, honour, wealth, et cetera) to people according to their degree of contribution to the state.

In medieval Europe, where the influence of Christianity was strong, the state was an authority given legitimacy as an earthly institution supporting God's work. It was an age in which it was considered the greatest good for both the state and the people to obey God's will, and to carry out God's will was believed to constitute justice. In addition, salvation was supposed to be granted in accordance with the extent of one's devotion to and faith in God, and it was thought that fair

Table 4.2: *Notions of justice/fairness in the history of Western thought*

Ancient Greece	Medieval Europe	Modern civil society
Perspective on the state The state is maintained by the wisdom of philosopher-rulers, the courage of soldiers, and the work of citizens	The state has legitimacy as a thing which supports God's works	The state is constituted in order to protect and expand the freedom, equality and independence intrinsic to the individual
Seigi (justice) The peace and prosperity of the state	The manifestation of God's will	Respect for the rights of the individual
Kōsei (fairness) Treatment according to each individual's contribution (execution of duty) to the state	Treatment (salvation) according to each individual's faith and devotion to God	Treatment according to individual ability, effort and achievement
Thinkers Plato	St Augustine	Rousseau, Rawls

treatment would be given according to one's 'balance sheet' which encompassed not only the land of the living, but the afterlife, as well.

Social contract theory is what formed the philosophical foundation of modern civil society. That is why, in the thought of Rousseau and Rawls, the individual takes priority over the state, and the state's *raison d'être* was deemed to lie in its protection of individual freedom and equality, its location as an instrumental organ for the expansion of that protection, and the extent to which it fulfilled that function. In such a society, it goes without saying that the very realisation of individual rights constitutes justice. For that reason, the distribution of resources in accordance with individual achievement and the treatment of people according to their ability and effort were taken as proper to the operation of a fair society.

In present-day Western European countries, the modern-civil-society-type justice principle is taken to be the social principle. However, notions of justice from ancient and medieval times are historical, which is not to say that they no longer exist in the current age. There are still totalitarian states around the globe in which the maintenance of their state system takes precedence over the rights of citizens. There is also no small number of people and groups who take God's will as justice, and see submission to that will as their supreme mission. Consequently, the three types of justice concept shown in Table 4.2 all now have their own respective zealous supporters, have an impact upon the values and behaviour of their respective states and citizens, and, at times, have become the trigger for serious social conflict.

The structure of justice and fairness

Fairness criteria and competence

Here, based on the differences among the notions of *seigi*, *kōsei* and *kōhei* discussed in the first section (Table 4.1), and the concepts of justice in the history of Western thought surveyed in the second section (Table 4.2), we will introduce a theoretical model relating to the meanings of justice and fairness and the connections between them.

A conceptual formula of fairness

Fairness (*kōsei*) is an assessment criterion for social behaviour, but, as illustrated by the lower portion of Figure 4.1, it can be expressed as the formula: 'Treatment / Deservedness.' 'Deservedness' refers to qualifications, entitlements, and rights (Olson, Roese, Meen and Robertson, 1994). We define *kōsei* as 'a certain action or decision treating the people involved in a manner befitting their qualifications and rights.' Let us consider a situation in which a parent is dividing some sweets between two children. If the parent thinks that the children have the same right to receive the sweets, then the parent will probably divide up the sweets and give the children half each. If the parent thinks that the older child deserves more sweets, then he or she might give each child a different quantity. Whichever the case, if the outcome of the distribution meets the qualification of each child, then we call that distributive fairness.

Sometimes, a parent might propose that the children play 'Rock, scissors, paper' with each other, the winner taking the sweets she or he likes, rather than the parent dividing up the sweets. If this method is employed, then there will be a range of outcomes, sometimes resulting in situations which could not always be described as distributive fairness. However, as 'Rock, scissors, paper' gives each child an equal chance of winning, it could be seen as affording treatment according to qualification, after all. Satisfying this formula in this manner,

Figure 4.1: The conceptual relationship between justice and fairness

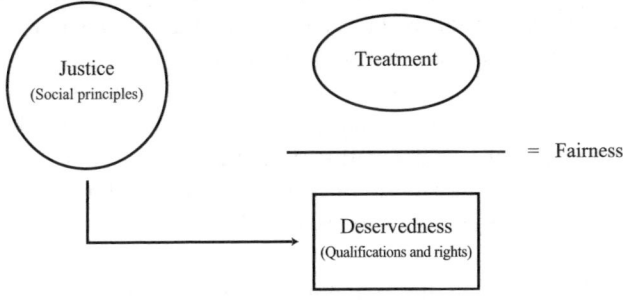

not by the outcome, but by its procedural aspect, is what is called procedural fairness.

The conditions for deservedness: equality, equity, need

We have thus defined *kōsei* as being a criterion for evaluating whether the treatment of involved parties is appropriate, in the light of their rights, qualifications, and entitlements – namely, their deservedness. What, however, might deservedness encompass? There are potentially many conditions which comprise deservedness. Deutsch (1975) suggested three types – equity, equality and need – as the criteria for resource allocation seen to be fair. The differences among them can be regarded as differences in deservedness.

First, let us think about equal distribution. When a parent gives an equal share of sweets to each of his or her children, then the children's qualification relates to their being members of that family. Children from other families are not the target of that distribution. In other words, deservedness in equal distribution means group membership. In Japan, the right to receive state-provided services such as education, medical care, welfare service, et cetera, is given equally to all citizens, but this distribution is limited to Japanese nationals, and the legitimate qualification for receiving this is group membership, in terms of being a Japanese citizen. Again, students of a particular university faculty have an equal right to attend lectures held by that faculty. As this right is not extended to students of other universities or other faculties, the legitimate qualification for receiving allocation of this resource is also group membership, in terms of being a student of that faculty. In other cases, too, such as with communities, companies, clubs, and so on, being a member of the group generates eligibility to receive an equal share of a certain resource. When giving or not giving a particular resource to a certain individual, membership constitutes one type of deservedness which forms the basis for judging if that is fair or not, and this is a rationale used in equal distribution.

In equitable distribution, a different condition for deservedness is employed as a basis. Companies and the like give good treatment, including high pay and promotion, to hard-working employees. In cases of equitable distribution like these, individual performance becomes the deservedness condition which determines disposition. In present-day society, most economic and social resources, including assets, prestige and status, amount to equitable distribution which is implemented by valuing individual performance. However, if the times and the culture change, then different conditions sometimes count for more. In our country, Japan, in the Edo Period (1603–1867), one's place of origin and family background were definitive qualifications. Peasants' children could only become peasants themselves, warriors' sons were destined to become warriors, too, and the stipend they received from the ruling clan (*han*) had also been fixed since their parents' generation. The only ones who could assume key positions in the clan administration were high-status sons from the clan, and most young men of low-status class remained in lowly positions, no matter how hard they tried.

In distribution according to need, deservedness equates to level of hardship – in other words, what quantity of resources are needed. In the kind of society in which it is normal to receive a fixed standard of education, to be healthy and to live a cultured life, helping those who could not attain these things by their own efforts alone, such as children, the elderly and people with disabilities, and especially providing them with social and material resources, would probably be regarded as fair distribution. In this case, eligibility for receiving such special distribution would depend upon the extent of people's hardship, meaning how poor they were.

Treatment: positive reinforcement and negative reinforcement
Treatment, incidentally, does not only have a positive value such as reward or enjoyment. There are some types, such as penalties or liabilities, which have a negative value. Employees have to pursue their duties according to their responsibilities, and university students have to pay their tuition fees, or else they will forfeit their enrolment. Paying taxes, too, is the duty of citizens. Attempts to evade such obligations without special reason are seen as unfair. In addition,

while penalties are meted out to those who commit offences or crimes, in those cases, fair treatment means giving penalties commensurate with the seriousness of that person's offence or crime.

Fair negative resource distribution, also, has the three standards of equality, equity and need. For example, neighbourhood association dues, PTA membership fees, taxes and so on are, as a general rule, imposed equally upon members of those various groups, namely the neighbourhood association, the PTA and the country of Japan, respectively. The equal distribution of negative resources, too, in the same manner as with positive resources, is carried out on a deservedness basis, in terms of group membership. Generally, taxation is equal, but special measures have been established for low-income households, such as reductions in or exemptions from tax. This can be considered as distribution according to need in relation to negative resources, in which eligibility equates to level of hardship. Criminal punishment is one example we can give of equitable distribution. When crimes committed in company are being tried in court, the one who played a more important role in the committal of that crime receives a heavier sentence as the main culprit, while someone whose role was smaller gets a lighter penalty, as her or his accomplice. In sentencing, the level of contribution towards the committal of the offence or crime constitutes their deservedness, and it is thought to be fair if the heaviness of the punishment is changed to fit that.

Justice as a social principle

Examples have been given of the many different deservedness conditions for fair resource distribution, as above. According to Deutsch (1975), the choice of which of these conditions of deservedness will be emphasised depends upon what the social group regards as it social goal. The term 'social goal' expresses a social principle relating to what kind of society people imagine, and what kind of society they are trying to create.

Seigi and *kōsei*

Deutsch stated that, in a social group which values productivity, the group will give priority to equitable distribution, but in a social group which values harmony among its members, equal distribution will be favoured. If resource distribution is to be carried out according to individual performance and contribution, then competition will be promoted among individuals and this will lead to an increase in the social group's productivity, but, on the other hand, trust and cooperation among members will tend to be afforded secondary importance. Conversely, with equal distribution, as being a group member is a condition for receiving resource allocation, people will strive for reconciliation and collaboration so as not to be ostracised from the group, but intra-group competition is suppressed, and productivity as a group probably tends to fall. In groups where resource distribution is conducted according to the criterion of need, compassion and consideration towards the weak are valued. That is a characteristic of societies which place value on education and social welfare.

Then again, what kind of deservedness conditions will be valued in fair distribution differs according to the times and the culture. That depends, after all, on what each respective society is aiming for – in other words, these are discrepancies arising from differences in social ideal. If we rephrase the term 'social ideal (principle)' as 'justice (*seigi*),' then, of the two elements which make up the fairness formula, it is justice which decides deservedness conditions, and we can say that justice guarantees and verifies the legitimacy of a certain fairness criterion. In the Edo Period, for example, resource distribution was carried out which made people's place of origin and family background its deservedness conditions, and this was regarded by people as fair, but what formed the rationale for this was the fact that the preservation of a social order based on a hierarchy according to a class system and Confucian social relationships was the social ethos (ideal) in that age. To build and maintain such a society was justice in the Edo Period, and, from such a perspective, resource allocation that relied on a certain hierarchy in the society was implemented, and that was endorsed by the people as a fair thing.

In this age of democracy, social ideals themselves are undergoing change. In contemporary society, individual freedom and equality are social principles, and to preserve and expand these is justice. In response to such changes in social philosophy, individual achievement has come to be valued in present-day society as a deservedness condition for carrying out fair allocation.

To summarise the preceding discussion, *kōsei* and *kōhei* mean treatment commensurate with deservedness, but it is the social ideal, namely justice, which determines which deservedness condition to take as a standard. Any number of kinds of standard for *kōsei* and *kōhei* can be created by replacing the deservedness conditions. In order for the use of a certain deservedness condition among them to be deemed appropriate, it must be one that reflects an ideal or ethos which people harbour in relation to society as something which 'should be this way.' In other words, *kōsei* and *kōhei* need to be justified by *seigi*. Figure 4.1 shows just such links among *kōsei*, *kōhei* and *seigi*.

Various kinds of *seigi*

Table 4.3 shows examples of the combination of typical deservedness conditions and the justice which forms their foundation. In societies which construe individual freedom and rights as justice (*seigi*), individual achievement is an appropriate deservedness condition in determining fair distribution. If social harmony were the social principle, then in such a society being a member of the group – in short, group membership – would probably amount to a qualification for fairness. In a society which valued social welfare and education, the developmental stage of the individual (infant, elderly, or the like), and whether there was any disability, would be likely to carry more weight in judgements of fairness. In a society in which the maintenance of a stratified social order was the ethos, family background and place of origin would be the deservedness condition for the fair distribution of resources. On the other hand, in a totalitarian society such as one in which the prosperity and preservation of the state itself constituted justice, each individual's loyalty and contribution to the state would probably be seen as a qualification for judging the fairness of resource allocation. Then again, in societies and groups which defined justice as the realisation of religious doctrine, the fact of having faith, or an individual's level of devotion, might become the qualification emphasised when fairly distributing social resources.

Table 4.3: Fairness criteria and social principles

	Fairness criteria	
Justice (social ideals)	**Deservedness** (qualifications and entitlements)	**Treatment**
Freedom and rights of the individual	Individual achievement	• Resources (assets; privilege; power, etc.)
Social harmony	Group membership	
Social welfare and education	Developmental stage; poverty; disability	• Liabilities (taxes; unpleasant environment, etc.)
Strata order	Ancestry; place of origin	
State order	Loyalty; role performance	• Penalties (criticism; criminal punishment, etc.)
Religious principles	Faith; devotion	

Social ideals thus change according to the times, culture, value system and so on, but the criteria for fairness also change. This is because the deservedness condition which comprises the criterion for fairness changes along with the social ideal, namely, what justice is.

Justice for the Japanese

The significance of psychological studies on fairness

In comparison with other social sciences, the history of psychological research on fairness is a short one, going back only about thirty years. Instead, it has been the task of jurisprudence and politics, in particular, to conduct research on the central theme of fairness and justice, and put it into practice. This is due to the fact that, in jurisprudence, laws and legal proceedings constitute the procedures for the systematisation and administration of conflict-resolution in accordance with the principles of fairness. In politics, the question has been how best to effect justice through social systems and policies. Political scientists and lawyers believe that the condition of fairness can have an objective existence; they design laws and systems to bring this about, and try to implement them. Fairness with such a connotation is called objective fairness. Psychology, on the other hand, deals not with impartial fairness, but with people's perceptions vis-à-vis conflict, and attempts to clarify the kinds of situations which people judge as fair. In that sense, psychological studies of fairness deal with subjective fairness.

Even in cases in which a certain resolution policy is judged as being fair from a legal viewpoint, the parties concerned might not necessarily think it is fair, nor adopt that method. In cases such as this where objective fairness and subjective fairness are incongruous, lawyers tend towards the view that people's judgement is narrow-minded and distorted, but, from the perspective of conflict resolution, that by itself is insufficient. Firstly, it is rare for ordinary people to make judgements about their own problems in the light of the law – on the contrary, a subjective viewpoint on fairness is indispensable for understanding people's conflict behaviour, because they are going to try to resolve the conflict based on their own judgement of fairness. Secondly, even if the interested party were to choose to appeal to the courts, it often happens that she or he does not accept the outcome when the court's verdict does not align with that person's sense of fairness, in which case the conflict becomes long drawn-out, and the efficacy of the lawsuit for ending the conflict is reduced. Thirdly, in cases where the law grossly deviates from people's sense of fairness, the law will probably lose people's trust, and its function as a system for conflict resolution is likely to deteriorate.

In contemporary society, not only the law, but all kinds of policies and systems, also, must gain the understanding and support of ordinary citizens, or else they will become unable effectively to carry out their functions to the full. That applies in Japan, too. That is why it is indispensable for research on conflict resolution to elucidate the mechanism of subjective fairness – in other words, what people use to judge something as fair, however distorted that may be, and how their behaviour is influenced by that judgement of fairness or unfairness. In that sense, nowadays, when civic participation in politics and societal decision-making is being promoted, the significance of psychological studies of fairness is vital.

Japanese notions of justice

Among Western scholars, there are some who view the Japanese as having no concept of fairness (Kidder and Muller, 1991). In Japan, during its period of rapid economic growth from the mid-1960s through the 1980s, there were many social systems which prevented free economic competition, and the majority of Japanese firms adopted a seniority (*nenkō*) system in an attempt to avoid competition within their organisations (Ohbuchi, 1998). That is why we can venture to say that, to the best of our knowledge, Western-type notions of justice such as respect for individual rights were weak among the Japanese, at least until recently. However, the social ideal which justice manifests is not merely respect for the rights of the individual. The Japanese have traditionally valued social harmony within groups, and have made it their most important social philosophy. The social systems and enterprise management in the period of rapid economic growth were things which reflected such a philosophy, and we can deduce that the kind of management which took equality as its criterion for fairness was being carried out in all realms of Japanese society, in accordance with this notion of justice. The seniority system, for example, combined with life-long employment, was a system in which most employees, if they continued to work for a particular company all their life, would gain, in total, around the same amount of remuneration. That is why Japanese society also has been run according to a certain type of justice concept, though not quite the Western idea of justice. As a result, the system of equality broadly permeated among the Japanese in the period of high economic growth, and, in the 1980s, ninety per cent of Japanese had arrived at the point of perceiving themselves as 'middle-class' (Chūō Kōron Henshūbu, 2001).

Since the 1990s, however, in the midst of its protracted escape from economic doldrums, there has been a rise in expressions of doubt about conventional equality-oriented social management, and now, a changeover to an American-style competitive society is being promoted in Japan, in both the public and private sectors. On the other hand, there is also considerable objection to this. This is a sort of clash between justices, and we can say that today's Japan is in the very thick of a confrontation between social ideals. What is important is that through this clash of philosophies, awareness of justice and fairness has gradually grown among the Japanese.

In those days, when they surrendered themselves to a comfortable optimism in the midst of high economic growth and egalitarianism, many Japanese uncritically trusted its systems and policies, be they of the nation or of enterprise, and left the running of them entirely up to the leaders. In the storm of lingering recession and system reform, many Japanese awoke from their dependence upon such leaders and spoke up about the condition of the various realms of society, including politics, economics and welfare, more frequently giving voice to their opinions. The impact of that has clearly emerged in the elections in recent years, and even the Prime Minister has lost the ability to maintain his position without the support of ordinary citizens. Japan being a democratic country, that would only be expected, but it is only in the past two or three years that the situation has been emerging in which the will of the people is strongly reflected in Japanese politics.

There is also a tendency to criticise such a political situation as pandering to the masses, but it is significant that the Japanese have begun to have a strong interest in social fairness. It is probably true to say that the future direction of reform in Japanese society will depend upon which social ideal the Japanese choose as justice.

5 Procedural Justification in Egalitarian Resource Allocation

Shinobu Kitani

Introduction

Canonical studies relating to the egalitarian allocation of resources can be divided broadly into two types, according to their research interest. The first investigates the issue of resource allocation methods vis-à-vis individuals' legitimate demand for resources, while the second scrutinises the content of the advantage which resources bring to individuals. In relation to the latter, by departing from the utilitarianism that originated from J. Rawls, controversy has erupted in the field of political philosophy over advantage – which ought to be equally allocated – and conceptual definition of the equalisandum has been carried out, this including Rawls' 'primary goods,' Sen's 'capability,' and Dworkin's 'resources.' In this chapter, however, I focus upon the former: that is to say, the canons and procedures relating to how to allocate resources when the total quantity of allocatable resources amounts to less than the sum of the quantities legitimately demanded by all of the individuals involved. Such a standpoint might be criticised for its avoidance of the latter's fundamental debate on egalitarian allocation, and for its commitment to technical methodology, but it is extremely difficult for scholars to agree on the concept of advantage, and, as a real issue, it is not valid in terms of a quantitative proposal on egalitarian allocation.

Admittedly, the concept of advantage is not fixed, but it is probably advisable to indicate the most mainstream views among the theories of distributive justice from recent years, because the efficiency and fairness of allocation are discussed in modern economics, with the premise that each individual has a utility function on the vector of goods to be allocated. I, however, wish to place the foundation of the egalitarian allocation principle not in utility, but in each individual's advantage, though the difference is merely a formal one in my main argument. Advantage is inter-subjective, differing both from utility, which can be subjectively measured, and from an objective quantity of goods, as in Rawls 'primary goods,' it being a concept located between the two (Cohen, 1989, p. 921). In other words, it is close to Sen's 'capability' (Sen, 1985), which is concerned neither with preference for the good to be allocated, nor with its quantity, but rather with what kind of function that particular good affords to each individual. In my view, Cohen's theory of equality emphasises equality of access to advantage, and the question of whether materials for advantage which have been equally allocated are directly put to good use is situated within the jurisdiction of each individual's responsibility, but, in the case of capability, the choice of function is within the jurisdiction of responsibility.

In this chapter, without considering the issue of individual responsibility, and taking the viewpoint that the egalitarian allocation of advantage means the egalitarian allocation of the materials for advantage, the quantity of the good to be allocated is assumed to be capable of objective measurement. Accordingly, the degree of each individual's advantage (advantage function) which an allocated good generates is assumed here to be linear. The advantage allocation standard must be one that establishes a functional such as would determine the advantage allocation point within the feasible advantage area. Here, I incorporate the same idea as in the mathematical formulation of the bargaining problem, which determines the allocation point from a feasible utility set. Several reasonable axioms for uniquely determining a functional which determines an allocation have been considered in bargaining theory, but, due to a dislike for the canonicity of those axioms, numerous methods have also been conceived for formulation of the allocation issue as a multi-stage, non-cooperative game, and the establishment of an allocation as its equilibrium position, because a canonically-established allocation is understood to have been procedurally justified if an allocation determined by an axiom can be attained in the form of an allocation determined as an equilibrium position.

As the concept of advantage has more objectivity than utility has, a consideration of its allocation might also need to focus upon canonicity when determining the allocation of advantage. In reality, the determination of an allocation by means of a non-cooperative game is just, in the respect that it is based on the utility-maximisation actions of each individual. However, in actuality, if we see an advantage-securing game as an assertion of rights to advantage on a judicial stage, then the determination of allocation by means of the formulation of a non-cooperative game is likely to have meaning in terms of procedural justification. In this chapter, also, I take this standpoint. In other words, by constructing a particular multi-stage, non-cooperative game, I will attempt procedurally to support the assertion that advantage ought to be distributed equally.

A determination method for resource-allocation

The basic formulation of resource-allocation problems

Now, I assume the type of good to be allocated as J type, and the total quantity (vector) as $\boldsymbol{S} = (S_1, S_2,..., S_J)$. Also, I consider there to be N number of individuals in a society, and the advantage which an allocation goods vector $\boldsymbol{s} = (\boldsymbol{s}^1, \boldsymbol{s}^2,..., \boldsymbol{s}^N)$ ($\boldsymbol{s}^i = (s_1^i, s_2^i,..., s_J^i)$) holds for individual i to be $u_i(\boldsymbol{s})$. However, I take i to be self-regarding, and this can thus also be written as $u_i(\boldsymbol{s}^i)$. Here, $\Sigma_{i=1}^{N} \boldsymbol{s}^i \leq \boldsymbol{S}$.

The problem is that, given a resource limit of $\Sigma_{i=1}^{N} \boldsymbol{s}^i \leq \boldsymbol{S}$, we see a distribution of advantage among individuals $(u_1, u_2,..., u_N)$, and can establish an allocation vector $\boldsymbol{s}^i$ ($i = 1, 2,..., N$) from an efficient and fair perspective. By efficiency, I mean so-called Pareto efficiency, which means a situation in which it is impossible for a particular individual to better his or her advantage without worsening any other individual's advantage. There are various ways of apprehending fairness according to how allocation situations are set up – in other words, by what kind of procedures this resource allocation is carried out. For example, perceptions of fairness in relation to an allocation decision in a situation where allocation is determined by bargaining among interested parties, rather than by the society (the government), will probably differ completely from those in a situation in which allocation is decided by the society. My argument focuses upon the Kalai-Smorodinsky solution, the epitome of the latter, but reinterprets it within the egalitarian-equivalent concept. Moreover, the Nash bargaining solution, which exemplifies the former, is one that takes the advantage-allocation balance into account, in the sense of equitable allocation.

Now, without losing generality, the total quantity vector $\boldsymbol{S} = (S_1, S_2,..., S_J)$ may be considered as $\boldsymbol{1} = (1, 1,..., 1)$ (it being sufficient to change the unit expressing the quantity of goods). At this time, we call

$$X = \{s = (s^1, s^2, \ldots, s^N) \mid \Sigma_{i=1}^{N} s^i \leq 1, s^i \geq 0 \ (i = 1, 2, \ldots, N)\}$$

$$\mathbf{B} = \{x \mid \exists s \in X; 0 \leq x \leq (u_1(s^1), u_2(s^2), \ldots, u_N(s^N))\}$$

a feasible advantage area. Generally, when we view u_i as a utility function of i, **B** is said to be a bargaining set. Here, advantage functions u_i are linear, and $u_i(\mathbf{0}) = 0$ for all i.

Figure 5.1 shows a feasible advantage area **B** where $J = 2$, $N = 2$, and u_i are linear functions: $u_1(s_1, s_2) = s_1 + s_2$, $u_2(s_1, s_2) = 2s_1 + 3s_2$. In this manner, **B** is a convex set bounded by the x_1-axis, x_2-axis and two straight lines.

The Nash bargaining solution

The Nash bargaining solution is an allocation in which it is stipulated that the advantage increment product $(x_1 - a_1)(x_2 - a_2)\ldots(x_N - a_N)$ from the initial situation $\mathbf{a} = (a_1, a_2, \ldots, a_N)$ of each individual within area **B** is made the minimum. For example, if we consider the initial situation to be $\mathbf{0} = (0, 0)$ in the case where no goods allocation is made, then an allocation which makes the advantage product $x_1, x_2, \ldots, x_N$ the minimum will be the Nash bargaining solution.

Figure 5.2 is one in which the Nash bargaining solution is sought in relation to the previous example. As the intersection of the curve $x_1 x_2 = k$ and area **B** is (1, 3), the goods allocations of Individuals 1 and 2 are (1, 0) and (0, 1), respectively. Here, because we assume a situation in which a third party allocates the goods to Individuals 1 and 2, we take the advantage distribution $\mathbf{0}$, in which no goods are allocated to either individual, to be the initial situation. However, in the case where Individuals 1 and 2 have an equal right to ownership of two goods, we might make the initial situation egalitarian allocation (the advantage distribution being (1, 2.5), accordingly).[1]

In this way, a Nash bargaining solution can be sought mechanically, but it is justified from different angles. Here, I wish to organise these from two viewpoints. The first is axiomatic justification. This considers a functional F corresponding to solution x from the bargaining problem set $\{(\mathbf{B}, \mathbf{a})\}$ which is defined by a bargaining set **B**, and uniquely determines the Nash bargaining solution as satisfying the necessary conditions of F. These are the five conditions called Pareto efficiency, symmetry, scale invariance, domain non-attribution, and mimesis through reduction, and if these conditions are reasonable,

Figure 5.1: Feasible advantage area

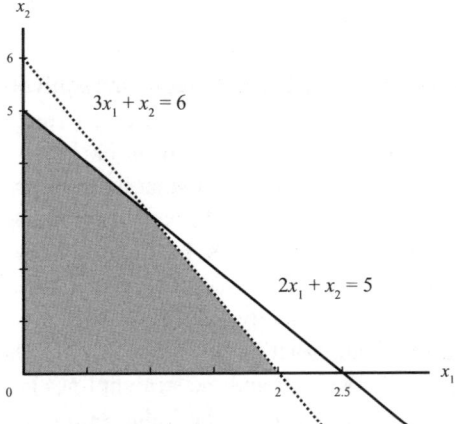

Figure 5.2: The Nash bargaining solution

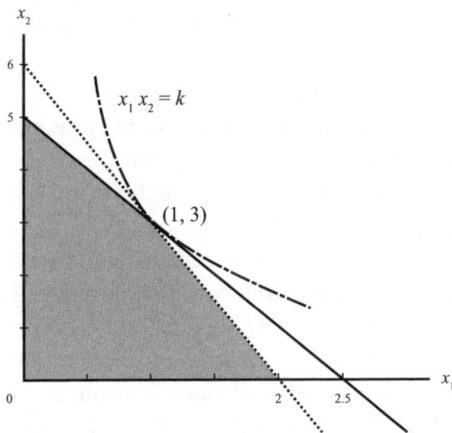

then allocation by means of a Nash bargaining solution will be justified. Another is procedural justification. By incorporating the cost vis-à-vis bargaining time (time preference), Rubinstein (1982) discussed goods allocation from a non-cooperative game framework, and proved that the Nash bargaining solution is realised as a sub-game perfect equilibrium (SPE) in an alternating offer game. In this game, players take turns making a goods-allocation offer, and allocation is determined at the stage when all players accept an offer. The point of this game is that, because the total quantity of the good to be allocated shrinks each time another offer is made, each player has an incentive to end the game as early as possible.[2]

The Kalai-Smorodinsky solution and egalitarian equivalent solutions

In the Nash bargaining solution, allocation bargaining is carried out fairly among various parties, and such bargaining attempts to establish the allocation which would result from it as constituting egalitarian resource allocation. The Kalai-Smorodinsky solution, on the other hand, is based on the Kantian categorical imperative which states that advantage ought equally to be allocated.

In relation to an initial situation $a = (a_1, a_2,..., a_N)$, the maximum point of intersection between **B** and the straight lines $(x_1 - a_1)/u_1(I) = (x_2 - a_2)/u_2(I) =...= (x_N - a_N)/u_N(I)$ is the Kalai-Smorodinsky solution. That is to say, this solution constitutes egalitarian allocation of advantage, in the sense that the allocated proportion of advantage from an initial situation vis-à-vis the maximum advantage each person can obtain in all allocation combinations is equal for all players.

When we seek the Kalai-Smorodinsky solution in the previous example, given an initial situation 0, as the maximum value among the intersections of straight lines $x_1/2 = x_2/5$ and area **B** is (12/11, 30/11), the goods allocation to Individuals 1 and 2 will be (1, 1/11) and (0, 10/11), respectively, as in Figure 5.3.

The Kalai-Smorodinsky solution can also be calculated mechanically, but, in the same way as the Nash bargaining solution, it can uniquely be determined from five conditions: Pareto efficiency, symmetry, scale invariance, unrestricted domain, and individual monotonicity. As for procedural justification, a concept close to the Kalai-Smorodinsky solution – an egalitarian equivalent solution – needs to be provided.

In relation to any individual i, when allocation $s = (s^1, s^2,..., s^N)$ satisfies the condition:

$$u_i(s^i) = u_i(k(1, 1,..., 1))$$

and is efficient, then s is said to be an egalitarian equivalent allocation.[3] Now, let us seek an egalitarian equivalent allocation in the previous example. First, we allocate the same quantity of goods (k, k) to individuals 1 and 2, which means granting them advantage $2k$ and $5k$, respectively. Then we increase goods 1 to individual 1 by x_1, but reduce the latter's goods 2 by y_2, and reduce goods 1 to individual 2

Figure 5.3: The Kalai-Smorodinsky solution

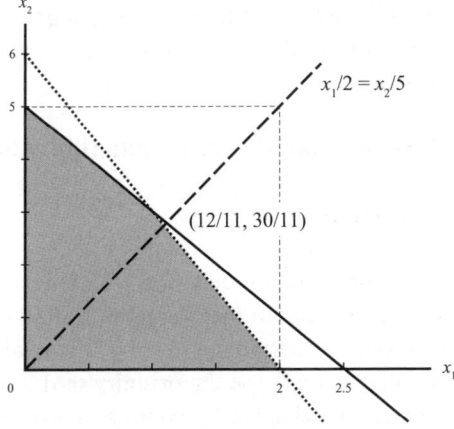

Table 5.1: The calculation of egalitarian equivalents

Individuals	Goods	
	1	2
1	$k + x_1$	$k - y_1$
2	$k - x_2$	$k + y_2$

by x_2, but increase the latter's goods 2 by y_2 so that their respective advantage does not change. In other words, the following equations are satisfied:

$$2k + x_1 - y_1 = 2k, \quad 5k - 2x_2 + 3y_2 = 5k.$$

Moreover, from the total quantity conditions of goods 1 and 2, the following equations are satisfied:

$$2k + x_1 - x_2 = 1, \quad 5k - y_1 + y_2 = 5k.$$

When we remove x_1, y_1, y_2 from the above equations, we can obtain

$$k = \frac{2 + \frac{1}{3}x_2}{4} \quad (0 \leq x_2 \leq k).$$

The maximum value of k is attained where $x_2 = k$, which will be $k = 6/11$, and the allocation $x_1 = 5/11$, $x_2 = 6/11$, $y_1 = 5/11$, $y_2 = 4/11$ is obtained. This allocation corresponds to the Kalai-Smorodinsky solution. Generally speaking, these do not correspond, but, as I will argue below, as both concepts become identical when the advantage function is linear, under local conditions in which goods allocation has a linear effect upon advantage, one may regard them as approximately the same.

A procedural justification of egalitarian allocation

Multi-stage auction games

The auction game I propose here is one which implements an egalitarian equivalent solution. In fact, something similar to this has already been proposed by Demange (1984).[4] This is an extremely complex game, as there is only one opportunity in the auction for a bidding value offer. In this chapter, by contrast, I attempt to realise an egalitarian equivalent solution by means of a multi-stage auction game.

The main strategy of N-tuple players is to offer a fraction k_i of the allocation goods (bidding value). In other words, Player i's making the offer k_i means that s/he makes a demand for rights towards k_i only, out of the total quantity of allocation goods I. At the same time, k_i becomes the bidding value i vis-à-vis the allocation goods, and the player who has proposed the highest bidding value gains the right to make an allocation proposal for the goods. The sequence in this auction game is as follows:

1. Let $r = 1$
2. N-tuple players make bids k_i as offers for assignment in relation to the allocation goods ($0 \leq k_i \leq r$, $i = 1, 2,..., N$).
3. The player who has made the greatest k_i offer proposes the goods allocation $s = (s^1, s^2,..., s^N)$. In cases where there are multiple players offering the maximum k_i, the player with the smallest i becomes the proposer. That is to say, in this game, when there are identical k_i offers, let there be a convention prioritising the player with the smallest i.
4. Players other than the proposer of allocation accept or reject the s of 3) in descending order of bidding value k_i. Where k_i ($0 \leq k_i \leq r$) all players accept, the goods allocation is decided to be s, and the game ends. Where there are any players who reject the offer, θ is allocated to the proposer and the game proceeds to stage 5).
5. Allocation to players who have rejected the offer is decided to be $k_i r$ ($r = (r, r,..., r)$), starting from the player with the largest bid. When the total of these bids is greater than r, then θ is allocated

to each player once r is surpassed, and the game ends. Where the total is no greater than r, the remainder is deemed to be a new r, and only the proposer and those who accepted his/her offer make bids k_i $(0 \leq k_i \leq r)$, and the game returns to 3).

The number of players participating in an allocation offer at the next stage in the auction is reduced by exactly the number of players rejecting the earlier offer, and, if there are no players rejecting, then the game ends at that point. Accordingly, this game will end at (N–1) auctions, at most. The advantage of rejecting players which is determined at 5), given the set of rejecting players as being $\{j_1, j_2,..., j_M\}$ $(k_{j1} \geq k_{j2} \geq ... \geq k_{jM})$ $(M < N)$, becomes

$$u_{jh} = \begin{cases} u_{jh}(k_{jh} r) & (0 \leq h \leq L) \\ u_{jh}((1 - \Sigma_{h=1}^{L} k_{jh}) r) & (h = L + 1) \\ u_{jh}(0) & (L + 1 < h \leq M) \end{cases}$$

Here, L is an integer which satisfies both $\Sigma_{h=1}^{L} k_{jh} \leq r$, and $\Sigma_{h=1}^{L+1} k_{jh} > r$.

Solutions of multi-stage auction games

Many Nash equilibria exist in the multi-stage auction games defined in the previous section. For example, given that s is an arbitrary resource allocation, it is a Nash equilibrium which elucidates the strategy in which 'all of N-tuple players offer a bidding value 1/N, the proposer offers s, and the other players accept only an allocation offer of s, rejecting all others.' I would like, then, to focus my investigation upon sub-game perfect equilibrium strategy. First, let me give one example of Nash equilibrium in a two-person game, which is the lowest-order sub-game in a multi-stage auction game.

(LEMMA) In a two-player, multi-stage auction game in which the total quantity of goods to be allocated is r $(= (r, r,..., r))$, the strategy in which 'the bidding value of both players is $k_1 = k_2 = k^*$, player i who makes an allocation offer proposes $s = argmax_s\{u_i(s) \mid u_j(s) = u_j(k_j r)\}$ $(j \neq i)\}$, and the other player j accepts if the advantage yielded by the allocation offered is no less than $u_j(k_j r)$, but rejects if it is less' constitutes a Nash equilibrium. Here,

$k^* = max\{k \mid \exists s \in W_r; u_i(s) = u_i(kr)\ (i = 1, 2)\}$

$W_r = \{s = (s^1, s^2) \mid s^1 + s^2 = r, s^1, s^2 \geq 0\}$

(PROOF) Now, let player 1 deviate from the strategy in the lemma, and offer a bidding value of k_1 $(< k_2 = k^*)$. At this point, player 2 proposes allocation $s = argmax_s\{u_2(s) \mid u_1(s) = u_1(k_1r)\}$. The advantage which player 1 can gain whether s/he accepts or rejects this offer is $u_1(k_1r)$, and this will be lower than $u_1(k^*r)$.

Next, let a bidding value of k_1 ($< k_2 = k^*$) be offered. At this point, if player 1 offers s in which $u_2(s) < u_2(k^*r)$, this will be rejected by player 2, and the final advantage that can be obtained, $u_1((1 - k^*)r)$, will be lower than $u_1(k^*r)$. This is due to $k^* < 1/2$, by definition. Accordingly, player 1 will propose an s which will maximise $u_1(s)$ while fulfilling $u_2(s) = u_2(k^*r)$.

Here, let us assume the existence of s' ($s' \in W_r$, $u_2(s') = u_2(k^*r)$) so that $u_1(s') > u_1(k^*r)$. Due to the linearity of u_i, there exists the following vector s^+, which has a sufficiently small norm:

$u_1(s' + s^+) > u_1(k^*r)$

$u_2(s' + s^+) > u_2(k^*r) \qquad (s' + s^+ \in W_r)$

As this contradicts the maximality of k^*, the ultimate player 1 cannot gain an advantage greater than $u_1(k^*r)$. By the above, there is no incentive to deviate from the strategy illustrated in the lemma. (END OF PROOF)

Next, in relation to the multi-stage auction game in which there are m-tuple players ($2 \leq m \leq N$), let us show that a similar strategy to that in the lemma constitutes a sub-game perfect equilibrium.

(THEOREM 1) In a sub-game of the multi-stage auction game by m-tuple players (the total quantity of allocation goods being r), a strategy where 'the bidding value offer is $k_1 = k_2 = ... = k_m = k^*$, player i proposes $s = argmax_s\{u_i(s) \mid u_j(s) = u_j(k_jr) \, (j \neq i)\}$, and the other player j accepts when the advantage yielded by the proposed allocation is no less than $u_j(k_jr)$, but rejects when it is less,' is a sub-game perfect equilibrium. Here,

$k^* = max\{k \mid \exists \, s \in W_r; u_i(s) = u_i(kr) \, (i = 1, 2,..., m)\}$

$W_r = \{s = (s^1, s^2,..., s^m) \mid \Sigma_i s^i = r, s^i \geq 0 \, (i = 1, 2,..., m)\}$

(PROOF) When $m = 2$, in accordance with the lemma, the above strategy constitutes a sub-game perfect equilibrium. By mathematical induction in relation to $m = m'(m' \geq 3)$, assuming that all of the above strategies in $m \leq m' - 1 (m' \geq 3)$ are sub-game perfect equilibria, it suffices to show that this strategy is a Nash equilibrium when $m = m$.'

Let player i deviate from the above strategy.

1. When $k_i < k^*$

   The Proposer j' ($\neq i$) proposes an allocation s which satisfies $u_i(s) = u_i(k_i r)$, $u_j(s) = u_j(k^* r)$ ($j \neq j,$' i). As all players other than i accept, if i accepts, then allocation will be determined at this s, but if i rejects, then allocation will rest on $k_i r$. Whichever the case, the advantage of i will not exceed $u_i(k_i r)$.

2. When $k_i > k^*$

   In this case, player i becomes the Proposer. If s/he makes proposal s to p-tuple players other than i so as to fulfil the condition $u_i(s) < u_i(k^* r)$, the other players will reject, and the allocation of these p-tuple players will be ascertained by $k^* r$. After this, the game will shift to an auction game sub-game concerning the total quantity $(1 - pk^*)r$, involving $(m' - p)$-tuple players, excluding these p-tuple players. However, as the allocation to player i will be 0 if $pk^* \geq 1$, p must be established so that i meets the condition $pk^* < 1$. From the assumption of mathematical induction, the equilibrium strategy in this sub-game will be

$$k^{**} = max\{k \mid \exists t \in W_{(1-pk^*)r}; u_j(t) = u_j(k(1-pk^*)r) (\forall j \in Y)\}$$

$$= max\{k \mid \exists t/(1-pk^*) \in W_r; u_j(t/(1-pk^*)) = u_j(kr) (\forall j \in Y)\}$$

$$< k^*$$

Here, Y is a set of player i and $(m' - p)$-tuple players who accepted i's proposal. Accordingly, i will offer k^* as the bidding value in this sub-game,

$$u_i(k^{**}(1-pk^*)r) < u_i(k^*(1-pk^*)r) < u_i(k^* r)$$

and i's advantage will not exceed $u_i(k^* r)$.

From the above, player i will have no incentive to deviate from the strategy of this Theorem. (END OF PROOF)

(THEOREM 2) That sub-game perfect equilibrium in the multi-stage auction game yields the Kalai-Smorodinsky solution.

(PROOF) By Theorem 1, in the multi-stage auction game, the initial bidding value offer $k_1 = k_2 = ... = k_m = k^*$ is made, player 1's proposal $s = argmax_s\{u_1(s) \mid u_j(s) = u_j(k_j r) (j \neq 1)\}$ is accepted by all players from player 2 to N, and the game ends. The payoff at this point is $u_i(k^* 1) = k^* u_i(1)$ ($i = 1, 2,..., N$) due to the linearity of u_i, this being the Kalai-Smorodinsky solution, because k^*, by definition, is the maximum k where $s \in W_r$ exists such that $u_i(s) = u_i(k1) = k u_i(1)$. (END OF PROOF)

Due to the linearity of u_j, the Feasible Advantage Area generally takes the form of a polygon. This assumption may be a little strong, but we can probably conceive of a process in which the total quantity of allocation goods is small, or when the goods are allocated a little at a time, and the starting point for bargaining is shifted. For the reasons stated above, this proposition could also be called a procedural justification for resource-allocation equality.

Conclusion

In my main argument, I have reduced a categorical imperative – equality of allocation – to a non-cooperative game formula, and ventured into the meta-ethics of egalitarianism. Specifically, I have focused upon the Kalai-Smorodinsky solution, which is taken to be the most egalitarian among bargaining problems. Also, I have shown that the Kalai-Smorodinsky solution can be obtained as a sub-game perfect equilibrium solution from a certain multi-stage auction game by assuming linearity on advantage functions, though this is limited. In actuality, this is something which leads to an egalitarian equivalent solution.

As I stated at the beginning, egalitarianism must begin with the question of what thing is going to be made equal, but this is difficult in matters of substance. The egalitarianism I have considered here is equality of advantage, something which cannot be divided up according to some standards held by the central government. However, in cases where there is freedom of assertion of rights in terms of individual advantage, then it is significant to examine whether equality of advantage is procedurally possible. It is fair to say that research into social fairness is the study of egalitarianism, but might it not be more natural to regard it, not so much as a study relating to goods-allocation quantities, but as research into the creation of rules for the allocation of goods?

Part II
Justice and Fairness in Social Relations

6 Forgiveness and Justice: Victim Psychology in Conflict Resolution

Naomi Takada and Ken-ichi Ohbuchi

In many conflicts, resolution is attempted according to either the principle of retribution or the principle of forgiveness. If, on the one hand, the principle of retribution is chosen, tit-for-tat aggression may escalate between both parties concerned and the conflict may grow fierce, while the principle of forgiveness, conversely, can be conducive to a constructive resolution to the conflict. The adoption of the principle of forgiveness is extremely advantageous, but it is not necessarily an easy thing for victims to carry out. This is because they would have to forgo the advantages brought about by retribution – in other words, the execution of justice. We wonder, however, if people who choose forgiveness have no alternative but to accept injustice. In this chapter, we compare the results of Western and Japanese research, focusing upon whether two values of forgiveness and fairness (*kōsei*) which people experience when they are harmed by others are mutually exclusive, and whether the relinquishment of justice (*seigi*) is mandatory in the pursuit of forgiveness.

Responses to unfairness: forgiveness and retribution

Retribution and forgiveness are two types of behaviour exhibited by people when they perceive unfairness. In this section, we describe what people feel is unfair, and how they respond to it on an affective level. Next, we discuss the reasons for people's aspirations towards retribution and forgiveness, which constitute responses on a behavioural level vis-à-vis injustice, and their concomitant advantages and costs.

Mikula, Petri, and Tanzer (1990) studied the conditions under which people perceive injustice. They elicited examples of unpleasant events from people in Austria, Bulgaria, Finland and the former West Germany, and classified these events into three classes of justice: distributive, procedural and interactional justice. Violations of distributive justice were injustices perceived in relation to the allocation of resources of value or benefits, the unbiased nature of judgements, the assignation of responsibility, the degree of penalty, and the evaluation of achievement and effort. By violations of procedural justice, they meant overemphasis of rules and authority, and injustices perceived in relation to the inappropriateness of the content and assessment of examinations. Violations of interactional fairness included a lack of consideration for others' feelings, breaches of promise, criticism, self-centredness, enmity and malice. Of these, the most frequently-cited unpleasant event was violation of interactional justice. This result shows that people are exposed to justice violations on a daily basis, and that such experiences are inevitable.

Victims' responses to such justice violations arise on cognitive, affective and behavioural levels. According to Morrison and Robinson (1997), the experience of injustice not only activates cognitive awareness, but also triggers strong negative affective responses such as pain or hurt (Leary, Springer, Negel, Ansell and Evans, 1998; Vangelisti and Sprague, 1998). This activates such cognitive effort as pursuing the cause of the incident, or speculating as to the outcome of the violation. Through such cognitive interpretation, further feelings may also newly be aroused. While there might be differences in the behaviour thus motivated, according to what emotions are stirred as a result of having received unjust treatment, anger and hatred generally motivate punishment and revenge towards the perpetrator (Fitness and Fletcher, 1993).

The motivation of vengeance

According to Frijda (1994), the desire to take revenge upon a perpetrator is a fundamental and powerful motivator in human beings, one which has also been seen as a common element among humans since ancient times. Why, we wonder, is the motivation for vengeance so strong? Deterrent theory assumes that social harmony and justice are best secured by deterring future re-offence, and prove the significance of vengeance in its function as something which minimises the likelihood of re-offence (Butterfield, Trevino and Ball, 1997). Vidmer and Miller (1980) established a hypothesis saying that people become especially punitive towards those particular criminals who are thought likely to re-offend in future, as they believe that this has a large deterrent effect against criminals and potential criminals. In identical manner to this behavioural control model, in several studies on the death penalty conducted in the United States (Ellsworth and Ross, 1983; Vidmar, 1974; Vidmar and Ellsworth, 1974), it is shown that people who were asked about the necessity for the death penalty tended to try to explain by stressing this deterrent effect.

The theory of retribution, on the other hand, is the idea that when an individual deviates from social norms by a certain act, causes harm to society, and destroys its equilibrium, which equilibrium will be restored by applying sanctions to the individual. If this is followed, perpetrators would receive punishment matching the degree of malicious conduct in which they were involved. In this case, people could be said to be motivated by the idea of having the perpetrator make up for the economic and psychological losses arising from the malicious act. In four experiments conducted with American participants, Alicke (1992) found that people tended to assign most responsibility for crimes to people deserving of moral censure. If the driver at a traffic accident scene were a gang member, American participants attributed the cause to the driver him- or herself, rather than to other factors (an oil slick on the road, an intersection with poor visibility, or the other driver, for example), but such internal ascription was not conducted if the driver were not a gang member. The fact that censure and penalties are strongly linked with the morality of acts shows that punishment is aligned with the principle of retribution.

There are also scholars who cite vengeance motivations other than behavioural control and recovery of damages. Gouldner (1960) emphasises reciprocity. People believe that perpetrators should neither continuously maintain the advantages they have unjustly gained, nor, through continuing advantage, stand in a superior position to their victims. The maintenance of justice based on the norm of reciprocity, expressed otherwise as *lex talionis*, or 'an eye for an eye,' reflects such a belief. McCullough et al. (2001) point out an imbalance of power. This refers to victims' attempts to restore their own social value when they are belittled against their will, due to the unjust conduct of perpetrators. There are also scholars who take up the restoration of self-esteem (Miller, 2001). People who have been victimised feel that their own rights have been disrespected, and, in many cases, experience a lowering of self-esteem. By avenging themselves against perpetrators, victims can demonstrate that they are not the kind of weaklings who take unjust treatment lying down (Miller, 2001). Moreover, recovery from (ordinary) mental anguish is also included in the vengeance motivation (Orth, 2004). Victims experience diverse negative feelings, such as anger and heartbreak, but they can ameliorate such feelings through vengeance. In this way, victims can compensate for psychological and social damage through retribution.

The costs of vengeance

Retribution, if successful, has various benefits, as described above. In the pursuit of vengeance, however, there are also accompanying costs. Firstly, the peace of mind gained from the execution of retribution is a transient thing, and there is sometimes no long-term improvement in victims' affective state (Orth, 2004). Caprara et al. (1992) discovered that there is a correlation between negative emotion and neurosis among Italian research participants, in terms of scores for aggressive behavioural tendencies following an occurrence of victimisation. Using American subjects, McCullough et al. (2001) also found that people with a high vengeance tendency had markedly low life satisfaction and high negative emotion. We, too, had Japanese university students recall actual experiences of being harmed, and had them evaluate how they responded to the harm (retribution, forgiveness, avoidance, or conciliation), as well as their well-being, satisfaction, and so on, after resolution of the conflict (Takada and Ohbuchi, 2003). On well-being and sense of satisfaction vis-à-vis the outcome of conflict resolution, participants who had taken revenge on perpetrators rated lower than those who had not (Takada and Ohbuchi, 2003). These research results show that even though a temporary psychological effect might be obtained from retribution, this is not sustained, and brings about a negative psychological outcome in the long term.

The second cost accompanying vengeance is censure from the surrounding people. Revenge can sometimes be judged as unpardonable, from a moral perspective. Kim, Smith and Brigham (1998) considered how American participants behaved towards perpetrators when treated unjustly by the latter, in situations where observers with either affirmative or negative opinions towards the restoration of justice were watching. As a result, under the eye of observers who attached negative value to vengeance, participants seldom took revenge. This finding illustrates that retributive behaviour is influenced by the expectation of criticism from surrounding people. In this manner, retribution has two types of concomitant cost, but analysis of such costs offers several suggestions for consideration of what orients people towards forgiveness.

The meaning and factors of forgiveness

Forgiveness is one of the virtues which have been given great importance since ancient times. Christianity's teaching about 'turning the other cheek' is all too renowned. Why, we wonder, is forgiveness esteemed and recommended to such an extent?

Forgiveness is defined as an 'intraindividual, prosocial change toward a perceived transgressor that is situated within a specific interpersonal context' (McCullough et al., 2000, p. 9). This means that the debt which has arisen as a result of a person having damaged or hurt another's advantage is cancelled by the party on the receiving end of such action – in other words, the victim (Exline and Baumeister, 2000). From the viewpoint of social interchange, such forgiveness equates to the relinquishment of restoration of equilibrium by such means as retribution or confrontation.

Why, though, might forgiveness be possible, given that it is clearly disadvantageous to victims? Social psychologists have explored what regulates forgiveness, and have found situational factors, perpetrator factors and victim factors. Situational factors include the seriousness of the harm (Boon and Sulsky, 1997; Mullet and Girard, 2000; Zechmeister and Romero, 2002), and the interpersonal relationship between victims and perpetrators (Fincham, Paleari and Regalia, 2002; Finkel, Rusbult, Kumashiro and Hannon, 2002; Karremans, Van Lange, Ouwerkerk and Kluwer, 2003). It has been found that the slighter the injury, or the closer the interpersonal relationship between victims and perpetrators, and the more commitment the victims feel towards the perpetrators, the greater is the degree of forgiveness. Examples of perpetrator factors include apology and confession (Darby and Schlenker, 1982; Ohbuchi, Kameda and Agarie, 1989; Girard, Mullet and Calahan, 2002), and public punishment (Weiner, Graham, Peter and Zmuidians, 1991). When such outcomes are obtained, victims intensify their empathy towards perpetrators, leading to a heightening of altruistic concern and the stimulation of forgiveness. Empathy towards perpetrators (McCullough, Rachal and Worthington, 1997; McCullough, Rachal, Sandage, Worthington, Brown and Hight, 1998); relationship commitment (Finkel et al., 2002); perspective-taking (Takaku, Weiner and Ohbuchi, 2001; Takaku, 2001); agreeableness – one of the 'Big Five' traits; and so on, can be cited as victim factors. All of these encourage empathetic cognition and mitigating attributions, consequently revealing the psychological process in which forgiveness escalates. Most of the factors found thus far are ones which promote victims' empathy and favourable cognition, and emphasise victims' empathy in the evocation of forgiveness.

Motivations for forgiveness

Empathy is a powerful factor in the stimulation of forgiveness, but there are also other factors which trigger it. We attempted an investigation into the forgiveness-motivation mechanism, using Japanese research participants (Takada and Ohbuchi, 2004). We had Japanese university students recall past experience of victimisation, and had them evaluate their own thoughts and behaviour at that time from the perspectives of how far they could forgive the other party, and why they decided to forgive them (forgiveness motivation). By reference to Cloke (1993), Exline and Baumeister (2000), and McCullough et al. (2000), we compiled eighteen items to test the motivation for forgiveness. When we subjected these items to factor analysis, six dimensions were discovered (Table 6.1).

These incorporate other-oriented motivation and self-oriented motivation. Other-oriented motivation, consisting of 'empathy and understanding,' was something which stressed the other person's welfare. 'Need for acceptance,' 'maintenance of relationship,' 'debt/endowment,' 'maintenance of harmony,' and 'prioritisation of own convenience' are self-serving motivations, and these are ones which represent the desire to pursue self-interest. As all of these motivations, bar the motivation of prioritisation of one's own convenience, show a significant positive correlation with forgiving behaviour (Table 6.2), it can be understood that not only altruistic motivations, but also various self-serving motivations, evoke forgiveness.

Next, again with Japanese participants, we investigated the motivation for forgiveness and the authenticity of forgiveness (Ohbuchi and Takada, 2004). Having defined a willingness to forgive perpetrators wholeheartedly as 'internal forgiveness,' and the exhibition of actual acts of forgiveness towards the other party as 'forgiving behaviour,' we divided the participants into two groups, accordingly. We called the people who rated highly on forgiving behaviour and internal forgiveness the 'true forgiveness group,' and those rating high on forgiving behaviour, but low on internal forgiveness, the 'hollow forgiveness group.' The 'true forgiveness group' scored highly on relationally-oriented motivations such as empathy and understanding, maintenance of harmony, and relationship-maintenance motivation,

Table 6.1: Motivations for forgiveness

Factors and items	α
Factor 1: Need for acceptance	0.805
I wanted to be understood and be sympathised with by others.	
I did not want to feel isolated from others.	
I wanted to avoid the stress caused by the offence.	
I wanted to protect my ideal self.	
Factor 2: Maintenance of relationships	0.809
I wanted to maintain the relationship with him/her.	
I miss him/her.	
I wanted to re-establish the relationship with him/her.	
Factor 3: Debt-endowment	0.670
I did not mind the offence that much because such things seem inevitable in social interactions.	
I did not want to be bothered by such things, as the same goes for both parties	
It did not matter much either way.	
Factor 4: Maintenance of harmony	0.867
I did not want to disturb the harmony of the social network we belonged to.	
I wanted to keep relations we had in common running smoothly.	
Factor 5: Prioritisation of own convenience	0.603
I wanted to do my work or continue with planned activities.	
I wanted to give priority to my job and role.	
Factor 6: Empathy and understanding	0.609
I felt sympathy toward my offending partner.	
I felt understanding for him/her.	

and also highly on satisfaction towards the outcome of conflict-resolution. The participants in the 'hollow forgiveness group,' on the other hand, showed high self-oriented motivation, including reduced guilt feelings and expectation of acceptance, and had low satisfaction with the outcome of conflict-resolution. This result shows that forgiveness is carried out not merely with consideration for the interpersonal relationship with the perpetrator, but also for the victim's relationship with the surrounding people. Might this be a characteristic of the Japanese, however?

Cloke (1993), a mediator in conflict-resolution, cites fifty practical strategies which mediators utilise in order to enhance Western

Table 6.2: Correlations between motives for forgiveness and forgiving behaviour

	Need for acceptance	Maintenance of relationship	Debt endowment	Maintenance of harmony	Prioritisation of own convenience	Empathy and understanding
Forgiving behaviour	0.121[a]	0.433[a]	0.236[a]	0.210[a]	0.087	0.470[a]

Note: a = p < 0.01

clients' forgiveness. We classified these into fourteen categories, and tested their efficacy with Japanese research participants (Takada and Ohbuchi, 2003). As a result, it was found that several of the strategies cited by Cloke did actually stimulate forgiveness in Japanese people, too. These included: placing importance upon the benefits arising from forgiveness; facing resolution with a constructive rather than a confrontational stance; and taking the other person's perspective. These showed a weak but positive correlation with scores on the self-reporting scale of forgiveness (r = .202 to .239) (Table 6.3). Such results suggest that there is a mechanism among Japanese people in which forgiveness arises from both altruistic and selfish interests, due to emphasis on the advantages of forgiveness and perspective-taking, and forgiveness is prompted by a heightened motivation to avoid the conflict spiral and to maintain a constructive stance (Rubin, Pruitt and Kim, 1994). This probably constitutes a psychological process of forgiveness shared by Westerners and Japanese, alike.

In the Japanese case, on the other hand, there were also measures that inhibited, rather than encouraged, forgiveness. These were strategies which dissipated feelings of anger; attempted to overcome the causes impeding the attainment of forgiveness; and considered whether it was possible to nullify the harm itself, and showed a negative correlation with forgiveness (r = −0.113 to −0.195). The latter two probably support the finding (McCullough et al., 2001) that rumination suppresses forgiveness. Results implying that the dissipation of angry feelings inhibited forgiveness might represent a trait unique to the Japanese. It is a traditional social norm in Japan to avoid dispute and to prevent the actualisation of confrontation (Ohbuchi, 1998), and there is a risk that the venting of anger will actualise confrontation, entangle the people involved in the conflict, and become something which disrupts harmony. As such unfavourable situations will arise, in consequence, the dissipation of angry feelings is thought to be something which hinders forgiveness. Such findings perhaps suggest that Japanese people's forgiveness

Table 6.3: Correlations between 14 strategies and forgiveness

Cognitive and emotive efforts	Forgiveness
Affective control: an attempt to assuage anger through reading and music	−0.063
Expression of anger: an attempt to vent anger by smashing things or by other means	−0.195[a]
Composure: an attempt to regain composure over time	−0.013
Risks of forgiveness: an attempt to accept the disadvantages of forgiveness	0.066
Advantages of forgiveness: an attempt to positively evaluate the advantages accruing from forgiveness	0.202[a]
The meaning of forgiveness: an attempt to understand the true essence of forgiveness	0.079
Overcoming unforgiveness: an attempt to organise and overcome reasons for an inability to forgive	−0.113[b]
Constructive stance: an attempt to foster an attitude of consideration and mercy	0.239[a]
Neutral thinking: an attempt to maintain a neutral and objective perspective	−0.015
Self-responsibility: an attempt also to pursue self-responsibility	0.032
De-victimisation: an attempt to negate the occurrence of the harm itself	−0.178[a]
Relational reconsideration: an attempt to evaluate the relationship with the other party and assign it value	0.080
Perspective-taking: an attempt to understand the other party's position and circumstances	0.216[a]
Amendment of expectations: an attempt to understand what is expected of the other party and oneself	0.107

Note: a = $p < 0.05$; b = $p < 0.10$

arises as a result of consideration for the maintenance of harmony among all those involved.

The advantages of forgiveness

As the analysis of motivations for forgiveness indicates, forgiveness has the potential to bring various benefits to victims. Many studies have been carried out in relation to the advantages of forgiveness, and these can be divided broadly into psychological advantages and interpersonal advantages. Hebel and Enright (1993) and Freedman and Enright (1996) conducted eight-week psychotherapeutic interventions with elderly American females who still harboured anger about deep hurt they had suffered in the past, and other American females who had been sexually abused in infancy, with the aim of reaching forgiveness towards the perpetrators. Comparison of pre- and post-intervention showed that, following the interventions, participants tended to have enhanced self-esteem and life-satisfaction, and lowered depression and anxiety.

Rose and Asher (1999) conducted a study with American elementary school students, instructing them to read a scenario while imagining themselves as the protagonist who was being insulted by other children, and to choose one response from among six behavioural patterns, which included forgiving behaviour and revenge. Participants who chose forgiving behaviour had many close friends, and were also well-adjusted in their class. The results of such research suggest that, by means of escalating their forgiveness, victims can not only acquire peace of mind themselves, but can also improve their relationship with the other party, and maintain cordial interpersonal relationships with people other than the perpetrators.

The costs of forgiveness

However much victims might consider the potential advantages of forgiveness, there are times when they cannot act in a forgiving manner. This is due to the fact that forgiveness comes with concurrent costs (Exline and Baumeister, 2000; Exline, Baumeister, Bushman, Campbell and Finkel, 2004).

The primary cost of forgiveness is the fear that the violation will be repeated (Enright, Gassin and Wu, 1992). This problem is especially important in serious, long-term types of harm such as family violence and sexual abuse (see, for example, Engel, 1989), but it could also be applied to any kind of violation. In studies using the prisoner's dilemma paradigm, Axelrod (1980a; 1980b) deemed a strategy which showed a competitive response to be a forgiving strategy only after an opponent had chosen a competitive strategy twice in a row (tit-for-two-tat), and he had participants play this against a tit-for-tat strategy based on reciprocity. The forgiving strategy resulted in more resources being seized by the other player, with the win ratio also decreasing, in comparison with times when a tit-for-tat strategy was employed.

Secondly, there is the fear of social recognition of one's own weakness and impropriety. Forgiveness can be interpreted as stemming from the weakness, cowardice or hypersensitivity of the person in question. There is also a risk that behaving in a forgiving manner will be seen as an admission of fault on one's own part. Though forgiveness is a virtue in the sense that one curbs the pursuit of self-interest and justice in accordance with a spirit of mercy, it can also be seen as a social weakness or defect. Victims often desire retribution more than forgiveness in order to avoid such risks, and to preserve their identity and self-esteem (Fagenson and Cooper, 1987).

The third cost is dissatisfaction towards the non-implementation of justice. There are people who, believing that approval of default on the repayment of debts contravenes the standards of justice, hesitate to express forgiveness (Enright et al., 1992; Enright, Santos and Al-Mabuk, 1989). If value is placed upon retributive justice, then victims will probably dislike the freeing of perpetrators from punishment without demand for compensation or acceptance of responsibility. The expression of forgiveness in such circumstances is not only difficult, but could also be regarded as morally negligent.

Loss of the advantage of being in the position of victim could be cited as the fourth cost. The position of victim triggers feelings of guilt in the other party, and gives the former the power to demand apology and compensation. Moreover, being seen as a victim is also effective in gaining help and sympathy from other people. For these reasons, relinquishment of the position of victim means losing such benefits (Exline and Baumeister, 2000).

The complementariness of forgiveness and justice

We have hitherto surveyed the respective advantages and costs relating to the pursuit of justice and forgiveness. As shown in Table 6.4, the costs of forgiveness include the cancellation of debt, the exposure of weakness and impropriety, and the increased possibility of repetition of the harm. These correspond to the advantages of carrying out retribution, such as recovery from harm, restoration of social resources, and prevention of re-offence. Conversely, the costs of revenge involve the risk of censure from the surrounding people, and a continuation of negative feelings, and these, in turn, correspond to the benefits of implementing forgiveness, such as an improvement in mood, and psychosocial support from the surrounding people. In this manner, analysis of the advantages and costs of forgiveness and vengeance shows that they complement each other. If this is the basis, then would not the most desirable strategy for victims be to achieve self-advantage and social advantage through forgiveness, and also

Table 6.4: The benefits and costs of forgiveness and retribution

Benefits	Costs
Retribution	
Restoration of justice	Censure from surrounding people
• Economic losses	Continuation of ill feeling
• Social resources (power)	
• Psychological losses	
Prevention of re-offence	
Forgiveness	
Improvement of feelings	Continuation of injustice
Gaining of social psychological support from surrounding people	Exposure of weakness and injustice
Maintenance of interpersonal relationships	Potential for repetition of harm

simultaneously gain benefit through retribution? In other words, even if victims do forgive, their being able to restore justice can be called the best solution on the victims' part.

The psychotherapist Enright analysed cases of clinical intervention which aimed for the achievement of forgiveness in clients with whom he worked in the United States, and this formed the basis for his model of the psychological process of forgiveness (Enright and the Human Development Study Group, 1991; Enright, 2001). Within this process there was a stage at which clients had to choose either to pursue justice or to forgive. Is it true that victims can choose only one or the other, as Enright and colleagues argue? If victims choose forgiveness, do they have to give up on the restoration of justice? In the next section, we outline previous studies relating to forgiveness and justice in various spheres, and explore the possibility of the compatibility of forgiveness and justice.

The compatibility of justice and forgiveness

Does the fulfilment of justice have to be abandoned, we wonder, for the sake of forgiveness? In this section, we survey research indicating how forgiveness and justice are positioned in people's minds when they face making decisions as to whether to forgive or take revenge.

Justice is rightness. People who have been hurt have an interest in rightness, but there are diverse types of rightness. There is one kind of rightness which says that retribution is natural, while there is another that says that it is a mature person that abandons the idea of reprisal.

In this section, we take up a variety of notions of justice, and consider what relationship they each have with the pursuance of forgiveness, and what measures are possible in striving for the compatibility of justice and forgiveness.

Forgiveness and the multidimensionality of justice

While forgiveness is one kind of prosocial value, justice also is essentially a prosocial value. In their analysis of the structure of values, Schwartz and Huismans (1995) classified forgivingness as a prosocial value, along with helpfulness, loyalty, honesty, and so on. They have also analysed the link between values and type of motivation, but, according to their research, justice and forgivingness are deemed to have the same motivational goal – in other words, to have been motivated by an increase in altruistic concern (Schwartz, 1992). From such a perspective, justice and forgiveness can be considered to focus on a common goal, and not necessarily to be in opposition, as values.

Karremans and Van Lange (2005) experimentally investigated the relationship between justice and forgiveness. When, in their first study, they asked Dutch university students to report what they thought of when they heard the word 'justice,' most respondents cited such examples as 'equal distribution' or 'everyone being treated equally.' As these concepts of justice refer to how society should treat people, these can be called social justice. If we go along with this notion, social justice will be presumed to promote vengeance, as the punishment of perpetrators will be consistent with equal treatment.

The results of the second study which Karremans and Van Lange implemented, however, contradicted this prediction. After the experimenters had primed the experimental participants with this notion of justice, they used the Transgression Narrative Test of Forgiveness (TNTF) (Berry, Worthington, Parrott, O'Connor and Wade, 2001) to measure participants' forgiveness. For the purposes of measurement, they presented five scenarios describing scenes in which the protagonist was hurt by someone, and had the participants answer from the standpoint of the protagonist as to how much forgiveness they would show towards the perpetrator. As a result, those participants who had been primed with the notion of justice had a greater tendency to behave in a forgiving manner than participants who had been primed with some other concept (ambition, for example), or those who had not been primed at all.

Karremans and Van Lange (2004) interpreted this as meaning that participants primed with justice enjoyed enhanced accessibility to the similarly prosocial values of helpfulness, faithfulness, sincerity and forgiveness, resulting in the fostering of forgiving responses.

The reason why participants primed with the concept of social justice became forgiving, contrary to expectation, was not simply that it had prompted associations with other social values, but that justice had yet another aspect, one also capable of influencing experimental participants' behaviour. Research suggesting this has been carried out by Batson, Bowers, Leonard, and Smith (2000).

Batson et al. called 'moral justice' a view which regarded justice as having feelings corresponding to ethics, standards and morals, and performing acts coinciding with these. The relationship between moral justice and forgiveness is influenced by the question of to whose actions such justice is applied. If moral justice is employed when judging perpetrators' behaviour, victims will evaluate the perpetrators' actions as evil and unjust, resulting in a reduction in forgiveness. If moral justice is applied to the victims' own actions, however, there is a possibility that this will cause a decline in retribution, and enhance forgiveness. This is because there is a moral law which says that others should be treated with mercy and forgiveness, even when there is a justifiable reason for vengeance. After Batson et al. had measured the strength of American university students' moral justice, they had the participants swap raffle tickets (tickets which, if drawn, would be exchangeable for a preferred item costing up to US$30). Their tickets were taken away by their negotiating partner, but, under one condition, they were led to believe that their partner had taken them for selfish reasons, while under a different condition they were informed that the confiscation had been determined by the flip of a coin. Later, when given the right to take their partner's tickets, participants with high moral justice curbed their retributive behaviour regardless of the perpetrators' intent. As people with a strong sense of moral justice control their own behaviour accordingly, they are understood to have avoided retribution and behaved in a forgiving way, irrespective of whether retribution was justified.

These research results show that justice is multi-dimensional, and while there is a kind of justice which is inconsistent with forgiveness, there is also a kind of justice which is consistent with it. Ohbuchi (2006, Chapter 4 of this volume) has asserted that justice is something which reflects social principles, and people with different principles have different views of justice. Retributive justice, which holds that the restoration of damages and honour should be guaranteed in relation to victims, and that perpetrators should receive punishment fitting their wrongdoing, is likely to be pursued among people who have the realisation of individual rights as their social principle. Among people who have social harmony as their social principle, however, priority will probably be given to conciliatory justice, which says that the mending of social relationships should be attempted by means of forgiveness rather than punishment. The studies of Batson et al. suggest that yet another type of social principle (moral justice) stimulates forgiveness.

Such theoretical analysis indicates that forgiveness and justice are not necessarily at odds, and that they can be compatible. While there are some societies which place importance upon retribution, there are others which do not. This equates to a difference of social principle. Within any one society, too, multiple social principles exist, and there is also the possibility that a single individual has a latent plurality of justice. If this be the case, then it might be possible to enhance people's forgiveness by evocation of forgiveness-friendly justice concern in conflict situations.

The punishment of perpetrators

Even if forgiveness-friendly justice were a realistic option, it could be denied that, within the plurality of justice, retributive justice is the relatively stronger dimension. For that reason, it is necessary to weaken this type of justice concern in order to stimulate forgiveness. From this section onwards, we will examine this issue.

It is well-known that perpetrators' apologies are effective in evoking forgiveness from victims (Worthington, 2003). Apologising means personally acknowledging wrongdoing, and Schmitt, Gollwitzer, Forster, and Montada (2004), using American participants, manipulated five meanings contained in apology to explore why apology has an effect on forgiveness. These five meanings were: that the perpetrators acknowledged wrongdoing on their part; that they recognised the enormity of the harm they had done to their victims; that they declared their guilt; that they sought pardon; and that they offered compensation. The authors systematically manipulated these and examined what combination was most instrumental in evoking forgiveness. As a result, it was found that seeking pardon had the greatest influence, and when this was combined with acknowledgement of the extent of victims' suffering and the offering of compensation, forgiveness was most greatly stimulated.

Apology is something that restores victims' economic and social resources (dignity and reputation), but it also means that perpetrators take on disadvantages (economic and social). Accordingly, when apology is conducted, victims probably feel that social justice has been restored by this means between themselves and the perpetrators. In other words, apology is something which satisfies victims' concern for social justice. In light of this, it is considered that apology by perpetrators weakens anti-forgiveness justice concerns, thus promoting forgiveness in victims.

The future restoration of justice: humanistic forgiveness

Forgiveness goes against social justice in the sense of approving of present injustice, but it can have the effect of guaranteeing the future restoration of justice. When victims refrain from retribution, a debt is sustained on the part of the perpetrators vis-à-vis the current disequilibrium, but if the victims have further non-punitive contact with them, the disequilibrium will expand, and a premium will be added to the perpetrators' debt. The perpetrators will come to shoulder a large debt, and they will sometimes seek to behave so as to restore justice themselves, to try to repay the debt (as an attempt to improve a situation in which they are unfairly advantaged).

Kellen and Ellard (1999) misled the American university students who participated in their experiment into thinking that they (the subjects) had broken a piece of laboratory equipment. The authors then compared the responses of participants between when the experimenter acted in a forgiving manner and when the experimenter was not forgiving. When the experimenter made an additional request of the participants which was not included in the original agreement, those participants who had been treated with forgiveness often acquiesced to this request, though it would normally be quite permissible to refuse. On the other hand, in cases where the experimenter had acted in a retributive manner – refusing to hand over payment, for example – those participants frequently refused the additional request from the experimenter. This study shows that forgiveness generates a psychological debt on the part of the perpetrators, and encourages them to restore social justice by themselves.

There is a type of humanism which tries to promote the rehabilitation of anti-social and non-social children and youths by treating them forgivingly, instead of penalising them. Such a principle is sometimes observed in the mother-child attachment relationship. It sometimes happens that fathers use direct influence to force children who tend to play truant from school to apply themselves to their studies, while mothers do not use this method, instead treating the children forgivingly. Such a maternal attitude has a tendency to stir feelings of guilt in the children, and to prompt them to attend school once more (Sommer and Baumeister, 1997). If forgiveness motivates voluntary justice-restorative behaviour in perpetrators, then this would be something that satisfies both social and moral justice, and could be said to be the most ideal effect of forgiveness. The question of whether perpetrators feel a psychological debt vis-à-vis forgiveness depends, though, upon the perpetrators' cognition. As has been often recorded (Exline and Baumeister, 2000, for example), if perpetrators were to use forgiveness for self-serving cognitive re-evaluation, including the justification of violence or the underestimation of the violation, then their psychological debt would be minimal, and the anticipated effect would not be obtained. Humanistic forgiveness is thus something which incorporates the risk of inviting an outcome which is contrary to justice.

The restoration of justice by third parties

How third parties deal with victims also constitutes a factor in forgiveness. Though forgiving behaviour is influenced by the perceived benefits and costs flowing from it, these can change according to the behaviour of third parties. Rape victims often happen to be accused by those around them of being partially to blame, because of their provocative clothing, their own carelessness, or suchlike. Criticism such as this from third parties is thought to function as social pressure that urges forgiveness from the victims, but, in actual practice, this is not the case. As to forgive the perpetrators means publicly acknowledging wrongdoing on the victims' own part, the latter are likely to hesitate to be forgiving, and, though they might bow to social pressure and reach a compromise, in their hearts they will probably never pardon the perpetrators. If victims of rape are on the receiving end of social criticism, as well, they will suffer a double disadvantage, and are likely to feel that there has been a great loss in the sense of social justice existing between themselves and the perpetrators. Victims are thus strongly motivated towards the restoration of social justice, the likely result being that they strongly demand punishment and retribution vis-à-vis the perpetrators.

In the opposite situation, however, if others were to protect the victims, reassuring them that they were not at fault, and publicly approve the rightness of that behaviour, then would not victims' feelings of resistance towards forgiveness decrease to some extent? At the very least, any further strengthening of the desire for social justice and retribution would probably be avoided. For that reason, third parties' perceptions vis-à-vis harm and victims can be considered to sway concern for social justice and exert an influence upon forgiveness.

We examined this issue experimentally (Takada and Ohbuchi, 2006). We gave Japanese university students scenarios in which we had manipulated the extent of victims' responsibility (the victims actually were responsible, or not), and third parties' attribution of responsibility (third parties voiced their recognition of appropriateness of victims' behaviour, or not). The participants read these from the standpoint of the victims, then evaluated their willingness for forgiveness, concern for social justice, and so on. As a result, when the victims felt that they shared responsibility, they were more willing to forgive, yet they became non-forgiving when they thought that they personally were not responsible. This shows that victims' own judgement about responsibility has an impact upon forgiveness. At the same time, though, regardless of their belief that they were not responsible, victims became more forgiving when third parties supported this than when the latter did not, as shown in Figure 6.1. Consequently, as we have already stated, it can be thought that censure from third parties excited victims' concern for social justice and intensified their motivation for vengeance, but, when third parties publicly recognised victims' social appropriateness, this concern was ameliorated, and the victims tended to become forgiving.

Related research findings are reported by Hewston, Cairns, Voci, McLernon, Niens and Noor (2004). In their study on victims' forgiveness and guilt in the troubles which arose in Northern Ireland, the development of victims' forgiveness was facilitated when third parties empathised with victims' suffering and exhibited behaviour which was strongly critical of perpetrators. This study, too, suggests that supportive behaviour by third parties contributes to the mitigation of victims' sense of injustice.

Figure 6.1: The content of third-party utterances and forgiving behaviour

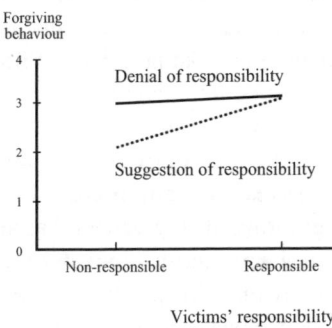
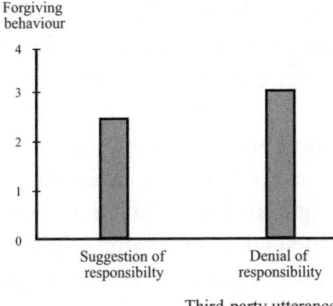

Though it is not generally well-known, the behaviour of third parties is an important regulatory factor which makes victims either forgiving or unforgiving, as we have argued in this section. There are, at present, a number of third-party institutions which help the resolution of social conflict, but their efficacy is not always clear. A variety of roles is expected of third parties in social conflict resolution, but, rather than directly intervening in the struggles, it may be more beneficial to reduce the desire for revenge and promote forgiveness by means of enhancing victims' sense of justice.

Conclusion

In this chapter, we have surveyed the advantages and costs related to two principles involved in conflict resolution. The forgiveness principle brings about harmonious resolution among the parties concerned, but, while the principle can discharge various kinds of justice – procedural, distributive and moral – there are costs in that it is not possible to implement rectification in the form of the restoration of justice, meaning recovery from the harm itself, restoration of social resources, and recovery from psychological injury. We have discussed how the kind of behaviour exhibited by disinterested third parties towards the victims and perpetrators in a conflict becomes a vital factor in reducing the costs concomitant with forgiveness.

At present, there is scant Japanese research into forgiveness, but we have conducted a series of investigations into the motivation behind Japanese people's implementation of forgiveness (Takada and Ohbuchi, 2004); how victims try to arrive at forgiveness (Takada and Ohbuchi, 2003); what kinds of interpersonal relationships are most conducive to the evocation of forgiveness (Takada and Ohbuchi, 2003); and whether the implementation of forgiveness enhances satisfaction towards the outcomes of conflict resolution (Ohbuchi and Takada, 2004). With Japanese people, when the opponents in a conflict were known to each other, there was a strong tendency to forgive the perpetrators, through a harmony-maintenance motivation – a desire to maintain social harmony among the surrounding people – and there was a high level of satisfaction towards the granting of forgiveness, based on such a motivation. This means that when victims consider the advantages and costs of forgiveness, they place emphasis not only upon how these things impact upon themselves, but also upon the benefits and costs which forgiveness brings to those around them. In Japanese conflicts, there is a possibility that victims recognise the parameters of the conflict as extending not merely to the interaction of the parties concerned, but also as encompassing interaction involving third parties, as well. If this be so, then the conduct of third parties can also be considered to have a powerful influence upon the forgiveness process of Japanese people, and there will probably be a call in future for the examination of psychological processes of forgiveness which include the conduct of third parties.

In this chapter, moreover, based on Ohbuchi's (2006a and b) multi-dimensional theory of justice, we pointed out that justice and forgiveness are not necessarily at odds, and that there is a concern for justice which promotes forgiveness. If it were possible to evoke harmonising justice and moral justice on the victims' side, then it might be possible to weaken their desire for retribution, and to encourage a forgiving solution. Empirical investigation of this matter remains a task for the future.

7 Justified Discrimination
Tōru Tamura

Since the dawn of history, there have existed many kinds of discrimination – slavery, class/hierarchical systems, apartheid, and the like. These have ranged from comparatively 'light' forms such as restriction of occupation or place of residence, for example, to exploitation and persecution, sometimes escalating even to brutal acts of aggression such as genocide and ethnic cleansing, which have brought about gruesome outcomes. This present age, permeated as it is by democracy and the notion of human rights, appears to function with the aim of making society one in which biased views towards others are discarded, and everyone is treated equally. Those who have been the victims of discrimination – people of colour, women, or people from hamlets known as *buraku*, the object of caste-like, systemic discrimination since feudal days in Japan – have taken a stand, launched movements aiming to improve their status and, by such means as legal enactments, seem to have obtained a certain degree of success. Among ordinary people, too, a hatred for bias and discrimination and a determination to censure those who overtly express such discrimination appear to have blossomed.

In reality, then, has discrimination vanished from our society? When asked such a question, the majority of people would probably reply: 'No, it hasn't.' The continuing presence of blatant discrimination is evidenced by such incidents as those in which unpleasant questions were asked only of female applicants at job interviews, thus dampening their desire to seek employment during the economic recession; or when numerous postcards inscribed with such words as: '[You] *Eta* (literally, 'filth,' a derogatory term for *buraku* people engaged in so-called noxious trades) have no human rights'; or '[You are] the root of all evil in Japan,' were sent to Tokyo businesses involved in the meat industry; or when female students at Korean high schools in Japan had their distinctive uniforms slashed in the train on their way to or from school. Through examples closer to home, as well, including the large number of real estate agencies which refuse to introduce rental properties to non-Japanese, and the graffiti maligning people from discriminated-against *buraku* that is sometimes seen in such places as subway station toilets, we are made aware of the deeply-rooted nature of discrimination towards such targets. It is also a frequent day-to-day experience for us, personally, to deprecate people whom we do not regard very favourably, even if this is not treatment directed at people belonging to certain specific groups. In other words, we are likely to see or experience a reality in which we cannot help being aware that discrimination certainly exists, in whatever shape or form, even though society itself might be moving towards disallowing it. If this be the case in a society which opposes discrimination, why, then, does it not cease to exist? What kind of processes might operate for it to be manifested in people's minds? In this chapter, I review the mental mechanism by which people counteract inhibition factors against contemporary social discrimination, whenever it is realised.

From inhibition to discrimination

That which can constitute the first inhibition factor for social discrimination is the threat of social sanction, which includes the disapproval of others. In present-day society, where egalitarian values are glorified, being tagged as prejudiced – as 'racist,' or 'sexist,' for example – carries the risk of deprivation of social resources and social ostracism. Consequently, in cases where people perceive that those around them hold such values, they are thought to suppress those discriminatory feelings, and to try not to declare them. In this respect, the popularisation through the mass media and school education of values asserting that it is bad to be prejudiced and to practise discrimination can be considered to have had a degree of efficacy towards the eradication of social discrimination. To cite an actual example, derogatory terms used to refer to Koreans residing in Japan and to people with physical disabilities, which were common some two decades ago, are no longer heard today. In Germany, as recently as about ten years ago, a travel company was apparently sued because of the 'displeasure' the plaintiff suffered due to having been accommodated at the same hotel as a group of people with disabilities, but surely nobody would think to do such a thing these days, and most people would probably doubt their own ears upon hearing that such a case actually stood up in court (Mummendy and Otten, 2004, p. 308).

Inhibition in such a form can hardly be called rock-solid, however, considering that it is shaped by external pressure. Discrimination comes to be practised in situations beyond the notice of others who hold anti-discriminatory values, for example. Discriminatory graffiti in toilets and the like falls into this category, as its writers exploit the opportunity to use demeaning language against specific persons when nobody else is present, therefore preventing the perpetrators being identified. It has been shown in many previous studies on stereotypes and bias that, even though inhibition due to external pressure might function very well in certain cases, it is capable of producing some unexpected by-products in circumstances where such constraint is perceived to be weak (Dovidio and Gaertner, 2004; Macrae, Bodenhausen, Milne and Jetten, 1994; Wyer, Sherman and Stroessner, 2000).

Stereotypes and prejudices, in the same way as discrimination, constitute a response which incorporates an interpretive judgement that is unfair, irrational, or unjustified, in the sense that it transcends the objective necessary requirements and facts of the situation (Hewstone, Rubin and Willis, 2002). In studies of inter-group bias, stereotypes, prejudices and discrimination are separated variously into cognitive bias, affective bias and behavioural bias, but, as cognitive and affective elements are essential as possible constituents of the basis upon which discriminatory behavioural responses are generated, the inhibition of stereotypes and prejudices is also important in considering the inhibition of discrimination. Next, then, by introducing studies relating to the inhibition of these responses, I shall examine the tenuous nature of the inhibition of discrimination when this is due to external coercion.

The rebound effect in stereotype-suppression

It has been made clear that stereotypes, from their very function, are very difficult things for people to avoid. This is because stereotypes categorise the countless objects of perception which exist in the real world as having some kind of coherence, and, as their basis lies in the natural human predisposition towards attempting efficiently to obtain information, stereotypes thus play an important role in people's social interaction. Thanks to the existence of stereotypes, people can, for example, efficiently form an impression of a target person belonging to a specific group (Brewer, 1988; Fiske and Neuberg, 1990), and, if they negatively stereotype the members of such groups, they can enhance or maintain their own self-esteem (Fein and Spencer, 1997; Tajfel and Turner, 1986). Due to this function, however, stereotypes have also been used to justify inequalities in resource-allocation (Jost and Banaji, 1994). Thus, for the same reason that social discrimination tends to be suppressed, the assertion of stereotypes is often not supported, and is inhibited. Scholars have been interested in what kind of effect stereotypes suppressed in this manner might have on the perceptions of people later on.

When a certain individual attempts to suppress a stereotype, s/he probably strives consciously not to think about that stereotype, or not to employ it. However, when we try to avoid or suppress a particular thought, we sometimes have the contradictory experience of it coming frequently to mind. In the research of Wegner, Schneider, Carter and White (1987), it was reported that experimental subjects who were instructed not to think about a certain target (a 'white bear,' in the study in question) more often thought of one than did experimental subjects who were told that they were allowed to think about that target. This indicates that an attempt to suppress thoughts about a particular target increases the likelihood of such thoughts later coming to mind – in other words, it enhances the accessibility of those thoughts.

This seems be the case with stereotypes. That is, the more an individual attempts to suppress a stereotype, the more accessibility to the stereotype may be heightened, which affects cognitive processes following it. Macrae et al. (1994) examined this phenomenon by using Britons' negative stereotypes of skinhead groups. In the initial stage of their work, Macrae et al. instructed half of their experimental participants to suppress stereotypes about skinhead groups, but did not give such an instruction to the other half. In consequence, it was shown that the participants who practised suppression did not use stereotypes as much as the non-suppression group. However, in the second stage, in which the researchers conducted lexical decision tasks concerning stereotype-related and non-related terms with these participants, it was shown that a greater rebound response to words related to stereotypes was fostered in the group which had exercised suppression than the group which had not. Moreover, it has been shown in other work by Macrae and colleagues that, as stereotypes whose accessibility is enhanced in this manner especially exert an influence upon subsequent cognitive processes such as impression-formation in the reverse direction to that intended by the suppression, the next members of that group whom participants encounter will be more markedly stereotyped than in a case where stereotype-suppression had not been attempted.

Wegner and Schneider (1989) have explained the operation of two processes in relation to the accessibility-increasing effect of thoughts repressed by thought-suppression. The first process is an automatic monitoring process which comes into play by intentional thought-suppression, and in which the thoughts which must be suppressed are identified. Next, when such thoughts are detected, the second control process tries to banish them by consciously 'jamming' them with other thoughts. The problem is that attention is all the more directed at the thoughts identified by the first process, leading to the enhancement of their accessibility. For that reason, because an insufficiency of cognitive resources due to some kind of obstruction induces a breakdown in the functioning of the second process which requires those resources, it becomes easier for those thoughts to be employed in judgements, and, as the thoughts which should be suppressed remain activated throughout the entire suppression process, this results in that suppression having an influence upon subsequent cognition, even after the suppression has finished.

Is the rebound effect unavoidable?

The results of Macrae et al. invite the pessimistic conclusion that the social restraint of stereotypes is always of short duration, and has the opposite effect of facilitating judgements in which stereotypes are reinforced. In not all cases, however, does such a reverse effect of suppression arise. In the racial-stereotype experiments of Wyer et al. (2000), the researchers posited that, as egalitarian values mean that people are usually motivated to suppress any stereotype deemed desirable of suppression, the rebound effect cannot occur because the suppression motivation always operates in situations where the target of judgement is a target to which that stereotype can be applied. However, they predicted that control would become difficult and stereotypes would be employed solely in cases where there was imposition of cognitive load impeding the control process, as Wegner and others have argued.

The American university students who participated in their experiments looked at a photograph of an Asian-American or an African-American male and described a typical day in his life. Here, half of the participants were told not to use stereotypes, while the remainder were not given any such instruction. The participants then were asked to read a story about a person who engaged both in behaviour matching the stereotype of an African-American (antagonistic and non-intellectual) and in behaviour matching the stereotype of an Asian-American (passive and intellectual), and to form an impression of that person. Consequently, in situations where the person's race was not made clear, participants who initially had suppressed stereotypes were more likely to form a stereotype-based impression of the target than did participants who had not practised suppression, whereas in cases where race was stipulated, there was no difference in impressions, irrespective of whether the participants had suppressed stereotypes. Moreover, when cognitive load was imposed, the rebound effect arose in participants who had suppressed stereotypes, and more stereotypical impressions of the target were formed, even if race were stipulated. From this result, Wyer et al. suggest that the rebound effect is not generated when the target of judgement is a target to whom are applied racial stereotypes which should be suppressed, and that the application of stereotypes to a target is efficiently suppressed by the motivation to suppress. They conclude, moreover, that that motivation loses efficiency and the rebound effect manifests itself particularly in circumstances such as when cognitive load is imposed.

Studies on these kinds of stereotype-suppression point out that the effect which corrects cognitive distortion through external coercion is one limited by the conditions under which said coercion is operating, and, when that is weakened, it is more likely to elicit a biased judgement than in situations where there is no suppression. Moreover, as such a biased judgement is taken as a rationale, there is high probability that a discriminatory response to the target will be brought to the surface within the individual concerned, as being the appropriate one in the circumstances.

However, let us separately reconsider the behavioural response we call discrimination and the cognitive response we call stereotyping, from the perspective of response bias. If we assume these are two different things, it would follow that even if stereotype-based, biased judgements tentatively were made, behavioural responses to that target need not be biased. Even if it were impossible to rectify distortion on a cognitive level, if discrimination on a behavioural level were always suppressed due to an awareness of the operation of external coercion, then at least outward fairness would be maintained. Could this actually happen? We subsequently deal with the question of to what extent external coercion would be effective in suppressing behavioural responses.

Aversive racism

In the United States of America, the home of a much greater number and diversity of racial and ethnic groups than Japan, social discrimination has long continued to be a huge problem. Though America was founded on the basis of the principle of freedom and justice for all, it took a great amount of time before people's fundamental human rights were guaranteed by law, and, furthermore, it still cannot be said that structural changes in such laws have gone so far as to be reflected in people's attitudes. There is continuing, deep-seated discrimination against people of colour, starting with those who are black, and there is a persistent disparity between whites and people of colour in various economic indicators such as indices of health and welfare, the gap even further widening in some cases (Jenkins, 2001). On the other hand, egalitarian values based on the spirit of freedom and equality which have existed since the founding of the nation have already become general and universal among the populace, racial integration having progressed in areas such as schooling, public transport, occupation and residence, and the expression of outwardly discriminatory attitudes seems substantially to have decreased. Dovidio and Gaertner (2004) employ a concept called aversive racism to analyse this kind of duality in US society. Aversive racists sympathise with victims of past inequality, support the principle of equality, and regard themselves as being devoid of prejudice, but, at the same time, they are also persons who unconsciously harbour negative feelings and beliefs vis-à-vis people of colour (Kovel, 1970). The way in which this discriminatory attitude is manifest is more indirect and subtle than the overt manner of expression traditionally seen, but the results it engenders are about as pronounced and injurious as with overt discrimination. It not being restricted only to racial discrimination, Dovidio and Gaertner's analysis might be useful in understanding the nature of the manifestation of discrimination in a society where external coercion driven by egalitarian values is in operation.

The nature of aversive racists
According to Dovidio and Gaertner, the pattern of social discrimination illustrated by aversive racists differs from that shown by conventionally overt, direct racists. As aversive racists acknowledge an awareness of egalitarian values, and desire not to be biased, they do not attempt to practise discrimination in situations where strong anti-discriminatory social norms are present. Because discrimination would directly jeopardise their egalitarian self-image and the cost would be too great, particularly in circumstances where a normatively appropriate response was unequivocal, such as when there was a clear definition of right and wrong, they do not attempt to reveal it, and

are motivated to avoid feelings, beliefs and behaviour which might be associated with discriminatory intent. For that reason, they tend to try to treat people of colour and white people equally, or to give preferential treatment especially to people of colour.

However, as they have uncomfortable feelings towards people of colour and minorities, those discriminatory feelings will be expressed as something indirect and rationalised in situations where the canonical structure is weak, such as when there is ambiguity in the guidelines for appropriate behaviour or in the basis for social judgements. This kind of discrimination is only expressed in cases where a negative response can be rationalised or justified on the basis of a factor other than race, so that such aversive racists can preserve their own egalitarian self-image and view their behaviour as not being racially biased. In other words, the decision as to whether discrimination will be expressed by aversive racists will depend upon whether it is a situation in which they, personally, and others around them, can attribute negative behaviour towards people who are the target of discrimination to a racial agenda.

Experimental investigation of aversive racism
Dovidio and Gaertner examined this prediction by means of a series of experiments, obtaining consistent corroboration relating to the nature of the discriminatory attitudes which aversive racists express. In their first field experiment regarding helping behaviour (Gaertner, 1973), they predicted that conservative whites would turn out to be more racially discriminatory than liberal whites. In this experiment, the targets of help appealed to participants over the telephone for aid because of a car breakdown, but the targets' race could be specified from their accents. Analysis of helping behaviour towards the targets revealed that conservatives clearly extended more help to whites than to blacks, and liberals showed about the same willingness to help either. However, it was shown that a higher proportion of liberals than conservatives tended to hang up, even before any request for help was given, in cases of calls from black people. In other words, as a clear-cut refusal of help would represent a deviation from societal norms, aversive-racist-type liberals carried out discrimination against blacks while avoiding deviation from social norms by circumventing any request for help by hanging up.

In other experiments using help-in-an-emergency situations conducted by Gaertner and Dovidio (1977), it was revealed that in cases where the onus of responsibility towards the person to be helped clearly fell upon the white participants, such as when there were no witnesses apart from the individual participants – in other words, in circumstances where social norms were unequivocal – participants gave help equally to whites and blacks, but, in situations where deviation from social norms was not clear-cut, such as when responsibility was diminished due to the presence of other witnesses, help was clearly extended less often towards blacks than towards whites.

A similar tendency towards indirect discrimination by aversive racists is also seen in other domains. In the experiments of Murrell, Dietz-Uhler, Dovidio, Gaertner and Drout (1994) and Dovidio and Gaertner (1996) which examined support for and perceptions of fairness relating to affirmative action, it was shown that white participants responded more negatively to the policy in situations where the target of affirmative action was black people than when people who were aged, disabled or Native American were targeted, and that resistance to the policy was further strengthened in cases where the stated purpose of the policy was to prioritise those people. Moreover, from the fact that such a response was mediated by perceptions of unfairness, it became obvious that when whites opposed affirmative action vis-à-vis blacks, they cited the unfairness of the policy as grounds for its rationalisation.

It has also been illustrated that in jury experiments involving white participants, in cases where some factor besides race is offered to enable the justification of a discriminatory verdict, black people tend consistently to receive a disadvantageous ruling (Johnson, Whitestone, Jackson and Gatto, 1995; Knight, Guiliano and Sanchez-Ross, 2001). In mock trial experiments with white participants as jurors, Dovidio, Smith, Donnella and Gaertner (1997) found that the accused's being white or black made no difference to white jurors' responses when the latter were questioned individually as to whether they would ask for the death penalty, but that they would more strongly insist on the death penalty for black defendants than for whites if they knew that a black juror had demanded the death penalty. This result could be attributed to the white jurors having been able to justify a discriminatory verdict without being conscious of racial discrimination, due to one other juror, who was black, having sought the death penalty.

A tendency such as this can also be seen in decisions to do with hiring or academic admission selection procedures. White participants in experiments involving mock hiring decisions (Dovidio and Gaertner, 2000) recommended black and white applicants for employment to an equal extent in situations where their academic transcripts clearly met the selection criteria, or where they clearly did not, but in cases where it was difficult to judge whether the criteria were satisfied, they recommended hiring white applicants more often than black ones. Additionally, in the mock university admission selection experiments of Hodson, Dovidio and Gaertner (2002), white participants with an especially strong discriminatory bent recommended white and black examinees equally when the candidates clearly fulfilled all of the multiple evaluation components, or when they clearly did not, but when some components were satisfied and some not, participants displayed a tendency to recommend more white than black examinees, and to give more weight to assessment components which justified such discriminatory decisions.

What aversive racism shows
The series of experiments by Dovidio et al. evokes the manner in which discrimination by aversive racists is asserted in an indirect, subtle form, all the while preserving rationality, in situations such as those in which the basis for judgement is obscure, or the basis for decision can be attributed to a factor other than race. The character Dovidio and his colleagues describe is that of a person who truly desires egalitarianism, yet who unintentionally displays discriminatory responses due to a conflict between that desire and the discriminatory feelings and beliefs which unconsciously exist within her or him. On this point, this portrait differs from that of a person who, while being aware of his or her own discriminatory feelings and beliefs, hesitates to declare them because of social coercion, and strives to suppress them. The latter type, when compared with the aversive racist discussed by Dovidio and others, could be said to be closer to the traditional racist.

The state in which the discriminatory response found by Dovidio and colleagues becomes obvious can also be interpreted as being a situation of weak social coercion, in terms of the impossibility of labelling the person concerned as prejudiced. In other words, in line with the results indicated by stereotype-inhibition studies, the suppression of social discrimination by external coercion can be considered something which is limited to situations where it is perceived that such coercion is in operation, and, in situations where such coercion is unconsciously perceived to be weak, social discrimination consequently appears in a way that gives rise to a harmful effect, to an extent comparable with any directly-expressed form. This condition also shows how deftly people's discriminatory awareness tries to claw aside or dive under the net of social inhibition and manifest itself.

As we have seen thus far, inhibition due to social sanction in the form of external coercion is insufficient for the eradication of social discrimination. With such coercion alone, as I have already argued at the beginning of this chapter, inhibition hardly functions in cases where social surveillance is perceived to be absent or weak. Conditions such as those seen in contemporary society, where discrimination continues persistently and forcefully to exist, certainly in places that elude the public eye, can be regarded as by-products of inhibition due to such external coercion.

Compared to the ages when the conduct of slavery and human trafficking were taken for granted, however, conditions of discrimination in times such as these can be said to have made considerable progress in an egalitarian direction. That means there has been a real increase in the number of people who genuinely embrace such values and, for that reason, such third parties will come to function as a compelling force. Naturally, this does not mean that people who truly embrace egalitarian values suppress discrimination because of external coercion. As they have internalised such values as a moral standard, they are motivated by inhibition to observe them. Here, we can find yet another type of inhibition relating to social discrimination. That constitutes empathy towards the target, and moral standards internalised on that basis.

Force counteracting moral inhibition

In studies of aggression, in particular, empathy has been seen as a powerful factor in its inhibition (Davis, 1994). Taking the viewpoint of the victim is thought to generate understanding and tolerance towards the victim's position, and to reduce animosity and aggressive responses towards the other person. Trying to share the victim's pain or empathetically experiencing an emotional response towards the victim's pain motivates the inhibition of aggression. According to Mummendey and Otten (2004), aggressive behaviour is one mode of social discrimination, but discrimination also has a mode in which advantage is disproportionately distributed. In short, discrimination does not necessarily involve injury to a target. However, empathising with the target in the unfair distribution of advantage can be presumed to give rise to vicarious experience of the target's dissatisfaction, anger or suchlike. Accordingly, empathy can be considered simultaneously to have an aggression-inhibition effect, and also to be effective in inhibiting discrimination. Furthermore, if moral standards were shaped on this basis, then discrimination would be constantly suppressed, even without the need for external coercion.

If inhibition of discrimination through empathy and morality are effective, however, why has discrimination not actually disappeared in real society? Our morality, according to Bandura (1999), while having but one standard, still changes flexibly according to circumstances and the person with whom we deal. Such inhibition of discrimination through empathy and morality is something which operates only in cases where we have acknowledged its target as existing within the scope of application of moral norms, and, in cases where we have decided that the target lies outside the scope of application, that inhibition will not function (Opotow, 1990). It has been made clear that our moral parameters can be easily narrowed in various situations, and there are also some cases of moral norms not being applied to a target when discriminatory acts are justified. Many psychologists are of the opinion that a cognitive disinhibition mechanism comes into play when moral parameters are narrowed, causing the act to be overlooked or justified in the mind of the perpetrator (Bandura, 1990, 1999; Baumeister, 1997; Opotow, 1990; Staub, 1990).

The disinhibition mechanism of discrimination

The moral disinhibition mechanism cited by scholars can be largely divided into four categories. The first is the cognitive reappraisal of reprehensible acts of exploitation or aggression as being socially acceptable. For example, people sometimes justify an act by saying, 'That's my job' or 'It's my duty,' or directing their gaze away from the fact that they themselves are engaged in immoral conduct, by regarding it as amusement or a game (Baumeister, 1997). To cite a different example, to call the killing of soldiers 'wasting,' or to rephrase the death of non-combatants in war as 'collateral damage' is taken as being effective in watering down the cruelty and tyrannical nature of the acts (Bandura, 1990, 1999). In scenes of destructive cults or group violence, also, the covering-up of the inhumane nature of acts has often been carried out through emphasis on lofty goals involving group ideology or the attainment of social ideals (Bandura, 1990, 1999; Opotow, 1990).

The second mechanism consists of the weakening of the agent's responsibility towards an act. In a situation where an authority guarantees the shouldering of responsibility for an outcome (Bandura, 1990, 1999; Staub, 1990), an agent can view exploitation and aggression as merely acts done on someone else's behalf, as s/he can shift responsibility for the act onto the authority. Additionally, in circumstances where anonymisation and job-sharing is practised (Baumeister, 1997; Opotow, 1990), as observers or victims cannot specify the person/s ultimately responsible for a detrimental outcome, fears of social sanction or retribution are mitigated.

The third mechanism is the disregard of detrimental outcomes caused by an action. In cases such as when, for example, a high-tech weapon is used to precision-bomb a target from a remote location, and the act and its outcome are physically and temporally removed from each other (Bandura, 1990, 1999), or when one thinks only of piloting a bomber or pressing the launch button of a missile in a timely manner, by concentrating not on the act as a whole or its meaning, but on low-order thoughts such as the operating procedure (Baumeister, 1997), it is easy for one's attention not to be directed towards such outcomes as victims' dissatisfaction or pain, and for even brutal acts to be executed without resistance.

The fourth mechanism is the changing of perceptions vis-à-vis the victim. If one thinks that punishment is natural because the victim provoked it in the first place (Bandura, 1990, 1999; Opotow, 1990), then not only exploitative behaviour, but even aggressive behaviour, also, can be justified as reprisal or defensive action. In cases, too, where the victim is disdained as barbaric and inferior, or as an inscrutable and dangerous target, aggressive behaviour is likely to be an easy choice. Furthermore, by dehumanising the victim, not merely consideration for the victim, but every iota of hesitation towards attacking that person will also be lost from an aggressor who treats a victim as an object without humanity, dignity or sensitivity.

It is clear that these cognitive mechanisms are sufficiently powerful to operate individually, and that one, by itself, is enough to facilitate the orientation of people towards exploitative or persecutory behaviour. In reality, however, it often happens that several of these mechanisms work in combination, thus enabling the more powerful release of moral inhibition on the aggressor's part, and even sometimes inducing a tragedy too horrible to behold.

The dehumanisation of victims

Many scholars have proceeded with analysis of phenomena relating to inequalities and injustices all over the world, and have identified the operation of these cognitive mechanisms, but it is the dehumanisation of victims, in particular, which is seen in cases of especially severe discrimination and in the majority of atrocious events in human history. Systems such as slavery, for example, which buys and sells human beings as if they were livestock, driving them relentlessly and abusing them, are the very epitome of dehumanisation in instances of discrimination. The black people who were forcibly shipped from the continent of Africa to America and Europe were shackled together, hand and foot, in the slave ships, and had to spend the voyage laid down like logs, and if they had the misfortune to die in that unsanitary environment, they apparently were simply tossed into the sea as if they were rubbish.

The dehumanising propaganda of wartime, too, enhances feelings of fear and hostile sentiment towards enemy countries, and has been regarded as common practice for the purpose of killing people without any awareness of wrongdoing. The portrayal of the people of an opposing country as insatiable, ferocious, malevolent 'enemies' bereft of human feeling, who would harm the women and children, property and livelihood of the home country, makes attacking the opponent a duty for protecting the people of the homeland from a dangerous presence which threatens their safety, and for attaining justice. The ruthless killing of 'Capitalist dogs,' 'Nazi pigs,' 'Jap rats' and suchlike during World War II and the Cold War was regarded as morally just, because, as dangerous and irrational animals, they might do something devious. Moreover, it is thought that, as far as soldiers are concerned, the lower the breeding of those who are thus imagined descends – to vermin, disease germs, or the like – the greater the authorisation granted to them to eradicate those harmful beings (Keen, 1986).

Such dehumanisation has also been observed on an ethnic-group level and an individual level. In the ethnic conflict in Rwanda, which started in 1994, the majority Hutus conducted mass slaughter within Rwanda, most of the casualties being minority Tutsis, but the Hutus who took part in the genocide assuaged their guilty feelings by calling the victims 'cockroaches' or 'snakes' deserving of annihilation, and 800,000 Rwandan citizens were slain, as a result (Opotow, 2005). At the notorious Jewish concentration camp in Treblinka, Poland, also, approximately 900,000 Jews were slaughtered between 1942 and 1943, and the Nazi officer who was head of the concentration camp at that time said in a later interview that when sending the stream of Jews who were transported there by train to the gas chambers, he tried to regard them as herds of livestock loaded onto freight trains (Moshman, 2005). In Argentina, under the military regime of the late 1970s, the poor and some thirty thousand university students and young people who had been working for social justice were murdered as dissident 'missing persons,' but a marine who was actually involved in the work of killing also said, in an interview where he was asked about those days, that he had tried to think of the victims who were thrown into the sea alive as just weeds (Moshman, 2005).

As the dehumanisation of victims in this way is predominantly seen in extreme cases of discrimination and violence, it can be regarded as one of the most precise materials for consideration in analysis of how people deal with anguish and guilt, or feelings of remorse and repentance, when they carry out discriminatory acts, and how they change the scope of application of moral norms. For this reason, psychologists (Bandura, 1973; Kelman, 1973; Zimbardo, 1970) have taken this up as a psychological factor which exacerbates aggressive behaviour, but empirical studies are few.

The work of Bandura, Underwood and Fromson (1975) was conducted in America, but constitutes one of the rare examples of direct examination of the effect which the dehumanisation of victims has upon aggressive behaviour. In groups of three, participants in Bandura et al.'s experiment assumed the role of site supervisors who had to convey to the targets an external assessment of the decision-making of the target group in a separate room. The decision-makers were specified as being either a group of repugnant 'animalistic,' or 'nice,' sensible, human people who had foresight, or else were not given any specific label. In situations where the decision-making was given an external assessment of 'inappropriate,' participants needed to penalise the target group by giving as strong an electric shock as participants personally considered apt. The electric shocks which the participants in this experiment chose were strongest in the cases where the targets had received dehumanising labels, middling in strength in neutral cases, and weakest in cases where the targets had been specified as human. Moreover, in post-experiment interviews, there were many responses which justified the use of electric shocks as penalties for dehumanised targets, while conversely proclaiming disapproval of the use of such penalties for humanised targets. It was further shown that participants who strongly justified the penalties utilised stronger shocks.

In Bandura et al.'s second experiment, moreover, in situations where an initial external assessment of 'inappropriate' was followed by a series of similar assessments, participants abruptly increased the intensity of the electric shock given to the dehumanised targets the second time, then continued to subject them to an extremely high level of shock. With neutral targets, however, despite the exhibition of a similar trend in assessments, the intensity of shocks remained at mid-level, and, with the humanised targets, participants intensified the shock a little on the first repeat, but progressively reduced it thereafter. This result indicates that the giving of dehumanising labels to targets will aggravate aggressors' punitive behaviour, and, because such dehumanising labelling induces a different interpretation of the behaviour to that meted out towards targets given humanising labels, that punitive behaviour will be justified.

The research of Bandura et al. shows that the dehumanisation of targets intensifies aggressors' exploitative and aggressive behaviour. As people negatively interpret a target's conduct, and see that conduct as the rationale and justification for giving even greater punishment, it is especially evident how such behaviour steadily escalates. This work dramatically shows how easy it is for people's cognition to become distorted merely because of a negative label given to a target, and whether punishment will be tolerated within those individuals.

In cases of dehumanisation in actual settings, however, not only such negative labelling as that seen in Bandura et al.'s research, but also a phenomenon in which people call the target by a dehumanising name can be observed, as in the examples cited above of 'Jap rats,' 'snakes,' 'cockroaches,' and so on. As such dehumanising labelling is a means of more concisely expressing the negative attributes of a target, in line with the messenger's intent, the pronounced image and impact it bestows thus gives such labelling the potential to exert a different influence from that of simple conveyance of salient features to people's cognition of a target. Scholars have not yet touched upon this, and, for that reason, we have become interested in such dehumanising labels.

Psychological studies of dehumanisation in Japan

The use of dehumanising labels can be observed in Japan, also, as is the case in other countries. During World War II, for example, the Japanese government notoriously built up its wartime regime on a national scale by calling the United States and Britain 'devils and beasts (*kichiku*).' It is also well known that the now-defunct Japanese Imperial Army called Chinese prisoners-of-war at that time 'logs (*maruta*),' and used them as human guinea pigs to test biological weapons. Even in our daily lives, such derogatory terms as '*zako* (minnow)' or '*kasu* (dregs)' are used to demean targets, and to emphasise that they have remarkably low worth, while in problems of bullying, especially, ostracised victims are called '*gomi* (rubbish)' or '*baikin* (germs).'

By fostering prejudice and disdain for targets, and exacerbating aggressive behaviour on the part of perpetrators, the use of dehumanising labels in such conflict situations can be presumed to make the conflict more serious. However, it has not yet been made clear by what kind of mechanism these labels exert such an effect. We thus experimentally investigated the effect upon aggressive behaviour of dehumanising labels, using Japanese participants as targets.

Aggressive behaviour intensification through dehumanising labels

It has been demonstrated in studies of stereotyping and stigmatisation that social labels such as 'WASP (White, Anglo-Saxon, Protestant)' and 'schizophrenic' cause their perceivers to make the sort of judgements which fit that label about their targets (Darley and Gross, 1983; Harris, Milich, Corbitt, Hoover and Brady, 1992). The effect of such a social label, by generating expectations in the perceiver in conformity with said social category, is to induce the perceiver to interpret, ascribe or reproduce the target's behaviour in a way that matches such expectations. As a result, judgements about impressions of the target come to be distorted in a direction corresponding with those expectations. Non-human labels which imply a negative nature are thought similarly to cause their perceivers to expect such a nature from their targets, and to facilitate the formation of negative perceptions fitting those expectations vis-à-vis the targets. Moreover, as the examples of dehumanisation indicate, because empathetic consideration towards targets thus negatively perceived is thought to diminish, we can presume that the occurrence of fierce attacks against those targets will be facilitated, in consequence.

Among the effects of dehumanising labels, there is also considered to be an action called the anonymisation of targets, irrespective of the nature which such labels exhibit. As the key to empathising with targets as fellow human beings is absent in relation to those whose social presence has diminished due to anonymisation, empathetic consideration is thought to develop with difficulty in this case, too (Baumeister, 1997; Opotow, 1990). In actuality, Worchel and Andreoli (1978) have shown that aggressors who do not remember information which sets targets apart as individuals carry out more violent attacks than aggressors who do remember such information. Accordingly, in order to show that the effect of dehumanising labels differs from the effect of simple anonymisation, it is necessary to conduct a comparison with neutral labels which do not suggest a negative nature. We (Tamura and Ohbuchi, 2006) used Japanese university students in our attempt to examine how their attitudes and behaviour towards targets would change in situations where dehumanising labels and anonymising labels were attached to the latter.

It has also been hypothesised that the effect of such dehumanising labels causes a lowering of inhibition in people who have become aggressive due to some kind of provocation (Bandura, 1990, 1999; Keen, 1986). However, it is thought not only that such labelling makes it difficult for people to suppress their heightened aggression by its rousing of such belligerent images as 'heinous' or 'not to be underestimated,' but also that the labels themselves have the potential to motivate aggression. We therefore decided to compare cases in which targets of labelling were extremely aggressive with cases where they were not, in order to investigate the aggression-motivating effect of dehumanising labels themselves.

Experimental investigation

We had male Japanese university students play a beat'em up-type game one-on-one with another participant. Participants were told that, for the duration of the experiment, they would be called by a nickname decided at random by a computer, but the participant's nickname was set at 'B,' while his opponent's nickname was one of the following: 'Rubbish (*Gomi*)' (a dehumanising label), 'A' (an anonymising label), or 'Nozato' (an actual surname). The beat'em up game was set up so that whenever a character sustained injury, noise sounded through that player's headphones, and participants were able mutually to choose how loud a dose of noise to give their opponent. The level of noise was deemed an indicator of aggressive behaviour. Half of the participants played against aggressive opponents who had chosen nothing but loud noise, while the remaining half played against

Table 7.1: Effect of dehumanising labels: means and standard deviations of social concerns, perception of hostility and aggressive behaviour

	Label	Anonymous	Real name
Social concern			
Aggressive opponent	4.37 (1.63)	4.53 (0.91)	4.80 (0.65)
Non-aggressive opponent	4.23 (1.16)	5.77 (0.66)	5.77 (0.94)
Perception of hostility			
Aggressive opponent	5.43 (1.09)	4.53 (0.99)	4.64 (0.93)
Non-aggressive opponent	2.91 (0.90)	2.17 (0.61)	2.38 (1.23)
Aggressive behaviour			
Aggressive opponent	5.86 (1.68)	5.76 (1.17)	5.68 (1.13)
Non-aggressive opponent	4.25 (1.18)	4.46 (1.47)	4.15 (0.93)

non-aggressive opponents who had chosen less loud noise. After the close of play, the participants answered questions about how hostile they had felt their opponent to be, and to what extent they had wished to be considerate towards that opponent.

Table 7.1 shows experiment participants' assessment of their perception of their opponent's hostility and their consideration for those opponents, and the loudness of the noise they chose for their opponent to hear. As can be seen in this table, participants who played against aggressive opponents were shown to have employed louder noise than participants who played against non-aggressive opponents, but no labelling effect appeared in the loudness of the noise. However, participants who played against targets who had been given a dehumanising label perceived stronger hostility in their opponents and had less consideration towards them than did participants who played against targets with an anonymising label or a real-name label. As no disparity was seen in participants' responses between those whose targets had anonymised labels and those with real-name labels, it was considered that anonymising labels had no effect, at least in terms of this experiment.

The path diagram in Figure 7.1 was obtained when we treated anonymising labels and real names as equivalent, and examined the effect of dehumanising labels by covariance structure analysis. From this diagram, it can be understood that dehumanising labels have a positive influence upon the perception of hostility from a target, and a negative influence on consideration for a target, while consideration has a negative influence upon aggressive behaviour. This means,

Figure 7.1: Path analysis of the effect exerted by dehumanising labels and the aggression of the other upon aggressive behaviour

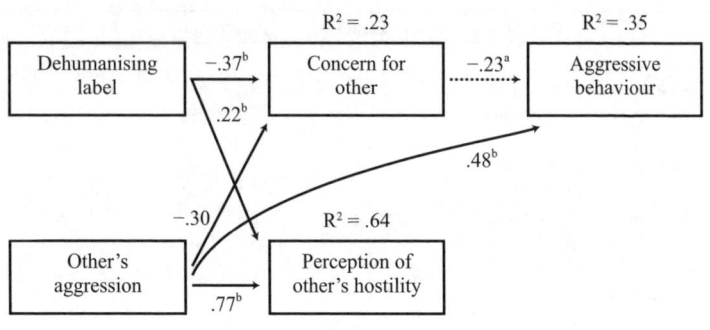

a = p < .05; b = p < .01; N = 63

in other words, that dehumanising labels strengthen perceptions of hostility from their targets while diminishing consideration for those targets, and a decrease in consideration intensifies aggressive behaviour.

This result shows that the application of dehumanising labels, unlike mere anonymisation, reduces people's consideration for their targets, and has the function of indirectly strengthening aggressive behaviour. In this experiment, especially, though the labelling was entirely arbitrary, the participants strongly perceived the hostility of those to whom it was applied, and reduced their consideration for the targets. This means that, through dehumanising labels, participants discovered a negative nature as the rationale that justified attacking the target, and this prompted them to decrease their consideration and step up their aggression. In addition, the fact that dehumanising labels also reduced consideration for the target in situations where the target was not aggressive means that participants found a rationale that justified an attack when, for some reason, there was the need to attack a target who had no just reason to be attacked, and this also coincides with the results of Bandura et al. (1975). In other words, this result shows how easily people's moral parameters can be narrowed, and suggests the possibility that discrimination towards a target is easily carried out, or is further strengthened, because when people practise discrimination for some reason, especially, they ascribe negative phenomena to targets due to arbitrarily-assigned dehumanising labels, and are thus granted the rationale for justifying that discrimination.

Conclusion

In Japanese society at present, it is far from a daily occurrence for social discrimination to be taken up by the mass media on any large scale. This probably means that, unlike in the United States, where various kinds of discrimination have become social issues, and Russia, China and European countries, in which ethnic struggles are always at flashpoint, there is comparatively little social discrimination in our society, and, even where it does exist, it takes a weak form, and thus is not very conspicuous. However, once it erupts in our society, in which people appear to have but a scant awareness of discrimination – as in the case of the so-called 'Herculano Incident' which occurred in Komaki City in Aichi Prefecture in 1997 – this graphically illustrates the fact that it has the potential to give rise to gruesome consequences. In this incident, a Japanese youth whose car had been damaged by a certain Brazilian youth gathered some companions in order to seek revenge; they, as a group, then violently attacked some Brazilian boys who were unrelated to the previous incident. Using a car, they abducted one fourteen-year-old boy, Herculano Reiko Lukocevicius, who was unable to escape in time, further beating and stabbing him to death (Borst, 1998; Laszlo, 1998).

Their blatantly discriminatory awareness towards Brazilian boys can be glimpsed from the fact that the Japanese youths in this incident attacked 'unrelated' Brazilian youths, and from a comment from one Japanese boy, who said: 'If we hadn't done it to them, some other Japanese would have done it, anyway' (Laszlo, 1998). At the same time, one can also grasp the danger which lay in inter-group contact. In light of this, one is prompted to reacknowledge the reality that the phenomenon of social discrimination is still very much in existence in Japan, too, without exception, and one cannot help thinking that it is a general phenomenon throughout humanity. It is possible to predict that there will be a heightening in awareness of people's human rights and consciousness of equality in Japanese society from here forward, along with the further advancement of globalisation, but, might not all manner of hitherto-hidden discrimination reveal itself as a distinct and conspicuous presence at the same time?

In this chapter, we have looked at the forces which work to inhibit discrimination, and at the mental mechanism of people who attempt to release that inhibition, in relation to the question of why discrimination does not cease to exist in contemporary society. From the research cited in this chapter, it appears almost as if people have the ability to elude the forces which inhibit discrimination by diverse means, and, though it is a great pity, we must come to the pessimistic conclusion that discrimination will not disappear from our society. As if to support this sad conclusion, many studies have shown that the stereotypes which form the foundation for discrimination are difficult things to obliterate, as they arise from a general tendency among people (Devine, 1989; Eberhardt and Fiske, 1996; Wyer et al., 2000). Moreover, as our own experimental work (Tamura and Ohbuchi, 2006) shows, such stereotypes also have the potential to be easily produced through arbitrary labelling, for the very reason that they justify discrimination. Accordingly, in society from here on, taking the existence of the phenomena of stereotyping and discrimination as a given, the question for us will probably be how to take heed of situations in which inhibition of these phenomena has no effect, and how skilfully to carry on dealing with them.

8 Self-recognition in Japanese Culture: Discrimination and Assimilation
Toshitake Takata

The cultural construal of self and the Japanese mode of self

How does one interpret each person, individually? In regard to cultural differences in self-construal or construal of humanity, Markus and Kitayama (1991) broadly classify self-construal into two types – independent and interdependent. The former understands the self as an independent being, separate from others, and is typical among the middle-class in the West, especially in North America. Here, the self is defined by various characteristics belonging to a certain individual (for example, ability, personality, motivation, etc.), but these are independent of surrounding conditions. The latter, on the other hand, considers the self as part of mutually-connected interpersonal relationships with others, and is said to be common in Asian cultures, including Japan's. Here, the self is defined by its relationships with others, and its characteristics fluctuate according to the properties of the surrounding conditions, including other people. The basic difference between these two types of self-construal lies not only in the definition of self, meaning how one grasps the relationship between oneself and others/society, but also extends over a broad realm encompassing the structure of self; the meaning of individual characteristics; tasks imposed upon individuals in society; the role of the other for the self; the basis of self-esteem; and so on.

Starting with the treatise by Markus and Kitayama (1991), numerous studies have been carried out in recent years on cultural differences in the self (see Oyserman, Coon and Kemmelmeier, 2002), but, of these, it is the research relating to the self-devaluative tendency of the Japanese that has become the particular focus of attention. Many empirical insights indicating the predominance among Japanese of a tendency towards self-devaluation in various aspects can be seen, including level of self-esteem (Diener and Diener, 1995); self-evaluation (Heine and Lehman, 1995; Karasawa, 2001); causal attribution of success and failure (Kashima and Triandis, 1986; Kitayama, Takagi and Matsumoto, 1995); and communication processes (Yoshida and Ura, 2003; Yoshida, Ura and Kurokawa, 2004).

Japanese self-devaluative behaviour

Self-devaluative social comparison

There is pioneering experimental evidence by Takata (1987) which confirms by experiment the tendency for Japanese people to assign a low value to their own ability. These experiments, which dealt with the social comparison of ability, showed that the results reported by Schwarz and Smith (1976) fundamentally are not replicated in Japan. In other words, Schwarz and Smith point out that, when one draws a conclusion as to the relative merits of self and others by comparing one's own and others' achievement scores, the level of ease of conclusion and the degree of certainty of the inferred result are regulated by statistical processing factors such as the mean difference between the scores of oneself and others, or the size of the variance, while a simultaneous bias towards self-enhancement can be seen, in which the conclusion that one is superior to others is easily reached, and the degree of certainty is also high. By contrast, in the results of Takata's experiments with Japanese subjects, conclusions reflecting statistical processing were completely absent, and a self-devaluative tendency alone was seen, in which the conclusion that the self was inferior was easy, and the degree of certainty, also, was high.

Heine, Takata and Lehman (2000) further examine this through comparative culture experiments using Canadian and Japanese university students as subjects. The subjects first attempted twenty trials in what was called an 'Integrative Cognitive Capacity' test. This consisted of participants counting the shapes, colours and number of shapes displayed on a computer screen and pressing keys to answer as rapidly as possible (for example, how many more red triangles were there than green squares). Next, as a 'Judgement under Uncertainty' task, the participants were asked to view part of their own and another's (an average of students' scores from the respondent's university) scores on the 'Integrative Cognitive Capacity' test, and decide which of them, on the whole, had scored more highly. Initially, scores for five trials were shown, and thereafter the scores for the participant and the other student were shown, one trial at a time, with subjects being permitted to stop at the point at which they thought

Figure 8.1: Intercultural disparity in the self-devaluative tendency

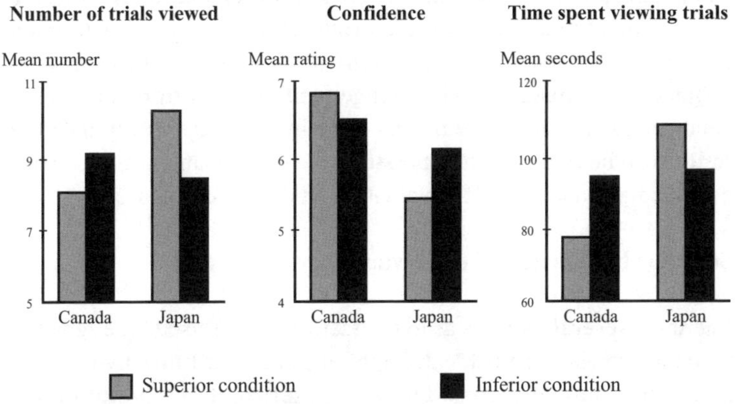

[Bar chart with three panels:

Number of trials viewed (Mean number, range 5–11): Canada — Superior ~8, Inferior ~9; Japan — Superior ~10.5, Inferior ~8.5

Confidence (Mean rating, range 4–7): Canada — Superior ~6.8, Inferior ~6.5; Japan — Superior ~5.5, Inferior ~6.2

Time spent viewing trials (Mean seconds, range 60–120): Canada — Superior ~78, Inferior ~95; Japan — Superior ~110, Inferior ~97

Legend: ■ Superior condition   ■ Inferior condition]

The range of number of trials is between 15 (highest) and 5 (lowest).
The range of confidence is between 7 (highest) and 1 (lowest).
The time shows the total of all trials.

Source: Heine et al., 2000

they could make a confident decision. The scores for 'self' and 'other' were pre-programmed, the variance of scores was large, and making a decision was quite difficult, but when the mean of all twenty trials was in superior condition, the respondent's own score was higher than the other's, while in inferior condition, the respondent's score was lower than the other's.

There were three main dependent variables: the number of scores seen before arriving at a confident judgement, the degree of confidence in the decision, and the time spent viewing trial scores before making a decision. Figure 8.1 shows the mean of these dependent variables in superior and inferior condition.

It is clear that when the number of scores viewed is small, confidence high and the time required for judgement short, this corresponds to superior condition with Canadians, but to inferior condition with Japanese. In other words, it can be said to have shown that though Canadians swiftly gain the confidence to claim that their own performance is better than average, based on little data, Japanese readily come to the conclusion that they are inferior. Furthermore, the trials themselves were quite challenging, as noted above, and there were also considerable numbers of subjects who made erroneous judgements, such as concluding that they were inferior even when they were in superior condition, or that they were superior even when in inferior condition. The results described above exclude such respondents but, from the proportion of subjects who made wrong judgements under each condition, it can be seen that Canadian subjects who made mistaken judgements tended to be in inferior condition, while Japanese tended to be in superior condition. These results can be said to lucidly illustrate the self-enhancement tendency of Canadians and the self-devaluative tendency of Japanese.

Self-devaluation as self-understanding

There are several theories as to the factors giving rise to the Japanese tendency towards self-devaluation, and these fall into two general categories, namely: consideration as self-understanding or self-evaluation – the view that understands the Japanese as having a basic tendency to perceive themselves suppressively; or, phenomena which accompany self-exposure – in other words, the view that Japanese are merely carrying out devaluative self-presentation, and that the true nature of their self-evaluation includes a tendency towards self-enhancement.

Heine, Lehman, Markus and Kitayama (1999), who emphasise Japanese devaluative self-recognition, point out the possibility, in relation to a tendency for self-enhancement that pursues a positive and high evaluation of the self, that this might be peculiar to Western culture, principally that of North America. Building on numerous findings, Heine et al. argue that the motivation for self-enhancement is not necessarily a universal phenomenon common to all people. According to Heine et al., the motivation for positively evaluating one's own self, especially the self-enhancement tendency in which individuals strive to maintain their self-evaluation at a high level, in a form independent from the surrounding social conditions, is not an important concern for the Japanese. Heine et al. claim that for the Japanese, a 'favourable' self-evaluation originates in the incorporation of characteristics which have value in Japanese culture, such as a high evaluation in terms of one's relationships with others, or being accepted by others, and it is not a positive evaluation in the form of assigning a higher value to the self than to others. Consequently, the Japanese tendency for self-devaluation or self-criticism, in order to align itself with the way of being that is expected of the self by others, is supposed to be based on a motivation for self-improvement, in which there is constant striving to direct attention towards the self's faults and failings, and to amend them.

However, there appears to be another facet which has not often been indicated in the past as a causal factor in Japanese devaluative self-understanding – a devaluative self-recognition which might be called the result of failure to secure '*amae* (dependence or indulgence) (Doi, 1973).' In his discussion of '*amae*,' Doi points out the existence of uniquely Japanese vocabulary items that relate to an inability to be dependent: '*suneru* (to be sulky),' '*higamu* (to be suspicious or jaundiced in one's attitude)' and '*hinekureru* (to behave in a distorted, perverse way...which involves feigning indifference to the other instead of showing *amae*)' (Doi, 1973, p. 29). He states that, in spite of the wish to be indulged originally having been present in all of these cases, things did not go as planned, and expectations were thwarted, thus giving rise to these feelings. Though there is some debate about the meaning of the concept of *amae*, Yamaguchi (2003), having summarised diverse points of contention to do with *amae*, regards its basis as being 'expecting that inappropriate behaviour or desires will be accepted by the other person.' In other words, in a self-other relationship, when there is a betrayal of one's (not always appropriate) expectations vis-à-vis the other with whom one fundamentally desires a merger, resulting in the failure of such a merger, a tendency to assign a low evaluation to oneself in desperation, with the idea that one is 'no good, anyway,' can be considered apparent among Japanese. Consequently, even if the self-devaluative tendency of the Japanese can be construed as being a phenomenon in the self-understanding or self-evaluation phase, several modes with differing fundamental directionality are thought to exist.

Self-devaluation as self-presentation

On the other hand, a social norm like the 'virtue of humility,' in which it is desirable for the self not to boast, but to behave humbly – the modesty norm – pervades East Asian culture generally, in Japan and in China, for example. The Japanese self-devaluative tendency is an issue related to self-presentation in public settings, as a result of the operation of such norms, and there are many opinions and insights which suggest that self-recognition itself has a self-enhancement orientation.

Kurman (2003), for example, investigates modesty- and self-enhancement tendencies by use of questionnaires aimed at high school students in Israel and Singapore. According to the measuring scale of Singelis, Triandis, Bhawuk and Gelfand (1995) used in this study, independent construal of self is dominant in Israel, while interdependent construal of self is dominant in Singapore. It was confirmed that the Singaporean respondents had a lower self-enhancement tendency than the Israeli respondents, but, at the same time, their humility tendency was also high. Moreover, when the measurement scores relating to humility were statistically controlled, the difference in self-enhancement between the two cultures disappeared. This, Kurman has concluded, shows that the norm which affirms humility in Singapore suppresses the public expression of self-enhancement, and it may be thought that a similar psychological mechanism is at work among Japanese, as well.

Recently, Greenwald and his colleagues (Greenwald and Banaji, 1995; Greenwald, McGhee and Schwartz, 1998) have developed a method called an Implicit Association Test, for measuring individuals' attitude and self-evaluation without being swayed by concerns of self-presentation. When this technique was used, though there was no difference in the degree of recognition of self-approval between Japanese and American university students, Kobayashi and Greenwald (2003) show that when measured with a questionnaire using the conventional self-esteem scale (Rosenberg, 1965), Japanese were more self-devaluative than Americans. Based on this result, Kobayashi and Greenwald conclude that cultural differences in the self-enhancement tendency are more a matter of expressive behaviour influenced by interests of self-presentation than of an implicit self-concept.

On the other hand, in regard to devaluative self-presentation, Yoshida (2003) points out that in cases where the presenter expects a response from the presentee which refutes the presenter's self-devaluation, and that response is received, then the maintenance and enhancement of self-evaluation can occur. There is a report of findings proving this (Yoshida, Ura and Kurokawa, 2004), and, combined with the findings of Gong, Suzuki and Yamagishi (2001), as shown below, this suggests the existence of self-devaluative presentation norms in Japanese culture. At the same time, Yoshida (Yoshida and Ura, 2003) has pointed out that self-enhancing presentation norms also exist in Japanese culture; that in either case there is individual variation in their degree of internalisation of these norms; and that, in people who have strong interdependent or independent construal of self, there is more of a tendency to internalise self-devaluative or self-enhancing presentation norms, respectively.

Furthermore, Gong et al. (2001) claim that because humility and modesty usually are highly valued in Japanese culture, a self-devaluative information-processing strategy has become the automatic default response activated by social conditions, without careful consideration of all information. For that reason, they assert, devaluative self-presentation is instantaneously set in motion in information-processing in social situations, though, if its assertion is inhibited, the self-devaluative tendency does not emerge. Gong et al., employing a similar experimental method to Heine et al. (2000), show that in cases where participants are taught that they will be rewarded for a correct judgement as to the relative merits of their own and others' performance, then the expression of self-devaluative presentation will be suppressed in order to meticulously process the information in anticipation of gaining reward, and Japanese respondents also become self-enhancing, but in cases where such teaching is absent, a self-devaluative response is generated.

Japanese self-enhancing behaviour

Indirect self-enhancement

As shown above, numerous opinions diverging from those of the study by Heine et al. (1999) have recently been put forward, advocating that a self-enhancing tendency can also be detected among Japanese. Piecing these together, Brown (2003) has concluded it is reasonable to understand that while a self-enhancement motivation exists universally, in Asian cultures as well, its expression can be inhibited by cultural norms. In such a case, might there be no difference between the Japanese mode of self-enhancement and that of Westerners? If there is a difference, how might it be?

In one of the previous debates which grew around this issue, there is a theory that Japanese carry out indirect self-enhancement through their interpersonal relationships. In other words, though they are self-devaluative towards themselves, they positively evaluate others with whom they have a deep connection (Endō, 1997), and they strive for self-enhancement by such ways as expectation of self-enhancing evaluations from intimate others (Muramoto and Yamaguchi, 1997; Muramoto, 2003). Under interdependent self-construal, in which significant others cannot be separated from the self, it is greatly possible that such others will become the foundation for self-enhancement, or will enhance others and groups with whom the self has integrated. There are, however, also positions which criticise this view (Heine, 2003b), based on such findings as that the tendency to enhance the group to which one belongs is more pronounced in Westerners than in Japanese (Heine, 2003a; Yuki, 2003), and that a group-serving bias which evaluates one's in-group more favourably than an out-group is not observed among Japanese (Heine and Lehman, 1997; Snibbe, Kitayama, Markus and Suzuki, 2003).

Self-enhancement towards out-group others

There is a view that Japanese also become self-enhancing towards out-group others with whom they have no emotional bond. Japanese interpersonal relationships are classified as comprising either *uchi*: those with whom *amae* (dependence or indulgence) applies; or *soto*: utter strangers (Doi, 1973), and it has been pointed out that Japanese frequently exhibit a discriminatory or self-centred attitude towards *soto* persons, and have a tendency to pursue self-interest by demeaning others (e.g., Kida, 1967; Yamagishi, 1998). In relation to this, Takata (2003) has conducted almost identical experiments with Japanese university students to those of Heine et al. (2000), which compared Japanese and Canadians. In that instance, Takata manipulated experimental conditions in order to induce respondents to recognise other respondents as *soto* others, by creating either a competitive condition which forced respondents to compete with each other for a prize to be awarded to the respondent with the superior score, or a non-competitive condition identical to that of Heine et al., in which there was no competition. The results are shown in Figure 8.2, and in each of the three indicators which show self-critical and self-enhancement tendencies, the same self-devaluative tendency as that of Japanese participants in the research by Heine et al. is replicated in non-competitive conditions.

By contrast, in the results for competitive conditions, a similar self-enhancing tendency to that of the Canadians indicated in Figure 8.1 was shown. Such a clearly self-enhancing tendency in the face of an other with whom a respondent has little emotional connectivity is also exhibited in the experimental results of Kitayama and Uchida (2003), and it must be said that it is difficult to agree with the view of Heine et al. (1999), which questions the very existence of a self-enhancement motivation among Japanese.

Self-enhancement as self-liking

There are several examples which indicate that Japanese exhibit a positive evaluation and feeling towards themselves in a form different from self-enhancement that attempts to place the self in

Figure 8.2: Disparity in self-devaluation/self-enhancement due to presence or absence of competition

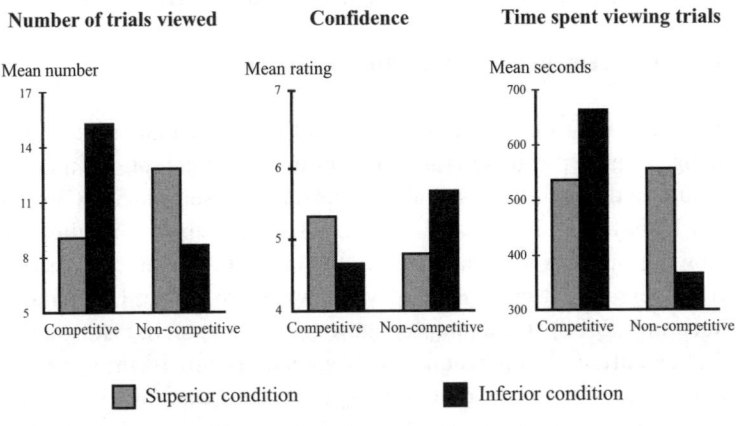

The range of number of trials is between 15 (highest) and 5 (lowest).

The range of confidence is between 7 (highest) and 1 (lowest).

The time shows the total of all trials.

Source: Takata, 2003.

a superior position to others. For example, James (1892) points out that it is normal to harbour warm feelings towards the self, in short, to have self-attachment. Japanese have this, also, but Kitayama and Karasawa (1997) argue that it is usually obscured because of the extreme permeation of a self-devaluative tendency due to a motive for self-improvement, as discussed above. Kitayama and Karasawa demonstrate through the name-letter effect (Nuttin, 1985) that it is only when implicit indicators (such as those where the self is not perceived in social contexts) are used that positive feelings towards the self can be perceived. This is a phenomenon in which one evaluates the letters contained in one's surname more favourably than letters which are not included, and not only did Japanese university students in the study clearly exhibit that tendency in the same way as Westerners, but they also assigned a relatively high value to numbers contained in their own birth-date. Kitayama and Karasawa interpret this as empathy towards the self when perceived critically, similar to sympathy directed at an unfortunate Other.

Indeed, this phenomenon corresponds to self-liking – one of the two dimensions of self-esteem (Tafrodi and Swan, 1995) and stems from the evaluation of others, contrary to self-competence based on experience of success, but there is also a view that, though Japanese certainly are not devaluative in regard to self-liking, they are self-devaluative on the dimension of self-competence (Heine, 2003b).

Self-enhancement due to self-other assimilation

In certain situations or cultures, the self's being equal to others, or being 'average,' can generate a favourable self-perception and contribute to the maintenance and enhancement of self-esteem (Brown and Kobayashi, 2002), and there are several reports of findings showing that this is pronounced in the case of Japanese. By means of surveys targeting Japanese over a wide age-range, Ōhashi and Harihara (2000), for example, show that self-esteem rises on the abovementioned dimension of self-esteem as self-liking (Tafrodi and Swan, 1995) in the case of people who feel that they are no different from the majority of others and are 'average,' and, moreover, who evaluate this as being a good thing – in other words, such Japanese tend to have a positive opinion of themselves. In this study, it is further illustrated that, among individuals who set no value upon being 'average,' there is a correlation between recognising the self as 'average' and low self-esteem, not only on the dimension of self-liking, but also upon that of self-competence.

Similarly, it is the findings of Takata (2000), through experiments with Japanese university student subjects, which confirm the possibility of self-other similarity bringing about the maintenance and enhancement of self-esteem. In this study, after the respondents had taken a 'Psychological Test of Cognitive Style,' they were given feedback as to their performance. In the experiment, respondents were assigned a superior condition (where their performance was better than the majority of university students), an equal condition (where equal), or an inferior condition (where worse), and respondents assigned an equal condition displayed the same level of satisfaction with their performance and with themselves as respondents assigned a superior condition. At the same time, when respondents were told their score, positive feelings such as cheerfulness grew stronger in equal condition (as in superior condition) than they did in inferior condition, while negative feelings such as gloom and frustration grew weaker (Figure 8.3).

Moreover, Takata (2001), while replicating the experimental method of Heine et al. (2000), adds a further consideration to

Figure 8.3: Self/other status and emotional experience

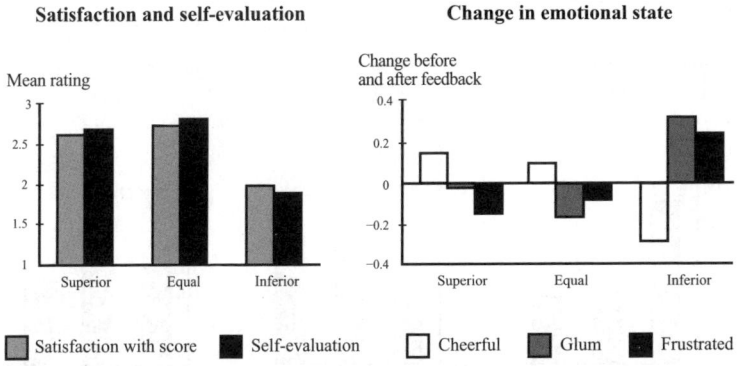

The range of rating is between 4 (highest) and 1 (lowest).

The emotional state ('Cheerful', 'Glum', 'Frustrated') is based on a factor analysis of 25 adjectives, a positive and negative value indicating that the feeling increased or decreased after feedback, respectively.

Source: Takata, 2000.

this issue. In the experiments of Heine et al., conditions were manipulated so that a participant was either in a superior condition, in which the score of an other with whom the participant was co-acting was higher, or in inferior condition, in which the partner's score was the lower, but in Takata's case, an equal condition in which the participant's score was about the same as that of a partner was additionally introduced. When the scores of self and other are approximately equivalent, this makes it all the more difficult to judge overall superiority, so the number of scores viewed before the final judgement should increase, the time required to make a decision lengthen, and the degree of certainty fall, but in actual fact, participants in equal condition reached a decision with similar promptness and certainty to those in inferior condition (Figure 8.4). At the same time, in this experiment, changes in the emotional experience before and after finding out the scores of self and other were also investigated, and, while positive feelings were enhanced to the same degree in equal condition as in superior condition, negative feelings diminished. Such results, it may be said, show that a condition in which the self and other are equal generates a positive emotional experience.

Figure 8.4: Self/other status and self-devaluative or self-enhancing tendencies

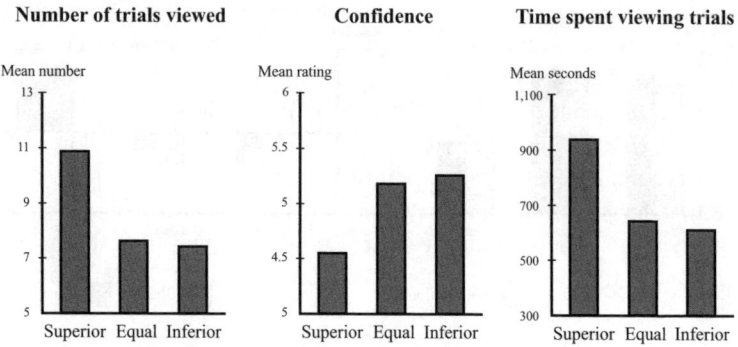

The range of number of trials is between 15 (highest) and 5 (lowest).
The range of confidence is between 7 (highest) and 1 (lowest).
The time shows the total of all trials.

Source: Takata, 2001.

The fundamental directions of self-recognition

If the characteristic of the Japanese self is its establishment of an interdependent self-construal as its foundation, then this probably does not stop at a mode of self-recognition such as a self-devaluative or self-enhancing tendency, but is likely to extend its influence also to the process of perception of the self – the very mechanism that determines how the self is recognised. The focus here is social comparison, in which the self is compared to others. Social comparison is a process concerned with recognising evaluations and judgements about the self and others (Taylor, Buunk and Aspinwall, 1990), and a process of considering information about others in relation to the self (Wood, 1996); that is to say, social comparison is functionally linked to modes of self-recognition, and it is probably appropriate to consider social comparison generally as one mechanism of self-recognition (Takata, 2004). In other words, within social interaction, social comparison is basically understood to be a mechanism of perceiving the self by reference to others in various forms.

In Japanese culture, where interdependent construal of self is dominant, it is thought that social comparison frequently occurs because harmony with the surrounding others and consensus are esteemed, and also that the result of comparison has great significance for self-recognition. Indeed, there are findings (Takata, 1993) which indicate that Japanese university students have a stronger tendency to conduct self-evaluation by social comparison than do American university students. Furthermore, Shoeneman (1981) shows that when subjects are made to recall the three sources to self-recognition – self-observation, social feedback, and social comparison – then self-observation is recalled overwhelmingly often, but in the results of a similar survey using Japanese university students and adults, though Japanese also most often recalled self-observation, the proportion was lower than in the American case, and the recall rate of sources including others as a medium, such as social feedback and social comparison, was relatively high (Takata, 1995). Japanese, it might be said, show a tendency to rely upon social mechanisms for self-recognition.

In this way, seen from the viewpoint of self-recognition through social comparison, which can be considered dominant in Japanese culture, one might assume the existence of two dimensions – realistic recognition *vs* hedonic recognition; and self-other assimilation *vs* self-other distinction – as a framework by which to gain a unified understanding of established theoretical and empirical studies. Below, the basic orientations of such self-recognition will be considered.

Realistic recognition and hedonic recognition

Adaptive force and hedonic force

The self-evaluative function of social comparison discussed by Festinger (1954) is presupposed to be an absolute necessity for social life to which an accurate and appropriate evaluation about the self has been adapted. However, social comparison is not ruled solely by such a factor. Brickman and Bulman (1977) state that two mutually-conflicting forces called adaptive force and hedonic force operate in situations where social comparison is carried out. Adaptive force is the force which leads an individual to compare her/himself with others, as one source of information for adaptively making one's own situation satisfactory. Festinger's argument deals mainly with conditions in which such a force is dominant, and, in cases where self-evaluation is uncertain, one conducts comparisons with others, in search of information, and the social reality gained as a result is supposed to generate feelings of satisfaction and stability, and lead to adjustment.

Hedonic force, on the other hand, is a force which leads the individual to avoid social comparison which provokes accurate self-evaluation, in order to circumvent all kinds of unpleasant feelings which self-other comparison can also trigger. If one compares oneself with others, oneself and the surrounding conditions certainly do become clear, but, in one respect, it means that the relative merits of the self and others also become distinct. Brickman and Bulman (1977) emphasise that such a situation is emotionally unpleasant. When one is inferior to others, one has feelings of inferiority and self-inadequacy, and is troubled by the gaze of others who look down upon one, and so on. Conversely, even when one is superior to others, others' jealousy and the nuisance of having to deal with it, anxiety over losing one's present status, and the discomfort of a sense of sin, shame or the like do arise. Moreover, even when one is equal to others, there are also cases where an unpleasant feeling is aroused by the loss of a sense of one's uniqueness (Snyder and Frokin, 1980).

The perspective of self-recognition

Under conditions where hedonic force is dominant, Brickman and Bulman (1977) suggest, phenomena differing from the prediction of social comparison theory arise, in order to avoid unpleasant feelings accompanying comparison. These comprise such things as the establishment of norms which try to keep comparison at a minimum, and a tendency to compare the self with someone different from oneself. Again, according to Festinger's (1954) hypothesis, though the desire for comparison arises and conditions dictate that one should seek contact with others, there are also studies (including Wilson and Benner, 1971; Takata, 1981; Takata and Hayashi, 1981; Strube and Roemmele, 1985) whose results show that, on the contrary, isolation is favoured. In other words, whatever the relative status between the self and others, the urge to elicit a comparative result favourable to oneself, avoiding the pain and discomfort which accompanies precise self-evaluation – a force which, if one seems about to arrive at the self-evaluation that one is inferior to others, produces the sort of comparison which would spawn the conclusion that one is superior or equal to others – can be called a hedonic force.

If one considers that there are many findings which support Festinger's (1954) basic hypothesis, then it probably goes without saying that a mode of self-recognition can be seen in which the adaptive force described by Brickman and Bulman (1977) is in operation. Accordingly, the basic perspective when one perceives how one looks by means of social comparison might be said to contain an orientation towards realistic self-cognition – an adequate self-evaluation based upon reality, for the sake of social adjustment – as well as an orientation towards hedonic self-recognition that is conducive to a conclusion favourable to oneself – a self-recognition which would not give rise to discomfort and pain (Takata, 2004).

Self-other distinction and self-other assimilation

The dual nature of human existence

Humans have a dual nature, being both individualistic beings and collective beings, and their self-recognition also has two aspects corresponding to that nature (Yamamoto, 1989; Itō, 1993). If one notes this point, along with focusing upon the individualistic aspect of human beings, the self will probably be recognised as an individual being differentiated from others, and if one focuses upon the collective or social aspect, then the self will probably be recognised as a social being that cannot exist without connections to others. Viewed in this way, it could be possible to cite one's way of perceiving one's relationship with others – whether perceiving oneself and others as individual beings distinct from each other, or perceiving the relationship between oneself and others as being inevitable – as another fundamental dimension when recognising the self. One might also consider that independent construal of self stresses a perception of humans as individualistic beings – as people differentiated from others, while interdependent construal of self emphasises a perception of humans as social beings – as people who cannot exist without their relationships to others.

Basing upon a comprehensive review of the literature on social comparison in connection with health and illness, Takata (1998) points out that, under conditions of heightened orientation towards self-recognition through social comparison, modes of self-recognition correspond to dimensions relating to the self-other relationship such as these. A situation where physical or mental health is impaired is one condition in which social comparison is likely to occur in both of the aforementioned orientations, realistic self-recognition and hedonic self-recognition. In other words, while there is a strengthening in the desire for realistic self-recognition, in terms of a wish to clarify one's medical condition, there is often ambiguity associated with perceptions relating to health and sickness for ordinary people who lack specialist knowledge (Sanders, 1982). On the other hand, as the occurrence of a health problem is a state in which one faces a threat to oneself (Gibbons and Gerrard, 1991), a tendency to move toward hedonic self-recognition, which avoids direct confrontation with reality and is convenient to the self, also strengthens (Wills, 1981; Taylor, 1982). In cases such as these, social comparison occurs in the various processes of self-recognition of one's state of health, response to illness, treatment of sickness, and aid (Sanders, 1982). Especially at times when comparison takes place in order to deal with a threat to oneself, basically, the following two orientations in cognition about the self-other relationship can be considered to exist.

Self-other distinction

The first of these is an orientation to hedonically perceive the self by emphasising self-other differences. For example, the phenomenon called unrealistic optimism, which rates one's likelihood of developing a disease dangerous to one's health as lower than other people's, is well-known (Weinstein, 1987; Hoorens and Buunk, 1993). Such an illusion of invulnerability, which assumes that one alone will be all right, is not limited to health issues, but also extends to underestimation of the probability of negative events in general, such as natural disasters or traffic accidents, happening to oneself, and behind such optimistic recognition, Perloff (1987) suggests, there lies a process of social comparison, and downward comparison, in particular. In other words, part of the reason for the birth of those illusions is making a downward comparison with another person who seems imminently likely to have bad things happen to him/her, and judging that one is less likely than the other person to have things happen. Downward comparison further includes a cognitive mechanism such as representative heuristics, in which one assumes an inappropriate standard for comparison (a fictional or real other person), then judges that one does not fit the criteria (Weinstein, 1980). Moreover, Perloff argues that when a schema related to negative events is activated, a priming effect, in which people who have negative characteristics appertaining to that schema are easily accessible, also constitutes one cognitive mechanism belonging to downward comparison.

Self-other assimilation

The second orientation is one which emphasises the similarity between self and other. For example, the phenomenon known as false consensus (Ross, Greene and House, 1977) means perceiving one's own behaviour as something that every other person also does, and Suls, Wan and Sanders (1988) point out that this is especially pronounced in relation to acts that are not good for one's health. In other words, there arises a perception that, because everyone else is doing it, one's own behaviour will be all right, even if it is a little bad for the health. Furthermore, Croyle and his colleagues have shown by a series of experiments (for example, Croyle and Ditto, 1990; Jemmott, Ditto and Croyle, 1986) that when the threat of falling ill is aroused, though one tends to perceive the threat as less grave and not attempt to take steps to deal positively with it where there are other people exposed to the same danger as oneself, in cases where one alone is in a different situation from others, there is a tendency to take the treat seriously and also to think of a way to address it. That is to say, by finding others in the same situation as oneself, a perception and response that are convenient to the self occur, and the threat to the self is removed.

If the studies from which these examples were taken are consolidated, it may be possible to conclude that there are basically the following two types of perception relating to the connection between self and other in comparisons demanding a response to threats to oneself; namely, (1) an orientation which tries to distinguish self and other, as seen in unrealistic optimism and downward comparison; and (2) an orientation which attempts self-other assimilation, as seen in false consensus and the effect of similar others, and so on. In these processes, the prominence of the diffusion and flexibility of social comparison as a cognitive mechanism is worthy of note (Wills, 1987; Gibbons and Gerrard, 1991; Taylor, Buunk and Aspinwall, 1990). In other words, persons with whom one is compared are not restricted to similar others who are effective for self-evaluation (Goethals and Darley, 1977), others who bring about a positive result for the self being chosen, and if that is impossible, then imaginary parties for comparison may even be fabricated (Goethals, 1986). Furthermore, in the case both of others with whom the self is compared, and of the dimensions in which comparison is carried out, those that are useful in hedonic self-cognition are chosen or created.

Basic orientations in self-recognition

Basic modes of self-recognition

As we have considered thus far, if we are to assume two dimensions as fundamental modes of self-cognition through social comparison: (1) realistic orientation and hedonic orientation; and (2) self-other differentiational orientation and self-other assimilational orientation, then the four fundamental modes of self-recognition below are surely conceivable. Figure 8.5 illustrates these respective modes of self-recognition, together with related theories.

1. Realistic and self-other-differentiational self-cognition: a mode of recognition, through adaptive force, of the self as a separate being from others, based on fact. The social comparison discussed by Festinger (1954) is originally this kind of self-recognition – a way of creating one's unique form that is different from others (Singer, 1980).
2. Realistic and self-other assimilative self-cognition: a mode in which one fundamentally perceives the self as moving towards assimilation with others, though, through adaptive force, the individual is oriented towards perceiving the self based on fact. Identification as a method of self-cognition and social comparison by proxy model, upon which Wheeler, Martin and Suls (1997) focused, can be said to have such a nature.
3. Hedonic and self-other-distinctive self-cognition: a mode in which one perceives the self hedonically, by setting the individual apart from others as a *figure*, in order to gain positive self-affection in the context of social relationships with others. Social comparison which has a self-enhancing function is useful in the maintenance and enhancement of self-esteem through the placing of the self in a superior position to others. Responses to threat by means of self-other distinction, including downward comparison (Wills, 1981), as reviewed in a previous section, constitute one example of this.
4. Hedonic and self-other-assimilative self-cognition: a mode in which one perceives the self hedonically, by integrating the individual as a *ground* amongst the surrounding others, in order to gain positive self-affection in the context of social relationships with others. Social comparison which has a self-harmonising function (Takata, 2004) prevents a lowering of self-esteem by understanding the self as equal to others. Threat-response strategies which strive for self-other assimilation, such as false consensus, constitute one example of this.

Figure 8.5: Basic modes of self-recognition and related theories

		Perspectives of self-recognition	
		Realistic self-recognition	*Hedonic self-recognition*
		(Self-evaluation by comparison)	(Self-enhancement)
Self-other relationship	*Self-other distinction*	Theory of social comparison processes[a] (Festinger, 1954) Self-assessment theory (Trope, 1983)	Downward comparison theory (Wills, 1981) Self-evaluation maintenance model[c] (Tesser and Campbell, 1983) Theory of social comparison processes[b] (Festinger, 1954) Unrealistic optimism (Weinstein, 1987)
		(Self-evaluation by assimilation)	(Self-harmonisation)
	Self-other assimilation	Proxy model (Wheeler et al., 1997) Pursuit of other's expectation[e] (Heine et al., 1999)	False consensus (Ross et al., 1977) Upward comparison theory (Collins, 1996) Self-evaluation maintenance model[d] (Tesser and Campbell, 1983) Failure of *amae*[e]

a = self-evaluation function; b = unidirectional push upward; c = comparison process; d = reflection process; e = Japanese self-devaluation tendency.

By considering the mode of self-recognition in these ways, it appears possible to gain a new perspective on the content and function of the human self from having comprehensively embraced the various studies on the self. For example, the two classifications, 'self-other distinction' and 'self-other assimilation,' as previously stated, respond to the different modalities of the self caused by culture, and by further adopting the classifications of 'realistic' or 'hedonic' orientation, it is possible to extend conventional debate on the modalities of the self in Japanese culture – the so-called 'typically Japanese self.'

Dominant modes in Japanese culture

As is known from the previous discussion, the Japanese also exhibit in various forms a tendency to strive for the maintenance and heightening of self-esteem by obtaining a positive evaluation in relation to the self. When these are examined from the viewpoint of the aforementioned basic orientations in self-recognition, all can be interpreted as hedonic self-recognition. Namely, what is contained in a hedonic and self-other distinctive trend is a self-enhancing tendency which Japanese display towards *soto* (out-group) others (Takata, 2003). A mode which strives for the maintenance and enhancement of self-esteem by means of positioning the self as someone more competent than others, in other words, the mode which is constantly seen in Western culture (Sedikides, 1993), constitutes self-cognition oriented towards self-other distinction which attempts to place the self in a superior position different to that of others, and when this is accomplished through social comparison, its self-enhancing function can be said to operate.

Conversely, it goes without saying that the maintenance and heightening of self-esteem arising from self-other equality (Takata, 2000; Takata, 2001) represents a moving toward self-other assimilation, and is pertinent to the self-harmonising function of social comparison (Takata, 2004). Again, indirect self-enhancement through interpersonal relationships (Endō, 1997) also can be said to be oriented toward self-other assimilation, because it constitutes self-enhancement in a form integrated with intimate others and members of the in-group. Furthermore, self-attachment (Kitayama and Karasawa, 1997), also, probably can be regarded as being based upon the mechanism of self-other assimilation, if one interprets sympathetic empathy for others as having been directed towards the self. In other words, it can be argued that, except for their self-other-distinctive orientation towards others who belong to the *soto* world, a self-other-assimilative trend is dominant in the self-enhancement exhibited by Japanese.

On the other hand, when Japanese tendency for self-devaluation is viewed in terms of self-evaluative standards, two alternative cases can be considered to exist: realistic orientation and hedonic orientation (See Figure 8.5). Firstly, given the fact that a situation in which one can only give oneself a low assessment provokes negative feelings (Takata, 2003), there can be thought to be, in the background, a more realistic orientation than hedonic orientation, namely, a stance that seeks to perceive the self appropriately. In this case, as self-devaluation focusing upon aspects of the self that cannot fulfil others' expectations (Heine et al., 1999) is triggered by a strong awareness of the presence of others, and the motivation to assimilate with them, it can be seen as oriented in the direction of self-other assimilation. On the other hand, in the case of self-devaluation as a result of *amae* (desire for dependence or indulgence) which ended in failure – of desperate self-devaluation when one feels that one is no good – while still hypothetical, it must be concluded that this has a hedonic orientation, due to the fact that it is not the result of sober self-exploration. In addition, as such a case is also the result of failure to self-harmonise with another person who aspires toward self-other assimilation, its fundamental orientation can be said to be toward such assimilation.

Uchi/soto demarcation

Judging from the above, one can probably see that in the Japanese case – whether with hedonic self-recognition which attempts to assess the self positively, or with realistic self-recognition which tries to perceive the self based on fact, even if this is painful – Japanese people are basically self-other-assimilative towards *uchi* others, and self-other-distinctive only towards *soto* others. Consequently, the argument that Japanese culture lacks a self-enhancement motivation (Heine et al., 1999), or that its self-devaluative tendency is entirely a matter of self-presentation, it being essentially self-enhancing (Kudo and Numazaki, 2003), is one-sided in either case. It is one aspect of self-recognition in Japanese culture to have both self-enhancing and self-devaluative tendencies in the background, one or the other of which can be thought to manifest itself under different conditions. The *uchi/soto* issue, in other words, self-other relationality, is considered to be one of the most important situational factors, but what other factors there might be remains a question for future investigation.

As considered thus far, there is controversy as to whether Japanese self-devaluation and self-enhancement should be perceived as matters of self-understanding and self-evaluation, or of self-presentation, but, at this stage, it is impossible to decide upon either. Even so, while the concept of the self in Japanese culture remains shaped on the basis of the relationship with the other, there does seem to be some room for thought about how self-evaluation and self-presentation can be clearly demarcated, in the same way as under an independent construal of self which defines the self as existing independently of others. Preferably, as it can be fully assumed that situational or individual differences in the degree of awareness of the existence of an other to whom the self is to be presented, as well as the nature of the self-other relationship, will exert an influence upon self-evaluation and self-presentation

(Tice, 1992), investigations from such perspectives will probably be even more important from here on.

Conclusion: discrimination and assimilation

In this chapter, starting with discussion of the Japanese self-devaluative tendency which heretofore has been much-debated, principally from the viewpoint of independent versus interdependent construal of self (Markus and Kitayama, 1991), the modes of self-recognition characteristic of Japanese culture were discussed, mainly based on the empirical data which the author has collected and the related theories. The following points were suggested, as a result:

1. Japanese people demonstrate not only a self-devaluative, but also a self-enhancing tendency, though several psychological mechanisms based upon how the self-other relationship is perceived operate in the background, and phenomenally identical self-devaluative or self-enhancing recognition can take on different psychological meanings.
2. Recognition of the self through social comparison has two basic orientations: (1) realistic recognition and hedonic recognition; and (2) self-other distinction and self-other assimilation, and Japanese self-recognition, whether having a realistic or a hedonic orientation, is basically self-other-assimilative towards *uchi* others, and self-other-distinctive towards *soto* others.

Such views suggest that two basic orientations of self-recognition – discrimination, a self-other-distinctive tendency towards others with whom the self cannot have emotional integration; and assimilation, a self-other-assimilative tendency vis-à-vis others of the same nature – are dominant in Japanese culture.

9 Intra-group Fairness, Group Identification and Inter-group Aggression

Tomohiro Kumagai

In this chapter, I focus upon how intra-group fairness promotes group identification, and whether it exerts an influence upon inter-group behaviour. The relationship between perceived fairness and group identification has been debated mainly by Western scholars. It is the aim of this chapter to verify the cultural universality of this issue, with the Japanese as its target. In the first section, I undertake a simple review of fairness studies; then, I review research supporting the hypothesis that intra-group fairness strengthens group identity, in the second part; and propose a theoretical model of group identification, and discuss its link with procedural justice, in the third. In the fourth section, I introduce the research I conducted on Japanese subjects, relating to the psychological process by which intra-group fairness impacts upon group identification and inter-group behaviour. Finally, in the fifth part, I discuss the significance of intra-group fairness and inter-group behaviour.

Theories of intra-group fairness

Given that human beings are social animals, their belonging to and living in groups are issues that cannot be avoided. In fact, it can be said that humans spend most of their lifetime as members of groups. Consequently, the majority of their desires and needs are related to collective life. Many intra-group needs have, as their goal, the maximisation of power and control. There are, however, some more interesting needs which, though there is no necessity for them to be maximised, are nevertheless ones which cause dissatisfaction if not met, and which motivate people to fulfil them. The epitome of these is the need for fairness. Fairness is defined as a certain act or decision which treats the person/s concerned in a way befitting his or her qualifications and rights. Within groups, people do not necessarily want the maximally desirable treatment – the allocation of the maximum amount of resources or the greatest assignment of control, for example – they being more concerned subjectively with whether the treatment they receive is appropriate to their own circumstances. Why, then, might people have such a strong interest in the maintenance of fairness? Here, I will discuss distributive fairness and procedural fairness, which are the usual classifications of fairness, and introduce the fairness motivation which can be postulated from them.

Distributive fairness

Distributive fairness means fairness related to outcomes. Research on distributive fairness has shown that people are not necessarily content simply when things are equally shared. This fact can be seen in equity theory, which comprises early fairness studies. According to Adams' (1965) equity theory, people's satisfaction and behaviour are greatly influenced not by objective outcome standards, but by whether the received outcome is judged to be equitable. Equity theory makes explicit the criteria used when individuals judge that their own pay or suchlike is equitable – namely, the balance between their degree of contribution, as input, and their benefit, as output. When people have not received an equitable outcome, an emotional response is generated, and they are motivated to try to restore a fair balance between input and output. Their emotional response in such situations is reported as also being manifest in measurements of psychological arousal (Markovsky, 1988).

According to Deutsch (1975), however, the perception of fairness also encompasses the principles of equality and necessity, in addition to equity. People's choice of principle is determined by the objectives they are trying to achieve within social relationships. In a corporate entity, for example, the principle for heightening productivity will be equity; for harmony in social relations, it will be equality; and, if welfare is emphasised, then the principle will be necessity (Barrett-Howard and Tyler, 1986). Irrespective of which of the principles of equity, equality or necessity applies, people will be strongly motivated by the fair distribution of resources, in all cases. The human perspective proposed in such studies on distributive fairness is a rational human perspective. In a rational human perspective, it is assumed that people strive to maximise resources in social settings. However, the simultaneous pursuit of such a thing by all members of society generates a competitive relationship among constituent members. People are thought to carry out fair distribution in order to minimise the conflict arising from such an outcome.

As studies relating to fairness progressed, however, it was found that people's interest in fairness was not limited merely to their attempts to maximise the allocation they obtained without conflict arising. It was an issue of procedural fairness, in which people were keenly interested in the distribution process itself, rather than the amount distributed to them.

Procedural fairness and group authority

It was Thibaut and Walker (1975) who pointed out that it was not only outcomes, but also perception of procedure, that had an influence upon people's judgements of fairness. This was discovered from research on the connection between fairness and authority (such as court judges, for example) within groups. However, an interest in procedural fairness was extensively seen, also being observed in organisational situations (Folger and Greenberg, 1985; Greenberg, 1987, 1990), interpersonal situations (Barrett-Howard and Tyler, 1986), political situations (Tyler, Rasinski and Spodick, 1985), and educational settings (Tyler and Caine, 1981). In conventional social exchange theory (Thibaut and Kelly, 1959) and realistic group conflict theory (Sherif, Harvey, White, Hood and Sherif, 1961; Taylor and Moghaddam, 1994), it was considered that people carried out mutual interaction with authority figures in order to gain benefit and avoid loss. In order to maximise benefit, people jointly develop resource-allocation relationships, abide by their rules, and expect that others, too, will follow those rules. If those rules are ones which generate long-term benefit, then people come to abide by them.

Similarly, people's interest in procedure, which Thibaut and Walker (1975) discovered, also was construed as being due to people's trying to secure control over desirable outcomes by maintaining procedural fairness. If this interpretation is followed, then the greater the possibility of process control, the fairer people might consider it to be (Folger, 1977). However, there is also the view that, when there is conflict, people do not always emphasise process control. According to Tyler (1988), though there is indeed an emphasis on control in conflicts of interest, it is reported that there is not that emphasis in situations of issue-resolution which are disputes over truth. This suggests that there are factors other than control involved in procedural fairness.

As a factor apart from control, Thibaut and Walker (1975) assert that uncertainty about outcomes enhanced interest in the fairness of procedure. Under conditions in which the outcome is uncertain, such as whether a judicial institution will attribute fault to the husband or wife in a divorce settlement, it is difficult to estimate if the outcome is fair. Accordingly, people judge the fairness of the outcome from the fairness of procedure. Evaluation of procedural fairness functions as a heuristic which enables prompt evaluation of the correctness of choice (Lind, Kulik, Ambrose and de Vera Park, 1993).

In this way, procedural fairness certainly has a strong influence in people's judgement of fairness, but this is thought to be something more than mere functionality in terms of the securing of control. According to social identity theory (Tajfel and Turner, 1986), people are motivated to form their own self-identity from groups and social categories. Moreover, in that process, people try to form a more favourable self-concept, self-esteem and self-evaluation. Lind and Tyler's (1988) group value model asserts that procedural fairness is employed as a means to procure information relating to that self. According to the group value model (Tyler and Lind, 1992), people construe from the fairness of procedure that the social relationship between themselves and groups or authority is favourable. If they have been meted an unfairly meagre outcome, have been treated rudely or insensitively, or have been unable to punish someone who injured them, for instance, then individuals interpret that they have received information showing that their own social position is marginal. Conversely, if they experience receiving a fair outcome, having others listen to their opinion, or see wrongdoers punished by way of retribution or restitution, for example, then individuals feel that they are respected and valued by the group.

Lind, Kanfer, and Earley (1990) studied the association between procedural fairness and relational concern. In their experiments with American university students, when participants were given their own opportunity for voice vis-à-vis the decision-making process, even after the outcome of that decision-making had emerged, they evaluated the procedure as fairer than in cases where they had no opportunity for voice. In this case, opportunity for voice equates to procedural fairness (Folger, 1977). If it were true that people have an interest because they think that procedure controls outcomes, then even if it were established after the outcome had emerged that procedural fairness had been observed, this would be unlikely to influence the judgement of fairness. In actual fact, however, irrespective of the outcome, people perceived fairness depending on whether they had opportunity for voice. What, then, would have been the factors regulating the evaluation of fairness of procedure? Tyler, Boeckman, Smith, and Huo (1997) asserted that the neutrality of procedure and trust in authority did have an impact, but other factors apart from those were the social position of individuals and the degree of respect for their standpoint in their communities. People thus can be considered to be motivated towards the maintenance of fairness by the influence of procedural fairness upon identity.

Procedural fairness and group identity

In the previous section, I introduced theories and research relating to the sense of fairness. Based on this, I will next discuss the influence upon identity of a sense of fairness. In the review conducted thus far, I stated that in people's fairness judgements there was a focus not only upon outcome but also upon the procedure, because this would provide them with information on how they themselves were evaluated. In other words, fairness is emphasised because of interest in identity. How, then, is interest in identity related to group process?

As the group value model suggests, people judge how they are evaluated by their group based on their perception of fairness within the group. In what form, then, do people experience that evaluation? In many cases, it is the members positioned in a group's upper strata – in short, the authority – who decides how members are treated. Tyler and Lind (1992) propose a relational model of authority in connection to the relationship between authority and procedural fairness. In this model, procedural fairness influences people's obedience towards or rebellion against authority. The model posits that this is influenced by perceptions of the relationship between the authority and members, in terms of how neutral and trustworthy are the authority, and how much it respects the group members.

In Tyler's (1989) study targeting American citizens, for example, it was indicated that the perceived fairness of the police and law courts determined people's attitudes towards the government and the judiciary. From perceived fairness, people affirmatively interpret their own position in society or in a group. This perception, moreover, impacts upon self-esteem, the social self, and self-worth. The relational model of authority posits that people shape their feelings about their own social worth, social status and reputation through the treatment they receive from authority (De Cremer and Tyler, 2005; Tyler and Smith, 1999). Similarly, Lind (2001) asserts that people find value in the fairness of procedures because it guarantees a sense of belongingness, and becomes a message of acceptance. This is also confirmed by Tyler and Blader (2002), and fairness of procedure can also be thought to provide information about the need to belong and social reputation.

Inspired by these findings, De Cremer and Tyler (2005) conducted experiments involving American university students. They posited that people estimate information on relationality – in other words, social reputation, the degree of belonging, the level of identity, and the amount of self-uncertainty – from the procedures that decide distribution. If fairness of procedure affects these factors, then fair dealing received from group authority figures will constitute information enabling people to fulfil such needs. As a result, people will consider a fair group more attractive, and, it is thought, will come to behave in a way that serves to benefit that group.

The need to belong and procedural fairness

The relational model of authority surmises that fairness of procedure conveys messages of acceptance and belonging (Tyler and Blader, 2002; Tyler and Lind, 1992; Tyler and Smith, 1999). In order to verify this point, De Cremer and Blader (2006) identified the influence of need to belong vis-à-vis procedural fairness. With Dutch university students as experimental participants, they first measured the strength of subjects' need to belong, then had the leaders convey to the participants the evaluations relating to the questions, and measured the self-evaluation of participants at that point. As a result, only those with a high need to belong showed a lowering of self-evaluation when the evaluation procedure was unfair.

Furthermore, De Cremer and Blader (2006) claimed that subjects with a strong need to belong employed a different manner of information-processing in relation to procedural fairness from those with a weak need. According to these researchers, people with a strong need to belong try harder than those with a weak need to systematically process information concerning procedural fairness and to make a precise judgement. This De Cremer and Blader validated through scenario experiments. After having measured the strength of need to belong of the participating Dutch university students, they had the subjects read a scenario. Each scenario related to a certain company's restructuring plan, and gave voice to employees about the matter. There were two types of scenario – one in which there was a strongly convincing reason for voice having been given, and another in which the rationale for giving voice was not very convincing. As a result, it was found that participants to whom a highly convincing reason was given made more positive evaluations of the fairness and reliability of the judgement concerning several changes in department, and this tendency was more pronounced in people with high need to belong than those with low need. Such studies show that procedural fairness supplies evaluative data concerning relationality, by which people gain a sense of belonging.

Group identification

In this section, I firstly review prior research relating to group identification, and then discuss the relationship between group identification and procedural fairness.

According to social identity theory (Tajfel and Turner, 1986), social groups have the function of ordering, structuralising and simplifying the world and making it predictable, and are indispensable as things which fulfil the needs of the individual and society. It is assumed in this theory that, in that process, people perceive group members as beings who share the same characteristics and have a high commonality, and recognise that they themselves are also such beings. It is also known that members who have identified with a group confuse group typicality and their own characteristics (Smith and Henry, 1996). Construing in-group membership as part of oneself in this way constitutes group identification in social identity theory (Cooper and Hogg, 2002; Otten, 2002; Smith, 2002; Wright, Aron and Tropp; 2002).

On the other hand, self-categorisation theory embraces group identification, placing greater emphasis on the cognitive aspect of the group. People categorise themselves in the same way as they categorise others (e.g., Turner, Hogg, Oakes, Reicher and Wetherell, 1987). In addition, Hogg (2004) states that social identity is shaped through assimilation with a prototype belonging to the category in question. Based on such debates concerning social identity, in this study I define social identity as self-concept based on social category. Here, I also define group identification as the identification of self-concept with a category or group prototype.

The four factors in group identification

In order for people to identify with a group, first those people need to form a group identity. According to Jackson and Smith (1999), group identity is mainly made up of four dimensions. These are (1) perceptions of the inter-group context; (2) in-group attraction; (3) belief in interdependence and a shared fate; and (4) depersonalisation. Here, I discuss how group identification arises, in each of these four dimensions, respectively.

Perceptions of the inter-group context

According to social identity theory, self-categorisation theory (Turner, et al., 1987) and optimal distinctiveness theory (Brewer, 1991; 1993), group identity is formed by inter-group differentiation. The common thread in these theories is their attempt to elucidate group identity and self-categorisation by emphasising in-group and out-group differentiation (e.g., McGuire, McGuire, Child and Fujioka, 1978; McGuire, McGuire and Winton, 1979). It is further posited that, when the difference between the in-group and out-group is small, people try to magnify that difference. It has been shown in previous studies that group identification is strengthened through that emphasis of difference. The dimension of comparison in which that influence has been especially frequently reported is inter-group status. According to Brown, Hinkle, Ely, Fox-Cardmore, Maras and Tayler (1992), people are motivated to recognise their own in-group as something which is more favourable and valuable. This is swayed also by status stability, and Ellermers and others have demonstrated that, in cases where the structure of group status is unstable, group identification grows stronger than in cases where it is stable (Doosje, Spears and Ellemers, 2002; Ellemers, Van Knippenberg and Wilke, 1990).

Moreover, when there is high inter-group permeability, there is a lowering among a low-status group's members of a sense of membership and satisfaction towards their own group (Ellemers, Van Knippenberg, De Vries and Wilke, 1988), while high-status group members conversely enhance their commitment towards their group (Ellemers, Doosje, Knippenberg and Wilke, 1992). As a heightened degree of inter-group permeability constitutes a threat to group identity, an attempt to compensate for this is thought to have resulted in the strengthening of identification towards the group by members of high-status groups. It is considered that people try to emphasise differences and boundaries in inter-group relations, and enhance group identification in the process.

In-group attraction
When a group has some kind of attraction for people, the latter will harbour favourable feelings towards that group, and it is thought that, as a result, people will form a social identity based on the group. When a certain company pays high wages, people probably will feel attracted to that company, and make being an employee of that company part of their identity. However, such material attraction is not the only kind to influence the creation of social identity, for psychological attraction plays an equal, if not greater, part.

Perception of similarity among in-group members has been given as an example of psychological attraction (Brewer, 1991, 1993; Brewer and Pickett, 1999; Turner, et. al., 1987). According to Brewer and Kramer (1986), simply by emphasising a vague and abstract similarity (for example, the fact of being students at the same university), group identification is enhanced, and an increase in cooperative behaviour can be seen. As similarity with others is a signal of the validity of one's own attitudes and actions, this functions as a psychological reward, resulting in its becoming an attraction. Moreover, from their perception of the validity of their attitudes and actions, people also come to identify with the group which provides assurance to their self-image (Swann, Kwan, Polzer and Milton, 2003). Furthermore, according to Branscombe, Spears, Ellemers and Doosje (2002), members who are respected by their group evaluate that group's worth highly, work even harder for the group, and strengthen their discrimination against out-groups. In addition, as I have already noted, it is known that fair treatment is construed as respect towards the self, and enhances identification towards the in-group (Lind and Tyler, 1988; Tyler, Degoey and Smith, 1996; Tyler and Lind, 1992). In this way, when a group offers psychological and material rewards to those belonging to it, then its members are seen as perceiving that group as being all the more attractive, and will intensify their identification with the group.

Belief in interdependence and a shared fate
Belief in interdependence and a shared fate shape social identity through perceptions of future well-being and in-group solidarity. Interdependence can be largely divided into two types: interdepend-

ence of fate and interdependence of task. Lewin (1948) saw groups as existing not because of any similarity among the various individuals constituting them, but because of interdependence of fate. Rabbie and Horwitz (1969) examined that by experiments in which Dutch children participated. The participants were divided into two groups and were supposed to perform tasks for which they would receive rewards. However, the experimenters told the participants that as there were not enough rewards to go around, only one group would be given rewards. In each instance, the experimenters gave one of three different explanations about which group would be rewarded, saying that it would be decided by the toss of a coin, or that the experimenters would unilaterally decide, or else they would give the right to decide to one of the groups. The experimenters additionally set up one more group as a control group, not providing any explanations. After the explanations, they carried out the distribution of rewards, and the participants evaluated members of their in- and out-groups by rating their personal attributes. In consequence, all participants except those in control condition evaluated members of their in-group more favourably than members of their out-group, no matter which method was used to allocate reward, and irrespective of whether they received a reward. Under control condition, such a disparity was not observed. This means that, irrespective of the commonality of situation which the participants faced, the mere fact of having had a shared experience determined favour towards the group.

Rosenbaum, Moore, Cotton, Cook, Hieser, Shover and Gray (1980) conducted experiments relating to interdependency of task. They gave their American university student participants the task of building a tower out of blocks in groups of three. They manipulated intra-group interdependence by giving different rewards to different participants. The condition for highest interdependence was equal distribution of rewards among group members. In the condition for lowest interdependence, the individual who stacked the most blocks within one group monopolised the reward. Between these, the experimenters employed both distribution methods, but also established three conditions in which proportions were varied (80/20, 50/50, 20/80). As a result, as interdependence among group members decreased, task productivity fell, the level of cooperation decreased, and the attractiveness of group members also dwindled.

The influence of interdependence upon group identification is thought to be the effect of assurance and well-being. Acting in concert with others within the in-group means less risk of isolation, and this information generates a sense of assurance in people. If a group does truly give assurance, then people are likely to rate it as highly attractive. In consequence, people are though to strengthen their identification with that group.

Depersonalisation

Depersonalisation occurs when people's degree of awareness of themselves as unique individuals weakens, and they form a social identity through being more strongly conscious of themselves as members of a group. This process has been reported in Sherif et al.'s summer camp experiments (Sherif et al., 1961), and minimal group experiments (Tajfel, Flament, Billig and Bundy, 1971). Recently, it has also been examined using the SIDE model (Social identity model of depersonalisation effects model, Postmes, Spears, Sakhel and de Groot, 1999), but what is assumed in these studies is a process of compensation, by means of a clear-cut social identity, for the blurring of individual identity in situations of high anonymity. By that process, people focus on their own social identity, emphasise the characteristics of the group, and strengthen their identification with the in-group prototype. It is anticipated that members of groups which have better-defined images and distinctive features consequently will be more likely to identify with their groups. One of the suggested factors in the clarity of group image is group entitativity (Campbell, 1958). Entitativity is defined as 'the degree of having the nature of an entity, of having real existence' (Campbell, 1958). Both a queue of people waiting for a bus and the employees of a particular company are the same in that their actions have a unified purpose, but the latter generally are perceived as being a group with high entitativity, while the former usually is not. It is reported from previous studies that the higher a group's entitativity, the more strongly people will identify with that group (Castano, Yzerbyt and Bourguignon, 2003; Sani, 2005).

Modelling of the group identification process

Jackson and Smith (1999) also note this point, but these four dimensions are not entirely independent of each other, there being some degree of mutual overlap. Here, then, I will discuss the relationship between those various dimensions, and propose my own model in relation to group identification, based on this.

Firstly, group attraction can be considered to be the thing that has the strongest influence upon group identification. Whether physically or psychologically, when a group offers reward to its members, the members will probably feel strong attraction towards that group, and be motivated to identify with it. What, then, constitutes an attractive reward that a group offers? If members are supplied with food or money by belonging to a group, then that group probably will become an attractive group.

Apart from such material attractions, what kind of psychological attractions might we imagine? I see relief as being one of these. I beg your recall of my point in the preceding discussion of group attraction, namely, that a perception of similarity functions as group attraction. I argued that these factors resulted in group attraction because they constituted information relating to self-legitimacy. The feeling that the self is not a socially deviant presence, but is socially accepted, generates a sense of relief. This relief, as a reward which a group offers, is thought to heighten the attraction of that group, and to enhance identification with it. Moreover, this relief is the point emphasised by Jackson and Smith (1999) in their dimension of belief in interdependence and shared fate. Having an interdependent relationship with others means the self is not in a socially isolated situation. This, too, gives people relief and makes the group attractive, and the identification of its members grows stronger. We can presume that, in this manner, group attraction and a belief in interdependence gives rise to a shared sentiment in terms of relief, and this promotes both group attraction and group identification.

Another group attraction apart from relief also comes to mind – self-definition. I have already explained that the group supplies self-verifying information. In similar manner, the group also provides its members with information which enables them to define themselves, and facilitates identity-formation. Such self-defining information is thought to be attractive to people whose self is in an ill-defined condition, and to promote their identification as group members. Reference to the connection between the blurring of self-concept and group identification has already been made in the discussion concerning Jackson and Smith's (1999) dimension of depersonalisation. Accordingly, there can be thought to be an association between group attraction and the dimension of depersonalisation. A causal relationship can be assumed in which the self-defining information possessed by the group prototype strengthens group attraction and promotes members' identification.

Now, how might these various factors tie in with the remaining dimension of inter-group context? The impact of inter-group context upon group identification arises from emphasis upon inter-group difference. This can be seen to have two effects. One is the formation

Figure 9.1: The dual group-identification model

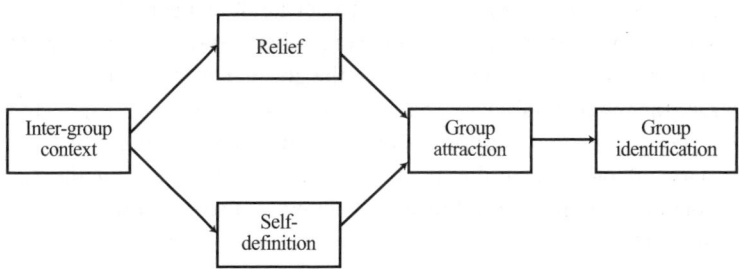

of a more positive identity, as is posited in social identity theory. It is thought that people seek a positive identity because it facilitates acceptance from others and membership of a group. Need to belong is a fundamental human need. Moreover, as people who are positively evaluated are liked more than those who are negatively evaluated, they are probably more easily accepted by others. Consequently, people who have stressed inter-group differences and have obtained a positive evaluation would be more likely to be accepted by society, and their relief, too, would increase. In consequence, the attraction of the group which gave them relief would grow, and the identification of its members presumably would strengthen.

In contrast to the provision of such relief, the emphasising of inter-group difference can be thought also to affect the factors for self-concept. As self-categorisation theory and optimal distinctive theory indicate, an emphasis upon inter-group difference is also an emphasis upon self-concept. Furthermore, as I have already discussed, because groups who supply information relating to self-concept become more attractive, it is assumed that members' identification also becomes stronger. Figure 9.1 is a model of the links between those various factors, based on the above discussion. In this model, inter-group difference – emphasised by inter-group context – moderates relief, on the one hand, and self-definition, on the other, these constituting attraction vis-à-vis the group. It predicts that the attraction held by the group will enhance people's identification towards the group.

The effect of procedural fairness upon group identification

How might this dual group-identification model be related to procedural fairness? The group value model of procedural fairness assumes that people perceive respect from fair treatment by the group, and identify with that group. If this is applied to the dual group-identification model, it can be conjectured that procedural fairness has an influence upon relief. The perception of respect which arises because of procedural fairness gives members a sense of acceptance and relief. That is considered to make the group more attractive, and to strengthen members' identification. This reasoning is also supported by De Cremer and Blader's (2006) results. The outcome of their research demonstrated that the strength of need to belong moderates perceptions of procedural fairness. This is because the more powerful a person's need to belong, the more eagerly they strive to gain a sense of acceptance by means of procedural fairness. I assumed the tendency was observed for people with a stronger need to belong to interpret procedural fairness as a sign of acceptance, as they could not gain a sufficient sense of acceptance with unfair procedure.

In this way, it has been presumed that procedural fairness moderates relief and intensifies group identification. However, this presumption was established mainly on the basis of data from Western scholars. Accordingly, in the next section, I will verify this point by using empirical data on Japanese subjects. Moreover, I will also validate the point that enhanced group identification influences inter-group behaviour. The aspect of inter-group studies which I have undertaken is inter-group aggression. In particular, I have identified the process which motivates people who themselves have not suffered any harm, but who have observed members of their in-group being harmed, to seek retribution upon the aggressors.

Group identification and third-party aggression

In this section, I use laboratory experimentation to verify the effect of procedural fairness upon group identification. To that end, I focus on factors from the dual group-identification model which contribute to relief, and identify the process by which these enhance group identification. Most debate concerning this process has been carried out by Western scholars, the inferences drawn having been based on the outcome of studies targeting participants from their respective countries. In my studies, therefore, I validate these assumptions using Japanese participants as subjects. Simultaneously, I also examined the effect of third-party aggression upon group identification.

Relief and procedural fairness

Of the various factors in group identification, it is relief which is the focus of the present study. Moreover, as I have noted in the foregoing discussion, relief is generated by a sense of acceptance, and I thus have used intra-group acceptance, in this study, as a mediating variable in group identification. On the basis of such a prediction, procedural fairness would be hypothesised as moderating acceptance and enhancing group identification (Hypothesis 1).

Here, I examined one more point, namely the impact upon inter-group interaction of group identification which has been enhanced by procedural fairness. This constitutes part of a study we conducted on third-party aggression (Kumagai and Ohbuchi, 2001, 2003, 2004). Third-party aggression signifies the engagement by a third party who has not directly been harmed in aggressive action towards the harm-doer in a conflict situation. I posited that third-party aggression is the outcome of third parties having equated the injury to one or more members of their in-group, and thus having been motivated to seek retribution. According to inter-group emotions theory (Mackie, Devos and Smith, 2000; Smith, 1993, 1999), when social identity is salient, related events and situations trigger emotions. Moreover, it has been reported that, even in the absence of individual involvement in such events or situations, emotions arise in people through their group having been harmed, or having been aided, and give rise to some kind of active or behavioural tendency (Devos, Silver, Mackie and Smith, 2002). The reasoning behind this assumption is also based on data concerning American university students. In this study, then, I validate this assumption, using Japanese students as subjects. On two points, inter-group emotions theory provides information which is useful in relation to the psychological process of third-party aggression. The first is that people respond emotionally not only to individual injury, but also to injury suffered on a collective level. When the victims are members of the in-group, and these victims are perceived as a symbol of the group, then third parties will probably feel negative inter-group emotion – in other words, animosity towards out-groups – and engage in aggressive action. The second is that inter-group emotion which arises due to events happening within the in-group is adjusted according to the strength of group identity. The following hypothesis can be drawn from these two points: that, through group identification, people would intensify their inter-group emotion and antagonistic attitude vis-à-vis the injury of in-group members, and aggressively react to harmdoers (Hypothesis 2).

Research findings

In order to verify these hypotheses, I conducted experiments with sixty-eight Japanese national university students as participants. The experimenter explained to the participants that the experiment would consist of three sessions, and that experiments would be conducted with six participants, simultaneously. In the first session, the experimenter said that they were going to measure participants' 'thinking styles' (Doosje, Spears and Koomen, 1995). The experimenter told the participants that people tended to be either deductive or inductive thinkers, and that he or she would first measure each participant's thinking style in the experiment. Based on its outcome, s/he further explained, out of the six who had participated at the same time, the experimenters would assign the three showing a stronger deductive thinking tendency to a 'deductive group,' and, conversely, the three showing a stronger inductive thinking tendency to an 'inductive group.' The task for measuring thinking style was a word association task. Participants were told the results of task analysis, but, in actual fact, all of the participants were assigned to the 'inductive group,' 'I 2.'

In the second session, the manipulation of procedural fairness was carried out. In relation to procedural fairness, we did operations in which there was either the presence or absence of opportunity for voice granted by authority. Specifically, the experimenter told the participants that they would have the leader of the group with the strongest inductive tendency write her or his opinion about an educational reformation which the university was to implement. Subsequently, the experimenter told participants in the voice condition that the leader wanted to take account of the opinions of other participants, and so he or she had expressed a wish to know their opinions. The participants were thus also given the opportunity to write their views. On the other hand, there was no such request from the leader to participants in the non-voice condition. Following this, participants responded to items on acceptance and group identification (using a seven-point scale).

The third session consisted of all participants observing another two participants distributing ten lottery tickets, after everyone had answered the question items. Allocation was conducted as follows: in the in-group condition, out-group members were the allocators and in-group members were the recipients. Conversely, in the out-group condition, both the allocators and the recipients were out-group members. All participants observed the distributors taking seven lottery tickets themselves, and handing three to the recipients. After observing the distribution, participants evaluated the fairness of the distribution carried out by the distributors (out-group members). Evaluation was carried out using a personal computer, and the experimenter instructed the participants to click on one of the nine buttons shown on the PC screen in relation to three points, comprising evaluation of the unfairness of the distribution, dissatisfaction towards the allocation, and how severely the distributors should be punished. At that time, the experimenter explained that the various buttons corresponded to unpleasant noises with different levels of loudness, and that noise at the level chosen by each participant would be played to a distributor for six seconds. The noise levels ranged from Level 1 (not at all unfair: 40 dB) to Level 9 (extremely unfair: 80 dB), and grew louder in 5dB increments.

Next, I will explain the results. Firstly, in order to verify the effect of manipulation of procedural fairness, I examined the item scores for acceptance and group identification by t-test comparing voice and non-voice conditions. Its outcome is shown in Figure 9.2.

Just as I hypothesised, the presence or absence of voice – in other words, procedural fairness – intensified acceptance and group identification. In addition, in order to examine the mediating effect of acceptance, I conducted a regression analysis using group identification as the dependent variable, and voice and acceptance as the independent variables. In relation to the voice factor, I coded the voice condition as 1 and the non-voice condition as 0, as dummy variables. Furthermore, as Step 2, I conducted a regression analysis with acceptance as the dependent variable and voice as the independent variable. Figure 9.3 is a path diagram composed using the significant paths gained as a result (the numeric value is beta-value). Voice mediated acceptance and enhanced group identification. This is an outcome which supports Hypothesis 1.

Figure 9.2: Average scores by condition in items on acceptance and group identification

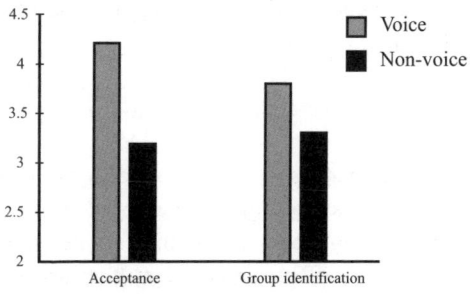

Figure 9.3: Results of path analysis on group identification due to voice and acceptance

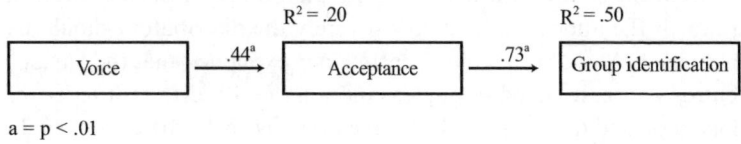

a = p < .01

Next, I will explain the outcome of third-party aggression which constitutes inter-group interaction. Figure 9.4 shows the results of an analysis taking as a measurement of aggression the mean value of the intensity of three noises that were given to allocators by participants in the third session. As Figure 9.4 indicates, after having observed in-group members receiving unequal distribution, participants who were given voice by group leader subjected allocators to more intense noise than did participants who were not granted voice. Such a disparity, moreover, was not seen in cases where it was out-group members who received the unfair treatment. This outcome shows that group identification which had been enhanced by procedural fairness strengthened aggression by third parties, as retaliation for injury to in-group members. This also is a result which supports Hypothesis 2.

In this study, I have examined the process by which intra-group procedural fairness mediates acceptance and strengthens group identification, and that, in turn, intensifies third-party aggression. Firstly, in relation to the group-identification process, this study has been one which, from among the group identification models I posed, focused upon the process in which acceptance mediated group attraction and enhanced group identification. Though I did not measure group attraction, an outcome supporting the fact that relief strengthens group identification was obtained. It also elucidated third-party aggression, in which people are motivated, through group identification intensified in the above way, to take aggressive action towards those who have harmed their in-group, in spite of themselves not having been harmed.

Conclusion

In this chapter, I have discussed the influence which intra-group procedural fairness exerts upon group members. With that aim, I posed a group identification model, and then examined the process in which procedural fairness affects group identification, and the inter-group aggression which arises as a result. Research on the relationship

Figure 9.4: Results of ANOVA by voice and victim in relation to intensity of aggression

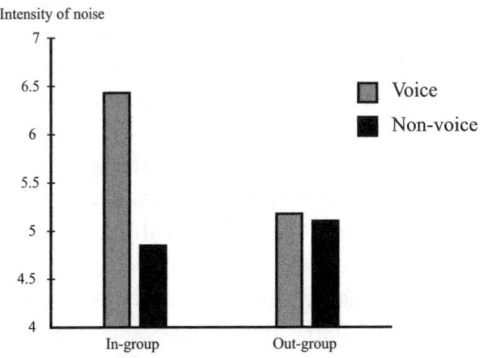

between fairness and group identification has hitherto been conducted principally by Western scholars. The group identification model proposed in this study was also something built on a foundation of Western research. In this study, then, I verified the predictions that could be drawn from pre-existing theories, using Japanese as subjects.

The central concern of this chapter has been to offer new theoretical insights into the process by which procedural fairness intensifies identification among group members. The outcome showed that procedural fairness enhances relief, and that, in turn, strengthens group identification. The process by which procedural fairness intensifies group identification is that which the group-value model already indicated. This study showed that a similar process applies in the same way when Japanese are the subjects. Moreover, my study can be considered to have further clarified the fact that procedural fairness comprises not control over the decision-making process, but interest in identity. The procedural fairness used in this study had an extremely weak influence in terms of control over decision-making. The voice which was granted to participants was voice vis-à-vis their leaders, but the leaders, too, were in a position of little influence over decision-making. Even though their leaders were in such a weak position, meaning they were weak authority, people were strongly motivated by having been treated fairly. This fact probably suggests that identity is the central concern of procedural fairness.

Additionally, it was shown in this study that interest in identity is satisfied by respect from others and relief that is gained from respect. However, in this study I did not directly measure relief as a dependent variable, but measured acceptance, which has a strong association with relief, and used that as a dependent variable. The strong links between the two have also been pointed out by researchers in sociometer theory (Leary and Baumeister, 2000). If one takes the experimental situation I used this time into consideration, then questions about acceptance can be seen to be easier for participants to answer than those about a state of mind such as relief, of which it is hard to be conscious. In order to more stringently validate the model, however, it will probably be necessary to devise a method of directly measuring relief. I intend to deal with this challenge in future research.

Another goal of this chapter was to examine whether procedural fairness intensified third-party aggression. As a result, it was seen that procedural fairness did enhance third-party aggressive reactions against the harm-doer, but this was only seen in cases where the victim was a member of the in-group, as illustrated in Figure 9.4. As it has been proven through this study that procedural fairness intensifies group identification, it can probably be said that third-party aggression is the outcome of group identification. The fact that procedural fairness mediates group identification and influences inter-group interaction has already been reported in relation to cooperative behaviour (De Cremer and Tyler, 2005). It was shown in the current study, however, that procedural fairness is effective, not only in the case of pro-social behaviour such as cooperative behaviour, but also with aggressive behaviour, which comprises anti-social behaviour. There is a strong human need to be treated fairly in an intra-group context, and, even more, it is deemed socially desirable. Accordingly, even if it be for the sake of conflict resolution, it is difficult for people to swallow intra-group unfairness, and it can be imagined that this makes it hard for them to suppress their participation in third-party aggression. Ironically, what this present study has shown is that it is precisely the ideal group where intra-group fairness is achieved and people are respected and feel relief within the group that is the very one at high risk of exacerbating inter-group conflict. In answer to these issues, as I have already noted, it might be effective to lead people towards alternative action by reinterpreting group stereotypes. More fundamentally, though, there is probably a need for further investigation in relation to why people are so concerned about fairness, and why they are so strongly motivated to maintain it.

It is a pity, however, that of the various factors in group identification, the current study was unable to delve into those to do with self-concept. I believe the latter factors also have a strong association with procedural fairness. As in Lind et al.'s (1993) discussion on the fairness heuristic, there might also be a process in which fairness of procedure, as a heuristic, provides self-concept information, this then constitutes group attraction, and enhances members' identification. This means, therefore, that procedural fairness provides group identification with both relief and self-concept, and exerts a great influence. In future study, there probably also will be a need to examine the effect of procedural fairness from the self-concept perspective, including the scale of its impact.

As I have already mentioned, one of the objectives of the present study was to use data on Japanese subjects to examine the relationship between the perception of fairness and group identification, which heretofore had been investigated mainly in the West. The results can be said to have supported the research outcomes obtained thus far. Accordingly, the psychological process involved in the perception of fairness and group identification can be seen to be not culturally specific, but universal. However, though the process might be the same, some cultural differences perhaps exist in terms of the intensity of interest in fairness and the strength of the group-identification tendency. I intend to examine these points in future, through international comparison.

This chapter is one which has investigated people's concern for fairness from the aspect of the social self. As I noted at the beginning of my argument, as long as it is an inescapable fact that human beings belong to groups, engagement with the issue of fairness perception from the viewpoint of the group will be a constructive method of dealing with them. This study has been an attempt to contribute one part of such theory. What this study has shown is the process by which procedural fairness destroys inter-group relations, but, naturally, many more constructive processes also exist. The question is in what direction will it lead a group identity which has been strengthened by procedural fairness; and politics and religion, culture, and psychology, too, are likely to play a great role in this.

10 Is Fairness Useful for Stress Management in Organisations?

Yōichirō Hayashi and Naotaka Watanabe

Foreword

The issues of justice (*kōsei*) and fairness (*kōhei*) are compelling ones for all individuals. Workplaces and organisations, in particular, are considered to be fields in which people often have first-hand experience of these issues (Takahashi, 1998). This is because activities within organisations intrinsically include problems which have a deep connection with fairness, such as decision-making, reward-allocation, and conflict-resolution.

Research debating workplace justice – a subject of great concern – increased in the 1990s, and, to date, there has been a considerable accumulation of theoretical and empirical studies (Colquitt, Greenberg and Zapata-Phelan, 2005). In consequence, researchers have proved that justice and fairness are vital and effective variables in realising appropriate management. It has been evident that justice, especially, exerts a positive influence upon various attitudes and actions of employees.

Studies have found that the concepts of organisational behaviour such as job-satisfaction, organisational commitment, organisational citizenship behaviour, work motivation, turnover (intent to change jobs) and counter-productive work behaviour, for example, have a deep connection with justice (Cohen-Charash and Spector, 2001; Colquitt, Conlon, Wesson, Porter and Ng, 2001). Such findings show that justice is an indispensable variable in organisational management.

The need for such justice has seldom been discussed, however, from the perspective of individuals' well-being or mental health. In fact, even though many commonalities have been found between the concepts and mechanisms addressed by justice studies and stress studies (Weiss, Suckow and Cropanzano, 1999; Zohar, 1995), there has been scant knowledge to tie the two together. In their eagerness to proclaim the need for justice from the positive viewpoint of organisational productivity or efficiency, the majority of conventional scholars could be accused of a lack of endeavour in examining organisational justice from a viewpoint which had more to do with employees' well-being and welfare, such as stress management or mental health. Accordingly, our research upon Japanese company employees aims to obtain some pointers as to how to put stress management into practice, by elucidating the association between mental health and organisational justice.

Stress and organisational justice

The notion of stress

Stress is one of the most popular concepts in social science (Buunk and de Wolff, 1992; Fried, 1993), and many scholars have offered various definitions. As such, it is difficult to present a clear definition, but the majority of definitions of stress can be considered to incorporate the following content, namely, the idea that stress is something experienced by individuals when they feel that they have to respond to demands from their environment that are beyond their own capacity (Carver, 1995; Vermunt and Steensma, 2001). In other words, this way of thinking regards stress as being the discrepancy between processing capacity and demands. Moreover, the cause which produces stress is called the 'stressor,' and the term 'stress response' is also commonly used to refer to the psychological, physical and behavioural responses which arise as a result of exposure to that stressor.

Most of the research conducted hitherto has identified stressors as triggers for stress. Such stressors are considered to be broadly divisible into the following four factors (Allegro, Kruider and Steensma, 1991; Vermunt and Steensma, 2001). The first is one related to work duties, thought to include such factors as work overload, lack of autonomy, role conflict/ambiguity, and so on. The second is exemplified by factors relating to the organisational system, such as human resources policy and the work environment, considered to include the remuneration structure, value system, promotion system, working hours and leave-acquisition, for example. Factors relating to interpersonal relationships within the organisation can be regarded as examples of the third, including poor leadership by bosses, interpersonal conflict, and a lack of social support. The fourth is thought to encompass factors external to the realm of work duties or the organisation, such as work/family conflict. Though other factors such as issues of career advancement or individual attributes can also be considered (Cooper and Marshall, 1978), stress studies have mainly focused their discussion upon the above-mentioned four factors.

Various stressors have thus been found, but, as there are numerous problems which have a deep connection with organisational justice, in the next section we will take a comprehensive look at research which has dealt with the link between the two.

Stressors in the workplace

Lack of autonomy is well-known as one of the work-environment factors which bring about a stress response. This represents a condition where the extent of employees' control or ability to carry out their work duties at their own discretion is limited (Karasek, 1979). On the other hand, Thibaut and Walker (1975), the scholars who led early justice studies, asserted that it was situations where people could control or exert influence upon decision-making, in particular, that constituted a factor which enhanced procedural justice. They also argued that problems in human resources policy and those inherent in the organisational system became stressors, but such issues relating to reward-allocation and evaluation procedures in organisations were linked with distributive justice and procedural justice (Cropanzano and Greenberg, 1997). Moreover, though we have already mentioned that poor leadership by bosses can become an interpersonal stressor, such a human-relations factor is both a highly isomorphic concept, and one with a highly interpersonal or affective dimension vis-à-vis fairness. Such an affinity suggests that fairness – and especially unfairness – can legitimately be regarded as a stressor.

It is also theoretically possible to assume that fairness affects the employees' stress response. In their uncertainty management theory, as well as in its earlier version, fairness heuristic theory, Van den Bos, Lind and Wilke (2001), and Lind and Van den Bos (2002), for example, state that people use fairness information in order to cope with situations of high uncertainty. While individuals come to feel a sense of security by confirming justice in the situation, their anxiety tends to be amplified by perceiving injustice.

In addition, other justice research models also incorporate the stress mechanism. According to the equity theory of Adams (1965), for one, individuals judge distributive justice by comparing the ratio of contribution to reward in their own case with that of others in a similar situation. Individuals are thought to feel tension and anxiety when they experience inequity, irrespective of whether that should constitute overpayment or underpayment, and to be motivated to resolve it.

Similarly, according to the referent cognition theory of Folger (1986), and Folger and Martin (1986), individuals who feel discontent at an outcome are considered to indulge in counter-factual imaginings to the effect that they might also have been able to obtain a different, better outcome. From information about the fairness of the determination procedures and processes, they estimate the possibility of such a (favourable) alternative truth being realised. If fair procedure has been carried out, then the individuals will consider the probability of a counter-factual outcome to be low, and accept the actual outcome: ('It was an outcome that was reached via proper procedure, so it cannot be helped, even though I am not happy about it.') On the other hand, if the procedure is judged to have been unjust, then individuals will not be able to accept an outcome about which there is lingering dissatisfaction: ('If procedure had been applied a bit more properly, then I would not have lost out/I would have got a better outcome.') Incited by such uncomfortable feelings, the individuals in question are thought to display anger, resentment and retaliation towards those who preside over the determination procedures and processes (people in authority).

The justice theories we have introduced here are all ones which emphasise the fact that the notion of a discrepancy between the treatment which individuals expect to rightly receive and the treatment which they actually do receive contributes to the formation of a concept of injustice. This is extremely close to the way of thinking of the Demand-Control model, which defines stress as the discrepancy between demand and the capacity to control (Karasek, 1979; Theorell and Karasek, 1996). The idea that thus regards fairness as a stressor which provokes a stress response (strain) can also be considered theoretically valid, but there has been little research directly investigating the ties between the two.

Elovainio, Kivimäki and Helkama (2001) elucidated the fact that procedural justice and relational justice are associated with the stress response (comprising nervousness, depression, and difficulty in concentrating). Tepper (2001) reported that distributive justice and procedural justice had an interactional effect upon emotional exhaustion, depression and anxiety. He made it clear that when distributive justice is low, the link between procedural justice and mental anxiety is strengthened. Judge and Colquitt (2004) illustrated that the four dimensions of justice – distributive, procedural, interpersonal and informational – are associated with the stress response and, further, that the relationship between the two is mediated by work–family conflict. In light of the above theoretical and experiential studies conducted in the West, there seems to be a clear connection between organisational justice and the stress response (strain).

Justice and stress in Japanese organisations

According to a report on a questionnaire survey as to 'the mental health efforts of workers' unions,' conducted in 2005 by the Mental Health Research Institute of the Japan Productivity Centre for Socio-Economic Development (JPC-SED), almost seven-tenths (68.7%) of workers' unions replied that 'emotional disorders' among union members had tended to increase over the previous three years.

In addition, the committee within the Japanese Ministry of Health, Labour and Welfare which investigates measures relating to mental health and overwork has pointed out that overwork is worsening employees' mental health, and has reported concrete figures such as the following, as evidence: the first is the issue of there having been more than 310 recognised cases in the past year of worker's compensation for brain or heart disease caused by overwork; the second is that there have been more than 34,000 suicides annually, approximately 9,000 of which have been of workers; the third is that recognised cases of workers' compensation for mental disorders have increased in recent years, the number of these identified as having led to suicide reaching 40; and the fourth is the problem of more than 60 per cent of workers having claimed that their work causes them intense stress and anxiety, as working hours have split into the two extremes of too long or too short, and non-scheduled working hours have tended to increase.

As such, the maintenance of employees' mental health is a pressing need in present-day Japan, and attempts to rectify this problem are being demanded from society as a whole. Of course, physical measures such as lightening employees' excessive workload are probably necessary, but there is also a call for the elucidation of psychological variables such as those which would ameliorate the stress response. The elucidation of such psychological variables offers suggestions for the clarification of measures to enhance the directionality of organisational management and employees' tolerance of stress. If one follows the aforementioned studies carried out in the West, then organisational justice can be considered a potentially powerful variable which influences employee stress. Justice is thought to be a universal feeling (Leung, 2005), and, in Japan, also, it is considered reasonable to assume that organisational justice exerts influence upon employee stress. If a link is found between the two, then we can anticipate efforts such as stress management and mental health maintenance through fairness.

In our present study, we examine the relationship between organisational justice and the stress response, using Japanese company employees as our subjects, but we assume that the relationship between the two is mediated by two variables. One is trustworthiness vis-à-vis the commutation relation with the organisation. If we follow Brockner (2002) and the abovementioned justice heuristic theory, then employees can be positioned as beings who always harbour anxiety as to how they will be treated by the organisation. Accordingly, employees can be thought especially to assess the trustworthiness of the commutation relation with the organisation, using fairness as a key, but we consider this trustworthiness to be a factor which directly affects the stress response. Also, many scholars have suggested that organisational justice strengthens the social commutation relation between individuals and organisations, and that this has an influence upon employee attitudes and behaviour (Masterson, Lewis, Goldman and Taylor, 2000; Moorman, Blakely and Niehoff, 1998; Rupp and Cropanzano, 2002; Tekleab, Takeuchi and Taylor, 2005; Wayne, Shore, Bommer and Tetrick, 2002). Based on the results of such Western research, we set up hypotheses regarding employees of Japanese organisations, as follows:

Hypotheses

As employees who perceive there to be justice in an organisation – though they experience stress within the organisation – have a strong sense of trust towards that organisation, this will probably result in a reduction of their stress response (Hypothesis 1). Another mediating variable in addition to trust in the organisation is a participative climate. Procedural justice is thought to give rise to a perception among employees that they are participating in decision-making. Also, it is considered that interpersonal and affective justice will obscure differences in power and status, and their distance, thus spawning a participatory atmosphere. According to the demand-control model, a situation endowed with a participative climate means that individuals are given a certain degree of discretion in their work duties. Again, it is considered easy for individuals who are favoured with a participative climate to obtain social support. A participative climate is, therefore, one factor which ameliorates the stress response. Based on the above argument, we made the prediction that organisational justice would mediate a participatory environment and lower the stress reaction (Hypothesis 2).

Participants and survey procedure

The experimental subjects were 399 employees working for two Japanese manufacturers, all Japanese nationals. 359 were male, 40 female, and one was of undetermined sex. Their average age was 42.36 years, and the standard deviation was 12.10. In terms of educational background, 158 were senior high school graduates, 190 were graduates of specialist colleges, polytechnics or two-year tertiary institutions, 166 had graduated from four-year university courses, 11 had Master's degrees, 6 had other education, and the academic backgrounds of 3 were unclear. Their positions were: 273 regular employees, including supervisors and subsection chiefs; 98 of middle-ranking management class, comprising section heads and deputy general managers; 16 of executive class, general managers and upwards; and 9 employees including those on secondment, part-timers and others. Moreover, in order to consolidate the subjects for analysis into regular employees only, the last 9 were excluded. Subjects whose responses were defective were further excluded, and the data from a final 387 respondents was used for analysis.

Measurement scales

Organisational justice
In order to measure perceptions of organisational justice, we developed our own unique scale based on the four-dimensional model of justice posed by Colquitt (2001). 'Four dimensions' indicates distributive justice, procedural justice, interpersonal justice and informational justice. Distributive justice is a concept which means the extent to which the rewards or outcomes one obtains are just. Procedural justice is a notion which expresses whether various decision-making procedures and processes in the workplace are consistent, or have bias. Interpersonal justice is a concept representing whether authority

figures in the workplace have shown consideration or respect for other employees when making some kind of decision. Informational justice is a notion expressing whether a workplace authority has given a thorough explanation of the reasons and rationale for a certain decision.

In the present study, we divided these four dimensions of justice into the four contexts of job assignment, resolution of conflict, performance appraisal, and promotion, and measured them. In relation to performance appraisal, for example, we had our subjects evaluate fairness from the four perspectives of whether: 1) it reflected the product of individual effort (distributive justice); 2) clear-cut standards were presented and objectively implemented (procedural justice); 3) the appraiser lent a sympathetic ear to individual opinions and utterances (interpersonal justice); and 4) reasons and rationales were presented and feedback given (informational justice). We multiplied the four justice dimensions by the four contexts, and measured using a total of sixteen items. When we calculated the trustworthiness coefficient (α), distributive justice was .64, procedural justice was .84, informational justice was .78, and interpersonal justice was .79. Distributive justice showed a somewhat low value, but the scores generally were at an acceptable level.

Organisational trustworthiness and participative climate
Trustworthiness in relation to an organisation is a concept representing whether it treats its employees with care, and we measured it using four items to do with perceived organisational support (for example: 'If I make a contribution for the sake of the company, the company will value that.'). Participative climate is a notion referring to the extent to which opinions and proposals are openly expressed, irrespective of status or occupational rank. This was measured using four items, making reference to West's (1990) team climate inventory (for example: 'Useful ideas are respected, regardless of occupational position or status.'). Moreover, the trust coefficient (α) for organisational trustworthiness was .86. Furthermore, the trust coefficient (α) for participative climate was .76.

The stress response (strain)
Our present study measured employees' stress response on the three scales of anger, depression and anxiety. The items were developed by us by reference to Yatomi's (1999) psychological stress response scale, using four items on each dimension to take our measurements. Examples of items are as follows: 'I become grumpy and prone to

anger when too busy at work' (anger); 'I sometimes have a sense of emptiness in the midst of a tranquil working life' (depression); 'I sometimes have a vague sense of anxiety as I work' (anxiety). On each scale, moreover, the trust coefficient was .88 for anger, .78 for depression, and .84 for anxiety.

Results

Organisational justice factor analysis

We conducted a confirmatory factor analysis based on the maximum likelihood estimation method (ML), in order to test whether a four-dimensional structure composed of distributive, procedural, interpersonal and informational justice would be found. For each variable, we have shown in Table 10.1 the mean value, standard deviation, and inter-variable correlation coefficient.

In our factor analysis of organisational justice, we considered the traits in the justice scales in our present study, and took the following steps. We first measured organisational justice (over four dimensions), in the four contexts of 'job assignment,' 'resolution of interpersonal conflict,' 'performance appraisal,' and 'determination of promotion.' As this is a situation in which multiple traits (the four dimensions of distributive, procedural, interpersonal and informational justice) are being measured from multiple content (the abovementioned four contexts), a so-called multi-trait-multi-method (MTMM) matrix can be obtained. In our own study, too, we carried out an analysis pursuant to an MTMM matrix. As I have already explained, the contexts from which perceptions of justice arise have been classified into four

Table 10.1: Mean values, standard deviations and correlation co-efficients

Variables	Mean	s.d.	1	2	3	4	5	6	7	8
1. Distributive justice	2.70	0.65								
2. Procedural justice	2.65	0.67	.71[a]							
3. Informational justice	2.48	0.68	.70[a]	.74[a]						
4. Interpersonal justice	2.66	0.67	.69[a]	.78[a]	.75[a]					
5. Trust	2.49	0.73	.56[a]	.51[a]	.58[a]	.56[a]				
6. Participation	3.02	0.67	.48[a]	.54[a]	.50[a]	.57[a]	.43[a]			
7. Anger	2.48	0.76	−.20[a]	−.25[a]	−.20[a]	−.23[a]	−.25[a]	−.19[a]		
8. Anxiety	2.25	0.79	−.12[b]	−.18[a]	−.13[a]	−.17[a]	−.22[a]	−.19[b]	.68[a]	
9. Depression	2.02	0.73	−.18[a]	−.25[a]	−.19[a]	−.25[a]	−.31[a]	−.30[a]	.65[a]	.80[a]

Note: a = p < .01; b = p < .05.

types, namely, 'job assignment,' 'resolution of interpersonal conflict,' performance appraisal' and 'determination of promotion,' but these four contexts can be broadly consolidated into two categories, according to their content. As job assignment and resolution of interpersonal conflict share a common aspect in that they are events experienced on a daily basis in the workplace, they can be regarded as one category. Performance appraisal and determination of promotion, on the other hand, are both issues to do with human resources policy, and so this pair can similarly be seen as a discrete category. We thus assumed two factors relating to context, in line with these broad categories, in addition to factors relating to traits (in this case, the four justice dimensions).

The first contextual factor was the 'workplace event factor,' comprising job assignment and conflict resolution, and the second contextual factor, the 'human resources policy factor,' was composed of performance appraisal and promotion. For the purposes of actual analysis, however, instead of assuming contextual factors, we assumed a correlation between the error variables of observed variables belonging to shared contexts. In other words, we assumed a correlation between disturbance in observed variables representing workplace events (meaning disturbance among all items measuring job assignment and resolution of interpersonal conflict), and, similarly, assumed a correlation between disturbance terms in all observed variables included in human resources policy (namely, among disturbance terms of all items measuring performance appraisal or determination of promotion). This is a method called the correlated uniqueness model (Marsh, 1989; Saris and Aalberts, 2003).

Figure 10.1 framatically shows the two-justice-factor model (which I describe below) + two-context-factor model. As sixteen observed variables are used in the actual analysis, it is an even more complex model. We beg your attention to the point that paths indicating correlation have been drawn among the disturbance terms of observed variables representing identical contexts. A fit index as in Table 10.2 was obtained as a result of analysis. AMOS5 was employed for analysis. The fit index in Table 10.2 shows that the four-justice-factors + two-context-factor model is the one which best fits our present data set, in comparison with other models.

The three-justice-factor model + two-context-factor model, however, is a model which merges interpersonal justice and informational justice into one factor, rather than separating them, while the two-justice-factor model + two-context-factor model is

Figure 10.1: Correlated uniqueness model

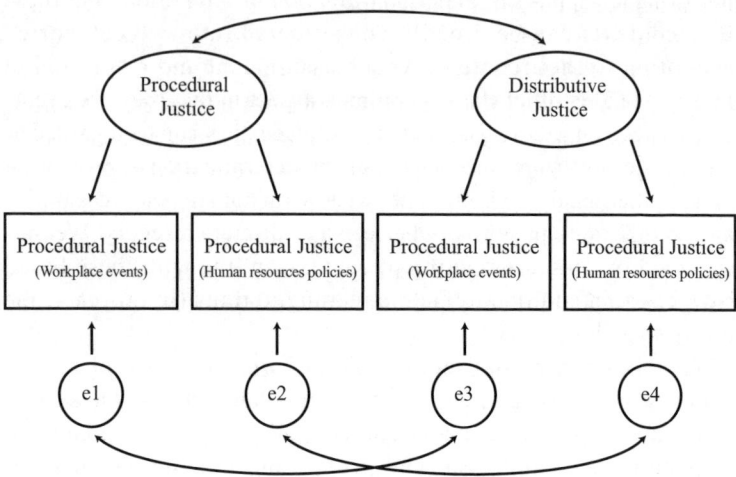

Table 10.2: Results of confirmatory factor analysis of organisational justice (fit index)

Model	χ^2	Number of observations	Degree of freedom	Probability	$\Delta\chi^2$	Δ Degree of freedom	Probability
4 factors	375.18	387	75	.000			
3 factors	386.88	387	78	.000	11.7	3	.010
2 factors	424.03	387	80	.000	37.15	2	.000

	AIC	CFI	RMSEA	IFI
4 factors	529.18	.91	.10	.91
3 factors	534.88	.90	.10	.91
2 factors	568.03	.89	.11	.90

one which regards interpersonal justice, informational justice and procedural justice as one factor, and amalgamates them. As a result of comparing the fit of the three-justice-factor model + two-context-factor model with the four-justice model + two-context factor model, using the difference between the χ^2 (chi-square) value and the degree of freedom, it was suggested that, on a $p < .01$ standard, the four-justice-factor model + two-context-factor model was the one with the better fit. With AIC, also, the four-justice-factor model + two-context-factor model showed the lowest values. This indicates the result that the four-justice-factor model + two-context-factor model best fits the data set. Accordingly, it was made clear that the four-justice-factor model posed by Colquitt (2001) is also supported in studies where Japanese people constitute the sample.

Causality analysis vis-à-vis the stress response
We established two hypotheses relating to the process by which organisational justice exerts influence upon the stress response. One hypothesis predicted that organisational justice would mediate trust towards the organisation and influence the stress response. The other hypothesis predicted that organisational justice would mediate the participatory atmosphere of the workplace and influence the stress response. Structural equation modelling (SEM) was used in order to test these hypothetical models which presume a mediating effect. AMOS5 was used for the purpose of analysis.

Analytical procedure consisted of the following two steps: a) testing of the measurement model; and b) testing of the structural model (Anderson and Gerbing, 1988). In the first step, the link between the observed variables and constructs (latent variables) was tested by confirmatory factor analysis. In the second step, we assumed multiple alternative models apart from the hypothetical model, and tested the validity of the hypothetical model by weighing the various fit indexes of the hypothetical and alternative models.

Figure 10.2 shows the analytical models and their results. We will explain the results in detail later, but first will discuss organisational justice and the observed variables of the stress response. As is clear from Figure 10.2, organisational justice is a latent variable which governs the observed variables comprising distributive, procedural, informational and interpersonal justice, but these observed variables are synthesis variables obtained by calculating scalar means made up of four items. In the same manner as this, the three observed variables of anger, depression and anxiety, which are governed by the stress response, are also scalar means comprising four items. We thus cannot regard these variables strictly as observed variables, but this is a method frequently used as an alternative to secondary factor analysis, or when incorporating high-order concepts into the analysis (Bagozzi and Heatherton, 1994). Conversely, organisational trustworthiness and participative climate are latent variables obtained with item values as observed variables. This sums up the measurement model, but when we compared this with a null model, a significant improvement in fit was found (see Table 10.3). This result demonstrates that it is valid to draw paths from structural concepts (latent variables) to observed variables.

Figure 10.2: Hypothesis (Full Mediation): A model to which alternative model paths have been added.

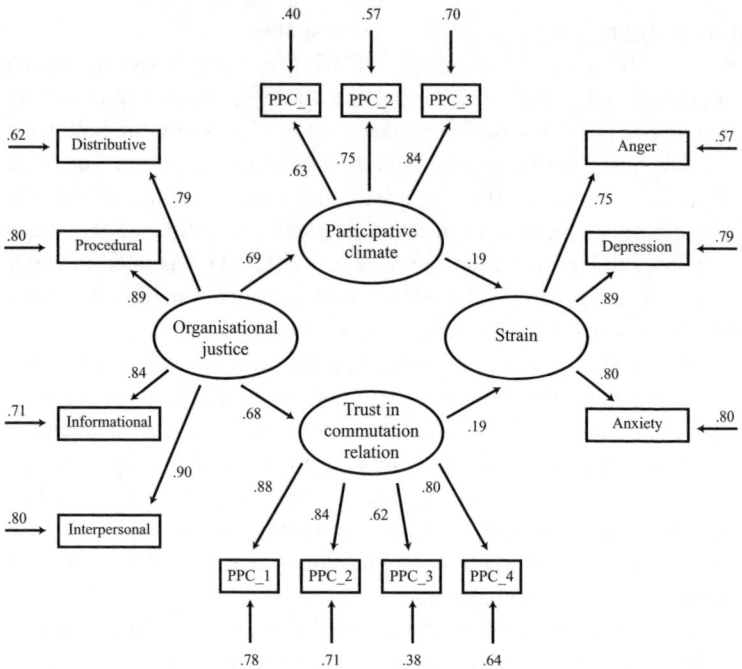

Note: The values on the solid lines are the standardised coefficients in the hypothetical model, and are all significant on a p < .001 standard. The dotted line is a path introduced in order to verify the Partial Mediation Model.

Table 10.3: Fit index of examined models

Model	χ^2	Number of Samples	Degree of Freedom	Probability
Null	3350.38	387	105	.000
Measurement	522.41	387	77	.000
Main Effects	487.22	387	74	.000
Partial Mediation	137.57	387	72	.000
Full Mediation (Hypothesis)	138.22	387	73	.000

	AIC	CFI	RMSEA	IFI
Null	3378.38	.00	.00	.00
Measurement	606.41	.86	.12	.86
Main Effects	577.22	.88	.12	.88
Partial Mediation	231.57	.98	.05	.98
Full Mediation (Hypothesis)	230.22	.98	.05	.98

In the second-step analysis, we drew paths between the latent variables selected by the measurement model, based on the model. Initially, we drew paths from justice variables to participative climate and organisational trustworthiness, then added paths from participative climate and organisational trustworthiness to the stress response. These are paths based on our hypothesis, and correspond to the solid lines in Figure 10.2. This is the model called 'full mediation (hypothesis)' in Table 10.3. It can be seen from Table 10.3 that the CFI and RMSEA exhibited sufficiently acceptable values, and all coefficient values of projected paths were significant, also. Furthermore, when the full mediation model was compared with the main effects model, the former obtained a significantly better fit: $\Delta\chi^2$ $(1, N = 387) = 349.00$, $p < .001$. The main effects model, on the other hand, is the model in which we assumed that justice variables, the trustworthiness of the commutation relation with the organisation, and participative climate would directly influence the stress response. In other words, we did not presume a mediation effect from trustworthiness and participative climate to extend to the relationship between organisational justice and the stress response. This result implies the validity of the hypothesis in our current study, to the effect that organisational justice does not operate directly to ameliorate the stress response, but rather exerts its influence through the mediation of organisational trustworthiness and participative climate.

Through comparison with the main effects model, it was suggested that the relationship between organisational justice and the stress response is mediated by trustworthiness and participative climate, but we decided to examine this way of mediation in detail. We tested which of the two hypothetical models – the full mediation model and the partial mediation model (see the dotted line in Figure 10.1), which presumes a direct path from justice variables to the stress response – had the better fit. According to a sequential χ^2 test, no significant difference in fit was found between full mediation and partial mediation: $\Delta\chi^2 (1, N = 387) = 0.65, p > .05$. If we consider the point that full mediation was the model with a higher degree of freedom (stronger constraint) than partial mediation, then it can be judged from the principle of parsimony in the explanation that the partial mediation model is the superior one. Moreover, the fact that the path coefficients from justice to the stress response were not significant can also be seen to confirm the validity of the full mediation model. From such results it can be judged that Hypothesis 1 and Hypothesis 2 which we proposed were supported.

Summary of findings and considerations

Our current study set up hypotheses saying that the connection between organisational justice and the stress response is mediated by the trustworthiness of the commutation relation with the organisation and by participative climate. SEM analysis supported these hypotheses of ours. This result suggests that justice does not directly lower employees' stress response, but, by leading the commutation relation with the organisation and the workplace atmosphere into a favourable state, it ultimately plays a role in ameliorating individuals' stress response.

As discussed above, the effect in which organisational justice brings a favourable air to the workplace is called the fair process effect, and it has mainly been North American scholars who have proved its validity, both theoretically and experientially. Our present study has proved that the fair process effect is a phenomenon which is also found in Japanese workplaces. However, it is difficult succinctly to describe the cultural differences between North America and Japan, and it is not considered necessarily a constructive exercise to try, but most studies up till now have reported that North America is more individualist than Japan, while Japan is more collectivist than North America (Hofstede, 1980). Moreover, Japan can also be said to be a society with a greater power distance than North America. Nevertheless, the effect in which fairness calls forth a favourable response in individuals shows that, regardless of such cultural disparities, it is still valid. Japanese firms have not been very eager to embrace it, but Japanese organisations should also take action to enhance employees' perceived fairness.

The full mediation model was supported in our research. In other words, no direct effect upon the stress response from fairness was found. Maybe this result can be interpreted as a unique trend in Japan. Japanese people perhaps have a strong tendency to be keenly aware of the instrumentality of fairness, using it as a key for knowing the organisation with which they have interchange, as well as their immediate workplace atmosphere. Folger (1998, 2001) argues that fairness is not a means, but an end in itself. In other words, individuals do not extrinsically focus upon fairness as a proxy indicator of certain interests, but are positioned as intrinsically focusing upon fairness, emphasising the value which fairness has as a moral and a norm. Still, Japanese employees perhaps are sensitive to its function as a heuristic for estimating the trustworthiness of the organisation and the quality of the workplace atmosphere. Fairness thus has not been found to have the effect of directly reducing the stress response, though a markedly indirect effect is thought to have been found in which it first enhances trustworthiness and participatory atmosphere, then lightens stress. Through his experimental work, Brockner (2002) reported that individuals with a dominant independent self had a higher level of concern for procedural justice than individuals with a strong interdependent self. If we assume that Japanese people have a stronger tendency to have an interdependent self, as has been conventionally thought, then this partially supports our reasoning. There still needs to be further research as to what kinds of variations might be discovered in the tendency to regard fairness as a means, or to see it as a moral which ought to be observed.

The results of our current study, however, were ones which reconfirmed the importance of fairness management (Hayashi, 2004; Sekiguchi and Hayashi, 2003). Fairness management was shown to be not only useful to organisations in the positive aspect of productivity enhancement, but also to be a notion which contributes to organisational welfare programs such as stress management. In terms of preventive psychiatry and public health, in particular, the aims of stress management can be divided into tertiary prevention (the treatment and optimum adjustment of people who have become ill), secondary prevention (the early detection of disease), and primary prevention (stopping people from becoming ill) (Watanabe, 2002). It is thought that stress management hitherto has been biased towards tertiary prevention, but, from here forward, measures to counter stress from the perspective of secondary and primary prevention will be desired. The management of organisational justice is considered to be a concept of particular use in primary prevention. Hereafter, comprehensive efforts to manage stress and fairness will be anticipated.

In closing, we will discuss the limitations of our current study and future research. The degree of stress is said to differ considerably according to age, but our study did not test the effect of such a demographic variable. Consequently, one could consider analysing the hypothetical models in our present research by age and social class (synchronous analysis of multi-population with mean structure). In addition, perhaps because the sample was not very large, the fit index of the organisational justice confirmatory factor analysis was not a sufficient value. One could consider there to be a need to further examine the factoral validity of organisational justice by increasing the size of the sample.

Part III
Justice and Fairness and Social Problem-Solving

11 Consensus-building in Public Development: Fairness Theory and the Creation of a New Field of Research
Toshiaki Aoki

Consensus-building in public development: Japanese research

The supply of social infrastructure hitherto has been an important task in Japan, and much public investment has been made for that purpose. As a result of the reduction in perceptions among residents in large urban areas of great inconvenience in daily life, the quantitative fulfilment of infrastructure can no longer be said to have important significance, apart from in certain areas and projects. On the other hand, new challenges have arisen in the form of problems relating mainly to the qualitative aspect of undertakings, such as consensus-building, environmental conservation and the improvement of the urban landscape. Accordingly, such improvements have become vital issues in present-day social infrastructure development.

The 'consensus-building problem' constitutes one of the most important examples among these challenges. By 'consensus-building problem,' I mean the issue of the enormous time costs generated in the building of consensus when development is undertaken. If great amounts of time are spent in consensus-building, then secondary problems will arise – not only will labour costs increase, but the provision of the service to be offered by the project also will be delayed. As a result, large social loss will arise, and the efficiency of the project will fall, as well. Loss on a national scale also occurs in the case of state projects, as exemplified by the delays in expanding Tokyo International Airport at Narita. If expansion is delayed, then the place of origin of international flights landing and taking off there will shift to other countries, resulting in great national loss to Japan. For that reason, consensus-building has become an extremely vital issue in current Japanese urban redevelopment.

Prior to the 1980s, the issue used to be consensus-building with such immediate stakeholders as landowners. Hence, the identification of negotiating partners was also relatively simple. Now, however, due to the diversification of social values and the fact that social infrastructure needs have, to a certain degree, been satisfied, the target for consensus-building has widened to include people in nature-conservation groups and the like, indirect though their interest may be. This has resulted in the emergence of a new problem, namely that of the necessity to obtain the consent of an unspecified number of people. The problem of consensus-building has, therefore, reached an even more difficult level.

In Japan, the problem of consensus-building in public development has been studied for many years in the fields of civil engineering and architecture, as it has a close association with urban planning and urban policy (Imamura, 1975). The majority of these consisted, however, of anecdotal accounts of cases of small-scale development, and no theoretical explanation relating to the psychological mechanism of the people involved was carried out. In the 1990s, though, conflict in large-scale projects began frequently to occur, and consensus-building became a vital social exercise. Consequently, public involvement (PI), which had a record of achievement in the United States, began to be trialled within Japan, as well. However, though studies introducing PI did increase on the research front, anecdotal reports comprised the majority of these, as always, and the psychological mechanism of consent remained unstudied.

In such a context, there grew in civil engineering, too, an emphasis on the necessity for research that employed a psychological approach (Fujii, 2001). Then, there appeared a string of studies which explored the psychological mechanism of consent, using a social psychological approach (Aoki, Hoshi and Satō, 2006; Aoki, Nishino, Matsui and Suzuki, 2003; Fujii, Takemura and Kikkawa, 2002). These studies basically were applications of social psychology, but, to their credit, they did introduce a scientific approach to a research field which previously had not ventured beyond anecdotal reports. Moreover, because of the strong awareness of practicality so typical of engineering that pervaded these studies, they can be characterised by their conduct of analysis which included factors not considered in previous social psychological research. Furthermore, as a result of the introduction of a social psychological approach, new theoretical development came to be anticipated – in other words, the perspective of the enhancement of practicality spawned a fresh analytical framework from existing research, and began to indicate the likelihood of that leading to the growth of new theory and fields of research.

In this chapter, I will thus conduct a review of research on consensus-building in public development implemented in Japan, and introduce some typical studies. In addition, I will discuss the potential for fresh theoretical development to which studies in consensus-building for public development have given rise.

Perspectives in consensus-building studies

In public development, the legitimacy of investment constitutes a vital factor in consensus-building. Moreover, as the existence of multiple stakeholders is assumed, the fairness of the project process also becomes an important consensus-building factor. If the framework of traditional negotiation studies proposed by US scholars is adopted (Kramer and Tyler, 1996; Lind and Tyler, 1988; Tyler, Boeckmann, Smith and Hou, 1997), the legitimacy of investment corresponds to 'distributive fairness' – meaning the fairness of the result of resource allocation; while the fairness of the project process corresponds to 'procedural fairness'– meaning the fairness of distributive processes. As the framework of fairness studies is something amply applicable to the consensus-building problem in public development, it is possible to elucidate the psychological mechanism of consent. Therefore, consensus-building studies are situated as being applications of fairness studies.

There are three points, however, upon which consensus-building studies differ greatly from fairness studies, namely: the former's dealing explicitly with social dilemmas (Dawes, 1980); its dealing explicitly with group situations; and its being based upon pragmatism.

Firstly, the presence of social dilemmas in public development is assumed because a structure of 'social profit' versus 'private profit' is always generated in the consensus-building process. In the case of dams, for example, people in downstream areas enjoy many benefits in such aspects as flood control and irrigation, so high social profit is expected from dam development. On the other hand, great private disadvantage arises for the people who dwell on the dam construction site, because they are asked to move. A social dilemma thus emerges for the landowners and leaseholders. This social dilemma is both a huge barrier to consensus-building and the greatest factor in the ballooning of negotiating costs. One could say that social dilemmas are, therefore, an unavoidable issue when dealing with consensus-building in public development.

Even in traditional negotiation studies, the existence of social dilemmas has been considered, though non-explicitly. Examples can be cited of such research which simultaneously considered distributive fairness vis-à-vis the group and procedural fairness vis-à-vis the individual (Brickman, Folger, Goode and Schul, 1981). However, social dilemmas are far from sufficiently incorporated in the analytical framework in these studies. This is where the two kinds differ.

Secondly, as many interested parties are present in public development, even in the case of a single project, the target of consensus-building will comprise multiple parties, including the residents of the project area, the owners of the land, and so on. In such cases, as the majority of people share interpersonal relationships through the community, they will pay attention to the opinions of community members. As a result, they will attune their opinions to those of local leaders and others. When such conformity occurs, positive/negative attitudes will be decided not by individual opinion alone, but also by the influence of the group's decision. For that reason, the impact of the group situation upon consensus-building in public development cannot be ignored.

The final point which can also be cited as a salient feature of research into consensus-building in public development is its employment of pragmatism. In Japan, this is attributed to technical experts in civil engineering and architecture having been the people to have taken most seriously the necessity for consensus-building in public development. In other words, technical experts implementing projects could be said to have valued 'practical research' because they appealed for a resolution of consensus-building problems. At such times, as engineers and researchers in civil engineering had no knowledge of psychology, they had no alternative but to conduct anecdotal-report-type field studies. In recent years, however, studies using social psychological approach have emerged, along with research employing micro-economics (Hatori, Matsushima and Kobayashi, 2003; Sakakibara, Isobe, Okada and Tatano, 2001), and diverse theoretical investigations relating to consensus-building in public development have come to be conducted. Even at present, a large number of anecdotal reports are in progress, but the theoretical approach is also steadily being established. Accordingly, the study of consensus-building in public development might be said to have reached a great turning-point in terms of its research paradigm.

Current state of consensus-building studies

Classification of consensus-building research

If one compiles an overall picture of research into consensus-building in public development in Japan, the result is as in Figure 11.1. Its theoretical research can be divided into two types: studies mainly describing causal relationships of various phenomena, and those elucidating structural elements of the phenomena. Empirical studies are taken to be studies which mainly substantiate the theories proposed in preceding research or the results deduced from them, in actual or hypothetical settings. Field studies are taken to be studies which report on actual phenomena, though their theoretical background is not always clear. In other words, I call anecdotal-report-type studies 'field studies.' Moreover, as my focus here has been on introducing research which includes a psychological perspective, I call your attention to the fact that there are also some research fields which I have not introduced, including conflict analysis employing game theory (e.g., Nagata and Sugima, 1993), studies using a micro-economical approach, and so on.

Theoretical studies

As I have stated above, the goal of theoretical research can be divided into the description of causal relationships and the discovery of factors

Figure 11.1: Classification of consensus-building studies relating to public development

Consensus-building studies relating to public development

- Theoretical studies
  Studies principally relating to such psychological mechanisms as attitude-formation and decision-making

- Theory-verification studies
  Studies which principally verify fair-process effect and attitude-formation theories

- Field studies
  Studies relating principally to workshop-management methods and the effect of residents' participation

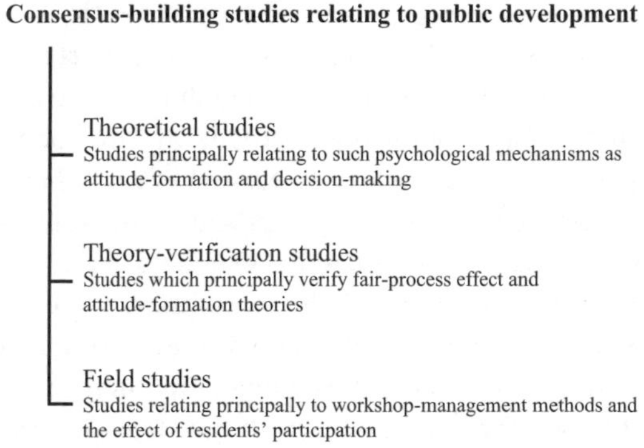

which constitute phenomena. The principal theme of such studies is the elucidation of the formation of positive/negative attitudes, and the mechanism of trust-building. First, then, our 'fairness attitude-change model' (Aoki, Nishino, Matsui and Suzuki, 2003) can be cited as an example of research dealing with the mechanism (causal relationships) in attitude-formation. Here, we examine the formation mechanism of citizens' positive/negative attitudes, focusing upon information-processing processes. We also carry out analysis of the shaping mechanism for cooperative intent in group situations (Aoki, Hoshi and Satō, 2003, 2006). We analyse the shaping mechanism for cooperative intent in cases where group pressure is applied, and we point out the likelihood of the perception of fairness being an important divisive factor in attitude-formation through conformity. I will discuss these points in detail in the following section.

Next, we can cite Fujii (2004) as a study relating to the psychological factors involved when positive/negative attitudes are formed. Fujii has conducted interview surveys with 1500 interviewees, and analysed the influence of the framing effect upon the intent to accept a proposal. As a result, Fujii has reported that positive perceptions of presented information are instrumental in the heightening of the intent to accept. These studies, having incorporated such new elements as the information-processing mechanism and cognitive frame, examine strategies for coping with theoretical explanations of phenomena and associated problems. Such studies, therefore, could be regarded as examples of applied fairness studies which reflect a fresh perspective.

The work of Nakayachi and Watabe (2004), on the other hand, exemplifies research on causal relationships in trust-building. They conducted two separate scenario experiments targeting students, and have analysed the influence of hostage-posting on the estimation of trustworthiness (n = 331, 230). As a result, they reported that, while voluntary information-disclosure was conducive to trust-building, there was a possibility that the disclosure of information in response to urging by others would provoke an erosion of trust. Fujii (2006) reported that thorough accountability is linked to trust-building, based on the results of his psychological experiments using 216 students. Furthermore, studies dealing with the role of trust in social dilemmas also offer many valuable insights, though they do not directly take consensus-building in public development as their research topic. Yamagishi (1998), for one, has carried out investigation into the classification of trust and its formation mechanism, and has found that, under uncertainty, expectation relating to intent is an important factor in trust. In studies targeting non-Japanese, also, it is reported that trust is an important factor in consensus-building. Flynn (1992) and Kramer and Tyler (1996), for example, each examine the role of trust with American subjects, from the viewpoints of risk- and organisational management, respectively.

In spite of there also having been some theoretical research regarding consensus-building in public development, as above, the number of studies remains small. For this reason, it is strongly hoped that there will be more theoretical research, to speed up the proposal of rectification strategies for actual problems and to establish this issue firmly as a new field for research.

Empirical studies

Studies relating to the fair process effect

The greatest majority of research which substantiates existing theories is probably that relating to the verification of the fair process effect. There are numerous reports of empirical studies in the US and the Netherlands on the fair process effect (Greenberg and Folger, 1983; Van den Bos, Lind, Vermunt and Wilke, 1997; Van den Bos, Wilke and Lind, 1998), but there are few which take public development as their subject matter. Under such circumstances, it has been reported in Japan that, resulting from scenario experiments, the fair process effect has also been detected in consensus-building in public development. Having had 240 citizens and 147 students read a scenario relating to the construction of a freeway and rubbish incinerator, then fill out a questionnaire, Aoki et al. have reported that the group which had received a detailed explanation indicated a significantly greater trustworthiness in the government and inclination to approve of the project than the group which had received a rough explanation (Aoki, Fukuno and Ohbuchi, 2004; Aoki, Hoshi and Satō, 2004). Fujii et al. also conducted a scenario experiment relating to the acceptance of the construction of a rubbish incinerator, and have reported that the inclination to accept was higher in cases where opportunity for voice was permitted, in comparison to those in which it was denied (Fujii, Takemura and Kikkawa, 2002).

We also carried out a questionnaire survey with 38 people eligible for compensation for land used in construction of an actual dam, and have reported that the fair process effect emerged even in an actual project (Suzuki and Aoki, 2003; Aoki and Suzuki, 2004). In other words, the landowners and leaseholders – who initially had showed distrust in the government and had also been opposed to the construction of the dam – changed their minds through having experienced fair process from the government, coming ultimately to trust the government and approve of the construction. Given that the emergence of the fair process effect in actual projects has been reported in road construction (Aoki, 2005) and environmental impact assessment (Takao, 2002), the development of the fair process effect can be considered possible in actual cases of public development. Moreover, as these reports show that procedural fairness plays an extremely important role in negotiating, fair process can thus be regarded as a key factor in smooth consensus-building.

Along with the growth in research relating to the fair process effect, there have also been seen some studies to do with factors in procedural fairness. The work of US psychologist Leventhal (1980) is a renowned example of research on factors in procedural fairness, but his fairness criteria include some which have no vital significance in public development. Bias suppression and ethicality, for instance, are presupposed in public development, and do not deserve treatment as special factors. On the other hand, though Leventhal does not cover them, there are also some other important factors which exist in actual situations. The Japanese engineer Baba (2002), as a result of having classified the factors in procedural fairness with reference to collections of notes from interview surveys he personally conducted and from IAP2 (the International Association for Public Participation), et cetera, suggests voice and debatability, access to information, and sincerity as factors for procedural fairness. We, too, conducted scenario experiments targeting ordinary adults and students ($n = 387$) in order to explore the causes of conflict which broke out in actual projects. In that instance, we set up a hypothesis based on the group value model (Lind and Tyler, 1988) to test whether the politeness of the explanatory attitude would constitute an important factor in procedural fairness. We found, as a result of our analysis, that the politeness of the explanation does have a fair process effect (Aoki, Fukuno and Ohbuchi, 2003).

Empirical studies on the fair process effect thus have culminated in the proposal of unique fairness criteria, by taking into account actual consensus-building problems. From this, it can be inferred that the resolution of real issues leads to the discovery of new research perspectives.

Research relating to the promotion of cooperative behaviour

At present, much public participation is being tried out in instances of public development. When facilities of a highly public nature such as freeways are being developed, public participation is positively implemented because broad-ranging consensus-building with interested parties is particularly essential in such cases. However, though people who have a direct interest, such as those eligible for compensation for land used, eagerly participate in such opportunities for involvement, other people are reluctant to participate. The current situation is one in which, in spite of the fact that the majority of citizens call for the reflection of public opinion and greater transparency, few citizens actually attend explanation sessions and the like. It is for that reason that measures are sought to promote positive participation in citizens' explanation sessions.

As attendance at citizens' explanation sessions is behaviour which expends attendees' own time for the sake of the community where they themselves live, it can be called a kind of cooperative behaviour in a social dilemma. In connection with this, it has been reported in fairness studies with American subjects that group-oriented cooperative behaviour has a close connection with the evaluation of fairness (Tyler, Degoey and Smith, 1996). We thus conducted a social survey of 4000 ordinary citizens (814 responses (20.4 per cent)) to test our hypothesis that citizens do not actively attend explanation sessions because they have the belief that fair process will not be carried out in public development. As a result, it was shown that, on the whole, citizens tend to have a negative impression of project procedures in instances of public development (Hikichi and Aoki, 2006). Moreover, when we used structural equation modelling to examine the causal relationships involved, the legitimacy which we had hypothesised could be detected (Figure 11.2). It can be inferred from this that fair process is an important factor promoting cooperative behaviour in a social dilemma situation.

In line with this finding, we conducted a detailed examination of the mechanism in which cooperative behaviour towards a community is enhanced by means of fair process. In that instance, we drew upon the group value model. In the group value model, the individual's affectional bond vis-à-vis the in-group is considered to be strengthened and group-oriented behaviour to be induced by a perception of procedural fairness (Lind and Tyler, 1988). We therefore hypothesised that citizens' cooperative behaviour would increase as affection for and pride in their community grew due to procedural

Figure 11.2: Procedural fairness and participatory behaviour

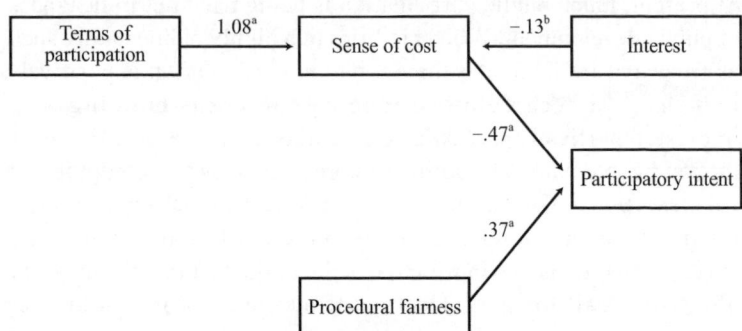

Chi square 459.57, df 205, p < .001 GFI .921, CFI .946, RMSEA .039. a = p < .01, b = p < .05. All non-standardised solutions

fairness, and we conducted a social survey targeting 3000 ordinary citizens (649 responses (21.6 per cent)). When we applied covariance structural equation modelling to the data obtained, it was found that fairness also played a vital role in the formation of affectional bonds such as love and pride towards people's locality, as shown in Figure 11.3 (Aoki and Suzuki, 2004; Hikichi and Aoki, 2005). This result supported our hypothesis that an affectional bond with citizens' own community, comprising 'love,' 'pride' and the like, would be fortified by a perception that their locality was being run fairly, and that this would find expression as cooperative behaviour towards that place.

These findings are deduced from the group value model, and perhaps have no great academic significance. However, seen from the viewpoint of city planning works, they do have important significance, for the reason that these findings suggest possibilities for remedying numerous urban problems, starting with traffic congestion, by strengthening citizens' place attachment and encouraging cooperative behaviour. Hitherto, the importance of increasing place attachment has been acknowledged in the field of city planning works, but there has been no discussion of methodology. However, it has been suggested through the aforesaid research that fairness enhances place attachment. For that reason, we can argue that the above-mentioned studies have proposed a new perspective for the rectification of problems, at least in the field of urban planning.

The potential of fairness studies
Generally speaking, social dilemmas are present at the root of most social problems (Daws, 1980). To resolve these, citizens' cooperative

Figure 11.3: The relationship between fairness and place-attachment/ community pride

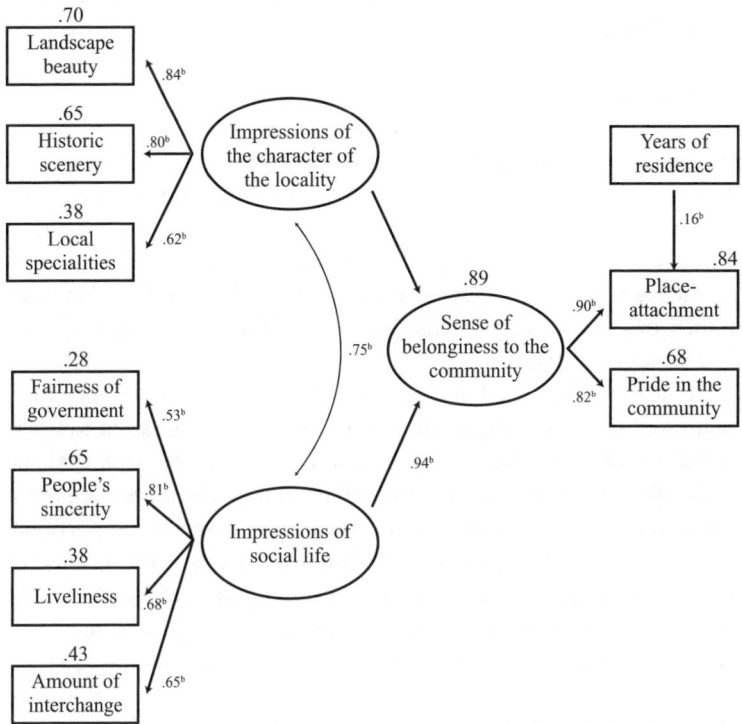

Chi square 219.83; df 33, p < .001; GFI .938, AGFI .897, CFI .938, RMSEA .093, AIC 263.83, b = p < .01. All non-standardised solutions

behaviour is essential. In this instance, when cooperative behaviour is promoted on the basis of utilitarianism, a secondary dilemma arises – that of who will pay compensation to the cooperators – and it becomes difficult to solve the problem. Accordingly, it is necessary to base the encouragement of cooperative behaviour on a philosophy other than utilitarianism. Fairness achieves importance, here. Fairness heightens group-orientation through the strengthening of affectional bonds. This results in an increase in citizens' cooperative behaviour. In other words, fairness has the ability to resolve social dilemmas without giving rise to secondary dilemmas, because it stimulates co-operative behaviour through the enhancement of intrinsic motivation.

If social dilemmas are remedied, then people will be able to secure a more pleasant and peaceful life. Moreover, if fairness is maintained, then the likelihood of that lifestyle continuing will also increase. From a practical viewpoint, therefore, we can say that fairness studies constitute an enormously promising field of research for consideration of our future lives.

Field studies

Research concerning participatory behaviour
As citizens' participation becomes vital in Public Involvement (PI), as I have already stated, many urban planning researchers have analysed citizens' participatory behaviour. Representative field studies relating to this include Terabe, Yai and Seki (1999); Yamaoka, Fujita and Matsui (2000); and Miyamoto, Fukui, Michigami, Kita, and Hinoya (2001).

Terabe et al. reported that people's willingness to participate in PI increased in direct proportion to their level of cooperation towards regular local activities. Yamaoka et al., in turn, advised that the collection of information was the principal impetus for participation, and that people's participatory motivation was inversely proportional to the distance between the development site and their place of residence. Miyamoto et al. reported that participatory behaviour was promoted by raising people's interest in a project by means of campaigns and so on, even in cases of small vested interest.

Research relating to the promotion of public participation
This type represents the largest proportion of studies concerning consensus-building in public development. Yai, Terabe and Seki (2000); Matsuda and Ishida (2002); Itō (2001); and Murata and Endō (1999) can be cited as the main examples. Yai et al. conducted questionnaire surveys, and reported notable points regarding methods of promoting PI which utilised survey sheets. Their report specifically states the need for government to take the lead in promoting PI, and for it to vary its response because cooperators and non-cooperators in such surveys do not share the same perceptions vis-à-vis the development of social infrastructure. Matsuda and Ishida, targeting the policy committee for a master plan in urban planning, measure changes in awareness among members during the deliberative process, and discuss methods of implementing such advisory panels. Specifically, they reported on the importance of ensuring transparency and allocating sufficient time for questions. Itō discusses how the consensus-building process

proceeds in community development and the tools it uses, based on his own professional experience as an urban planner. In concrete terms, he talks about how workshop participants reach consensus via five different stages of awareness, and how opportunity for communication is vital in consensus-building. Lastly, Murata and Endō examined residents' participation in the formulation of a reconstruction plan for public housing, and reported on the process in which an adversarial relationship between the administration and residents evolved into one of cooperation.

The significance of field studies
No theoretical explication is carried out in field studies such as those introduced here. However, such research does carry out 'detailed reporting of phenomena,' which constitutes essential information for the development of theory. Without such information, it would be difficult even to grasp the phenomena themselves, let alone to construct theories to describe those phenomena. That is why studies like these can be seen as a valuable source of information for theoretical researchers. Moreover, the theory established by theoreticians provides opportunities for experimental researchers to understand a phenomenon as a general model. For that reason, it can be argued that theoretical and empirical studies have a mutually stimulating relationship in which they grow in concert with each other. In other words, they both can be said to provide the other with fresh research perspectives. Such roles assume all the more importance as the phenomena needing elucidation grow more complex. Consequently, both types of research are vital, and we researchers need to pay attention to both kinds of studies, in order to elucidate the causes of problems and propose solution measures for complex phenomena such as urban issues.

New theory: the attitude-change model

Clarifying attitude-formation mechanisms

Fairness studies incorporate the accumulation of many insights. It is hard to say, however, that there is now an ample body of findings relating to the kind of information which undergoes processing during the formation of positive/negative attitudes, and how this is processed. In other words, insights concerning social cognition and the fairness effect are still not sufficient integrated. Though the process of positive/negative attitude-formation has been clarified to a certain extent, from the practical standpoint of policy-making, there can be seen a necessity for studies which describe citizens' change of heart in finer detail, to enable the design of policies which will encourage smooth consensus-building. If one considers the present situation, in which a negative image is widely held regarding public development (Aoki, Nishino, Matsui and Suzuki, 2003), it becomes necessary to use this as the premise upon which to examine the formation mechanism of positive/negative attitudes.

In public development consensus-building there are, however, two distinct negotiating situations: individual and collective. The former occurs when the entity implementing a project and an individual stakeholder conduct negotiations. The scene of negotiation over compensation for land is a prime example. Conversely, the latter is when interested parties organise themselves into a group and hold negotiations with the project-implementing entity, such as in the case where an entire area is to be developed. Negotiations over environmental conservation could be cited as a main example. In this case, unlike as in negotiations in individual situations, group pressure is thought to affect the mentality of participants on the citizens' side because negotiations are being conducted on a collective basis (Asch, 1951). Furthermore, in collective consensus-building situations relating to public development, there is also reported to be an increase in citizens' emotional utterances (Aoki and Nakai, 2004). It can thus be said that consensus-building in group contexts differs from that in individual contexts.

With such perceptions as noted above, we then conducted an investigation of citizens' positive/negative attitude-formation mechanisms in those respective circumstances, based on an 'attitude-change model of fairness.'

The attitude-formation mechanism in individual negotiation settings

If we follow the traditional framework of fairness studies, as Figure 11.4 shows (Lind and Tyler, 1988; Tyler, Boeckmann, Smith and Hou, 1997), individuals are thought to decide upon such attitudes as approval/opposition or cooperative intent, based upon the twin criteria of 'distributive fairness,' meaning the legitimacy (fairness) of the result of distribution of resources, and 'procedural fairness,' meaning the legitimacy (fairness) of the distribution procedure.

As it is usual, in this instance, for distributive fairness to be understood as the legitimacy of the result vis-à-vis the person making the judgement, personal legitimacy becomes the sole factor in judging distributive fairness. In the case of public development, however, due to its very public nature, there exist the dual aspects of 'private profit' and 'social profit.' The former, being a fundamental factor in the assessment of personal legitimacy, can be said to be micro-level distributive fairness (Brickman, Folger, Goode and Schul, 1981). The latter, on the other hand, being a fundamental factor in the assessment of the social legitimacy of a project, can be called macro-level distributive fairness.

As previously noted, opportunity for voice, the amount of information disclosure, and so on, can be considered factors contributing to procedural fairness. In this instance, if information disclosure is inadequate, dialogue between citizens and the government will not be sufficiently established, so we place particular emphasis upon information disclosure, from among the many factors in procedural fairness. We thus consider that citizens base their judgements concerning the legitimacy of a project upon these two kinds of fairness – distributive fairness and procedural fairness.

Moreover, with public development, it is not unusual for citizens' living environment to change greatly, due to that development. In such cases, anxiety arises in relation to the risks meant by change. For that reason, there is a necessity to compensate for that anxiety, so that consensus-building will proceed smoothly. In this instance, it is trust in the government which plays a role in offsetting anxiety (Yamagishi, 1998). Accordingly, trust can also be called an important factor in attitude-formation. In addition, it has been pointed out that prototypes relating to the object of judgement also become an important factor in attitude-formation, in instances of social judgement (Aoki, Nishino, Matsui and Suzuki, 2003; Gibbons,

Figure 11.4: The framework of general fairness studies

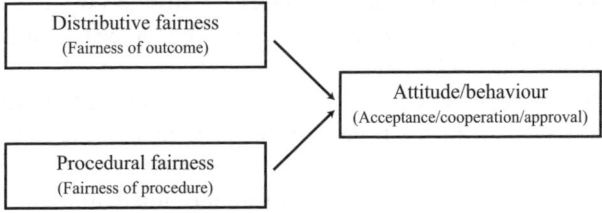

Gerrard, Blanton and Russell, 1998). Here, 'prototype' is a generic term for any impression, perception (schema), preconceived notion, or the like, held by a judge towards the object of judgement. It is reported that, in cases of public development, citizens often hold onto negative prototypes (Aoki, Nishino, Matsui and Suzuki, 2003). The strength of negative prototypes, in particular, appears to regulate citizens' positive/negative attitudes, for that very reason.

As the five factors of distributive fairness (both micro-level and macro-level distributive fairness), procedural fairness, trust, and prototypes can be considered to be formative factors in positive/negative attitudes towards public development projects, if the above line of reasoning is followed, we can posit these as attitude-formation factors. Furthermore, while the degree of civic-mindedness or the like could also be seen as an important factor in shaping positive/negative attitudes, we do not consider this explicitly in our model, making any variables other than the five factors described above subject to individual variability.

Hypotheses relating to the attitude-formation mechanism

It is known from attitude-formation models typified by the Heuristic Systematic Model (HSM) and Elaboration Likelihood Model (ELM) that the mechanism of attitude-formation differs according to the degree of self-relevance (Chaiken, 1980; Chaiken, Liberman and Eagly, 1989; Petty and Cacioppo, 1986). When self-relevance is high, because information-processing motivation rises, people form their own attitudes after careful consideration of information showing content directly relevant to the object of judgement (systematic judgement), but in cases of low self-relevance, because information-processing motivation is low, people form their attitudes by processing information with little deliberation, using such peripheral information relating to the object of judgement as prototypes (heuristic judgement). As such an attitude-formation mechanism can be detected in regard to a wide range of objects, positive/negative attitudes towards public development projects are also thought to be shaped by a similar mechanism.

Firstly, when procedures are not sufficiently fair (when information-disclosure is inadequate), if the project is low in self-relevance, then the formation of positive/negative attitudes will be mainly based on peripheral information, because information-processing motivation is weak. At this time, in cases where the project has high self-relevance, citizens will make efforts to collect as much information as possible, because information-processing motivation rises. For that reason, positive/negative attitudes come to be formed after consideration of both project information and peripheral information. Peripheral information, in this instance, can be thought to include prototypes related to public development and trust towards the project implementing body (the government).

On the other hand, when fair process has been carried out (when adequate information-disclosure has been implemented), if the project is low in self-relevance, then information on the project will not be taken into account even if there has been ample disclosure, and the formation of positive/negative attitudes will be based on peripheral information, because information-processing motivation will be weak. At this time, if the project has high self-relevance, citizens are thought to make efforts to collect as much information as possible. However, as there will be a lesser need to rely on peripheral information in circumstances where ample information on the project has been disclosed, positive/negative attitudes come to be formed on the basis of project information. An organised form of the above hypothesis is shown in Figure 11.5.

Analytical Results

In order to examine the hypothesis noted above, we conducted an experiment in which we manipulated the level of self-relevance (high versus low) and the amount of information disclosure (much versus little), using a scenario relating to the pros and cons of freeway construction. We set up an experimental site within a members-only Website on the Internet, and elicited responses from 200 cooperators in the experiment. After they had finished reading the scenario, we asked them to rate using a six-point scale on the screen (1. Completely disagree; 6. Completely agree). We subjected the data thus gained to structural equation modelling, resulting in the obtaining of the same model structure, irrespective of whether self-relevance was high or low, but here, in Figures 11.6 and 11.7, I illustrate the results when self-relevance is low.

Firstly, in the case where information-disclosure was insufficient, the inclination to approve was determined on the basis of trust towards the project-implementing body and the assessment of macro-

Figure 11.5: The theoretical structure of the attitude-formation mechanism

(a) The situation of inadequate information-disclosure (low self-relevance group)

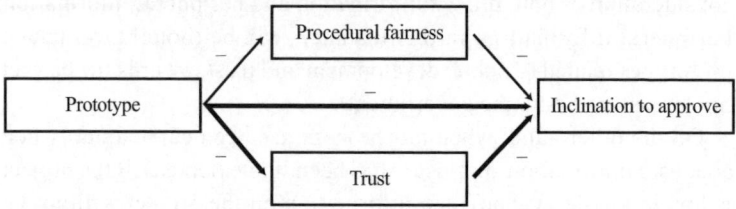

(b) The situation of adequate information-disclosure (low self-relevance group)

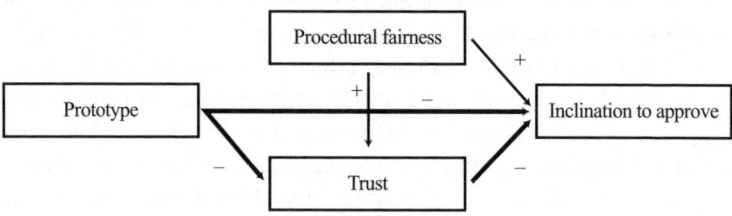

(c) The situation of inadequate information-disclosure (high self-relevance group)

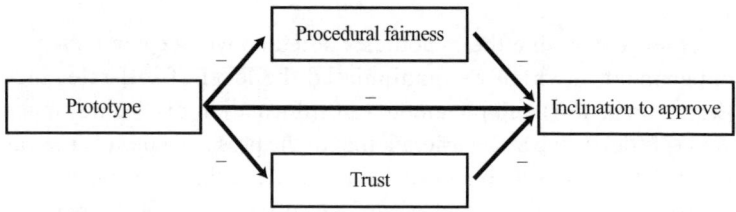

(d) The situation of adequate information-disclosure (high self-relevance group)

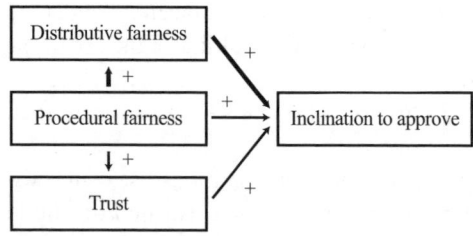

The comparative thickness of the diagram lines indicates the degree of influence.

level distributive fairness, regardless of self-relevance. For that reason, these factors can be understood to be important in attitude-formation when procedural fairness is less than ample, regardless of the level of self-relevance. Moreover, from the fact that the path coefficient value between macro-level distributive fairness and the inclination to approve is greater than the path coefficient between trust in the project-implementing entity and the inclination to approve, it can be seen that participants in the experiment based their decision about their own affirmative or negative attitude on project information, irrespective of self-relevance. This differs from projections based on the elaboration likelihood model, meaning that the inclination to approve is shaped mainly on the basis of project information, even in cases of low self-relevance. Consequently, the analytical results diverged from our hypothesis that project information would not be valued in cases where self-relevance was low.

Figure 11.6: Attitude-formation when there is inadequate presentation of information (low self-relevance group)

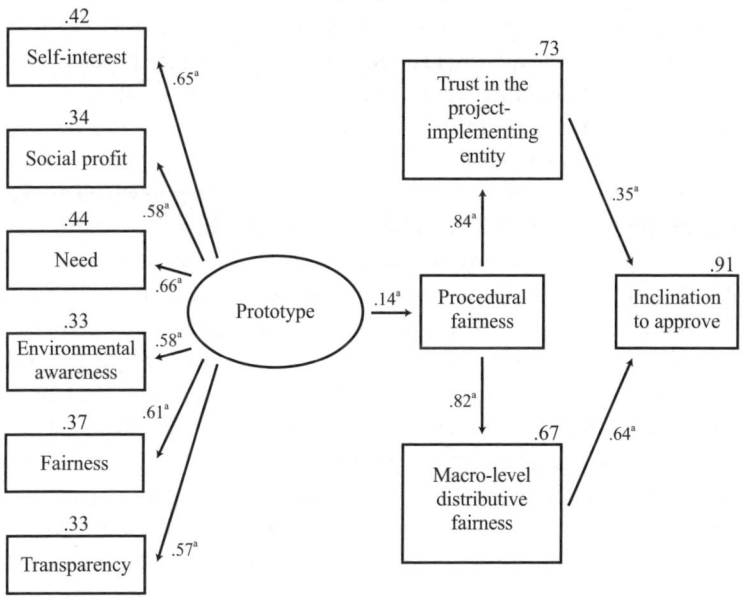

Chi square 122.34, df 71, p < .01. CFI .96, GFI .90, RMSEA .06. a = p < .01. All standardised solutions

Figure 11.7: Attitude-formation when there is adequate presentation of information (low self-relevance group)

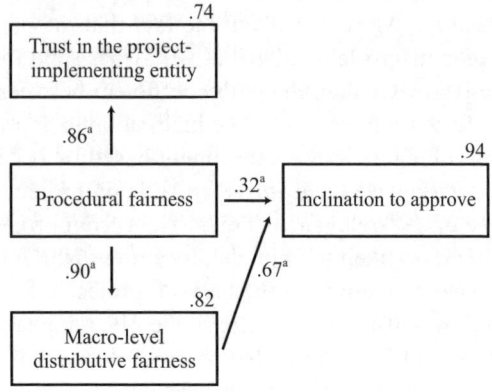

Chi square 8.55, df 5, p = .13. CFI .98, GFI .99, RMSEA .06. a = p < .01. All standardised solutions.

In cases of high self-relevance, on the other hand, the influence that prototypes exerted upon trust was enhanced. This means that participants in the experiment attached more importance to peripheral information in deciding whether they approved when self-relevance was high than when it was low. In this connection, the results supported our hypothesis.

Next, when we conducted analysis relating to cases in which ample disclosure of information had been carried out, here, too, there was the same model structure, irrespective of the level of self-relevance. As no significant path between the trustworthiness of the project-implementing body and the inclination to approve was detected in either case, whether self-reliance was high or low, peripheral information under conditions of sufficient information disclosure can be considered not to have an important role when attitudes are formed. This diverged from our projection that peripheral information would become important in cases where self-relevance was low. Even so, when self-relevance was high, on the other hand, trust in the project-implementing body lost importance. This means that if information-disclosure is sufficiently conducted in projects with high self-relevance, peripheral information will cease to be utilised in attitude-formation. In this connection, it was a result that supported our prediction.

Peripheral information and procedural fairness

It was predicted that attitude-formation would be based on peripheral information in cases of low self-relevance, regardless of the extent of information-disclosure, but the experimental result diverged from that prediction. We have considered three possibilities: cases in which citizens' interest in public development is high can be considered as the first possibility. In other words, as their taxes are poured into public development, there is the possibility that citizens will have a high level of interest, even in cases where they personally have no direct stake, and will decide on a stance of approval or rejection through careful deliberation. As a result, it is thought that project information would be used in attitude-formation even if self-relevance were low. Positive/negative attitudes are thus decided after careful deliberation in cases such as these, in the same way as in cases of high self-relevance.

Next, we can cite the possibility in which the judgement itself has been carried out heuristically, though reference is made to project information. In other words, though people might consult project information because they have a certain level of interest in public development, such interest is not considered great enough to induce them to think deeply about it. It is considered that if insufficient disclosure of information were carried out in such cases, participants in the experiment would evoke a negative cognitive frame from the unfairness of procedure, negatively interpreting the project information heuristically, and forming a negative inclination to approve. Conversely, it is thought that once they had received sufficient disclosure of information, experimental participants would evoke a positive cognitive frame through fair process and, as a result of heuristically interpreting project information in a favourable manner, form affirmative attitudes.

Finally, a possibility that constituted a phenomenon unique to the experimental scenario can be cited. In other words, there is also a possibility that if we had made the condition-setting for the low self-relevance group even lower, we might have obtained the projected result. It will be necessary to conduct more research into these possibilities, as a challenge for the future.

Some deeply interesting results were also obtained, however, in relation to the role which procedural fairness played in attitude-formation. The effect which perceptions of procedural fairness exerted on attitudes was approximately equivalent in both groups, but if attitude-transformation theory is followed, the method of attitude-formation in each group will be different. That is to say, in cases of high self-relevance, attitudes are thought to be determined after careful deliberation, but, when self-relevance is low, to be determined heuristically. In this way, when the mechanism of attitude-formation is different, there is the possibility that the role of procedural fairness will also differ. We have also considered this.

According to attitude-transformation theory, people will shape their own attitudes heuristically in projects with low self-relevance. If this be true, then this implies that assessments of trustworthiness and legitimacy will carried out heuristically from fair process. In this instance, the act known as procedural fairness will directly comprise the material for judgement. In attitude-formation towards an event with low self-relevance, therefore, the act of fair process itself can be considered to have an important significance.

By contrast, in projects with high self-relevance, positive/negative attitudes will be determined after careful deliberation. In other words, the inclination to approve will be shaped as a result of painstaking consideration of the project content. If this follows, then the results of our analysis can be interpreted to mean that the project content has been appropriately understood due to fair process having been implemented, leading to a heightening of the approval rating. In this case, procedural fairness can be thought to remain an indirect source of material for judgement. Accordingly, if this line of reasoning is pursued, then the content of procedural fairness can be thought to become important in attitude-formation towards events with high self-relevance.

From these facts, it can be inferred that the role played by procedural fairness in attitude-formation has the potential to vary in accordance with the level of self-relevance.

Research issues for the future

The following three points, at least, can be posed as issues in the attitude-change model relating to fairness. Firstly, we can cite the case in which, under conditions of low self-relevance, there is ambiguity in the reasons for project information having become a strong factor in attitude-formation. In my discussion, I named three possibilities, starting with the level of information-processing motivation vis-à-vis public development, but these probably need prompt verification.

Next, based on deductions from the attitude-transformation model and the results of covariance structure analysis, we have looked at the way the role played by procedural fairness in attitude-formation varies according to self-relevance, but we have not directly conducted a confirmation of this. Examining this by a direct method can therefore be proposed as a second issue.

The current lack of consideration of the influence of 'civic-mindedness,' which comprises a vital factor in cases of attitude-formation in social dilemmas, can also be named as the final challenge. If civic-mindedness is at a high level, then even if sufficiently fair process is not able to be carried out, the emergence of a strong fair process effect can still be anticipated. Accordingly, the incorporation of factors such as this into the theoretical frame can also be said to be an important task.

Attitude-formation in group consensus-building

Divergence in superficial acceptance and internal acceptance

Group situations are characterised by the emergence of group pressure. We thus conducted experiments using the three factors of private profit, procedural fairness and group pressure as variables, in order to examine the fair process effect in situations where group pressure has arisen (Aoki, Hoshi and Satō, 2006). The first round of experiments was conducted with three parties: one experimenter, one participant, and three cooperators (decoys) each time, for a total of 153 times (n=153). In the experiment, the experimenter asked the participants to undertake a cleaning task, and employed a formula calculated to have them reveal their cooperative intent toward the job. In that instance, private profit was manipulated by whether reward was offered. As for procedural fairness, the case in which a large amount of information was presented in a polite manner of speaking was deemed to be a condition of high procedural fairness, while the case in which scant information was given in a gruff tone was taken to be a condition of low procedural fairness. Group pressure was manipulated by the response sequence. In other words, when the situation was in 'pressure mode' for group pressure, the three cooperators first expressed their agreement, while a response was elicited from the participant first, in 'non-pressure mode.' Under such conditions, we had the participants reveal their cooperative intent. After that, participants filled out a questionnaire relating to their perceptions of private profit, group pressure and procedural fairness (comprising the two variables of feelings of sincerity and information disclosure), respectively (on a six-point scale).

As a result of using binomial logistic regression analysis to analyse the effect of the various factors upon cooperative intent, we found that perceptions of private profit and group pressure exerted a significant influence upon the formation of cooperative intent (Table 11.1). This supported our projection. However, no significant effect could be detected in relation to sincerity and information-disclosure which we had set up as variables in procedural fairness. That is to say, no fair process effect could be recognised. This suggests that peer pressure is an element which has a greater impact than procedural fairness.

There are, however, two kinds of cooperation in response to a request – that in which it is accepted willingly (internal conformity), and that in which compliance is grudging (superficial conformity) (Allen, 1965). While these both constitute cooperative behaviour, there is a vast gap between their respective motivations. In the latter case, especially, its indication of *unwilling* cooperation means there is the potential for a trifling matter to escalate into conflict. For that reason, identification of the divergence factor and promotion of internal conformity become vital when attempting to rectify a social-dilemma situation. Being mindful of the many previous studies which argued that fairness enhances commitment in that instance, we predicted that fairness would be the divergence factor for superficial and internal conformity. When we asked participants to fill out the questionnaire, in order to investigate the true meaning of their cooperative intent, we had them choose one from among the following alternatives: 'I revealed my true feelings'; 'Contrary to my true feelings, I expressed cooperation'; 'Contrary to my true feelings, I expressed non-cooperation.'

Table 11.1: Results of binominal logistic regression analysis

Variables	B	SE B	Wald	Odds
Private profit	0.84	0.21	15.96[a]	2.31
Group pressure	0.81	0.19	18.70[a]	2.26
Sincerity	0.18	0.28	0.43	1.20
Information disclosure	−0.03	0.24	0.02	0.97
Constant	−5.56	1.25	19.68[a]	0.01

Note: a = $p < .01$.

We divided the sixty participants who had declared their cooperation into two groups – the forty-eight who answered that they had revealed their true feelings (internal conformity group) and the twelve who replied that they had acted contrary to their true feelings (superficial conformity group) – and subjected them to a t-test relating to a rating scale of perceptions of the four criteria: group pressure; private profit; information-disclosure; and sincerity. In consequence, as Figure 11.8 demonstrates, the perception of group pressure was significantly higher in the superficial conformity group. On the rating scale for perceptions of private profit and information disclosure, however, the internal conformity group rated significantly higher. Considering these results, we can see that though the people who had felt strong group pressure merely conformed on a superficial level, there was a tendency towards voluntary conformity among those who had paid attention to the advantages accompanying cooperation, or who had felt that the reason for the request had been amply explained.

If we go along with the above results, we can argue that one method of facilitating smooth consensus-building in group consensus-building contexts is to arrange matters so that people do not feel excessive peer pressure, while we simultaneously devise ways of disclosing information so that they perceive it to be fair process. In addition, though it is not permissible intentionally to enhance the sense of private profit in public development, it can be argued that there is a necessity for efforts to be made to dissipate citizens' biases and misapprehensions through proper conduct of information disclosure, and, at least, to have them gain an appropriate understanding of private profit.

Figure 11.8: Comparison between a superficial conformity group and an internal conformity group (ratings)

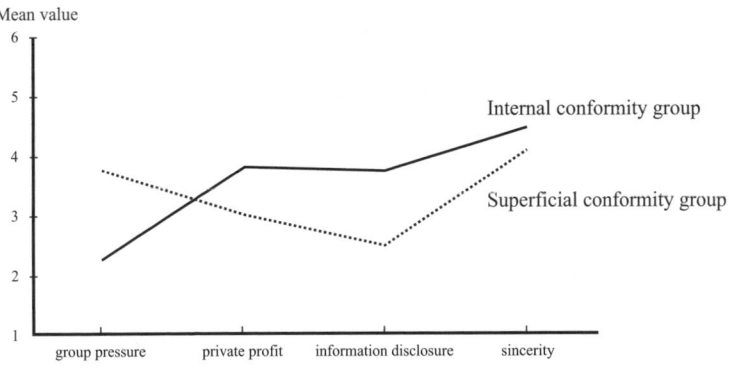

The relationship between group pressure and procedural fairness

Generally, group pressure and procedural fairness are considered independently to exert influences upon cooperative intent. We, however, have discovered that there are times when procedural fairness is the channel through which group pressure impacts upon cooperative intent (Aoki, Hoshi and Satō, 2004). In other words, it is possible that there are two different routes by which peer pressure and procedural fairness influence cooperative intent, as shown in Figure 11.9. We have also carried out analysis relating to this.

First, there would be the case in which group pressure was independent of procedural fairness, and both operate in parallel (Route 1). Then again, as in Route 2, there would also be the possibility that group pressure, by reducing procedural fairness, also had a negative influence upon cooperative intent. In such a case, an ultimate cooperative intent is thought to be formed as the sum of the downgrading effect of group pressure upon procedural fairness and the cooperation-promoting effect of procedural fairness.

We then conducted linear regression analysis, and examined the routes of group pressure influence. As a result, we found that procedural fairness is eroded only in cases where group pressure is particularly strongly felt. Accordingly, we came to the conclusion that though the effect of group pressure generally is shown as Route 1, the Route 2 effect can also arise, solely in cases where group pressure is extremely strongly felt, such as in situations in which group pressure is recognised as an intimidation factor.

Future issues

There are many remaining challenges that relate to the formation mechanism of positive/negative attitudes in group consensus-build-

Figure 11.9: The route of influence of peer pressure

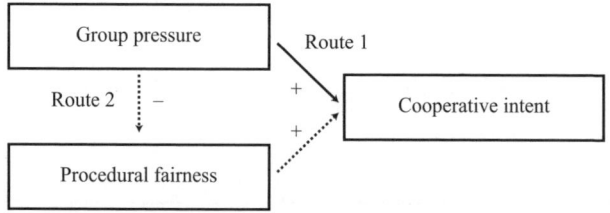

Note: Peer pressure is directed at promoting cooperation

ing. Firstly, from an academic viewpoint, we can cite the fact that the influence exerted upon the attitude-formation mechanism by self-relevance levels is yet to be ascertained. Secondly, from a practical perspective, we can see that, while it is important to elucidate the attitude-formation mechanism in cases where fair process has been carried out in situations in which the majority has expressed an opposing opinion, we have not yet gained sufficient insights regarding this issue. If we consider that procedural fairness has the potential for rectifying NIMBY problems, we can argue that this issue is extremely important.

Research on group consensus-building is still scant, and there are too many issues to even begin to enumerate. However, if we can throw light on its mechanism, and propose measures to cope with it, then there is a strong possibility that many social problems will be remedied. For that reason, we can argue that group consensus-building studies are socially vital, and, at the same time, a matter of urgency.

Conclusion: the potential for new fields of study

In order to solve many social problems, including social dilemmas, there is a need to implement policies which have high efficiency, after gaining a deep understanding of the phenomena in question. To accomplish this, the formation mechanism of cooperative attitudes must first be elucidated.

In that they allude to the formation mechanism of cooperative attitudes, fairness studies are extremely beneficial in the search for remedies for social dilemmas. Moreover, if we consider that fairness studies incorporate explanations of attitude-formation using the notions of interest and morality with which human beings are thought inherently to be equipped, then such studies can be seen to enshrine the potential to constitute a general theory relating to consensus-building. However, fairness studies hitherto have limited themselves to relational analysis of specific factors, and can hardly be said to have ample findings for resolving actual problems. Thus, if we consider new factors within the theoretical frame of fairness studies, in order to improve practical issues, that will make for more effective theory in fairness studies than hitherto. Moreover, if such attempts proceed, fairness studies might possibly develop into a general theory of consensus-building. It is therefore necessary to have a deep understanding of real consensus-building, and to choose new factors which should be incorporated into the frame of fairness studies. In other words, theoretical researchers need a deep understanding of field studies, commencing with anecdotal reports, and empirical researchers need a deep understanding of theoretical studies.

In reality, however, it is neither easy for theoretical researchers to conduct exhaustive field studies or empirical research, nor for empirical researchers to conduct theoretical studies. If, then, theoretical and empirical researchers work collaboratively towards the solution of real-life problems, taking full advantage of their respective fields of expertise, such problems will be solved. If that happens, we can also expect the rectification of social problems. Additionally, new academic insights are also likely to be gained, as theory will be built from new perspectives. That is to say, academic interchange between differing fields will enable great social contributions, and new academic contributions, as well.

Examples of the key to solutions being found through cooperation between theoretical and empirical researchers are by no means limited to consensus-building studies. At least, in our areas of research, namely, 'central city invigoration' and 'improvement of urban structure,' the same effect can be predicted. Numerous urban issues like these exist. That is why, if there is greater cooperation between urban researchers/planners who have been responsible mainly for empirical studies, and social psychologists who have principally concerned themselves with theoretical research, then we can probably anticipate the development of new fields of study, such as research which integrates both. If this happens, we will eventually see the birth of many planners who understand human behaviour and mentality, and a living environment in which people can enjoy a true sense of affluence will be developed. When that comes to fruition, we will be able to hail the rebirth of Japanese urban policy as one in which people take central place.

12 Sociological Perspectives on Environmental Justice: The Case of a German Residents' Movement

Sōko Aoki

Introduction: 'Fairness/justice' theories in sociology

The aim of this chapter is to take up the concept of 'fairness,' which has had little opportunity to be discussed within Japanese environmental sociology until now, situate it within the theoretical framework of environmental sociology through use of theories of 'environmental justice,' and elucidate its contemporary significance.

The debate around 'fairness/justice' has been carried on since Socrates, mainly in the sphere of philosophy. In modern times, utilitarian justice theories, epitomised by Bentham and J.S. Mill, and Rawls' Theory of Justice (1971), which aimed to better the former, form the two great lineages of the normative theory approach to 'fairness/justice.' However, while the normative-theory approach to 'fairness/justice' possesses immense scholarly reserves, its sociological reserves – apart from Saitō (1998), who conceived the 'sociology of justice' – can hardly be called sufficient, as these are limited to fairness evaluation studies.[1] In the markedly scant background to the experiential-theory approach relating to 'fairness/justice' theory, the existence of such a situation can be noted, namely, a paucity of 'fairness/justice' theory in sociology.

In these circumstances, environmental justice theory is a comparatively new, experiential 'fairness/justice' theory (Bryant 1995; Bullard, 1994) which gained momentum in the United States in the 1980s. In American society, in which both racial diversity and strata disparity are significant, criticism has intensified since the 1980s towards the concentrated occurrence of damage due to environmental pollution in neighbourhoods inhabited by people of colour and people on low incomes. In particular, residents who protested, understanding the concentrated locating of disposal sites for hazardous waste in residential districts of African-Americans as 'environmental racism,' put their experience in the civil rights movement to good use as they developed a social movement seeking the simultaneous achievement of environmental conservation and social justice – in other words, 'environmental justice.' Here, what was made the principal issue was the fact that the distribution of advantage and loss in relation to the environment was not carried out fairly among races and social strata, and the environmental justice movement aimed to eliminate this unfairness. In that sense, environmental justice theories emanating from the US are debates on the distributive justice of environmental destruction and damage due to pollution, namely, 'justice in the narrow sense' (Ikeda, 2005), and on the social fairness of distribution.

At the same time, debate over environmental justice can hardly be called adequate in Japan, either. As I will discuss later, it is obvious that the theoretical foundation of Japanese environmental sociology has unwittingly involved environmental justice-like issues. However, it must be said that debate relating to justice itself, and arguments focusing upon the relationship between these and existing theory and methodology, are still insufficient. As a result of a December 2004 symposium entitled 'Theories of justice and legitimacy surrounding the environment: time, history, memory,' a special edition on that same theme was compiled in the October 2005 issue (no. 11) of *Kankyō Shakaigaku Kenkyū* (Journal of Environmental Sociology), and overall debate on environmental justice at last began in earnest, but the boundaries of concepts such as justice, fairness and legitimacy remain vague.

In this chapter, therefore, I firstly undertake a comprehensive ordering of Japanese debates over environmental justice. Next, with this as a basis, I demonstrate the contemporary significance of the issue of environmental justice, in the context of concrete examples.

Theories of environmental justice in Japan

In his paper in above-mentioned special edition, Ikeda (2005) conducts a systematic organisation in relation to theories of environmental justice in Japan. Ikeda situates justice as the assumed issue in justification, which 'tries to achieve what people think is right, in relation to the environment.' In his argument, he ventures a restrictive interpretation of the polysemic concept of 'justice,' and considers, from a sociological viewpoint, the question: 'What kind of things do people think are right, in relation to the environment?' Derived from this are 'four theories of environmental justice as background hypotheses of environmental sociology,' comprising 'environmental justice in the community,' 'utilitarian environmental justice,' 'environmental justice as distributive justice' and 'environmental justice as a remedy to passive environmental injustice,' and Ikeda indicates that the task of environmental sociology is to dredge these up subjectively and establish theories of environmental justice as medium-spectrum normative theories (2005, pp. 5–7). In this section, in line with Ikeda's argument, I will first organise the salient features of the four theories of environmental justice which the environmental sociology approach includes as its underlying hypothesis, then add 'participatory-democracy-oriented environmental justice,' which strives to conquer elitism, as a new point of contention in environmental justice theory, and clarify the situation of 'fairness' within Japanese environmental sociology, from its relationship with theories of environmental justice.

'Environmental justice in communities'

Both life-environmentalism (including Torigoe, 1997, 2004; Kada, 1995; Furukawa, 2004) and commons theory (such as Miyauchi, 2001a, 2001b; Fujimura, 2001) are environmental-sociological approaches built up through an accumulation of on-site fieldwork. Life-environmentalism is a way of thinking that 'places supreme value upon the preservation of local people's system of living,' rather than upon the natural environment or modern technology (Torigoe, 2004, p. 66). Here, the emphasis is upon what community inhabitants 'remark,' as well as their 'local knowledge,' and these become the criteria for the judgement of 'rightness' in relation to the environment. Commons theory, on the other hand, is the view that the conservation of the natural environment, native mountains and landscape is possible through their use as 'commons,' in which local residents jointly utilise and manage them. What is valued is the life-knowledge of the community dwellers, and there is the presumption of a value-judgement that local inhabitants can relate in the most 'correct' manner to the environment. In that sense, both life-environmentalism and commons theory have, as their underlying hypothesis, the 'environmental justice of communities,' underpinned by the justice theories of communitarianism, represented by the work of Walzer (1983). In other words, both are approaches which consider ways of relating to the environment, relying upon 'pluralistic and particularistic standards' of 'rightness' (community justice) inherent in each community.

If the problem is limited to one region, then community justice will probably be an appropriate criterion for judgement, and an approach which relies upon it is likely to be effective. However, environmental problems generally expand beyond community boundaries, and it is therefore quite rare for issues to be resolvable within a single community. There are also numerous cases in which confrontation over environmental justice occurs among several different communities. It is obvious that, with pluralistic and particularistic environmental justice alone, it is not possible to address all actual environmental issues. In order to respond to the environmental issues of today, in which there is a need for debate that is expanded spatially to a global scale, and temporally to a cross-generational perspective, it could be said: 'There must be emphasis on a "theory of universal justice" on various scales – in other words, a justice theory that can be constructed solely from the midst of conflict and struggle over numerous examples of pluralistic and particularistic community justice in transgressive space and time' (Ikeda, 2005, pp. 14–15).

'Utilitarian environmental justice'

Social dilemma theory has as its point of departure a focus upon dilemma conditions in which the most rational behaviour for increasing benefit for the majority of individuals gives rise to an irrational result, namely a decrease in benefit to society as a whole (Funabashi, 2003, pp. 190–197). Mathematical sociologists such as Umino introduce an approach based on social dilemma theory to environmental sociology, and explore the mechanisms and control methods of environmental issues, based upon rational choice theory (Seiyama and Umino (Eds), 1991; Misumi, 1993; Kanji, 1997 and others). Here, what is implicitly inherent in the combination of rational choice theory and social dilemma theory is the presumption that 'if the pursuit of gain is carried out based on the rational choice of each individual, then the benefit to society as a whole ought to be amplified.' Social dilemma theory – focusing its attention upon the fact that, contrary to the above premise, advantage to society as a whole declines – adheres quite faithfully to the utilitarian mode of thinking which says that justice is precisely the maximisation of 'utility,' meaning the degree of attainment of well-being of society as a whole, and it has utilitarian environmental justice as its underlying hypothesis (Ikeda, 2005, p. 16). Funabashi, on the other hand, building on the work of Umino and others, has conducted a typological treatment of social dilemmas surrounding the environment, and employs the term '"self-damaging-type" social dilemmas' to describe those social dilemmas in which the benefit recipients and adversity sufferers, who constituted the targets of Umino and colleagues' research, overlap. He further pinpointed the existence of an 'offensive dilemma,' in which benefit-recipients and adversity-sufferers do not overlap (Funabashi, 1989, 1995).

Utilitarian theories of justice have been sharply criticised by theories of social contract justice, represented by the work of Rawls (1971), as 'lacking a deep appreciation of the differences among individuals' (p. 183), and similar criticism of utilitarian theories of justice and the social dilemma theory of Funabashi et al, which takes utilitarian theories of justice as its underlying hypotheses, can also be anticipated. When aiming for the maximisation of utility for society as a whole, it is a challenge to know how to respond to the unfairness and bias which arise among constituent members of society, and it is Funabashi's indication of the 'offensive dilemma,' and the 'benefit zone–victimised zone theory' which I will discuss next, that focus upon this point.

Environmental justice as distributive justice

Benefit zone–victimised zone theory is an approach built up from the group research of Takamichi Kajita, Harutoshi Funabashi, Kōichi Hasegawa and others, through case studies associated with disputes over traffic-related pollution and issues with construction of incineration plants (Kajita, 1979; Funabashi, Hasegawa et al., 1985). 'Benefit zone' means the aggregate of persons and groups who enjoy some kind of benefit due to a given undertaking or decision, and 'victimised zone' refers to the aggregate of persons who, conversely, suffer loss or pain. In benefit zone–victimised zone theory, it has been pointed out that the form and manner of distribution of the benefit zone and victimised zone largely govern the process of expansion of pollution problems and residents' movements opposed to them; and, moreover, that the 'diffusion of the benefit zone and focalisation of the victimised zone' is advancing in contemporary society (Funabashi, 2001).

Benefit zone–victimised zone theory problematises social situations in which benefit and damage arising from environmental changes caused by human action are unfairly distributed. Benefit zone–victimised zone theory involves social justice, which focuses upon fair distribution of benefit and damage in relation to the environment as its underlying hypothesis. In that sense, benefit zone–victimised zone theory is backed by Rawls' theory of distributive justice, which says that a just society is one in which 'basic social assets ' are fairly distributed, and we can note here a commonality with 'theories of environmental justice in the narrow sense' which have been developed in the United States (Ikeda, 2005, p. 16).

Remedying passive environmental injustice

Perpetrator–victim structure theory, an analytical framework for a comprehensive understanding of pollution damage, was formulated and refined by Nobuko Iijima, a pioneer in Japanese environmental sociology. From the results of analysis of various pollution problems, starting with Kumamoto Minamata Disease and Niigata Minamata Disease, Iijima illustrated the mechanism of occurrence and amplification of damage, and the 'perpetrator structure' and 'victim structure' models which regulate the nature of victims' movements centring upon local inhabitants (Iijima, 1970, 1984, 1993, et cetera). Her work defines four levels of damage belonging to pollution issues: 1. Life and health; 2. Personality and mentality; 3. Lifestyle; and 4. Local society, plus the degree of damage at each of those levels. Iijima points out that these levels and degrees of damage are strongly governed by social factors such as the groups with which victims are affiliated, victims' social stratum, their local community, the offending enterprises, and the mass media, and she makes particular note of the reality that the social perception of damage does not progress, due to the groups to which victims belong, and their social stratum.

In addition to the injustice itself which victims face, there probably exists, in the background of such a perpetrator–victim structure theory, a strong issue-awareness that injustice to victims has to be recognised within society and rectified, yet either have not been recognised or, even if they are recognised, have been tacitly approved and allowed to go unchecked. Such issue-awareness corresponds to what Shklar has termed 'passive injustice': 'the refusal by both officials and by private citizens to prevent acts of wrongdoing when they could and should do so' (Shklar, 1990, p. 5). She asserts that, in cases of passive injustice, '[t]he voices of the victims must always be heard first,' thus giving direction to the remedying of conditions of passive injustice which are characteristically understood only by the victims, and hard for surrounding people and perpetrators to see (Shklar, 1990,

p. 81). In light of this, the perpetrator–victim structure theory, which focuses upon elucidation of the actual state of injury, can be noted as incorporating Shklar's theory of justice as its underlying hypothesis (Ikeda, 2005, p. 17).

As seen from the above, Japanese environmental sociology has been developed in four theoretical streams, each involving a different theory of environmental justice as its underlying hypotheses. In regard to this current situation, Ikeda (2005, p. 18) concludes: 'Environmental sociology needs subjectively and critically to dredge up the environmental justice theories upon which it has hitherto implicitly relied, and internalise them theoretically.' By contrast, the 'participatory democracy-oriented environmental justice' theory which I discuss next is not a background hypothesis to another theory or approach, but is a new perspective which criticises the elitism of contemporary society and explores the possibility of its conquest, starting with unfairness and injustice connected with the environment.

Participatory democracy-oriented environmental justice

It was Kiyoshi Toda who opened full-fledged debate in Japan, stimulated by the 'environmental justice' theories from the US which I mentioned at the outset. Toda (1994) focuses attention upon the elitism structurally embedded in environmental issues. A shared feature seen within such divergent societies as developed and developing economies, the socialist system, and the South–North relationship (global society) is an elitist structure in which 'in an "environmental problem cycle" consisting of 1) the causes of environmental destruction; 2) their impact; and 3) countermeasures,' it often happens that: 1) the main responsibility for environmental destruction lies with the elite; 2) the burden of its impact is foisted onto the weak; and 3) corrective measures cater to the interests of the elite (Toda, 1994, p. 18). Toda understands this structure to be an artefact of 'modern industrialised society,' which is characterised by: 1) the progressive view of history, expansionism and existentialism; 2) cycle-breaking; 3) uniformity; 4) the molecularisation of individuals; and 5) hierarchy and centralisation, and, in order to overcome this, he advocates the necessity for a changeover to a 'sustainable society' characterised by: 1) sustainability; 2) cyclicality; 3) diversity; 4) the enrichment of social relationships, and 5) self-government and horizontal networks. This changeover would be enabled by 'the simultaneous achievement of environmental conservation and social justice' – specifically, the way to accomplish this is presumed to be through the establishment of 'participatory democracy' within the process of countering environmental destruction. This precisely means the achievement of democratisation in the three dimensions; the domestic issue of the North and the South, and the North–South relationship (Toda, 1994, p. 249).

The distinctive features of such a theory of 'participatory democracy-oriented environmental justice,' focusing upon elitism, include its pinpointing of the unfair distribution of damage due to the occurrence and impact of environmental problems, and its emphasis upon the standpoint of the people concerned and the equal distribution of opportunities for participation, in relation to countermeasures. In light of the existing theoretical framework of environmental sociology outlined above, it can be seen that the theory of 'participatory democracy-oriented environmental justice' comes close to benefit zone–victimised zone and perpetrator–victim structure theories, in relation to occurrence and impact; and life-environmentalism, in relation to countermeasures, and, in that sense, shares the same issue-awareness as 'distributive justice as environmental justice,' 'environmental justice as a remedy to passive environmental injustice,' and 'environmental justice in communities.'

As discussed above, the 'fairness' concept has been greatly associated with the formation of the basis for fundamental issue-awareness in environmental sociology, which problematises the unfairness of distribution of advantage and disadvantage arising from environmental change. This issue-awareness has been tacitly incorporated as an underlying hypothesis in benefit zone–victimised zone and perpetrator–victim structure theories, and hypotheses from the United States on 'environmental justice in the narrow sense.' In regard to 1) what constitutes 'fair' distribution; and 2) from whose viewpoint does one see distribution as 'fair,' it has already been pointed out that conflict over 'fair' distribution cannot be controlled by power relations, though sufficient conscious debate is yet to be conducted. Debate over environmental justice, which has begun to gain momentum in recent years in environmental sociology, has the task of re-conceptualising 'fairness,' using the pluralistic concept of 'justice,' and can probably be located as the stimulation of issue-awareness, which hitherto implicitly has been viewed as an underlying hypothesis.

How, then, could we interpret actual examples, once they are passed through the filter of debate surrounding 'fairness,' or the environmental justice theory described above? Moreover, in these real cases, how might we subject 'fairness' and environmental justice to the scrutiny of debate? From the next section onward, I will specifically consider such points in line with issues to do with nuclear power-related facilities, and clarify the relationship of mutual interaction between experiential studies of environmental issues and the 'fairness' concept.

Case study of social unfairness: A German protest movement

Shifting the environmental burden 'outside'

As a rule, there is a strong tendency for atomic energy facilities such as nuclear power stations and facilities related to radioactive waste to be planned and constructed in a country's 'periphery,' avoiding its 'centre.' In this case, the 'centre' means an area which is in a position of relative advantage in comparison to other areas, in terms of concentration of population, economic vibrancy, political clout and governmental decision-making power, and culture; the 'periphery,' by contrast, refers to areas which are in a position of disadvantage in comparison to others (Funabashi, 2005). In Europe, for example, atomic energy facilities are often located near national borders. This is because there are fewer 'local inhabitants' there to influence policy-making, for though residents outside of those borders live in the vicinity of planned atomic energy facilities, their declarations of intent towards the policy-making of other countries have no legal force. Moreover, border areas are not only a country's 'periphery,' geographically speaking, but often also constitute an industrially and culturally backward 'periphery,' with a high unemployment rate. Construction plans for atomic energy facilities are presented in the guise of a definitive trump card for regional development in such 'peripheral regions' along borders. When seen from the viewpoint of benefit zone–victimised zone theory, this corresponds to the 'centre as benefit zone' and 'periphery as victimised zone' relation.

Funabashi paraphrases this relationship as the structure of 'shifting the environmental burden "outside."' This is when a certain area or group in society does not take on the environmental burden generated through its own production and consumption, thrusting it instead upon a different area or group which is spatially or temporally separated from it (Funabashi, 2005, p. 3). If we apply this to atomic energy facilities, we can note a 'centre/periphery' relation in which the centre, as the benefit zone, has enjoyed the electric power generated by a nuclear power station, but has pushed the environmental burden, consisting of the risk of radioactive contamination and accident that accompanies its operation, onto external locations. Furthermore, in connection to facilities dealing with nuclear waste, such as reprocessing plants and storage facilities, we see that the radioactive waste discharged along with electricity generation and the environmental burden concomitant with spent nuclear fuel not only are thrust upon the spatially-distant 'periphery,' but are also forced upon temporally-separated later generations. Such circumstances to do with nuclear power could be called typical examples of the unfair distribution of environmentally-related benefit and damage.

In this section, the campaign against the construction of a nuclear power facility which I take as an example is situated as a process that tries to perceive, critically confront, and defeat such social unfairness. I have previously taken up the case of the Wackersdorf protest campaign (1981–89) which, even among German anti-nuclear protest movements that have overwhelming people-mobilisation ability in comparison with other advanced countries, forced the cancellation of plans for the construction of a spent nuclear fuel reprocessing facility and led the federal government to abandon the plan of domestic reprocessing, and I have conducted an analysis focused upon the maintenance strategy for the movement frame[2] carried out in relation to local inhabitants by the leading group (*Träger Gruppe*) in the movement, and the movement frame of the local residents who were its recipients (Aoki, 2004, 2005). In this chapter, based on Aoki (2005), which focused upon local residents' movement framing, and conducted an analysis using the 'Letters to the Editor' column of a local newspaper, *Mittelbayerische Zeitung* (first published 1945, circulation approximately 80,000, hereafter called *MZ*), and interview data,[3] I will delve deeply into the movement framing which the local residents formed and transformed during the protest campaign development process, from the perspective of fairness and justice.

The movement setting and pre-site-occupation development process

The setting for the movement

Wackersdorf, the site both for the planned construction of a spent nuclear fuel reprocessing facility and for a movement against it, is a village of some 4,000 residents situated about in the middle of Schwandorf County (population approximately 140,000), in the

Oberpfalz administrative region (population approximately 1,090,000) of the State of Bavaria, some thirty kilometres west of the Czech border. The central metropolis of the county – the city of Schwandorf (population approximately 28,000) – lies adjacent to it. The village once thrived due to coal from the Wackersdorf coal mine which was opened in 1906, and in the 1970s it boasted the highest tax revenue in the State of Bavaria. However, when the mine was abandoned in 1982, the economic situation instantly worsened. Even from a county-wide perspective, though the Maxhütte mine situated in the southern part of the county was producing iron ore, its productivity also dwindled, and from 1982 onwards, economic stagnation became chronic. The whole of Schwandorf, which lined the Austrian and Czech borders, was cut off from the state's west, which embraced the state capital, Munich, and the famous tourist destination known as the 'Romantic Road,' and was situated in the so-called 'periphery' of Bavaria, not merely geographically, but also economically and culturally (Figure 12.1).

In Bavaria, there is an overwhelming majority of devout Roman Catholics. They constituted a strong power-base for the Christian-Social Union (CSU), a conservative political party, and supported the 'dictatorship' of Strauß, the State Premier. Wackersdorf and its hinterland were no exception, either, and conservative residents were numerous, especially in rural areas. Additionally, due to the fact that it was inhabited by many coal- and iron-mine workers, the region in question was viewed by the state government as being well-suited to the location of an atomic energy facility, its residents being submissive

Figure 12.1: The geographical location of Wackersdorf, Germany

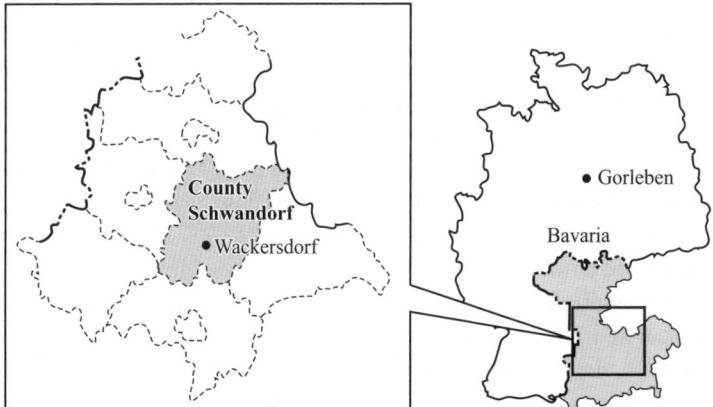

and accustomed to menial labour. In the background to the choice of Wackersdorf as the site for a spent nuclear fuel reprocessing facility, there can be noted an interest-linked structure common to the site-selection of atomic energy facilities – namely, the shifting outside of an environmental burden, taking advantage of the vulnerability of a peripheral region which is economically stagnating.

Formation of a protest campaign by local groups

In relation to this plan, rumours in Schwandorf County about candidate sites been unceasing since before the formal decision in 1985, and from 1981 on, a number of residents' groups were established, and an opposition movement centring upon petition campaigns and publicity activities was begun. There were groups of various sizes involved in the movement,[4] and the one which played the most central role was the *Bürgerinitiative* Schwandorf (Schwandorf Citizens' Action Committee, hereafter called BIS), which was established in 1981 by volunteers resident in Schwandorf County.[5] BIS was a comparatively large action group which covered the whole of Schwandorf County, and while having local chapters (*Ortsgruppen*)[6] in the form of cells in each district, it simultaneously played a leading role within all the groups in the Oberpfalz Administrative District. What BIS tackled in its inaugural period was the establishment of a regional foundation for the protest movement in the local area.

As the Bavarian state government and the Deutsche Gesellschaft für Wiederaufarbeitung von Kernbrennstoffen GmbH (German Company for the Reprocessing of Nuclear Fuels, hereafter called DWK) had proposed the construction plan, ostensibly 'leading to the creation of new employment,' there initially was no small number of residents that consented to the plan without understanding what sort of facility was to be built. In order to counter the sweet-talk of the project promoters, BIS needed to offer local residents correct information upon which to make their decision, by pointing out the problematical aspects of the planned facility, for instance. The approach to residents was made on a chapter basis, flyers being distributed which both indicated the points at issue with the plan, and simultaneously made clear the standpoint and policy of BIS. What was emphasised at that time was the fact that BIS was 'thinking seriously about the future of the area, and was a citizens' action group that transcended political, religious or business boundaries,' and that it 'was not a violent, radical group.' In addition to flyers and pamphlets, advocacy advertisements by BIS with the message: 'We are not the kind of foolish country bumpkins who would accept a nuclear power facility without complaint' were published frequently in the local newspaper, *MZ*. Physicists and chemists from the faction opposed to the project stressed the risks of a reprocessing facility. In the early stage of the protest campaign, BIS first emphasised the social unfairness contained in the construction plan, and their intention to expand their crusade against it by the legitimate means of non-violence, and aimed to increase the mobilisation of local residents.

Movement frame of local people in early stages of the movement
The first time that the spent nuclear fuel reprocessing facility issue made its appearance in the 'Letters' column of the local newspaper, *MZ*, was at the beginning of 1981, not long after the State Premier had made a declaration of acceptance for facility construction in Bavaria. From then until 1984, letters to do with the construction plan, relating to the pronouncements of politicians and the project proprietor, DWK, in the local legislature and public hearings, and from such viewpoints as the risks, merits and demerits of a reprocessing facility, were published at a rate of one per week. At this point, while criticism was concentrated towards DWK and the unfair methods of the State Premier, Strauß, who tried to force the plan ahead, hardly any criticism was seen to be directed towards the federal government. As far as the local residents were concerned, the current 'opponents' were DWK and Strauß, the Bavarian Premier, and more time needed to elapse before the federal government, lurking in the background, came to be recognised as 'the opponent.'

This trend, seen in the content of letters during the initial period of the movement, is thought to be the outcome of local residents' acceptance of the BIS approach, which emphasised the movement's local orientation. At that time, the movement frame of BIS, expressed in its publicity campaign, could be said to have resonated with that of local residents, on the point that theirs was 'a legitimate struggle to protect their area from the social injustice of having a nuclear facility imposed upon them.' From the initial stage of the movement, the movement frame of BIS was accepted by the local residents. The number of participants in petitioning and protest meetings against the plan steadily grew. At that point, letters referring to the movement style were yet to be seen.

Escalation of the movement and advent of *Autonome*
In February 1985, the federal government, Bavarian state government and DWK announced the formal decision to construct a spent nuclear fuel reprocessing plant in Wackersdorf, and the village authorities voiced their acceptance of the facility. In the movement's early period, BIS had continued comparatively moderate activities such as petitioning and publicity campaigns, but from February 1985, when the location was formally decided, the movement also arrived at a big turning point. As I show in Table 12.1, moves relating to the construction plan accelerated in 1985, with a tentative site occupation (August), and a fully-fledged site occupation (December–January the following year) to oppose the start in December of forest clearing at the projected construction site, and so on. Comparatively radical members in BIS stepped up their influence, and their mode of opposition increasingly involved direct action, resulting in some arrests. It was also around this time that violent youth called *Autonome* began to turn up at the planned construction site from urban areas all over the German Federation.

Against the backdrop of these circumstances, an increasing number of letters relating to the construction project and the protest campaign were published in the 'Letters to the Editor' column from 1985, making a total of 116, more than double the fifty of the previous year. References to violence began to be conspicuous, and most were critical of violent action. There were repeated letters from local residents arguing that violent youth should not be accepted for the sake of the success of the protest campaign, and these threw doubt upon the movement policy of BIS, which tacitly approved their participation.[7]

From 1985 onwards, when *Autonome* began to participate in the movement and protest action gradually escalated, there was growing aversion among local residents towards those young people who were committing violent acts on the momentum of the anti-nuclear crusade, and irritation towards the way the behaviour of these youths was giving the police an excuse to intervene. At this point, as far as the residents were concerned, the opposition movement was 'a legitimate motion of objection, conducted as legally as possible, in order to preserve their home area from the social injustice of the one-sided imposition of radioactive contamination,' and it was thought that *Autonome*, who employed the illegitimate means of violence, ought not to become involved in the movement scene. There was strong

Table 12.1: Events related to the nuclear reprocessing plant in Wackersdorf

Month and Year	Principal Events
Sep 1979	Federal-state agreement on Nuclear Reprocessing Plant (NRP) construction in (West) Germany.
Dec 1980	Bavarian State Premier, F. J. Strauß, announces Bavaria's acceptance of NRP.
Oct 1981	*Formation of 'Bürgerinitiative (Citizens' Action Committee) Schwandorf (BIS).'*
Nov 1981	Demonstration (about 2,000 participants in Regensburg).
Dec 1981	Deutsche Gesellschaft für Wiederaufarbeitungsanlage Kernbrennstoffen GmbH (DWK) (German Company for the Reprocessing of Nuclear Fuels) announces three possible NRP sites (Steinberg, Teublitz, *Wackersdorf*).
May 1982	Protest assembly (about 15,000 participants in Schwandorf).
Sep 1982	Protest assembly (about 10,000 participants in Regensburg).
Feb 1985	*DWK formally decides to construct NRP at Wackersdorf.* Protest assembly in Schwandorf and other cities and towns (about 3,000 participants in Schwandorf).
Aug 1985	*Trial site occupation (in Taxöldener's Forest).*
Oct 1985	Protest assembly and protest march (about 50,000 participants in Munich).
Dec 1985	*Commencement of tree-felling in Taxöldener's Forest.* Short ground occupation. *Protest assembly (about 40,000 participants in Wackersdorf). Start of the long ground occupation (with about 2,000 participants).*
Jan 1986	Culture Festival at the occupied site. *Forced clearance of site occupation. Resumption of forest-felling work.*
Mar 1986	Demonstrators and police clash at construction site. First death among protesters. Easter March (6,000–10,000 participants in Wackersdorf).
April 1986	*Reactor disaster in Chernobyl.*
May 1986	'Pfingsten March' (in Taxöldener's Forest).
	'Anti-NRP Festival' (in Taxöldener's Forest).
Oct 1986	Anti-NRP classical music concert held in Regensburg; performance of Haydn's oratorio, *Schöpfung*.
Oct 1987	Protest assembly (in Taxöldener's Forest); protesters clash with Berlin riot police.
Apr 1989	VEBA, a principal company in DWK, suggests an alliance with the French company, COGEMA, in relation to the NRP. Prime Minister Helmut Kohl also announces a 'two-pillared (Franco-German)' policy.
May 1989	*DWK decides to cease construction.*
June 1989	Germany and France sign a formal agreement to process nuclear fuel used in German reactors at La Hague (France).

rejection by the local residents of participants from elsewhere, who were mainly young people, and the movement remained closed to outsiders.

Site occupation and local residents' movement frame

Outline of the site occupation in Wackersdorf

Even within BIS, opinion was divided as to how to distance itself from *Autonome*, but when the construction plan went ahead and forest clearing was begun, the protest campaign side implemented a site occupation in earnest, in order to take a stand against it. On 21 December 1985, some 2000 out of the approximately 40,000 participants in the protest meetings held in the village moved into the forest where the projected construction site lay, and formed a 'solidarity village (*Hüttendorf*).' In this 'solidarity village,' dubbed the 'Freie Republik Wackerland (Liberal Republic of Wackerland),' about twenty huts were built, and the village was also equipped with a communal kitchen, information bureau, assembly hall, and so on. An onsite radio station was also established, and access broadcasts were made over shortwave. Most of the inhabitants of the 'solidarity village' were young people who had come from outside the local area, but local residents also sometimes stayed overnight in the huts. Large quantities of food and daily necessities were sent in by the local residents. A Mass was celebrated on Christmas Eve, and a get-together to mark the New Year was held on New Year's Day, and, in addition, a culture festival was held on 5 January 1986. Various items were staged, including a rock concert, chalking up approximately 15,000 attendees.

In the early morning of 7 January, two days after the culture festival, the 'solidarity village' was forcibly cleared by a police squad that was sent in, closing the curtain on the site occupation after sixteen days. During the eviction, the police squad used helicopters, water cannon trucks and armoured vehicles to smash the huts, and drove the 'residents' away. As well as a large number of arrests,[8] there were quite a number of casualties, the majority being youths who had come from outside the local area.

The dynamic state of local residents' movement framing

Through its launch into direct action, meaning the site occupation, the movement exerted a powerful impact upon the community at large, and caught the media limelight. How, though, were such activities interpreted by residents who had originally hoped for moderate action?

As I have previously stated, many young people from outside the local area came to the site occupation. Among them were some black-masked *Autonome* members, as well, but it was guitar-carrying, long-haired 'hippie youth' and 'punk youth' with hair dyed red and green that constituted the majority of 'solidarity village dwellers.' At first, it seems that there was embarrassment among some local residents at coming into contact with the hippie and punk youth. However, the experience of taking in food and suchlike and spending time together with them in the day-time, or occasionally conversing with them until late at night around the bonfire progressively changed local residents' preconceived notions about the young people. In response to a letter to the newspaper from the pro-project faction which criticised the site occupation as 'a bunch of thugs,' there was even a letter of rebuttal from a resident, saying: '[M]any people have spent several days at the site and come into contact with the thinking of the squatters...You, who have no knowledge of the scene, should have no right to criticise.'[9]

On the other hand, when the site occupation came to an end with its forced removal, it was letters confessing the fear and bewilderment felt by local residents at the time of the eviction that were sent to the 'Letters' column.[10] This was because the police at that time differed from those sent in previously. Until then, supervision had been provided by the Bavarian State Police, and, in many cases, especially, local police officers were deployed. It was not rare for the protesting residents and the police to know each other, and the police were perceived as 'friendly.' By contrast, it was federal border police and riot police from Berlin that were deployed for the first time in this forced eviction. Being alien to the locality, they ruthlessly went ahead with the task of clearance, without feeling. The eviction scene was filled with an unprecedented, formidable atmosphere.

Such an experience of coming into conflict with the newly-deployed, hostile police squad and having a sense of personal danger was something unexpectedly traumatic for the local residents. The federal border police and riot police were the embodiment of state power, and, through this experience, the local residents were led willy-nilly to a realisation of the power of the state. The target of the forced expulsion was not *Autonome* alone. Not only were hippie and punk youth forced into patrol wagons, but there were also even incidences of local residents being restrained. At this stage, local residents were made to realise[11] that 'in fact, [they], too, had come to be viewed by state power as the enemy.'[12] After January 1986, when the camp was removed, destructive action by *Autonome* at the construction site escalated in intensity, and there were numerous fierce clashes between them and riot police, who retaliated with water cannons and tear gas.[13] However, following the forced clearance, letters criticising *Autonome* were seldom seen. In their stead, there was increasing criticism towards the riot police and the federal government which had sent in the riot police to subdue the scene.[14]

The process of transformation from a movement which was, for the residents, 'a legitimate struggle to protect their area from the social injustice of having a nuclear facility imposed upon them,' to a 'confrontation with state power, which could undermine its own justice,' becomes clear from an ordering of the dynamic state of local residents' movement frame before and after the site occupation. An examination of the relationship with the movement frame upheld by BIS shows that, initially, the movement frames of local residents and BIS were in sympathy on the point that theirs was 'a legitimate struggle to protect their area,' and this encouraged the mobilisation of local residents. However, when *Autonome* began to appear on the scene and the movement intensified, a gap opened between the movement frames of BIS and local residents over the pros and cons to do with the question of 'how far the movement should commit to non-violence.' As discussed in detail in Aoki (2004), BIS was prepared to accept violence by *Autonome*, using the logic of a double standard of violence, but local residents' criticism of *Autonome* did not cease. During the site occupation which BIS had launched while still burdened with this issue, local residents also experienced confrontation with the police at the time of the forced clearance. As a result, even the local residents themselves, who had criticised the existence of *Autonome* as 'illegitimate,' came to be seen in the eyes of state power as an 'illegitimate' presence, and they strongly perceived that the movement itself also was being labelled 'illegitimate.' As I will elaborate later, this represented to the local residents an erosion of 'the justice granted by the state (legitimacy),' and, at the same time, resulted in the formation of a new collective identity.

Local residents' movement frame and development of the movement

What kind of impact, then, might such a transformation in the movement framing of the local residents have had on the actual development of the movement? Let us consider this issue by focusing upon the structure of conflict over the social fairness, legitimacy and justice which arose between the project promoters and their opponents.

The structure of confrontation prior to the site occupation
The thing that existed from the time of the movement's initiation between the promoters of the plan and its opponents was a fundamental disagreement as to the advisability of the social fairness of the very policy of constructing a reprocessing facility in a peripheral area.

The promoters advocated that the reprocessing facility construction plan was a valid policy for enabling a stable supply of energy and for upgrading the domestic industrial base, and that it was an action that incorporated social justice, leading also to the invigoration of a depopulated area. Their response was that opponents of the plan constituted an unjust presence that ignored the shared benefits of a stable supply of energy, and that the protest campaign lacked legitimacy. In counter to this, to the local residents who were anxious about the risk of radioactive contamination, and who objected to being seen as 'compliant,' and having a 'hazardous facility' thrust upon them, it was their natural right to oppose the plan in order to guarantee the safety of their own lives and protect their livelihoods, and the protest movement was 'a valid defence against social injustice.' It was the local residents' assertion that it was the promoters' way that lacked justice, as they attempted to push a 'hazardous facility' onto a peripheral area, sweet-talking the populace and exploiting the area's weakness in terms of economic stagnation; and that it was the construction plan itself, in which total safety was not guaranteed, that ought not to be allowed.

At the same time, there existed two different movement styles in response to the imposition of a 'hazardous facility' – one which condemned the promoters' wrongs by committing itself to non-violence, and adhering to orthodox resistance; and another which saw as inevitable the resort to violent force in order to fight injustice. It was BIS and the local residents that took the former standpoint, while it was *Autonome* that took the latter. The local residents saw their own movement style as legitimate, offering resistance by non-violent means, and perceived *Autonome*, which resorted to violence, as an illegitimate presence, and the disjuncture between the local residents and *Autonome* was decisive on this point. In contrast to this, the promoters saw all their opponents as adversaries, irrespective of their movement style, and all their adversaries as an illegitimate presence. They denounced as illegitimate the existence of *Autonome*, the perpetrators of violent acts, and, in the same way, also called illegitimate the existence of the local residents who (in their view) had accepted *Autonome*. It was the promoters' logic to use legitimate means, namely the deployment of police, to suppress the opposing force which (in their eyes) had turned into a mob.

As the above illustrates, the structure of confrontation prior to the site occupation consisted of two axes of conflict relating to the social justice of the reprocessing facility plan itself and the legitimacy of movement styles. The pro-construction actors were the trio made up of the federal government, the state government and DWK, but, at that time, it was the state government of Bavaria and DWK that regarded the local residents as direct 'adversaries' (Figure 12.2).

The structure of confrontation after the site occupation

This conflict structure changed dramatically through the site occupation. The local residents who had come face-to-face with

Figure 12.2: Structural outline of the confrontation (prior to site occupation)

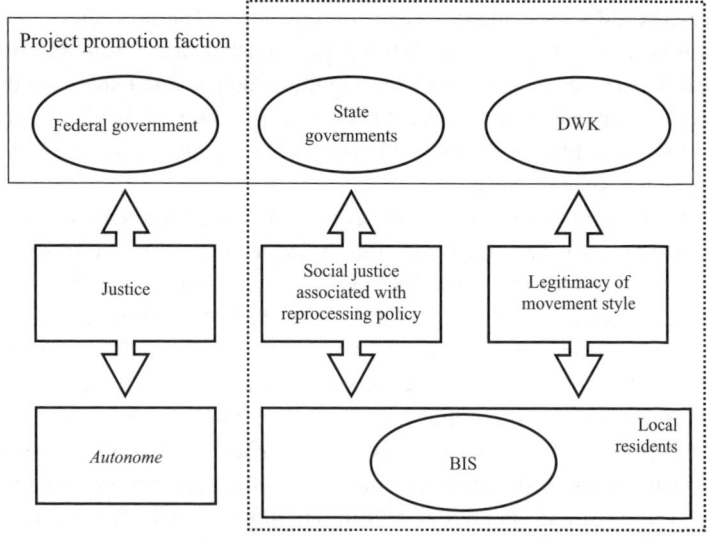

·········· Extent of the 'movement' perceived by local residents

state power at the time of forced eviction were made to realise that their 'adversaries' were not only the state government and DWK. At the same time, committed as they were to non-violence, the local residents who were on the receiving end of the deployment by state power of brutal police came to a realisation that non-violence was not going to secure their own legitimacy, and that even they themselves, who were merely 'exercising their rights,' were nothing but an illegitimate group in the federal government's opinion, and that they were being stripped of their legitimacy. It was not only the residents who happened to be on the scene of forced removal who arrived at this conclusion. The majority of local residents who did not happen to be present at the scene saw, amid the scenes of forced eviction that were repeatedly screened on the evening news, the figures of neighbours standing dazed with shock at the deployment of riot police, and those of acquaintances vigorously protesting. The local residents, some of whom were BIS members, came to share a movement frame of 'confrontation with state power which could destabilise their own legitimacy,' and went on to develop a confrontational stance vis-à-vis the federal government.

What was most important for local residents at this time was to win justice for opposition to the reprocessing policy. The axes of conflict to do with social fairness in relation to reprocessing policy and the legitimacy of movement styles, which had hitherto been duplicated, were consolidated into an axis of conflict surrounding the justice of their very existence. To the local residents, their own justice was something which no longer was protected by the legitimacy granted by the state, but something that they themselves had to preserve, and win from the state. Among those local residents who self-consciously began the struggle to preserve their own justice there arose an empathy towards *Autonome*, which had been labelled an illegitimate presence by state power, as they themselves had been, and, in addition, there was growing concern for other locations, such as Gorleben, where temporary and permanent storage facilities for high-level radioactive waste were located. For local residents, 'we' meant 'people confronting state power over the issue of the justice of their own existence,' and this point enabled an alliance with *Autonome* that transcended the difference in their movement styles, and partnership with the residents of other locations also became possible (Figure 12.3).

In this chapter, using the example of a protest campaign against a spent nuclear fuel reprocessing facility in Wackersdorf, I have examined the transformation process in the movement frame of

Figure 12.3: Structural outline of the confrontation (after site occupation)

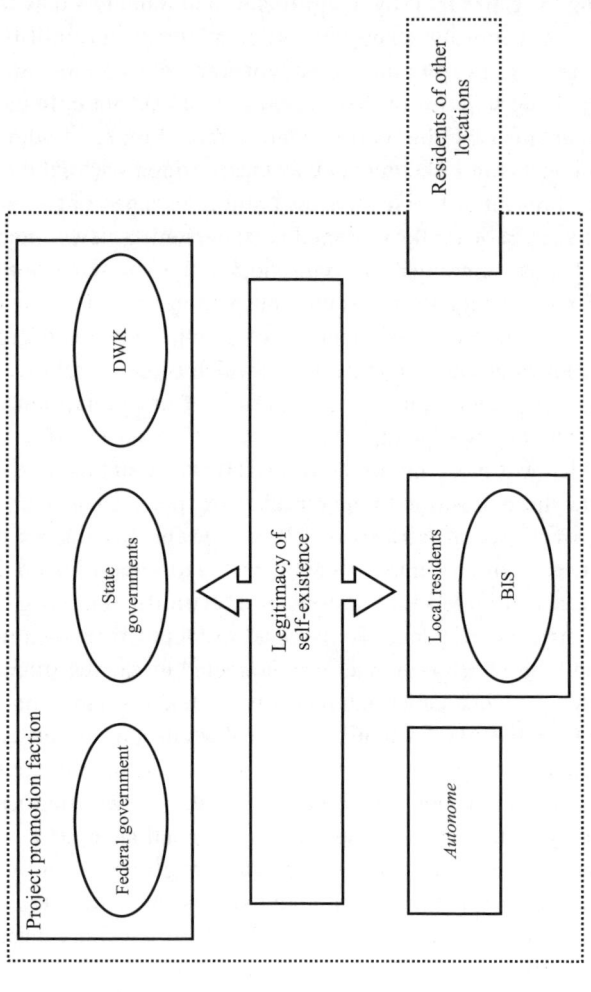

········· Extent of the 'movement' perceived by local residents

the local residents opposed to the facility, and the influence of that transformation. What this illustrates is the process by which local residents that had been forced to change their collective identity attempted de-authoritarianisation, even while feeling bewilderment. The reason why many locals headed for the site of conflict, even though the actual action came to contradict the movement's original ethos, was not because they accepted the strategy of the leading groups, but because they sensed a danger in their own justice having been shaken by state power, and they came to share a movement framing that the local residents themselves formed through their own actual experience. The local residents who were denied the collective identity of 'we who alert society through legitimate means to the wrongdoing of the "opponent",' and who had to take on the collective identity of 'we who have been stripped of legitimacy by state power,' attempted to overcome the undermining of their justice by state power by the shaping of a new movement frame: 'struggle over self-legitimacy.' Relying on this new movement frame, the local residents made the axis of conflict with the promoters of the project converge with the axis to do with the justice of the reprocessing policy and nuclear energy policy itself, and, by extension, the very justice of their own existence, and simultaneously went on to expand the parameters of 'we.' At that time, it even became possible to subsume the violent *Autonome*, and their alliance with other localities which had a similar relationship with state power pushed forward.

If we view this from the perspective of environmental justice theory, we can appreciate it as a process of conversion from community justice, which involves life-environmentalism and commons theory, to universal justice. Initially, a kind of environmental justice peculiar to the area in question, which said, 'Violence is absolutely out of the question, even to save the environment,' was predominant among local residents, but, through the site occupation, a universal environmental justice able to be shared with other groups and groups in other areas, which said, 'If it is to save the environment, then a certain degree of violence is permissible,' became ascendant. Sublimation occurred here, starting from a kind of community justice in the area at issue – which, in answer to the question: 'Should we protect the environment even if it means sacrificing our own legitimacy?' held that: 'The securing of legitimacy should take priority' – and moving towards justice for the common good, which said: 'The environment should take priority.'

Suggestions for Japanese environmental justice studies

In this chapter, through the medium of environmental justice theory, I have located the concept of 'fairness' in environmental sociology, and have applied this to actual case studies. It has become clear from my analysis that there is a dual meaning embedded in the concept of 'fairness' assumed by environmental sociology – a concept of 'fairness' corresponding to Rawls' 'distributive justice' and a concept of 'fairness' corresponding to a state in which the 'passive injustice' described by Shklar has been rectified. Both of these are implicitly underlying hypotheses to the perpetrator–victim structure theory and the benefit zone–victimised zone theory, which are used for an objective understanding of the problem structure surrounding examples. Through the examples in this chapter, I have indicated the circumstances of 'the shifting outside of an environmental burden' relating to atomic energy facilities, from the viewpoint of benefit zone–victimised zone theory. Moreover, from the perspective of the perpetrator–victim theory, the occurrence of 'passive injustice,' whose circumstances are apparently difficult for operating bodies and state and federal governments to apprehend, has also been made clear. The first refuge for inhabitants of an area who resist such social injustice is environmental justice in the community, which is a background hypothesis to life-environmentalism and commons theory. In the examples in this chapter, this environmental justice in the community has been identified as a sublimation process leading to universal environmental justice, in the process of development of movements.

The majority of environmental movements which have been targeted by Japanese environmental sociology are those in the form of residents' campaigns which the local residents of a given area developed with the goal of solving an environmental problem or achieving coexistence with the environment. Of these, protest movements against large-scale public-works projects such as dam construction and crusades by local residents against so-called 'nuisance facilities' such as nuclear energy facilities have tended to be disparaged as 'regional egotism' or 'NIMBY (Not In My BackYard) movements.' The logic used by those who promote the construction of large-scale public works projects and 'nuisance facilities,' and by the 'centre,' which tries to impose nuisance facilities onto the 'periphery,' says: 'While refusing to accept "nuisance facilities," they themselves "enjoy the blessings" (of those facilities)…and reap the benefits. That's egotistical.' (Takagi, 1999, p. 202). Debate on the need to incorporate 'universal environmental justice' into movements is just beginning in Japanese environmental sociology, with the aim of defeating such criticism.

Up until now, however, it was understood in Japan that universal environmental justice was intrinsically incorporated in German local protest movements. This is due to the fact that though the 'citizens' action committee (*Bürgerinitiative*)'[15] movement style peculiar to German local protest movements actually had the dual nature of both a citizens' and a residents' movement, it was interpreted as being a 'citizens' movement' within the context of the 'citizens'/ residents' movements' typical of Japan. Honda (2001) assesses the *Bürgerinitiative*, which is an organisation open to outsiders, as being different from a Japanese residents' movement, which has a strongly exclusionist character, and he points out that the universal value orientation which German protest movements have is intrinsic to those movements from the beginning. However, what the case study in this chapter makes clear is the actual conditions in a movement where, at the start, there was a strong, residents'-movement-like character, especially in that it was closed to violent participants from outside. It was in the process of the local residents forcefully hammering out an opposing stance against state power, and in the process of asking the government 'What is legitimate policy?' and demanding rectification of social injustice, that this closed nature was breached.

Specifically, it was universal environmental justice, which the local residents thus gained in exchange for the wavering of their self-justice, that was the condition for the granting of openness to local protest movements, and what made possible the acceptance of participants from outside, as well as the formation of networks between movements spanning regional margins.

The point of this chapter, that 'universal environmental justice,' which had been understood to be essentially inherent in German local protest movements, was actually something which was won through trial and error by movement leaders, in the process of movement development, can be said to furnish a clue with which Japanese environmental sociology and the environmental movement itself can face and conquer criticism of 'regional egotism' and of the 'NIMBY' movement.

13 The Procedural Fairness of Public Participation in Environmental Planning: The Karlsruhe Project

Yukio Hirose

Introduction

What might be the prerequisites for the social acceptance of controversial environmental planning? Given that merely providing information as to the social dividends which could be anticipated from a particular plan is insufficient for consensus to be built in the whole community, it has begun to be argued that the establishment of a wide range of opportunities for public participation in the plan-drafting process is indispensable. In response to the antipathy which has arisen between the public and stakeholders, with their diverse values, and the concomitant failure of communication between experts and ordinary citizens, various participatory conference methods for consensus-building for the sake of resolution of environmental issues, including consensus conferences and planning cells, have been developed in recent years, mainly in the European Union (EU) (Renn, Webler and Wiedemann, 1995; Smith, 2003; Shinotō, 2005). In fact, participatory conferences aimed at consensus-building through discussion among the general public and stakeholders, they having been provided with information from experts, have already been employed in cases of environmental planning relating to such matters as traffic or waste, but it has not yet been made clear what kind of participatory procedures would be evaluated as fair, and, moreover, whether a plan would gain public acceptance if the procedures were judged to be fair.

Examples of research fields related to this theme include procedural justice studies in social psychology and studies of public participation procedures in political science and sociology. However, these respective studies have been carried out independently of each other, and theoretical interchange and synthesis hitherto has not been undertaken. While the former has consisted mainly of empirical research through experiments and surveys investigating the effect of procedural justice upon beneficiaries' degree of satisfaction, in terms of the conditions of distribution of resources from those in power in groups or society to the recipients of those benefits (Lind and Tyler, 1988), the latter has concentrated principally upon the development of procedures for deliberation which would bring into effect legitimate public participation in the policy-making process and the provision of information; and prescriptive studies as to what kind of requirements must be met in order for the above participation procedures to be fair (Renn, et al., 1995). In procedural justice studies in social psychology, process- and outcome controllability has been posited as a prerequisite for the constitution of procedural fairness, while concrete meeting protocols such as representativeness and information disclosure have been problematised as procedural prerequisites for the fulfilment of fairness in participatory conferences, in research into public participation procedures in political science and sociology, but there is yet to be any cross-referencing between these two branches of study. Research which deals with the development of environmental planning proposals made through participatory conferences, and which throws light upon the link between the public acceptance of plans and the procedural fairness of public participation, can be considered to have significance as a theoretical and practical expansion of social justice studies.

In this chapter, therefore, I survey the participatory conference model which has been implemented heretofore, and, after organising the criteria which constitute fairness in its participatory procedures, I discuss the example of a citizens' participation project implemented in public transport planning in the German city of Karlsruhe; by means of content analysis of project data, I conduct a normative investigation into whether the criteria for fairness in its participatory procedures was met; and, taking these together, I use statistical analysis of a social survey targeting the general public to consider whether evaluation of the procedural fairness of the citizens' participation project governed public acceptance of the planning.

A review of participatory-conference development

The participatory conferences which have been tried in the West and in Japan can be roughly classified into three types: stakeholder conferences, involving stakeholders; citizens' panel conferences, involving ordinary citizens; and hybrid conferences, which are a synthesis of the other two. Stakeholder conferences are participatory conferences involving representatives of different interest groups, typical examples of which are the scenario workshops of Denmark (Wakamatsu, 1999) and the community advisory committees of the United States (Linn and Kartez, 1995; Petts, 2001). Citizens' panel conferences are participatory conferences involving ordinary citizens who have a wide array of values, representative examples being the planning cells of Germany (Dienel, 1999; Dienel and Renn, 1995), Denmark's consensus conferences (Andersen and Jæger, 1999; Klüver, 2002), and US citizens' juries (Crosby, 1995; Smith and Wales, 1999). Hybrid conferences are those in which interested parties and a citizens' panel attend meetings separately, at different phases. The Dutch National Debate of the Netherlands (Mumpower, 1995), Germany's cooperative discourses (Renn, Webler, Rakel, Dienel and Johnson, 1993; Schneider, Oppermann and Renn, 1998) and Japan's agent role-playing conferences are typical examples (Kitani, Hasebe, Arai and Hiramatsu, 2002).

Characteristics and challenges of stakeholder conferences

The distinctive feature of stakeholder conferences is that different interest groups search for common ground among their respective private interests, through the mediation of a neutral facilitator. Representatives of groups and organisations which have a strong concern and interest in the issue participate. It can also happen that members of the general public participate as citizens' representatives. Though certain stakeholders such as business and the government might possess sufficient specialised information and knowledge, citizens' groups seldom have the opportunity to find out such things prior to meetings, and it is thus the role of experts to make sure that participants share an equal standard of knowledge and information about the issue in question (Linn and Kartez, 1995).

There are several problems with stakeholder conferences, which have such characteristics as these. Unless real representatives of interest groups participate in the meetings, compromise and consensus will not be reached, but, as members who lack responsibility and competence attend the meetings, the conferences often fail to make any progress. Moreover, coordination among interest groups often takes place behind the scenes in the form of lobbying, et cetera, rather than at formal meetings, and the conferences themselves can become a mere faēade. In addition, as participants have a strong commitment to the group interests which they represent, and they are strongly aware of the expectations of their affiliated group, it is said to be difficult for them to change their attitudes and opinions with any flexibility (Smith, 2003). Furthermore, even if members of a particular citizens' group do participate as representatives of the interests of citizens as a whole, there is also the problem that a specific individual cannot represent the entire citizenry, which encompasses a diverse range of opinion.

Characteristics and challenges of citizens' panel conferences

Citizens' panel conferences are distinctive in that they make recommendations on proposals for solutions which are based on a common understanding of issues from the standpoint of the general public, which diverges from that of the government and experts. From the perspective of public interest for society as a whole, citizens discuss issues with each other and seek common ground. Accordingly, interested parties are excluded from participation in the conferences, but often are involved in the capacity of witnesses who express opinions from their own standpoint, and supply information (Crosby, 1995). The participants at these conferences – ordinary citizens who have been randomly selected or who have answered a public call for members – are given the opportunity to hear information necessary for discussion from experts, and to deepen their understanding through interactive communication with such experts.

There are several problems with citizens' panel conferences, also. Even if the citizens' representatives are chosen by random selection, their rate of participation in meetings is sometimes low. For reference, according to Dienel's interview surveys, examples of planning cell meetings showed a participation rate of about ten to twenty per cent. Moreover, when citizens' panels are chosen by the random selection method, there is a risk that the views of one portion of citizens (stakeholders), who suffer disadvantage in such NIMBY (Not in my backyard) issues as landfill siting, will not be sufficiently reflected (Webler, 1995). Furthermore, in cases of public recruitment, the opinions of the participants sometimes happen to be skewed away from the opinion distribution of the parent population. In addition, it is sometimes difficult to gain the understanding of interested parties and the general public who were unable to participate in the conferences towards the conclusions reached by a panel in which only a portion of citizens – those whose interest was high – took part.

Characteristics and challenges of hybrid participatory conferences

What was considered as a solution to the problems with stakeholder conferences and citizens' panel conferences was the hybrid conference model (Renn, et al., 1993). The salient feature of this model is its aiming at a shared understanding of the issues through the participation of stakeholders, ordinary citizens and experts. At the stage of establishment of objectives and organisation of evaluation criteria for the planning proposal, interested parties present their opinions from the respective viewpoints of their private interests, and cover as wide a range of objectives and evaluation criteria as possible. Next, at the stage of assessing issue-resolution options, members of the general public participate from the perspective of mutual benefit, and seek common ground. In addition, experts make efforts to secure a common understanding by means of a two-way dialogue involving citizens and interested parties.

There is the implication in hybrid conferences that, in cases where agreement cannot be reached simply by debate among interested parties, the drawing of conclusions will be entrusted to ordinary citizens standing on the footing of mutual benefit (Renn, et al., 1993). However, there are also cases in which stakeholders oppose the delegation of decision-making powers to citizens. Furthermore, when the conclusions made by citizens' panels do not fulfil stakeholders' own interests, there remains the possibility that the latter will not accept those conclusions. Moreover, as two types of meetings are held in hybrid conferences, there is also the problem of high costs of implementation.

The Karlsruhe participatory project

There are three reasons why I have chosen the example of Karlsruhe from among the many participatory conferences held on environmental planning, both within Japan and elsewhere. Firstly, in this case, it had become a keenly contested issue over which citizens were divided into two opposing camps, and it was questioned whether citizens would accept the outcome of a civic referendum implemented immediately after the citizens' participation project to determine the pros and cons of the plan. Secondly, as information was provided not only by the administration, but also by NPOs and the media, citizens supposedly had a high degree of interest in the content and procedures of planning. Thirdly, it was considered that diverse opportunities for participation had been established by the hybrid conference model, involving stakeholders and citizens who were publicly recruited or randomly selected, and the prerequisites for fairness in the participation procedures had, to a certain extent, been satisfied.

Such cases enable normative investigation of the fairness of concrete procedures in participatory conferences, as well as evaluation of the procedural fairness of participatory conferences held in relation to planning, and empirical analysis of its effect upon the public acceptance of plans. Starting from 2002, we thus collected material on public participation and implemented interview surveys of people involved in the project in question and members of citizens' groups; then, in 2003, we carried out a questionnaire survey targeting the general public (Hirose, 2003; Hirose, 2005; Hirose, Ōtomo, Ōnuma, 2004).

Background to the public participation project

My explanation of the background to the Karlsruhe public participation project is based on City 2015 material (an urban redevelopment project master-plan), environmental groups' newsletters and interview surveys of municipal employees in charge.[1] The topic for discussion in this project was a future plan for a public transport system in Karlsruhe, using trams. The current public transport system is known as the 'Karlsruhe model,' which enables the carriage of passengers from neighbouring areas to the commercial and cultural facilities in the central district of Karlsruhe without changing from one transport medium to another, with an economical, integrated-fare system spanning multiple modes of transport – trains, trams and buses. In Germany in recent years, the general trend has been for public transport to decline due to an increase in vehicular traffic, and for commercial areas in the centre of small- to medium-sized cities to atrophy because of people driving to large-scale, suburban shopping malls to do their shopping. However, in Karlsruhe, the rate of growth of public transport has surpassed that of vehicular traffic, thanks to its unique public transport system, and the inner-city commercial district has maintained and expanded its function as a shopping centre. However, this transport system had problems, at the same time. Trams heading for the central city from outlying areas would bank up at the junction of multiple lines, the service was slow, and there was traffic congestion. The city asserted that there was also an increased risk of traffic accidents.

In 1996, the Karlsruhe city council proposed a plan to alleviate congestion in the central district by sinking only the S-bahn suburban tram lines running through that zone, but a majority of citizens in a civic referendum opposed the plan, and it did not eventuate. Matsuda (2002) cites high construction costs, a lengthy construction period and safety issues with underground tram stops as reasons for that outcome. The absence of opportunity for discussion and engagement through public participation between the plan having been proposed and the referendum could also be considered a factor in the failure to gain the understanding of the citizens.

Even after the referendum, traffic congestion in the central urban district worsened due to the opening of new lines and the extension of existing lines into outer suburbs. The city council decided that a plan was needed to solve the problem of congestion in the central district and to address projected future passenger increase, and proposed a comprehensive urban redevelopment project, City 2015, three years after the previous civic referendum, following the lifting of a moratorium. In its promotion of the project, the city council made the following recommendations: 'Goal-setting, planning and options need to be examined by the open method of public participation, and thoroughly debated by citizens and visitors from other centres. It is especially imperative for there to be extensive talks among citizens before any policy resolutions by the city council or the referendum to follow,' and it set up a citizens' participation project management committee consisting of councillors from various parties in the city council.

An outline of the public participation project

Figure 13.1 shows an outline of the public participation process up till a civic referendum on the transportation plan. The public participation process can be divided largely into five phases, namely: a report on the transport reform plan by stakeholders, including the transport alliance and retailers; a report on the transport reform plan by a citizens' panel conference made up of ordinary citizens recruited by public subscription; comments by a group of experts on the publicly-recruited citizens' panel's recommendations on the transport reform plan; and a report by a citizens' panel conference of ordinary citizens randomly selected from within the city and surrounding areas. After this is the referendum, the most important thing in which all citizens can directly participate. The period between the stakeholders' report

Figure 13.1: Procedures of citizen participation in Karlsruhe

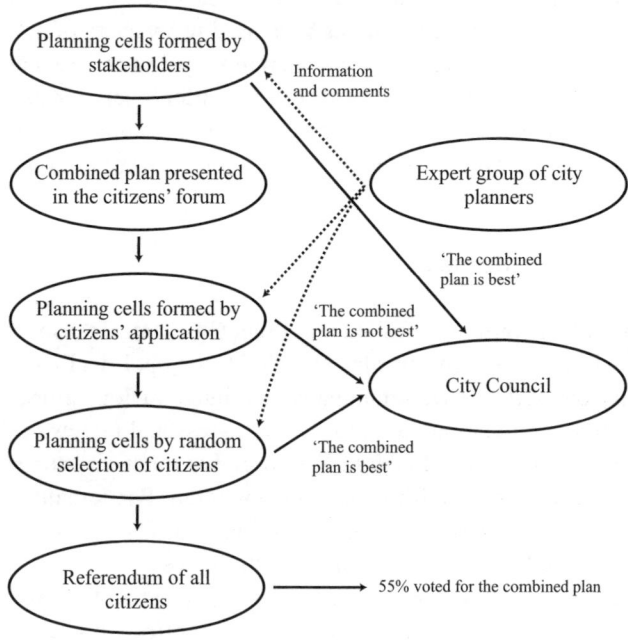

Source: Hirose et al., 2004

to the city council and the referendum was approximately one year and four months.

The principal opportunities for public participation in which citizens could voice their opinions on the planning proposal and be involved in reporting on it were the stakeholder conference and the two types of citizens' panel conference. Whichever the conference, the procedure followed that of planning cells, creating multiple groups dealing with the same agenda, and employing the method of independent and parallel debates.

'Planning cells' mean a collection of small 'cells' which have the function of examining the same plan simultaneously with other cells. An ample number of citizens – between 100 and 500 – is chosen at random to form a single 'work circle' (plenary session), and 'working groups' are set up by dividing participants into multiple 'cells,' each with twenty-five members. When discussion is to take place, these are often further divided into subgroups of about five members each. According to Dienel (1999), in formal planning cells, participants meet for sixteen sessions of ninety minutes each over four consecutive days, and create a report as a whole. This method was devised in the 1970s, and has been used in a variety of planning in countries such as Germany, Switzerland, Spain and Israel at both community and state level. At all of the conferences in Karlsruhe, meeting time was reduced to half that of formal planning cells, and participants in two out of the three conferences were not randomly selected.

Stakeholder conferences

A stakeholder conference called the 'Inner City Tram Transportation Work Circle,' representing such stakeholders as political parties on the city council, the tram company, retailers, various guilds, and community associations, was formed to assess and review multiple options for settling the dual issues of resolving inner-city congestion and securing capacity for tram transportation. Participants broke into a number of working groups for discussion. The focus of debate was upon the following three solution strategies:

The first was a proposal to reduce tram traffic on the inner-city Kaiserstrasse by laying additional surface tramlines in streets to the south, including Kriegstrasse. The second strategy proposed first to sink suburban tramlines underground, and then move the city tramlines from Kaiserstrasse to somewhere else, in order to banish surface trams altogether from Kaiserstrasse. The third proposal was to leave the Kaiserstrasse tramlines in place, and sink only the suburban tramway underground.

Representatives of each of the working groups brought their own recommendations to the plenary session, and, after discussion, the representatives voted, a great majority agreeing with the proposal for an underground tramway. The proposal to leave the tram network above ground did not achieve a majority. The stakeholder conference's recommendation was for a plan combining the sinking of the suburban tramway under Kaiserstrasse and the laying of extra lines in Kriegstrasse.

The publicly-recruited citizens' panel conference

The project management committee held a citizens' forum to call for participation in a publicly-subscribed citizens' panel conference. At the forum, a group of five urban planning experts first reported on the basic concepts relating to future planning for the central district, then, a question-and-answer session was held between the experts' group and the citizens in attendance. As well, there was a request for participation in a citizens' panel conference in which the general public would report to the city council on the planning proposals.

Some 500 citizens applied to join the citizens' panel conference scheduled for January and February 2002. Each applicant joined a working group with a theme of interest to her/him, from among a range of themes about future planning for inner-city transportation (inner-city tram transportation; expansion of pedestrian zones; motor vehicles and bicycles; and so on). Any one working group comprised a maximum of thirty members, and a total of nineteen groups were formed, but a whole twelve groups discussed 'inner-city tram transportation,' the same topic as at the stakeholder conference.

Each working group met once per fortnight for a total of four meetings, each lasting three hours on a weeknight at a local primary school or the like, in the presence of a neutral facilitator. The sequence of the four meetings was as follows:

The main topic for discussion at the first meeting was an analysis of the current situation. Participants aired their own opinions on the merits of having tramlines in the inner city (the various functions of the lines, and so on), and its demerits (problems including traffic congestion and accident risk). Through the task of classifying the content of every opinion, all members shared a wide-ranging awareness of the merits and demerits of having trams in the inner city. They discussed what material would be necessary for consideration of the plans, and requested the secretariat to prepare such material for the next meeting.

The main topic at the second meeting was the setting of future objectives. Members heard explanations of the material, such as projected passenger numbers stemming from the sinking of the suburban tramway and financing of the construction costs, and discussed the contents. Next, they broke into sub-groups of five to discuss the goals that inner-city transport ought to achieve in future. Finally, all the members held a discussion in order to coordinate the objectives coming from each sub-group.

The principal item on the agenda at the third meeting was solution strategy proposals for realisation of the future objectives. Participants tabled options for achieving those goals, and went on to bring them together through discussion. In the process, they also considered the merits and demerits of each solution.

At the fourth meeting, the main topic was the compilation by the whole group of a report based upon analysis of the present situation, future objectives and resolution strategies. The four meetings of the working group ended with the election of a representative to attend the plenary session, which would combine all of the reports.

At the plenary session, the recommendations of each group were reported by its respective representative. All twelve groups which discussed the resolution of congestion in the inner city agreed to a reduction in tram traffic in the central district. As a solution strategy, ten groups endorsed the relocation of lines to the more southerly Kriegstrasse, while seven approved of the sinking of the suburban tramway under Kaiserstrasse, but all of the groups positioned as an alternative the proposal to sink the suburban tramway but to leave the city tramlines on the surface. The citizens' panel conference recommended that the main solution strategy be the relocation of tramlines from the central district to other streets, but that sinking the suburban tramway would be a next-best strategy in case the tramline-relocation strategy were not effective. This diverged from the recommendations of the stakeholder conference, which offered the sinking of the suburban tramway as the best solution.

The experts' group forum

Five groups of experts made comments on the reports from the publicly-recruited citizens' panel conference and the concrete resolution strategies. As a solution strategy to inner-city congestion, they saw the relocation of city tramlines as being insufficiently effective as a sole remedy, the sinking of the suburban tramlines being assessed as the only way to solve the problem. At an expert forum held over two days in May 2002, the experts' groups announced the results of their evaluation of the feasibility and effectiveness of the solution strategies proposed by the publicly-subscribed citizens' panel conference, and had a question-and-answer session with citizens.

The randomly-selected citizens' panel conference

A citizens' panel conference made up of seventy Karlsruhe residents and seventy residents from outside the city, each selected at random, was planned for July 2002. The reason for the addition of residents from outside Karlsruhe was that, as tram users, they were judged as being in the same position as the city-dwellers. From Karlsruhe, a sample of 500 people was chosen in line with the sex ratio, age composition and district population of the entire parent population of citizens, requests for participation were made, and about 100 replied that they were willing to participate. Seventy of them took part, comprising nine working groups. 300 residents from outside the city, also, were randomly selected by the same procedure from a number of towns, but as only about twenty actually participated, they made up a sole working group. Two separate weekend meetings were held, implementing the same procedure as the publicly-recruited citizens' panel conference. They discussed the recommendations from the publicly-subscribed citizens' panel conference and the experts' comments about them, and chose desirable solution strategies from among multiple options. In consequence, ninety-five per cent of participants endorsed the proposal to sink the suburban tramlines, and so all ten working groups recommended that the proposal to sink suburban tramlines in the central district was the best.

Direct voting by citizens

In September 2002, a civic referendum was held to question the pros and cons of a combined plan (*Combiplan*) for the sinking of suburban tramlines under Kaiserstrasse and the relocation of city tramlines to Kriegstrasse. It was held on the same day as the German national elections, and fifty-five per cent of voters approved the plan. The referendum brought the public participation project to its conclusion.

Normative analysis of the Karlsruhe public participation project

Public participation in Karlsruhe is an example of a hybrid-type conference – a conference with a format comprising multiple planning cells. Its main participatory phases were the stakeholder conference and two types of citizens' panel conference. Here, I will analyse whether the specific procedures of the participatory project, which was composed of three conferences, meet the criteria for fairness. To that end, I will review the normative studies relating to the criteria which should be used for the evaluation of participatory conferences. While making reference to prior research, I will first organise the principal low-order criteria constituting fairness in the participatory procedures of participatory conferences, then attempt an assessment of the participation procedures from the Karlsruhe example.

Review of normative studies on the participatory conference model

Social psychology studies relating to procedural justice also set in order the prerequisites for procedural fairness (Leventhal, 1980; Tyler and Lind, 1992). Leventhal (1980), for instance, identifies consistency, bias suppression, accuracy, correctability, representativeness and ethicality as the principal requirements for procedural fairness, but each of these requirements is organised mainly in association with the behavioural style of authority figures who allocate resources. By contrast, studies which assess the procedural fairness of participatory conferences and the reasonableness of conference outcomes (Abelson, Forest, Eyles, Smith, Martin and Gauvin, 2003; Baba, 2002; Petts, 2001; Smith, 2003; Webler, 1995) focus not upon the authorities who ran the conferences, but upon conference procedures themselves, and discuss what kind of concrete procedures are required to guarantee fairness.

Webler (1995) cites fairness and competence as metacriteria for the evaluation of various participatory conferences, and argues that, in order for these criteria to be met, there needs to be openness, meaning that everyone has the opportunity to participate; representativeness, meaning that participants are chosen so as to represent citizens as a whole; involvement in deciding upon conference procedure, such as determining the agenda; sufficient opportunity for the voicing of opinion and engagement in discussion; the reflection in planning of debate outcomes; and the provision of information necessary for discussion, and study opportunities.

Abelson et al. (2003), following the protocol for proceedings in participatory conferences, lists as the four prerequisites for fairness: the securing of the representativeness of conference participants; citizen control in the deciding of conference procedure and in discussion; provision of information at conferences; and legitimacy and accountability of decisions. Smith (2003), too, names inclusiveness and representativeness of conference participants, equality of voice, unconstrained dialogue, and a decision rule which does not limit participants' freedom as assessment criteria for participatory conferences.

Here, with reference to the preceding studies, I will classify the prerequisites for the fairness of participatory procedures under the four headings of representativeness of conference participants; provision of information to conference participants and the general public; opportunity for the expression of opinion and debate in public participation; and the legitimacy of consensus-building in participatory conferences, then go on to consider whether the Karlsruhe participatory project has fulfilled the various requirements.

Representativeness of conference participants

There is debate as to which of the two methods, random selection or public recruitment, is the fairer procedure for picking participants. With random selection, if an adequate sample is chosen, unbiased representation can be obtained from the community as a whole. This has the merits of all citizens being guaranteed an equal chance of being chosen as representatives, and, simultaneously, of realising all-inclusive participation through the gathering together of citizens with a wide range of opinions and backgrounds. However, if those out of the chosen sample who actually participate account for only ten to twenty per cent of the total, as in the EU case, then the criteria for representativeness would not be completely met. On the other hand, with the public subscription method, as any citizen who wishes to participate basically can do so, open opportunity for participation is guaranteed and voluntary, positive participation can be anticipated. However, as there is a strong likelihood that only one portion of the population which has a high interest in the agenda and stakeholders will take part, and the great majority of citizens who have no strong concern or interest will not participate, the criteria for representativeness are not satisfied. In other words, this means that one or the other method will be adopted, depending upon whether equality of opportunity to participate or openness of participation takes priority.

As the Karlsruhe public participation project implemented randomly-selected and publicly-subscribed citizens' panel conferences, and a stakeholder conference, as well, it meets both of the criteria for representativeness, namely, equality of opportunity for participation and openness of participation. The fact that about 500 citizens took part in the publicly-recruited conference means that it was not a gathering of activists and members of interest groups comprising just one segment of the public that had particular, strong views, and it can be considered highly likely that people who held a great diversity of opinion were chosen from the whole mass of citizens. Moreover, even at the randomly-selected conference, twenty per cent of the sample of 500 expressed a willingness to participate, in response to the city's request. This was the same as the highest participation rate in the examples of formal planning cells. It can be judged from the above that this participation project does fulfil the 'representativeness' criteria for fairness.

Provision of information to conference participants and citizens

One of the prerequisites for procedural fairness in participatory conferences is the sufficient provision to participants of information relating to the topic under discussion. The management committee and experts must, for example, set up opportunities for participants to gain basic knowledge about the issue to be debated through talks by specialists and onsite tours, and explain about any questions which arose during meetings or any information deemed necessary. It is desirable for there to be discussion and exchange of opinion through mutual dialogue, rather than a one-way flow of information from experts to the public.

Let us now examine the sufficiency of information-provision in the Karlsruhe public participation project from the two perspectives of conference participants and citizens as a whole.

According to the minutes of meetings in the three types of conference based on the planning cells model, it appears that neither the provision of information to participants nor the opportunity for learning was adequate, and there was bias in the way experts supplied information. For example, participants received an explanation from the conveners' side about the material necessary for debate on the public transport plan in just one of the four meetings, and it is hard to imagine that in a single, three-hour meeting there would have been sufficient time for an explanation of the material and a question-and-answer session. As there was twice the meeting time in the formal planning cells, there were many opportunities set up for information to be supplied, but in the case in point the provision of information cannot be called adequate. Moreover, there was insufficient dialogue between experts and conference participants. For example, it was not until after the close of meeting that detailed comments were made by the experts on the recommendations of the publicly-recruited citizens' panel conference, and there was no opportunity for discussion about the gap in understanding between the conference participants and the specialists. At the randomly-selected citizens' panel conference, the report from the publicly-subscribed citizens' panel and experts' negative comments towards it were presented at the beginning of the conference, but it also cannot be denied that this one-sided presentation of information might have influenced the nearly unanimous approval of the proposal to sink the tramlines – the one favoured by the experts, but not that recommended by the publicly-recruited citizens' panel. Furthermore, one characteristic of a hybrid conference is its advantage of being able to institute opportunities for communication between stakeholders and the general public, but this merit is not sufficiently utilised in the current example. It can be seen from the above argument that there was not ample provision of information to conference participants.

What was the situation, then, with the supply of information to ordinary citizens? Throughout the period of the participation project, the planning proposals, minutes of the various conference meetings and their reports were distributed at the information centre in the central district, and a bus called the 'Infobus' drove around all parts of the city, providing information. In addition, explanatory sessions were held at community associations. The progress of the planning proposals and the participation project was reported at the citizens' forum and the experts' forum, and opportunities also were set up for citizens to have discussions with the conference conveners and specialists. At the citizens' forum held prior to the publicly-recruited citizens' panel conference, there was explanation of the planning proposals from a number of urban planning groups who were the experts and publication of their comments on the stakeholder conference's report. These facts suggest that, in terms of provision of information to the general public, the tentative criteria for fairness were met.

Opportunity for open and public debate

In terms of specific opportunities for citizens to voice their own views, the public participation project had the publicly-subscribed citizens' panel conference and the forum of citizens and experts, and all participants were able to express their opinions and engage in discussion. In the citizens' panel conference, there was only half the time afforded to formal planning cells, but opportunities were set up for working groups of up to twenty members and further sub-groups of five to share and discuss their respective views.

The method of splitting conference participants into subgroups and holding discussions without fixing their membership, however, is one attempt to promote fair participation in the expression of opinion and debate (Dienel, 1999). In any group, it is usual for members to divide, as time goes on, into those who have a lot to say and those who say little. The more members there are in a group, the greater tends to be the domination of the floor by one portion of members. This is because, while members who monopolise the discussion are scarcely influenced by the social inhibition of speech due to the presence of others, the utterances of taciturn members become all the more strongly inhibited as the number of people in the group increases. Accordingly, the fewer members there are at a meeting, the smaller will be the differential among members in the amount of utterances. Small-group deliberation has the function of equalising members' participation in debate. In the public participation conferences in Karlsruhe, also, working groups of up to twenty members would be split into four subgroups, as needed, and, because discussion took place without the membership of the subgroups being fixed, all participants had greater opportunity to speak unreservedly – this, arguably, resulting in fair opportunity for voice. Consequently, one could say that the criteria for expression of opinion and opportunity for voice were being fulfilled both within and outside the meetings.

Legitimacy of consensus-building in participatory conferences

The legitimacy of consensus-building incorporates aspects of reasonableness and reliability, and methods of group decision-making and representative-selection are associated with each.

Was consensus-building in the public participation project reasonable? In other words, was the determination of conference recommendations carried out in an unbiased, rational manner? As a procedure for summing up the recommendations of multiple working groups, representatives report the conclusions of each group at the plenary session, and confirm the groups' mutual differences and commonalities.

Furthermore, the representatives of each group vote as to what has been the general consensus. When overall agreement is obtained as a result of the poll, this is deemed to be the recommendation of the plenary session. When opinion is divided, or when there are minority views, these facts are incorporated into the report.

Methods which enable a detailed understanding of the distribution of debate and the consensus in the plenary session have been adopted. From the above points, the criteria for reasonableness in relation to consensus-building in the participatory conferences could be assessed as having been met.

The random selection of planning cells can be seen as a method which considers both the representativeness of participants and the reliability of group determination by way of meetings. It is thought that, due to the repeated choice of multiple working groups from a parent population of citizens in general, participants as a whole correspond to the distribution of citizens in general with their diverse views, and, at the same time, the distribution of conclusions from the working groups also probably corresponds to the conclusions drawn in hypothetical situations which all citizens can discuss with each other. The reason for the adoption of a group-determination method in relation to a single topic debated by multiple groups seems to be that it is considered possible to deduce common ground based on the distribution of conference conclusions made by representatives chosen from society as a whole. This is probably because, if only the results of group deliberation by means of a single conference involving a small number of representatives are taken into consideration, the reliability of conjecture as to the consensus of citizens as a whole is judged to be low.

In each of the three types of conference in Karlsruhe, the conclusions of the multiple working groups converged into one, and consensus as a work circle was built. In the randomly-selected citizens' panel conference, for example, the conclusions from ten working groups were identical, and they reported that the proposal to sink the suburban tramlines was the best. At the publicly-recruited citizens' panel conference, the conclusions from the twelve groups which discussed tram transportation in the inner city largely concurred on the proposal to sink the tramlines, saying it was the next-best strategy. If each conference is taken in isolation, the reliability of its consensus-building could be considered high, but the fact that the conclusions of two conferences differed lowers the reliability. The first reason for this is the possibility that a majority of participants in the publicly-subscribed citizens' panel conference were opposed to the proposal to sink the suburban tramlines. In the social survey which the city implemented prior to the participation project, responses were split between for and against, and if one considers the outcome in which the fors only slightly outnumbered the againsts, it suggests that participants in the publicly-subscribed citizens' panel conference were skewed more towards opposing the rail-sinking proposal than towards approving it. The second reason, moreover, is that participants' judgement of the plan is likely to have been influenced by the previously-noted fact that the provision of information from experts in the randomly-chosen citizens' panel conference was, in one sense, biased. After consideration of these two reasons, there still remain some problems relating to the reliability of consensus-building in the Karlsruhe conferences as a whole.

Overall procedural fairness evaluation of the project

The Karlsruhe example of a hybrid conference can be thought to fulfil the requirements for fairness of participatory procedure on each of the two points – participant representativeness, and opportunity for debate and voicing of opinion. However, as for the requirement for provision of information in the conferences, it meets the standard in terms of supplying information to the general public, but there was insufficient provision of information to conference participants. The legitimacy of consensus-building in the citizens' panel conferences also remains in doubt.

However, debate opportunities *were* established for all kinds of citizens, including stakeholders; citizens in general, both publicly recruited or selected at random; visitors; and community associations, as well. Provision of the information necessary for decision-making in the civic referendum was also carried out not only by the administrative side through its citizens' forum or the information centre, for example, but also by the newsletters of environmental groups opposed to the sinking of the suburban tramlines, street-corner public relations campaigns, and so on. These probably gave citizens sufficient insights for discussion and making judgements about the issue, and the fact that all citizens had the opportunity to engage in decisions about the pros and cons of the plan through the referendum makes it possible to evaluate this public participation project as a whole as having fulfilled, to a certain extent, the criteria for procedural fairness of public participation, does it not?

Social survey research on the Karlsruhe project

Normative studies on public participation marshal the evaluation criteria constituting fairness, stating that all of them are necessary for procedural fairness. It is not clear, however, what kind of specific procedures conference participants and ordinary citizens might decide are important, or whether they would judge the procedures as being fair if those requirements were actually met. The Karlsruhe public participation project is thought to have offered citizens a wealth of information to help them evaluate a variety of aspects of the participatory procedure and to decide whether to accept the plans. Now, by means of a social survey targeting the general public who did not take part in the conferences, it should be possible to clarify what sort of assessments of concrete meeting procedure had a deep connection with the procedural fairness of public participation, and, in addition, to examine whether the fairness of conference procedures had any influence upon the public acceptance of the plans. Here, to that end, let me cite Hirose, Ōtomo and Ōnuma (2004), and introduce a summary of the outcome of our social survey conducted in Karlsruhe.

With earlier studies relating to procedural justice and public participation (Lind and Tyler, 1988; Renn and Webler, 1995) and a normative analysis of the Karlsruhe public participation project as its basis, our social survey set up a hypothesis such as the following: Firstly, as a factor directly regulating the social acceptance of the public transport plan, we postulated that an assessment of fairness vis-à-vis the procedures in the public participation project was just as important as the evaluation of the contents of a draft transport plan for the inner city. Next, we posited that the procedural fairness evaluation of the public participation project was governed by whether the three undermentioned prerequisites for participatory procedures were being fulfilled. In short, these were assessments as to the adequacy of disclosure to citizens of information about the plans, the opportunity to participate through debate and expression of opinion, and the representativeness of the conference participants. In consideration of the difficulty for ordinary citizens who did not participate in the conferences of making a decision in regard to the legitimacy of consensus-building, which was another requirement taken up in relation to conference procedures, this was not included among the survey items. Thirdly, we postulated that the overall evaluation of the contents of the draft public transport plans was regulated by assessment of the dividends to be generated by the plans and the costs which would arise because of it. In other words, this meant evaluation of the safety aspects intended by the plans, such as the alleviation of traffic congestion and accident risk; assessment of the planning costs, including the expenditure that accompanied the plans and noise during the works; and evaluation of the convenience aspects, such as the inconvenience of having to change from one mode of transport to another – something which was not originally designed in the plans, but was a cause for concern.

Social survey methodology

In October 2003, one year after the civic referendum, we conducted a social survey targeting citizens of Karlsruhe, selecting a sample of 300 by quota-selection based on population statistics relating to sex, age and family size in the parent population, and obtaining 280 valid responses by visiting respondents to interview them.

The question items used in an analysis of the survey results quoted here were as follows: 1) we measured social acceptance of the public transport plan with the two items: 'The outcome of the referendum is hard to accept,' and, 'I am satisfied with the outcome of the latest referendum;' 2) we measured the comprehensive assessment of the effectiveness of the plan with the two items: 'The combined plan is superior, from an overall perspective,' and, 'The combined plan is satisfactory, from an overall perspective;' 3) with seven items, we measured individual assessments of the plan's effectiveness, including: 'The traffic congestion in the inner city can be solved by the public transport plan'; 'The costs needed for the plan will be a big financial burden for the city'; and, 'When the plan becomes reality, it will be more inconvenient than it is now to change trams'; 4) we measured the evaluation of procedural fairness in public participation with the two items: 'The current public participation project was, on the whole, conducted with fair procedures,' and 'The procedures in the public participation project conducted by the city can be evaluated positively, overall'; and 5) again with seven items, we measured individual assessments of the participatory procedure, such as: 'There were some people who were not able to participate in the citizens' panel conference, even though they wanted to'; 'The city adequately explained the points at issue with the public transport plan'; and 'Citizens had ample opportunity to state their opinions.'

Results and discussion on the social survey

Firstly, from a simple tabulation of the survey items, let us examine how Karlsruhe citizens evaluated the procedures in the participatory project. It can be understood that the general public does not evaluate the public participation conferences as having met the standards for representativeness from the fact that forty-three per cent answered in the affirmative and eleven per cent in the negative to the question item on representativeness: 'There were some organisations or groups that were unable to take part in the public participation project,' while forty-nine per cent answered in the affirmative and twenty-six per cent in the negative to: 'The conference conclusions do not represent the opinions of citizens in general, because only those citizens who wanted to discuss the issue participated in the citizens' panel conference.' Next, in the question item opportunity for voicing of opinion and discussion: 'Anybody could have participated in the public participation project,' seventy-two per cent of respondents agreed and eleven per cent disagreed, while sixty-four per cent agreed and fifteen per cent disagreed with the statement: 'Citizens had ample opportunity to state their opinions in the citizens' forum and citizens' work circle,' so the criteria for opportunity for voice and debate were assessed as having been met. Moreover, as fifty-six per cent were in agreement, while twenty-nine per cent in disagreement with one question item on disclosure of information: 'The city adequately explained the problematical issues in the combined plan to the citizens,' and fifty-seven per cent for and twenty-five per cent against another statement: 'Information about the combined plan was provided in a way that was understandable to any citizen,' the criteria for provision of information in the public participation project were assessed as having been fulfilled.

In relation to the criteria for opportunity for expression of opinion and debate, and the provision of information to the general public, the survey results above were largely congruent with the normative evaluation of conference procedures in the preceding section. However, in the normative analysis, the criteria for representativeness were evaluated as having been met, though citizens gave a different assessment. This showed that citizens in general took a stern view of the bias among participants in the publicly-recruited citizens' conference and the lack of all-inclusive participation by attendees at the stakeholder conference.

How about the evaluation of procedural fairness in the public participation project? Sixty-eight per cent replied in the affirmative and fifteen per cent in the negative to the question item: 'The current public participation project was, on the whole, conducted with fair procedures.' Sixty-five per cent agreed and seventeen per cent disagreed with the statement: 'The procedures in the public participation project conducted by the city can be evaluated positively, overall.' From these results, it can be considered that the general public judged that the procedures in the public participation project were fair, overall. This result corresponds to the evaluation by normative analysis in the previous section.

Next, then, let us look at the connection between the public acceptance of the plan and its determinant factors. Five factors were obtained as a result of conducting a confirmatory factor analysis regarding the fourteen items comprising individual items on plan effectiveness and on procedural evaluation, respectively. As anticipated, the individual assessments of plan effectiveness were divided into three factors corresponding to traffic safety, transport convenience, and planning cost. The individual assessments of participatory procedure divided into two factors, contrary to expectations: disclosure of information and opportunity to participate combined into one, while representativeness branched off to become the other factor.

As a result of applying the Structural Equation Model in order to examine the links among the postulated factors, with reference to the above confirmatory factor analysis, the structure in Figure 13.2 was obtained. It was confirmed that this had a latent variable structure identical to the hypothetical model.

Figure 13.2: Structural model of public acceptance of the plan

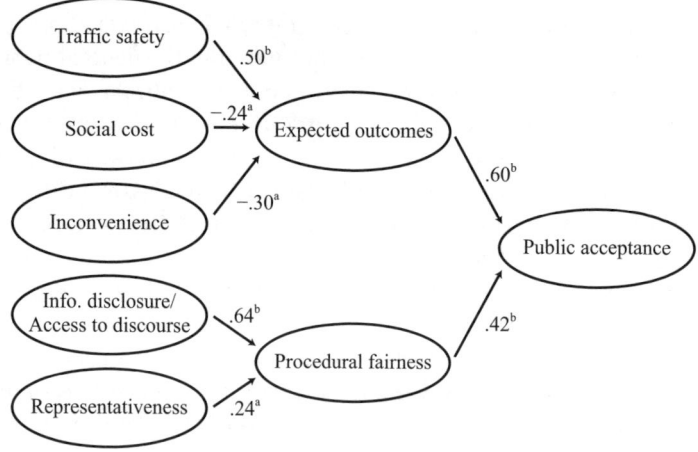

a = p < .01; b = p < .001
Source: Hirose et al., 2004

The public acceptance of the public transport plan, or, in other words, the degree of acceptance of the decision, was determined by assessments both of plan effectiveness and of the procedural fairness of public participation. As regards the acceptability (or not) of transport policy, it was shown that though it may be natural for the effectiveness of the planning it spawns to be assessed as excellent, there is a simultaneous need for the public participation procedures leading up to a residents' referendum on the pros and cons of the plan to be assessed as fair. Moreover, it was also confirmed that whether participatory procedures are fair depends upon fulfilment of the criteria requiring the adequate disclosure of information about planning, and sufficient opportunity to discuss the content of the plans and state opinions, as well as needing a wide range of citizens' views to be aired at conferences and for it to be demonstrated that the conference conclusions represent citizens as a whole. For the ordinary citizens who did not participate in the conferences, though, it was an outcome which suggested that, in terms of standards for judging whether procedures were fair, the representativeness of conference participants was made a separate criterion on its own, but the disclosure of information in the public participation project and the opportunity to discuss and voice opinions were not recognised as independent criteria.

Implications for public participation projects in Japan

I have conducted normative and empirical research in the intersecting field between procedural justice in social psychology, and public participation procedure studies in political science and sociology. I have reviewed research on the participatory conference model heretofore implemented principally in the EU, and on the evaluation of those conferences, and have classified the criteria constituting the fairness of participatory procedures into four: representativeness; opportunity for expression of opinion ('voice') and discussion; provision of information; and legitimacy of consensus-building. Subsequently, I took up the example of a public participation project implemented in public transport planning in Karlsruhe, and, through content analysis of conference material, conducted a normative examination as to whether its participatory procedures met the four criteria for fairness. At the same time, by means of statistical analysis of a social survey aimed at ordinary citizens, I considered whether assessment of the procedural fairness of the public participation project had regulated social acceptance of the public transport plan.

The results confirmed that the procedural fairness of public participation is a vital prerequisite for the social acceptance of plans created through such public participation. In addition, it was revealed that citizens recognise the importance of securing participant representativeness in meetings which recommend the plans; the establishment of opportunities to debate the plans and express opinions; and the disclosure of plan-related information, as criteria for assessing meeting procedures involving citizens' participation as fair. Furthermore, in the Karlsruhe case discussed in this chapter, upon conjunctively conducting a normative analysis of specific conference procedures and an empirical analysis by means of a social survey targeting ordinary citizens, then comparing the respective results, I was also able to confirm a certain measure of correspondence between the conclusions obtained from these two differing methods. However, with regard to the evaluation of representativeness, a disparity could be seen in the results of the two analyses. While it is necessary to apply the two methods concomitantly in order to examine whether specific participation procedures are fair, there will probably be a need in future to reconcile not only the procedural evaluations given by the general public who did not take part in participatory conferences, but also the assessments from participants who actually were involved in the conferences. It has become increasingly common for decisions on such environmental planning matters as waste disposal or transport to be made by referendum, in cases where public opinion is sharply divided. My results suggest that, for the nay-sayers to accept the result of the referendum, it is necessary for public participation procedures leading up to the referendum to be conducted fairly. Though I dealt with the sole case of Karlsruhe, there probably is a need for mutual comparison of multiple examples of public participation, not only in the EU, but also in Japan, in order to further examine what kind of participatory procedures are necessary to meet the criteria for fairness.

In Japan, too, there is a growing number of examples in which environment-related planning has been formulated through public-participation procedures. The stipulation of participation as one of the long-term goals in the 1994 Japanese Basic Plan on the Environment (*Kankyō kihon keikaku*) provided the impetus for many local authorities to adopt some public-participation procedures when developing their own basic plans on the environment and waste management. Moreover, public-participation procedures such as public hearings came to be stipulated as necessary in plan-drafting for river upgrades, thanks to the 1997 amendment of the Rivers Law. Various kinds of public-participation procedures have come to be adopted in such plan-drafting, including public recruiting of some members of plan-drafting committees, giving ear to public opinion by means of citizens' forums or questionnaires, or seeking public comment on the planning proposals, but hardly any normative or empirical analyses have been conducted thus far as to what kind of participatory procedures fulfil the criteria for procedural fairness. While there have been several recent attempts at social experimentation using public participation methods implemented in the EU (Wakamatsu, 2003; Kobayashi, 2004, Shinotō, 2005); and assessments have been made of the competence of meetings by such means as interviews with forum participants, almost no empirical studies have been carried out relating to the fairness of meeting procedures. This is why it will be necessary henceforth to build up a body of research as to what kinds of procedural fairness criteria govern the public acceptance of planning, with reference to prior studies and my research, and targeting concrete examples of public participation in Japan.

For example, by means of a social survey targeting the citizens of Tsushima City, which used public participation in its formulation of a basic plan for waste management, we (Hirose, Ōtomo, Asai and Shoji, 2005) found that the fairness of plan-drafting procedures are governed by four criteria: the representativeness of participation; provision of information; opportunity for debate and expression of opinion; and their reflection upon decision-making. It appears that citizens in Japan, too, judge the fairness of basic planning procedures in their own municipalities by almost the same criteria as in the results of the survey of the German public participation project. It is highly likely that the low-order criteria which constitute procedural fairness are shared, these criteria transcending socio-cultural differences. However, survey results from Hirose et al. (2005) also include results which refute the hypothesis that the procedural fairness of public participation is a principal regulatory factor in the public acceptance of basic plans for waste management. This result differs from that of Karlsruhe. In the Karlsruhe case, as it was an issue in which there was a conflict of opinion among citizens regarding the pros and cons of the plan, assessment of the procedural fairness of the citizens' forum could be considered also to have been the main regulating factor in the public acceptance of the plan. In examples of basic planning for waste disposal in Japan, perhaps ordinary citizens are not as interested in public participation in plan-drafting and its procedural fairness because it is not an issue upon which citizens are divided. It is with precisely such a contentious issue as that in the Karlsruhe case, where there was sharp disagreement among the citizens, that there is also a strong possibility that the fairness of participatory procedures will play a vital role.

Whichever the case, in future, there is likely to be a need to promote the theoretical and practical development of social fairness, through the accumulation of normative and empirical research into public participation in environmental planning and its procedural fairness

Notes

Chapter 2

1 For a detailed treatment of the development of studies on the 'sense of unfairness' issue in SSM Surveys, found at the beginning of the first three sections of this chapter, see Umino (2000b).
2 On the issue of fairness in stratum consciousness studies, see Saitō (1994). In relation to justice encompassing the issue of fairness, see Saitō (1998).
3 The terms 'affective evaluation' and 'cognitive evaluation' are not general terms. Though the orthodox attitudinal components of social psychology are cognitive, affective, and evaluative (or behavioural), I have ventured to use such terms in the context of our own object of analysis.
4 On Japan's social strata in general, focusing on insights from SSM Surveys, see Hara and Seiyama (1999) and Hara and Seiyama (2005).
5 The results of the Fourth SSM Survey have been published in four volumes by Tōkyō Daigaku Shuppan Kai as *Gendai Nihon no kaisō kōzō* (The stratification structure of contemporary Japan).
6 The results of the Fifth SSM Survey have been published in six volumes by Tōkyō Daigaku Shuppan Kai as *Nihon no kaisō shisutemu* (The stratification system in Japan).
7 See Umino and Saitō (1990) for detail on this section.
8 'Elaboration' basically is a method of cross tabulation comprising (at least) three variables, the results of which are used to estimate a causal relationship (Zeisel, 1985).
9 The statements in this section are mainly based upon Oda and Abe (2000), and Umino (2003).
10 Even among respondents who had completed only the mandatory minimum of schooling, a high per centage (seventy-four per cent) answered affirmatively to the opinion: 'Just because one has a high educational level, it does not necessarily follow that one will be advantaged in terms of income.' At first glance, this fact seems to contradict the description given in the main text. However, this can be explained by the age- and employment structure of these respondents.

Chapter 3

1 As shown in Figure 3.1, however, when the relationship between the persons concerned was unfavourable, the utility of people's satisfaction rose in direct proportion to the advantageousness of their outcome in comparison with the other person.
2 See Roth, Prasnikar, Okuno-Fujiwara and Zamir (1991); Costa-Gomes and Zauner (2001); Buchan, Croson and Johnson (2004); and Oosterbeek, Sloof

and van de Kuilen (2004) for discussions relating to cultural differences in ultimatum bargaining behaviour.
3 A similar report is found in Charness and Rabin (2002).
4 If the presence or absence of information on the total pie did indeed effect a change in the criteria for judgement of offers, then it might be possible to propose a cognitive framing effect as a psychological process which mediates between them (Tversky and Kahneman, 1981). By cognitive framing, I mean a tendency for different preferences to arise according to the placement of the point of reference for judgement. There are positive and negative sides in cognitive framing, the positive frame oriented towards the outcome from the perspective of advantage, and the negative frame from that of loss, respectively. As the positive frame generally shifts its focus to the increment of advantage, this spawns a tendency to seek sure advantage, even if the increment is small, and, as the negative frame spotlights the shortfall in comparison with the ideal condition, then this gives rise to a tendency to seek an outcome which will minimise loss, even if this is uncertain. Might the rareness of rejection even of low offers be attributable to the fact that a positive frame took shape because experimental participants who were told no information about the total pie set the benchmark for judging offers at ¥0, and aspired towards sure advantage, I wonder? On the other hand, the generation of a negative frame, the suppression of compromise, and the occurrence of rejection behaviour perhaps were facilitated by the fact that participants who were given information about the total pie set the benchmark for judgement at an equal amount of ¥1000.

Chapter 4

1 Translator's note: The stereotypical Japanese housewife prepares breakfast for family members.

Chapter 5

1 Allocations established by the Nash bargaining solution differ according to their initial situation. Generally, an allocation is sought so as to maximise the product relating to increments of advantage within Area **B** $(x_1 - u_1 (S/N))$ $(x_2 - u_2 (S/N))...(x_N - u_N (S/N))$. In the example here, which sets advantage allocation at (1, 2.5), because the intersection of Curve $(x_1 - 1)(x_2 - 2.5) = k$ and Area **B** is (13/12, 11/4), the allocation to both parties according to the Nash bargaining solution becomes (1, 1/12), (0, 11/12).
2 If alternating offers are repeated ad infinitum, this produces a utility level of the initial situation. Moreover, the justification of a procedural-theory-like Nash bargaining solution by means of such a multi-stage game is called the 'Nash program,' and many of these have been proposed.
3 On egalitarian equivalents, see Young (1994), pp. 146–150.
4 It was Crawford (1979) who first proposed such an auction game, but its shortcomings were pointed out by Demange (1984), and it was modified. The modified game, however, is considerably more complex than the game described in this chapter.

Chapter 12

1 The fairness evaluation model has two theoretical streams: the equity theory of J. Adams and others, and the expectation states theory of J. Berger and the like; but these both focus mainly upon explanations relating to pay and reward-distribution within small groups and each has accumulated unique insights in connection with the macro level. Fairness evaluations regarding income (Alwin, 1987; Mirowsky, 1987), treatment (Robinson and Bell, 1978), and society as a whole (Umino and Saitō, 1990); exploration by means of social surveys into the links between socio-economic status (Umino, 1988; Kimura, 1990) and personality (Iwama, 1994); and attempts to elucidate the fairness evaluation process have been carried out.

2 The term 'frame' is defined as 'schemata of interpretation' which 'enable individuals to locate, perceive, identify and label occurrences within their life space and world at large' (Snow et al., 1986, p. 464). Snow employed the term 'collective action frames' as an interpretive framework relating to points of contention or associated issues presented by movement organisations, or the movements' goals and strategies, emphasising that these frames were 'action-oriented sets of beliefs and meanings that inspire and legitimate the activities and campaigns of a social movement organisation' (Benford and Snow, 2000, p. 614).

3 Data was collected from a field survey conducted from 14 January - 13 February and 22 October – 10 November 2004, as well as 28 January to 17 March 2005.

4 Examples of groups on record include local groups such as BI Altdor, BI Amberg, BI Cham, BI Hersbruck, BI Kallmünz, BI Mitterteich, BI Oberviechtach, BI Regenstauf, BI Schwaben, Jugentzentrum im Städtedreieck, BI Sulzbach-Rosenberg, BI Weiden and BI Löchow-Dannenberg; Christian groups including BIWK (established at the University of Regensburg), der Arbeitskreis Theologie und Kernenergie, der Bund der Deutsche Katholischen Jugend, and Katholischen Land-Jugend Bayern; nationwide environmental groups such as BUND, BBU, and Öko-Institut; and doctors' and physicists' groups.

5 Full membership was restricted to county residents, so residents from outside the county could only become auxiliary members. Auxiliary members did not have voting rights at general assemblies. Regular membership numbers peaked at about 1500, and were around 1000 in 1989.

6 Local chapters included Ortsgruppe Schwandorf, Ortsgruppe Nittenau, Ortsgruppe Schwarzenfeld, Ortsgruppe Bruck, Ortsgruppe Nabburg, Ortsgruppe Pfreimd, Ortsgruppe Neunburg v. W., Ortsgruppe Bodenwöher, and Ortsgruppe Stadtdreieck.

7 For concrete details of the letters, see Aoki (2005, pp. 185–186).

8 According to BIS records, 763 people were arrested.

9 Letter from N.L., a Regensburg citizen, published 4 February 1986.

10 For concrete details of the letters, see Aoki (2005, p. 186).

11 Citation from an interview with 'K.,' a Schwandorf resident who frequently travelled to the site occupation at that time (25 January 2004).

12 There could even be seen a somewhat self-mocking letter, saying: 'Residents opposed to the plan have grown used to being criticised as 'chaos' (in the same way as *Autonome*)' (Extract from the letter of E.B., a villager from Hirschau, published 18 January 1986).
13 According to BIS records, in 1986 alone, about 4000 people were arrested and charged, and, of these, more than 2000 were convicted.
14 For concrete details of the letter, see Aoki (2005, p. 186).
15 The 'citizens' initiative' or 'citizens' action group' (*Bürgerinitiative*) emerged in the early 1970s as a defensive response by regional urban communities to public transport policy and urban redevelopment policy, and its wave progressively shifted to farming regions faced with huge development projects. Among these groups, in areas included in a string of plans to construct nuclear power facilities, it was the local residents opposed to such plans who established citizens' action groups called 'XX *Bürgerinitiative*' (place-names being inserted in place of XX) in every corner of the federation, and became the leading actors in the protest movement. In this process, *Bürgerinitiative* took on the ambiguous meaning of a 'citizens'/residents' movement group.'

Chapter 13

1 The description of the project is based on the following materials:
- Beteiligungskonzept City 2015, Entwicklung des offentlichen Personennahverkehrs als Baustein fur die Aufwertung der City, pp. 1–9.
- Beteiligungskonzept City 2015, Emphehlung des Arbeitskreises 'OPNV in der Karlsruher Innenstadt' an den Gemeinderat, pp. 1–3.
- Beteiligungskonzept City 2015, Emphehlungen der Arbeitskreise – Synopse, pp. 1–44.
- Beteiligungskonzept City 2015, Emphehlung der Arbeitsgruppen, pp. 23–47.
- Beteiligungskonzept City 2015, Expertenforum; Zusammenfassung der Ergebnisse, pp. 1–4.
- City 2015 Ergebnisse des Beteiligungsverfahrens nach Offener Burger beteiligung, Facharbeitskreisen und Ergebniskonferenz, pp. 1–11.
- VCD (Verkehrclub Deutschland) kraisfairkehr Karlsruhe e. V., 2001 (Weinnachten), 2001/2002 (Winter), 2002 (Sommer).

Bibliography

Abelson, J., Forest, P. G., Eyles, J., Smith, P., Martin, E., and Gauvin, F. P. (2003). Deliberations about deliberative methods: Issues in the design and evaluation of public participation processes. *Social Science and Medicine*, 57, 239–251.

Adams, J. S. (1965). Inequity in social exchange. In L. Berkowitz (Ed.). *Advances in experimental social psychology* (Vol. 2, pp. 267–299). New York: Academic Press.

Alicke, M. D. (1992). Culpable causation. *Journal of Personality and Social Psychology*, 63, 368–378.

Allegro, J., Kruidenier, H., and Steensma, H. (1991). Aspects of distributive and procedural justice in quality of working life. In H. Steensma and R. Vermunt (Eds). *Social justice in human relations* (Part 2, pp. 99–116). New York: Free Press.

Allen, V. (1965). Situational factors in conformity. In L. Berkowitz (Ed.). *Advances in experimental social psychology* (Vol. 2, pp. 133–170). New York: Academic Press.

Alwin, D. F. (1987). Distributive justice and satisfaction with material well being. *American Sociological Review*, 52, 83–95.

Andersen, I. E., and Jæger, B. (1999). Danish participatory models. *Science and Public Policy*, 26, 331–340.

Anderson, J. C., and Gerbing, D. W. (1988). Structural equation modeling in practice: A review and recommended two-step approach. *Psychological Bulletin*, 103, 411–423.

Aoki, S. (2004). Kōgi undō ni okeru furēmingu: Bōryokuteki 'yosomono' no juyō o meguru senryakuteki jirenma to sono kokufuku (Framing in protest movements: A strategic dilemma over the acceptance of violent 'outsiders' and its solution). *Shakaigaku Kenkyū* (The Study of Sociology), 76, 189–210.

———(2005). Rōkaru kōgi undō ni okeru undō furēmu to shūgōteki aidentiti no hen'yō katei: Doitsu, Vakkāsudorufu saishori shisetsu kensetsu hantai undō no jirei kara (The process of transformation of movement frames in local protest movements and collective identity: A case study of the movement against the construction of nuclear fuel reprocessing facility in Wackersdorf, Germany). *Kankyō Shakaigaku Kenkyū* (Journal of Environmental Sociology), 11, 174–187.

Aoki, T. (2005). Tetsuzukiteki kōsei ga motarasu sho kōka no jisshōteki kenkyū: Dōro no bariafurī jigyō o daizai ni (An empirical study on the fair process effect: A verification using a road development project). *Kensetsu Manējimento Kenkyū Ronbun Shū* (Journal of Construction Management), JSCE, 12, 1–8.

Aoki, T., and Nakai, Y. (2004). Shakai shihon seibi ni kansuru shimin kōza no hitsuyōsei (The necessity for public lectures about social infrastructure development). *Kensetsu Manējimento Kenkyū Ronbun Shū* (Journal of Construction Management), JSCE, 11, 427–432.

Aoki, T., and Suzuki, A. (2005). Shakai shihon seibi ni okeru sanpi taido no keisei: Kōsei no kizuna riron to taido hen'yō moderu no tōgō (Positive/negative attitude-formation in the consensus-building process for social infrastructure development: The integration of fairness-bond theory and the attitudinal-transformation model). *Jikken Shakai Shinrigaku Kenkyū* (The Japanese Journal of Experimental Social Psychology), 45(1), 42–54.

Aoki, T., and Suzuki, Y. (2004). Isawa damu kensetsu ni taisuru ippan shimin no sanpi taido no keisei kikō (The formation mechanism of ordinary citizens' attitudes for and against the Isawa Dam Construction Project). *Doboku Keikakugaku Kenkyū Kōen Shū* (Proceedings of Infrastructure Planning), 30, CD-ROM.

Aoki, T., Fukuno, M., and Ohbuchi, K. (2003). Setsumeisha no inshō ga umidasu botan no kakechigai genshō (Impact of an elucidator's impression on the acceptance towards a project). *Doboku Keikakugaku Kenkyū Kōen Shū* (Proceedings of Infrastructure Planning), 27, CD-ROM.

Aoki, T., Hoshi, K., and Satō, T. (2004). Furieki hi-sōki-gata no dōchō atsuryoku no sayō ka ni okeru rigai kankeisha no sanpi taido no keisei (Positive/negative attitude formation in a non-connected group). *Kensetsu Manējimento Kenkyū Ronbun Shū* (Journal of Construction Management), JSCE, 11, 27–34.

——— (2006). Shūdan jōkyō ni okeru kyōryoku ikō no keisei kikō: Dōchō atsuryoku to tetsuzukiteki kōsei ga kōteiteki ni sayō suru baai (The mechanism of cooperative attitude-formation in group situations: In cases where group pressure and procedural fairness have a positive effect). *Doboku Gakkai Ronbun Shū* (Journal of Infrastructure Planning and Management), JSCE, 807 (IV–70), 55–65.

Aoki, T., Nishino, H., Matsui, K., and Suzuki, A. (2003). Kōkyō jigyō ni taisuru jōhō teikyō to taido keisei (Disclosure and attitude-formation in a consensus-building process for public development). *Doboku Gakkai Ronbun Shū* (Journal of Infrastructure Planning and Management), JSCE, 737(IV–60), 223–235.

Asch, S. E. (1951). Opinions and social pressure. *Scientific American*, 193, 31–35.

Axelrod, R. (1980a). Effective choice in the prisoner's dilemma. *Journal of Conflict Resolution*, 24, 3–25.

——— (1980b). More effective choice in the prisoner's dilemma. *Journal of Conflict Resolution*, 24, 379–403.

Baba, K. (2002). NIMBY shisetsu ritchi purosesu ni okeru kōheisei no shiten: Bunpaiteki kōsei to tetsuzukiteki kōsei ni yoru jūmin sanka no hyōka furēmu ni mukete no kisoteki kōsatsu (The fairness perspective in the process of siting NIMBY facilities: A basic consideration in terms of distributive and procedural justice, aimed at an evaluative framing of residents' participation). *Toshi Keikaku Ronbun Shū* (Papers on City Planning), pp. 295–300.

Bagozzi, R., and Heatherton, T. (1994). A general approach to representing multifaceted personality constructs: Application to self-esteem. *Structural Equation Modeling*, 1, 35–67.

Bandura, A. (1973). *Aggression: A social learning analysis*. Oxford, England: Prentice-Hall.
——— (1990). Selective activation and disengagement of moral control. *Journal of Social Issues*, 46, 27–46.
——— (1999). Moral disengagement in the perpetration of inhumanities. *Personality and Social Psychology Review*, 3, 193–209.
Bandura, A., Underwood, B., and Fromson, M. E. (1975). Disinhibition of aggression through diffusion of responsibility and dehumanization of victims. *Journal of Research in Personality*, 9, 253–269.
Barrett-Howard, E., and Tyler, T. R. (1986). Procedural justice as a criterion in allocation decisions. *Journal of Personality and Social Psychology*, 50, 296–304.
Batson, C. D., Bowers, M. J., Leonard, E. A., and Smith, E. C. (2000). Does personal morality exacerbate or restrain retaliation after being harmed? *Personality and Social Psychology Bulletin*, 26, 35–45.
Baumeister, R. F. (1997). *Evil: Inside human cruelty and violence*. New York: W. H. Freeman and Company.
Bazerman, M. H., Loewenstein, G. F., and White, S. B. (1992). Psychological determinants of utility in competitive contexts: The impact of elicitation procedure. *Administrative Science Quarterly*, 37, 220–240.
Benford, R. D., and Snow, D. (2000). Framing process and social movements: An overview and assessment. *Annual Review of Sociology*, 26, 611–39.
Berry, J. W., Worthington, E. L. J., Parrott, L., O'Connor, L. E., and Wade, N. G. (2001). Dispositional forgiveness: Development and construct validity of the transgression narrative test of forgiveness (TNTF). *Personality and Social Psychology Bulletin*, 27, 1277–1290.
Bies, R. J. (1987). The predicament of injustice: The management of moral outrage. In L. L. Cummings and B. M. Staw (Eds). *Research in organizational behavior* (Vol. 9, pp. 289–319). Greenwich, Connecticut: JAI.
Bies, R. J., and Moag, J. S. (1986). Interactional justice: Communication criteria of fairness. In R. J. Lewicki, B. M. Sheppard, and M. H. Bazerman (Eds). *Research on negotiation in organizations* (Vol. 1, pp. 43–55). Greenwich, Connecticut: JAI.
Blount, S. (1995). When social outcomes aren't fair: The effect of causal attributions on preference. *Organizational Behavior and Human Decision Processes*, 63, 131–144.
Blount, S., Bazerman, M. H., and Neale, M. A. (1995). Alternative models of negotiated outcomes and the non-traditional utility concerns that limit their predictability. In R. J. Bies, R. J. Lewicki, and B. H. Sheppard (Eds). *Research on negotiation in organizations* (Vol. 5, pp. 95–116). Greenwich, Connecticut: JAI.
Bolton, G. E., and Ockenfels, A. (2000). ERC: Theory of equity, reciprocity, and competition. *American Economic Review*, 90, 166–193.
Boon, S. D. and Sulsky, L. M. (1997). Attributions of blame and forgiveness in romantic relationships: A policy-capturing study. *Journal of Social Behavior and Personality*, 12, 19–44.
Borst, A. (1998). *The Situation of Brazilians in Japan*. Report given at a press conference at the Foreign Correspondents' Club, Tokyo, Japan (FCCJ), 1 October. *http://www.debito.org/Bortzpressconf.html* (accessed 8 June 2006).
Boucher, D., and Kelley, P. J. (1994). *The social contract from Hobbes to Rawls*. London: Routledge.

———(1997). *Shakai keiyaku ron no keifu: Hobbuzu kara Rōruzu made* (The genealogy of social contract theory: From Hobbes to Rawls). S. Iijima and S. Satō (Trans.). Kyōto: Nakanishiya Shuppan.
Branscombe, N. R., Spears, R., Ellemers, N., and Doosje, B. (2002). Intragroup and intergroup evaluation effects on group behavior. *Personality and Social Psychology Bulletin*, 28, 744–753.
Brewer, M. B. (1988). A dual process model of impression formation. In T. K. Srull and R. S. Wyer, Jr. (Eds). *Advances in social cognition* (Vol. 1, pp. 1–36). Hillsdale, New Jersey: Lawrence Erlbaum Associates, Inc.
——— (1991). The social self: On being the same and different at the same time. *Personality and Social Psychology Bulletin*, 17, 475–482.
——— (1993). The role of distinctiveness in social identity and group behaviour. In M. Hogg and D. Abrams (Eds). *Group motivation: Social psychological perspective* (pp. 1–16). Hamel Hempstead, UK: Harvester Wheatsheaf.
Brewer, M. B., and Kramer, R. M. (1986). Choice behavior in social dilemmas: Effects of social identity, group size, and decision framing. *Journal of Personality and Social Psychology*, 50, 543–549.
Brewer, M. B., and Pickett, C. (1999). Distinctiveness motive as a source of the social self. In T. R. Tyler, R. M. Kramer, and O. P. John (Eds). *The psychology of social self* (pp. 71–87). Hilldale, New Jersey: Erlbaum.
Brickman, P., and Bulman, R. (1977). Pleasure and pain in social comparison. In J. M. Suls and R. L. Miller (Eds). *Social comparison processes: Theoretical and empirical perspectives* (pp. 149–186). Washington DC: Hemisphere.
Brickman, P., Folger, R., Goode, E., and Schul, Y. (1981). Microjustice and macrojustice. In M. J. Lerner and S. C. Lerner (Eds). *The justice motive in social behavior* (pp. 173–204). New York: Plenum.
Brockner, J. (2002). Making sense of procedural fairness: How high procedural fairness can reduce or heighten the influence of outcome favorability. *Academy of Management Review*, 27, 58–76.
Brockner, J., Cremer, D. D., Van den Bos, K., and Chen, Y. (2005). The influence of interdependent self-construal on procedural fairness effect. *Organizational Behavior and Human Decision Process*, 96, 155–167.
Brown, J. D. (2003). The self-enhancement motive in collectivistic cultures: The rumors of my death have been greatly exaggerated. *Journal of Cross-Cultural Psychology*, 34, 603–605.
Brown, J. D., and Kobayashi, C. (2002). Self-enhancement in Japan and America. *Asian Journal of Social Psychology*, 5, 145–168.
Brown, R., Hinkle, S., Ely, P. G., Fox-Cardmore, L., Maras, P., and Tayler, L.A. (1992). Recognizing group diversity: Individualist-collectivist and autonomous-relational social orientations and their implications for intergroup processes. *British Journal of Social Psychology*, 31, 327–342.
Brumfitt, J. H. (1972). *The French enlightment*. London: Macmillan.
——— (2004), *Furansu keimō shisō nyūmon* (Introduction to French enlightenment philosophy). I. Shimizu (Trans.). Tokyo: Hakusuisha.
Bryant, B. (1995). *Environmental justice: Issues, policies, and solutions*. St. Louis: Island Press.
Buchan, N. R., Croson, R. T. A., and Johnson, E. J. (2004). When do fairness

beliefs influence bargaining behavior?: Experimental evidence from Japan and the United States. *Journal of Consumer Research*, 31, 181–190.

Bullard, R. (1994). *Unequal protection*. San Francisco: Sierra Club Book.

Butterfield, K. D., Trevino, L. K., and Ball, G. A. (1997). Punishment from the manager's perspective: A grounded investigation and inductive model. *Academy of Management Journal*, 39, 1479–1512.

Buunk, A. P., and de Wolff, C. (1992). Social psychological aspects of stress at work. In P. Drenth, H. Thierry, and C. de Wolff (Eds). *New handbook of work and organizational psychology* (pp. 447–496). Houten, the Netherlands: Bohn, Stafleu, Van Logham.

Camerer, C. F. (2003). *Behavioral game theory: Experiments in strategic interaction*. New York: Princeton University Press.

Campbell, D. T. (1958). Common fate, similarity, and other indices of the status of aggregates of person as social entities. *Behavioural Science*, 3, 14–25.

Caprara, G. V., Berbarabelli, C., and Comrey, A. L. (1992). A personological approach to the study of aggression. *Personality and Individual Differences*, 13, 77–84.

Castano, E., Yzerbyt, V., and Bourguignon, D. (2003). We are one and I like it: The impact of ingroup entitativity on ingroup identification. *European Journal of Social Psychology*, 33, 735–754.

Caver, C.S. (1995). Stress and coping. In A. S. Manstead and M. Hewstone (Eds). *The Blackwell encyclopedia of social psychology* (pp. 635–639). Oxford: Blackwell.

Chaiken, S. (1980). Heuristic versus systematic information processing and the use of source versus message cues in persuasion. *Journal of Personality and Social Psychology*, 39, 752–766.

Chaiken, S., Liberman, A., and Eagly, A. H. (1989). Heuristic and systematic information processing within and beyond the persuasion context. In J. S. Uleman and J. A. Bargh (Eds). *Unintended thought* (pp. 212–252). New York: Guilford Press.

Charness, G., and Rabin, M. (2002). Understanding social preferences with simple tests. *Quarterly Journal of Economics*, 117, 817–969.

Chūō Daigaku Shakaikagaku Kenkyūjo (Ed.). (1996). Nihonjin no kōseikan (Japanese perceptions of social justice). *Chūō Daigaku Shakaikagaku Kenkyūjo Kenkyū Hōkoku*, No. 17.

Chūō Kōron Henshūbu (2001). *Ronsō, chūryū hōkai* (Controversy on the demise of the middle class). Tokyo: Chūkō Shinsho Rakure.

Cloke, K. (1993). Revenge, forgiveness, and the magic of mediation. *Mediation Quarterly*, 11, 67–78.

Cohen, G. A. (1989). On the currency of egalitarian justice. *Ethics*, 99, 906–944.

Cohen, R. L. (1991) Justice and negotiation. In M. H. Bazerman, R. J. Lewicki, and B. H. Sheppard (Eds). *Research on negotiation in organizations* (Vol. 3, pp. 259–282). Greenwich, Connecticut: JAI.

Cohen-Charash, Y., and Spector, P. E. (2001). The role of justice in organizations: A meta-analysis. *Organizational Behavior and Human Decision Processes*, 86, 278–321.

Collins, R. L. (2000). Among the better ones: Upward assimilation in social comparison. In J. Suls and L. Wheeler (Eds). *Handbook of social comparison: Theory and research* (pp. 159–171). New York: Kluwer Academic/Plenum.

Colquitt, J. A. (2001). On the dimensionality of organizational justice: A construct validation of a measure. *Journal of Applied Psychology*, 86, 386–400.

Colquitt, J. A., Conlon, D. E., Wesson, M. J., Porter, C. O. L. H., and Ng, K. Y. (2001). Justice at the millennium: A meta-analytic review of 25 years of organizational justice research. *Journal of Applied Psychology*, 86, 425–445.

Colquitt, J. A., Greenberg, J., and Zapata-Phelan, C. P. (2005). What is organizational justice? A historical overview. In J. Greenberg and J. Colquitt (Eds). *Handbook of organizational justice* (pp. 3–58). Mahwah, New Jersey: Lawrence Erlbaum Associates, Publishers.

Cooper, C. L., and Marshall, J. (1978). Sources of managerial and white collar stress. In C. L. Cooper and R. Payne (Eds). *Stress at work* (pp. 81–105). Chichester, England: Wiley.

Cooper, J., and Hogg, M. (2002). Dissonance arousal and the collective self: Vicarious experience of dissonance based on shared group membership. In J. P. Forgas and K. D. Williams (Eds). *The social self: Cognitive, interpersonal, and intergroup perspectives* (pp. 327–342). New York: Psychology Press.

Costa-Gomes, M., and Zauner, K. (2001). Ultimatum bargaining behavior in Israel, Japan, Slovenia, and the United States: A social utility analysis. *Games and Economic Behavior*, 34, 238–269.

Crawford, V. P. (1979). A procedure for generating Pareto-efficient egalitarian equivalent allocations. *Econometrica*, 47(1), 49–60.

Cropanzano, R. and Greenberg, J. (1997). Progress in organizational justice: Tunnelling through the maze. In C. L. Cooper and I. T. Robertson (Eds). *International Review of Industrial and Organizational Psychology* (vol. 12, pp. 317–372). New York: John Wiley.

Crosby, N. (1995). Citizen juries: One solution for difficult environmental questions. In O. Renn, T. Webler and P. Wiedermann (Eds). *Fairness and competence in citizen participation* (pp. 157–174). Dordrecht: Kluwer Academic Publishers.

Croyle, R. T., and Ditto, P. H. (1990). Illness cognition and behavior: An experimental approach. *Journal of Behavioral Medicine*, 13, 31–52.

Darby, B. W., and Schlenker, B. R. (1982). Children's reaction to apologies. *Journal of Personality and Social Psychology*, 43, 742–753.

Darley, J. M., and Gross, P. H. (1983). A hypothesis-confirming bias in labeling effects. *Journal of Personality and Social Psychology*, 44, 20–33.

Davis, M. H. (1994). *Empathy: A social psychological approach.* Boulder, Colorado: Westview Press.

——— (1999). *Kyōkan no shakai shinrigaku: Ningen kankei no kiso* (The social psychology of empathy: The foundation of human relationships). (A. Kikuchi, Trans.), Tokyo: Kawashima Shoten.

Dawes, R. M. (1980). Social dilemmas. *Annual Review of Psychology*, 31, 169–193.

De Cremer, D., and Blader, S. L. (2006). Why do people care about procedural fairness? The importance of belongingness in responding and attending to procedures. *European Journal of Social Psychology*, 36, 211–228.

De Cremer, D., and Tyler, T. R. (2005). Managing group behavior: The interplay between procedural justice, sense of self, and cooperation. In M. P. Zanna (Ed.). *Advances in experimental social psychology* (Vol. 37, pp. 151–218). San Diego, California: Academic Press.

De Dreu, C. K. W., and Van Lange, P. A. M. (1995). The impact of social value orientations on negotiator cognition and behavior. *Personality and Social Psychology Bulletin*, 21, 1178–1188.

De Dreu, C. K. W., Weingart, L. R., and Kwon, S. (2000). Influence of social motives on integrative negotiation: A meta-analytic review and test of two theories. *Journal of Personality and Social Psychology*, 78, 889–905.

Demange, G. (1984). Implementing efficient egalitarian equivalent allocations. *Econometrica*, 52(5), 1167–1177.

Deutsch, M. (1975). Equity, equality, and need: What determines which value will be used as the basis for distributive justice? *Journal of Social Issues*, 31, 137–149.

Devine, P. G. (1989). Stereotypes and prejudice: Their automatic and controlled components. *Journal of Personality and Social Psychology*, 56, 5–18.

Devos, T., Silver, L. A., Mackie, D. M., and Smith, E. R. (2002). Experiencing intergroup emotions. In D. M. Mackie and E. R. Smith (Eds). *From prejudice to intergroup emotions: Differentiated reactions to social group* (pp. 111–134). New York: Psychology Press.

Diekmann, K. A., Samuels, S. M., Ross, L., and Bazerman, M. H. (1997). Self-interest and fairness in problems of resource allocation: Allocators versus recipients. *Journal of Personality and Social Psychology*, 72, 1061–1074.

Dienel, P. C., and Renn, O. (1995). Planning cells: A gate to 'fractal' mediation. In O. Renn et al. (Eds). *Fairness and competence in citizen participation* (pp. 117–140). Dordrecht: Kluwer Academic Publishers.

Dienel, P. C. (1999). Planning cells: The German experience. In U. Khan (Ed.). *Participation beyond the ballot box* (pp. 81–93). London: UCL Press.

Diener, E., and Diener, M. (1995). Cross-cultural correlates of life satisfaction and self-esteem. *Journal of Personality and Social Psychology*, 68, 653–663.

Doi, T. (1973). *The Anatomy of Dependence*. J. Bester (Trans.). New York: Kodansha International.

Doosje, B., Spears, R., and Ellemers, N. (2002). Social identity as both cause and effect: The development of group identification in response to anticipated and actual changes in the intergroup status hierarchy. *British Journal of Social Psychology*, 41, 57–76.

Doosje, B., Spears, R., and Koomen, W. (1995). When bad isn't all bad: Strategic use of sample information in generalization and stereotyping. *Journal of Personality and Social Psychology*, 69, 642–655.

Dovidio, J. F., and Gaertner, S. L. (1996). Affirmative action, unintentional racial biases, and intergroup relations. *Journal of Social Issues*, 52, 51–75.

——— (2000). Aversive racism and selection decisions: 1989 and 1999. *Psychological Science*, 11, 319–323.

——— (2004). Aversive Racism. In M. P. Zanna (Ed.). *Advances in Experimental Social Psychology* (Vol. 36, pp. 1–52). New York: Academic Press.

Dovidio, J. F., Smith, J. K., Donnella, A. G., and Gaertner, S. L. (1997). Racial attitudes and the death penalty. *Journal of Applied Social Psychology*, 27, 1468–1487.

Eberhardt, J. L., and Fiske, S. T. (1996). Motivating individuals to change: What is a target to do? In C. N. Macrae, C. Stangor and M. Hewstone (Eds). *Stereotypes and stereotyping* (pp. 369–415). New York: Guilford Press.

Ellemers, N., Doosje, B. J., Van Knippenberg, A., and Wilke, H. (1992). Status protection in high status minority groups. *European Journal of Social Psychology*, 22, 123–140.

Ellemers, N., Van Knippenberg, A., and Wilke, H. (1990). The influence of permeability of group boundaries and stability of group status on strategies of individual mobility and social change. *British Journal of Social Psychology*, 23, 233–246.

Ellemers, N., Van Knippenberg, A., De Vries, N., and Wilke, H. (1988). Social identification and permeability of group boundaries. *European Journal of Social Psychology*, 18, 497–513.

Ellsworth, P. C., and Ross, L. (1983). Public opinion and capital punishment: A close examination of the views of abolitionists and retentionists. *Crime and Delinquency*, 29, 116–169.

Elovainio, M., Kivimäki, M., and Helkama, K. (2001). Organizational justice evaluations, job control, and occupational strain. *Journal of Applied Psychology*, 86, 418–424.

Endō, Y. (1997). Shinmitsu na kankeisei ni okeru kōyō to sōtaiteki jiko hikaku (Enhancement and relative self-comparison in close relationships). *Shinrigaku Kenkyū*, 68, 387–395.

Engel, B. (1989). *The right to innocence: Healing the trauma of childhood sexual abuse*. Los Angeles: Jeremy Tarcher.

Enright, R. D. (2001). *Forgiveness is a choice: A step-by-step process for resolving anger and restoring hope*. Washington, DC: APA LifeTools.

Enright, R. D., and the Human Development Study Group (1991). The moral development of forgiveness. In W. Kurtines and J. Gewirtz (Eds). *Moral behavior and development* (Vol. 1, pp. 123–152). Hillsdale, New Jersey: Erlbaum.

Enright, R. D., Gassin, E. A., and Wu, C. R. (1992). Forgiveness: A developmental view. *Journal of Moral Education*, 21, 99–114.

Enright, R. D., Santos, M. J. D., and Al-Mabuk, R. (1989). The adolescent as forgiver. *Journal of Adolescence*, 12, 95–110.

Exline, J. J., and Baumeister, R. F. (2000). Expressing Forgiveness and Repentance. In E. M. McCullough, K. I. Pargament, and C. E. Thoresen (Eds). *Forgiveness: Theory, research, and practice* (pp. 133–155). New York: Guilford Press.

Exline, J. J., Baumeister, R. F., Bushman, B. J., Campbell, W. K., and Finkel, L. J. (2004). Too proud to let go: Narcissistic entitlement as a barrier to forgiveness. *Journal of Personality and Social Psychology*, 87, 894–912.

Fagenson, E. A., and Cooper, J. (1987). When push comes to power: A test of power restoration theory's explanation for aggressive conflict escalation. *Basic and Applied Social Psychology*, 8, 273–293.

Falk, A., Fehr, E., and Fischbacher, U. (2003). On the nature of fair behavior. *Economic Inquiry*, 41, 20–26.

Fehr, E., and Schmidt K. M., (1999). A theory of fairness, competition, and cooperation. *Quarterly Journal of Economics*, 114, 817–868.

Fein, S., and Spencer, S. J. (1997). Prejudice as self-image maintenance: Affirming the self through derogating others. *Journal of Personality and Social Psychology*, 73, 31–44.

Ferguson, T. J., and Rule, B. G. (1983). An attributional perspective on anger and aggression. In R. G. Geen and E. Donnerstein (Eds). *Aggression: Theoretical and empirical reviews* (Vol. 1, *Theoretical and methodological issues*, pp. 41–74). New York: Academic Press.

Festinger, L. (1954). A theory of social comparison processes. *Human Relations*, 7, 117–140.

Fincham, F. D., Paleari, F. G., and Regalia, C. (2002). Forgiveness in marriage: The role of relationship quality, attributions and empathy. *Personal Relationships*, 9, 27–37.

Finkel, E. J., Rusbult, C. E., Kumashiro, M., and Hannon, P. A. (2002). Dealing with betrayal in close relationships: Does commitment promote forgiveness? *Journal of Personality and Social Psychology*, 82, 956–974.

Fiske, S. T., and Neuberg, S. T. (1990). A continuum of impression formation, from category-based to individuating processes: Influences of information and motivation on attention and interpretation. In M. P. Zanna (Ed.). *Advances in experimental social psychology* (Vol. 23, pp.1–74). New York: Academic Press.

Fitness, J., and Fletcher, G. J. O. (1993). Love, hate, anger, and jealousy in close relationships: A prototype and cognitive appraisal analysis. *Journal of Personality and Social Psychology*, 65, 942–958.

Flynn, B. J. (1992). Trust as a determinant of opposition to a high-level radioactive repository: Analysis of a structural model. *Risk Analysis*, 12, 417–429.

Folger, R. (1977). Distributive and procedural justice: Combined impact of 'voice' and improvement on experienced inequity. *Journal of Personality and Social Psychology*, 35, 108–119.

——— (1986). Rethinking equity theory: A referent cognition model. In H. W. Bierhoff, R. L. Cohen, and J. Greenberg (Eds). *Justice in social relations*, New York: Plenum.

——— (1998). Fairness as a moral virtue. In M. Schminke (Ed.). *Managerial ethics: Moral management of people and processes* (pp. 13–34). Mahwah, New Jersey: Erlbaum.

——— (2001). Fairness as deonance. In S. W. Gilliland, D. D. Steiner, and D. P. Skarlicki (Eds). *Research in social issues in management* (Vol. 1, pp. 3–33). New York: Information Age Publishers.

Folger, R., and Cropanzano, R. (1998). *Organizational justice and human resource management*. Thousand Oaks, California: Sage.

Folger, R., and Greenberg, J. (1985). Procedural justice: An interpretive analysis of personal systems. In K. Rowland and G. Ferris (Eds). *Research in personal and human resources management* (Vol. 3, pp. 141–183). Greenwich, Connecticut: JAI.

Folger, R., and Martin, C. (1986). Relative deprivation and referent cognitions: Distributive and procedural justice effects. *Journal of Experimental Social Psychology*, 22, 531–546.

Freedman, S. R., and Enright, R. D. (1996). Forgiveness as an intervention goal with incest survivors. *Journal of Consulting and Clinical Psychology*, 64(5), 983–992.

Fried, Y. (1993). Interesting domains of work stress and industrial relations: Introductions and overview. *Journal of Organizational Behavior*, 14, 397–399.

Frijda, N. (1994). The lex talionis: On vengeance. In S. H. van Goozen, N. E. van de Poll, and J. Sergeant (Eds). *Emotions: Essays on emotion theory* (pp. 263–289). Hillsdale, New Jersey: Lawrence Erlbaum.

Fujii, S. (2001). Doboku keikaku no tame no shakaiteki kōdō riron: Taido tsuijū-gata keikaku kara taido hen'yō-gata keikaku e (Social behaviour theories for infrastructure planning: From planning that pandered to public attitudes to planning for attitudinal modification). *Doboku Gakkai Ronbun Shū* (Journal of Infrastructure Planning and Management), 688(IV–53), 19–35.

———(2004). TDM no juyō mondai ni okeru ishi kettei furēmu (The decision frame of TDM (transportation demand management) acceptance). *Doboku Keikakugaku Kenkyū Ronbun Shū* (Infrastructure Planning Review), 21(4), 961–966.

———(2006). Seifu ni taisuru kokumin no shinrai: Taigi aru kōkyō jigyō ni yoru shinrai no jōsei (People's trust in government: Trust development due to implementation of public works with justice). *Doboku Gakkai Ronbun Shū* (Journal of Infrastructure Planning and Management), JSCE, No. 807(IV–70), 29–41.

Fujii, S., Takemura, K., and Kikkawa, T. (2002). 'Kimekata' to gōi keisei: shakaiteki jirenma ni okeru rikoteki dōki no yokusei ni mukete (The decision-making process and consensus-building: A strategy to an egoistic motivation in social dilemmas). *Doboku Gakkai Ronbun Shū* (Journal of Infrastructure Planning and Management), JSCE, 709(IV–56), 13–26.

Fujikawa, Y. (1984), *Seigiron no rekishi* (The history of justice theory). Tokyo: Ronsō Sha.

Fujimura, M. (2001). 'Minna no mono' to wa nani ka: Mura no tochi to hito (What is 'everybody's'?: Village land and people). In M. Inoue and T. Miyauchi (Eds). *Shirīzu kankyō shakaigaku 2: Komonzu no shakaigaku* (Environmental sociology series 2: The sociology of commons) (pp. 32–54). Tokyo: Shin'yō Sha.

Fukuno, M. (1999). Kōshō ni okeru jiko rieki to kōsei kanshin: Saishū teian kōshō paradaimu ni yoru bunseki (Self-interest and fairness concern in negotiation: Analysis by the ultimatum bargaining paradigm). *Kōdō Kagaku*, 38, 29–38.

Fukuno, M., and Ohbuchi, K. (2001). Saishō teian kōshō ni okeru ukete no kyohi dōki no bunseki: Dōitsusei hogo no shiten kara (An analysis of respondents' refusal motivation in ultimatum bargaining: From the perspective of identity-preservation). *Shakai Shinrigaku Kenkyū*, 16, 184–192.

———(2003). Procedural fairness in ultimatum bargaining: Effects of interactional fairness and formal procedure on respondents' reactions to unequal offers. *Japanese Psychological Research*, 45, 152–161.

———(2005). *Preference information and social value orientations as offerer's intention in ultimatum bargaining*. Manuscript submitted for publication.

Funabashi, H. (1989). 'Shakaiteki jirenma' toshite no kankyō mondai (Environmental issues as a 'social dilemma'). *Shakai Rōdō Kenkyū* (Society and Labor), 35, 23–50.

——— (1995). Kankyō mondai e no shakaigakuteki shiza: 'Shakaiteki jirenma ron' to 'shakai seigyo shisutemu ron' (A sociological viewpoint on environmental issues: The 'social dilemma hypothesis' and 'social control system hypothesis'). *Kankyō Shakaigaku Kenkyū*, 1, 5–20.

——— (2001). Kankyō mondai no shakaigakuteki kenkyū (The sociological study of environmental issues). In N. Iijima, H. Torigoe, K. Hasegawa and H. Funabashi (Eds). *Kōza kankyō shakaigaku, dai-ikkan: Kankyō shakaigaku no shiten* (Environmental sociology course, Vol. 1: Perspectives of environmental sociology) (pp. 29–62), Tokyo: Yūhikaku.

——— (2003). Shakaiteki jirenma ron (The social dilemma hypothesis). In H. Funabashi and T. Miyauchi (Eds). *Shintei kankyō shakaigaku* (New edition environmental sociology) (pp. 190–209). Tokyo: Hōsō Daigaku Kyōiku Shinkyō Kai.

——— (2005). Genshiryoku seisaku no naihō suru konnansa ni tsuite no shakaigakuteki kōsatsu (Sociological considerations on the difficulty involved in atomic energy policy). *Mutsu–Ogawara kaihatsu, kaku nenryō saikuru shisetsu mondai chōsa hōkokusho* (Survey report on Mutsu–Ogawara development and nuclear fuel recycling facility issues), pp. 1–30.

Funabashi, H., Hasegawa, K., Hatanaka, M., and Katsuta, H. (1985). *Shinkansen kōgai: Kōsoku bunmei no shakai mondai* ('Bullet Train' pollution: the social problems of rapid civilization). Tokyo: Yūhikaku.

Furukawa, A. (2004). *Mura no seikatsu kankyō shi* (The life-environment history of the village). Kyoto: Sekai Shisō Sha.

Gaertner, S. L. (1973). Helping behavior and racial discrimination among liberals and conservatives. *Journal of Personality and Social Psychology*, 25, 335–341.

Gaertner, S. L., and Dovidio, J. F. (1977). The subtlety of white racism, arousal, and helping behavior. *Journal of Personality and Social Psychology*, 35, 691–707.

Gibbons, F. X., and Gerrard, M. (1991). Downward comparison and coping with threat. In J. Suls and T. A. Wills (Eds). *Social comparison: Contemporary theory and research* (pp. 317–345). Hillsdale, New Jersey: Lawrence Erlbaum Associates.

Gibbons, F. X., Gerrard, M., Blanton, H., and Russell, D. W. (1998). Reasoned action and social reaction: Willingness and intention as independent predictors of health risk. *Journal of Personality and Social Psychology*, 74, 1164–1180.

Girard, M., Mullet, E., and Callahan, S. (2002). The mathematics of forgiveness. *American Journal of Psychology*, 115, 351–375.

Goethals, G. R., and Darley, J. M. (1977). Social comparison theory: An attributional approach. In J. Suls and R. L. Miller (Eds). *Social comparison processes: Theoretical and empirical perspectives* (pp. 259–278). Washington DC: Hemisphere.

Goethals, G.R. (1986). Fabricating and ignoring social reality: Self-serving estimates of consensus. In M. Olson, C. P. Herman, and M. P. Zanna (Eds).

Relative deprivation and social comparison. The Ontario Symposium (Vol. 4, pp. 135–157). Hillsdale, New Jersey: Lawrence Erlbaum Associates.

Gong, L., Suzuki, N., and Yamagishi, T. (2001). Beyond cultural construal of self: Self-effacing heuristics among Japanese. Paper presented at the 4th Annual Conference of the Asian Association of Social Psychology, Melbourne, Australia.

Gouldner, A.W. (1960). The norm of reciprocity: A preliminary statement. *American Sociological Review*, 25, 161–178.

Greenberg, J. (1987). A taxonomy of organizational justice theories. *Academy of Management Review*, 12, 9–22.

——— (1988). Equity and workplace status: A field experiment. *Journal of Applied Psychology,* 73, 606–613.

——— (1990). Organizational justice: Yesterday, today and tomorrow. *Journal of Management*, 16, 399–432.

Greenberg, J., and Folger, R. (1983). Procedural justice, participation, and the fair process effect in groups and organizations. In P. B. Paulus (Ed.). *Basic group process* (pp. 235–256). New York: Springer-Verlag.

Greenwald, A. G., and Banaji, M. R. (1995). Implicit social cognition: Attitudes, self-esteem, and stereotypes. *Psychological Review,* 102, 4–27.

Greenwald, A. G., McGhee, D. E., and Schwartz, J. L. K. (1998). Measuring individual differences in implicit cognition: The implicit association test. *Journal of Personality and Social Psychology*, 74, 1464–1480.

Güth, W., Schmittberger, R., and Schwarze, B. (1982). An experimental analysis of ultimatum bargaining. *Journal of Economic Behavior and Organization*, 3, 367–388.

Hara, J. (1998). SSM chōsa no rekishi to tenbō (The history and outlook of SSM surveys). *Yoron*, 88, 74–86.

Hara, J. (Ed.). (1990). *Kaisō ishiki no dōtai* (The dynamics of stratum consciousness). Tokyo: Tōkyō Daigaku Shuppan Kai.

Hara, J., and Seiyama, K. (1999). *Shakai kaisō: Yutaka na shakai ni okeru fubyōdō* (Social stratification: Inequity in an affluent society). Tokyo: Tōkyō Daigaku Shuppan Kai.

——— (2005). *Inequality amid affluence: Social stratification in Japan*. B. Williams (Trans.). Melbourne, Australia: Trans Pacific Press.

Harris, M. J., Milich, R., Corbitt, E. M., Hoover, D. W., and Brady, M. (1992). Self-fulfilling effects of stigmatizing information on children's social interactions. *Journal of Personality and Social Psychology*, 63, 41–50.

Hatori, T., Matsushima, K., and Kobayashi, K. (2003). Purojekuto jōhō no teikyō to jūmin no gakushū (Providing project information and citizens' learning). *Doboku Keikakugaku Kenkyū Ronbun Shū* (Infrastructure Planning Review), 20, 163–174.

Hayashi, Y. (2004). Kigyō soshiki ni okeru kōsei to sono kizuna kinō no kenkyū (A study of justice in corporate organisations and its bonding function). Sendai: Tohoku University (Unpublished doctoral thesis).

Hayashi, Y., and Ohbuchi, K. (1999). Jūgyōin no soshiki ni taisuru kōsei chikaku to soshiki shikō: Keizaiteki kōkan moderu to shūdan kachi moderu (Employees' perceptions of fairness relating to organization and group-orientedness: The economic-exchange model and group-values model). *Sangyō/Soshiki Shinrigaku Kenkyū*, 12, 99–110.

Hebel, J. H., and Enright, R. D. (1993). Forgiveness as a psychotherapeutic goal with elderly females. *Psychotherapy*, 30, 658–667.
Heine, S. J. (2003a). Self-enhancement in Japan? A reply to Brown and Kobayashi. *Asian Journal of Social Psychology*, 6, 75–84.
——— (2003b). Making sense of East Asian self-enhancement. *Journal of Cross-Cultural Psychology*, 34, 596–602.
Heine, S. J., and Lehman, D. R. (1995). Cultural variation in unrealistic optimism: Does the West feel more invulnerable than the East? *Journal of Personality and Social Psychology*, 72, 595–607.
——— (1997). The cultural construction of self-enhancement: An examination of group-serving biases. *Journal of Personality and Social Psychology*, 72, 1268–1283.
Heine, S. J., Lehman, D., Markus, H. R., and Kitayama, S. (1999). Is there a universal need for positive self-regard? *Psychological Review*, 106, 766–794.
Heine, S. J., Takata, T., and Lehman, D. R. (2000). Beyond self-presentation: Evidence for self-criticism among Japanese. *Personality and Social Psychology Bulletin*, 26, 71–78.
Hewston, M., Cairns, E., Voci, A., McLernon, F., Niens, U., and Noor, M. (2004). Intergroup forgiveness and guilt in Northern Ireland: Social psychological dimensions of 'The Troubles.' In N. R. Branscombe and B. Doosje (Eds). *Collective guilt: International perspectives* (pp. 193–215). New York: Cambridge University Press.
Hewstone, M., Rubin, M., and Willis, H. (2002). Intergroup bias. *Annual Review of Psychology*, 53, 575–604.
Hichibe, N. (2002). Nihon no fukōheikan: Fukōheikan kenkyū no rebyū to arata na kasetsu no teiji ni mukete (Perceptions of fairness and justice in Japan). *Soshiorojikaru Pēpāzu*, 11, 1–28.
——— (2003). 'Fukōheikan' no shakaigaku: 'Fukōhei shakai' to iu hyōshō no hyōshutsu no kaimei ni mukete (The sociology of perceptions of justice: Toward an understanding of representation of 'unjust society'). *Soshiorojikaru Pēpāzu*, 12, 27–56.
Hikichi, H., and Aoki, T. (2005). Chiiki ni taisuru aichaku keisei no shinri katei no kentō (A study on the psychological mechanism of place attachment). *Keikan Dezain Kenkyū Kōen Shū* (Proceedings of Landscape Design), JSCE, 1, 232–235.
Hikichi, H., and Aoki, T. (2006). Machizukuri no keikaku katei ni taisuru sanka kōdō no kiteiin to sono chiiki sa (Determinants of participation behavior to planning process for city planning and the regional differences). *Infrastructure Planning Review*, 23, 237–42.
Hirose, Y. (2003). EST dōnyū no tame no gōi keisei purosesu: Kārusurūe no kōtsū keikaku o jirei to shite (The consensus-building process for EST introduction: A case study of the Karlsruhe public transport plan). *Heisei 14-nendo Kankyōshō chikyū kankyō kenkyū sōgō suishinhi kenkyū seika hōkukusho* (Ministry of the Environment report on results of research receiving comprehensive funding for the promotion of global environment studies, 2002–2003), pp. 132–143.
——— (2005). Kankyō hairyo kōdō no kiteiin ni kansuru Nichi-Doku hikaku chōsa (A Japan-Germany comparative survey into regulating factors in

pro-environmental behaviour). *Heisei 14-, 15-, 16-nendo kagaku kenkyūhi hojokin kenkyū seika hōkokusho* (Report on results of research funded by scientific research grants, 2002–03, 2003–04, 2004–05).
Hirose, Y., Ōtomo, S., and Ōnuma, S. (2004). Kōtsū keikaku no shakaiteki juyō to sono kiteiin toshite no tetsuzukiteki kōsei hyōka to keikaku kōka hyōka: Kārusurūe no shimin sanka jirei (The public acceptance of transport planning and the evaluation of its procedural fairness and planning effectiveness: the example of Karlsruhe citizens' participation) (Unpublished paper).
Hirose, Y., Ōtomo, S., Asai, N., and Shōji, T. (2005). Gomi shori kihon keikaku de no shimin sanka to sono sanka tetsuzuki no kōseisa ni tsuite no chōsa kenkyū (A survey study on public participation in basic planning for waste-disposal and the fairness of its participatory procedures) (Unpublished paper).
Hodson, G., Dovidio, J. F., and Gaertner, S. L. (2002). Processes in racial discrimination: Differential weighting of conflicting information. *Personality and Social Psychology Bulletin*, 28, 460–471.
Hoffman, E., McCabe, K. A., Shachat, K., and Smith, V. L. (1994). Preference, property rights, and anonymity in bargaining games. *Games and Economic Behavior*, 7, 346–380.
Hofstede, G. (1980). *Culture's consequences*: *International differences in work related values*. Beverly Hills, California: Sage.
Hogg, M. A. (2004). Uncertainty and extremism: Identification with high entitativity groups under conditions of uncertainty. In V. Yzerbyt, C. M. Judd, and O. Corneille (Eds). *The psychology of group perception: Perceived variability, entitativity, and essentialism* (pp. 401–418). New York: Psychology Press.
Honda, H. (2001). Genshiryoku o meguru Doitsu no funsōteki seiji katei (2): Hangenpatsu undō no zenkokuka (1975–77) (The disputational political process in Germany relating to atomic energy (2): The nationwide spread of the movement against nuclear power generation) (1975–77). *Hokkai Gakuen Daigaku Hōgaku Kenkyū*, 36, 43–107.
Hoorens, V., and Buunk, B. P. (1993). Social comparison of health risks: Locus of control, the person-positivity bias, and unrealistic optimism. *Journal of Applied Social Psychology,* 23, 291–302.
Iijima, N. (1970). Sangyō kōgai to jūmin undō: Minamata-byō mondai o chūshin ni (Industrial pollution and residents' movements: Centring on the Minamata disease question). *Shakaigaku Hyōron* (Japanese Sociological Review), 21, 25–45.
———(1984). *Kankyō mondai to higaisha undō* (Environmental issues and victims' movements), Tokyo: Gakubun Sha.
Iijima, N. (Ed.). (1993). *Kankyō shakaigaku* (Environmental sociology), Tokyo: Yūhikaku.
Ikeda, K. (2005). Kankyō shakaigaku ni okeru seigiron no kihon mondai: Kankyō seigi no yonshurui (Fundamental justice-theory issues in environmental sociology: Four types of environmental sociology). *Kankyō Shakaigaku Kenkyū*, 11, 5–21.
Inamura, H. (1975). Chiiki jūmin no hannō to rosen sentei (The response of regional residents and route selection). *Doboku Gakkai Ronbun Shū* (Journal of Infrastructure Planning and Management), JSCE, 238, 93–106.

Itō, M. (1993). Kojin shikōsei/shakai shikōsei shakudo no sakusei oyobi shinraisei/datōsei no kentō (An analysis of the creation and reliability/validity of egocentricity/sociocentricity scales). *Shinrigaku Kenkyū*, 64, 115–122.

Itō, M. (2001). *Kenchiku/machizukuri keikaku ni okeru jūmin sanka shuhō toshite no wākushoppu no kenkyū* (A study on workshops as a tool of public participation for construction and city planning) (Unpublished manuscript, Chiba University).

Iwama, A. (1994). Shakaiteki fukōhei no ninchi mekanizumu: Ken'i shugi oyobi muryokukan to no kanren (The cognitive mechanism of social unfairness: the link between authoritarianism and feelings of powerlessness). *Gendai Shakaigaku Kenkyū* (Studies in Contemporary Sociology), 7, 100–122.

Jackson, J. W., and Smith, E. R. (1999). Conceptualizing social identity: A new framework and evidence for the impact of different dimensions. *Personality and Social Psychology Bulletin*, 25, 120–135.

James, W. (1892). *Psychology: Briefer course.* New York: Holt. H. Imada (Trans.) (1992). *Shinrigaku (Ge)* (Psychology) (Vol. 2 [of 2]). Tokyo: Iwanami Shoten.

Jemmott, J. B., Ditto, P. H., and Croyle, R. T. (1986). Judging health status: Effects of perceived prevalence and personal relevance. *Journal of Personality and Social Psychology*, 50, 899–905.

Jenkins, R. R. (2001). The health of minority children in the year 2000: The role of government programs in improving the health status of America's children. In N. J. Smelser, W. J. Wilson, and F. F. Mitchell (Eds). *Racial trends and their consequences* (Vol. 2, pp. 351–370). Washington, DC: National Academy Press.

Jinji, N. (1997). 'Kyōyūchi no jirenma' moderu saikō: Umino moderu no saikentō to ippan moderu no kōchiku (A reconsideration of the 'commons dilemma' model: A re-examination of the Umino model and the formulation of a general model). *Riron to Hōhō* (Sociological Theory and Methods), 12, 15–30.

Johnson, J. D., Whitestone, E., Jackson, L. A., and Gatto, L. (1995). Justice is still not colorblind: Differential racial effects of exposure to inadmissible evidence. *Personality and Social Psychology Bulletin*, 21, 893–898.

Jost, J. T., and Banaji, M. R. (1994). The role of stereotyping in system-justification and the production of false consciousness. *British Journal of Social Psychology*, 33, 1–27.

Judge, T. A., and Colquitt, J. A. (2004). Organizational justice and stress: The mediating role of work-family conflict, *Journal of Applied Psychology*, 89, 395–404.

Kada, Y. (1995). *Seikatsu sekai no kankyōgaku: Biwako kara no messēji* (Lifeworld environmental studies: A message from Lake Biwa), Tokyo: Nōsan Gyoson Bunka Kyōkai (Rural Culture Association).

Kahneman, D., Knetsch, J. L., and Thaler, R. (1986). Fairness and the assumptions of economics. *Journal of Business*, 59, 285–290.

Kajita, T. (1979). *Funsō no shakaigaku: 'Juekiken' to 'jukuken': 'Daikibo kaihatsu mondai' ni okeru tekunokurāto to seikatsusha* (The sociology of conflict: The 'benefit zone' and 'victimised zone': Technocrats and people

living their lives in 'large-scale development issues'). *Keizai Hyōron* (The Economic Review), 28, 101–120.
Karasawa, M. (2001). Nihonjin ni okeru ji-ta no ninshiki: Jiko hihan baiasu to tasha kōyō baiasu (Self-other awareness among Japanese: Self-critical biases and other-enhancement biases). *Shinrigaku Kenkyū*, 72, 195–203.
Karasek, R. A., Jr. (1979). Job demands, job decision latitude, and mental strain: Implications for job redesign. *Administrative Science Quarterly*, 24, 285–308.
Karremans, J. C., Van Lange, P. A. M., and Paul, A. M. (2005). Does activating justice help or hurt in promoting forgiveness? *Journal of Experimental Social Psychology*, 41, 290–297.
Karremans, J. C., Van Lange, P. A. M., Ouwerkerk, J. W., and Kluwer, E. S. (2003). When forgiving enhances psychological well-being: The role of interpersonal commitment. *Journal of Personality and Social Psychology*, 84, 1011–1026.
Kashima, Y., and Triandis, H. C. (1986). The self-serving bias in attributions as a coping strategy: A cross-cultural study. *Journal of Cross-Cultural Psychology*, 17, 83–97.
Keen, S. (1986). *Faces of the enemy: Reflections of the hostile imagination.* San Francisco: Harper and Row.
———(1994). *Teki no kao: Zōo to sensō no shinrigaku* (Faces of the enemy: The psychology of hatred and war). (T. Satō and Y. Satō, Trans.), Tokyo: Kashiwa Shobō.
Kellen, R. C., and Ellard, J. H. (1999). An equity theory analysis of the impact of forgiveness and retribution on transgressor compliance. *Personality and Social Psychology Bulletin*, 25(7), 864–872.
Kelman, H. C. (1973). Violence without moral restraint: Reflection on the dehumanization of victims and victimizers. *Journal of Social Issues*, 29, 25–61.
Kida, M. (1967). *Nippon buraku* (The Japanese hamlet). Tokyo: Iwanami Shoten.
Kidder, L. H., and Muller, S. (1991). What is fair in Japan. In H. Steemsma and R. Verton, (Eds). *Social justice in human relations: Social and psychological consequences of justice and injustice* (Vol. 2, pp. 138–152). New York: Plenum.
Kim, S. H., Smith, R. H., and Brigham, N. L. (1998). Effects of power imbalance and the presence of third parties on reactions to harm: Upward and downward revenge. *Personality and Social Psychology Bulletin*, 24, 353–361.
Kimura, K. (1990). Kaisō ishiki toshite no fukōheikan (Perceptions of unfairness as stratum consciousness). In M. Umino and K. Katase (Eds). *Kyōiku to shakai ni kansuru kōkōsei no ishiki: Dai-2-ji chōsa hōkokusho* (Upper secondary school students' awareness about education and society: Report on the second survey) (pp. 73–88). Sendai: Tōhoku Daigaku Bungakubu Kyōiku Bunka Kenkyū Kai.
Kitani, S., Hasebe, T., Arai, K., and Hiramatsu, N. (2002). Chiiki-zukuri o daizai ni shita kankyō kyōiku no jissen: Rōrupurēingu gēmu o mochiita Yamagata-ken Kanayama-chō no jirei (The practice of environmental education based on community development: the example of Kanayama Town, Yamagata Prefecture, which used role-playing games). *Heisei 11–13-nendo kagaku kenkyūhi hojokin kenkyū seika hōkokusho*) (*Kenkyū*

daihyōsha, Hasebe Tadashi) (Report on results of research funded by scientific research grants, 1999–2000~2001–02) (Research representative: Tadashi Hasebe), pp. 153–176.
Kitayama, S., and Karasawa, M. (1997). Implicit self-esteem in Japan: Name letters and birthday numbers. *Personality and Social Psychology Bulletin*, 23, 736–742.
Kitayama, S., and Uchida, Y. (2003). Explicit self-criticism and implicit self-regard: Evaluating self and friend in two cultures. *Journal of Experimental Social Psychology*, 39, 476–482.
Kitayama, S., Takagi, H., and Matsumoto, H. (1995). Seikō to shippai no kiin: Nihonteki jiko no bunka shinrigaku (Attribution of success and failure: The cultural psychology of the Japanese-type self). *Shinrigaku Hyōron*, 38, 247–280.
Kluegel, J.R., Mason, D.S., and Wegener, B. (Eds). (1995). *Social justice and political change*. New York: Walter de Gruyter.
Klüver, L. (2002). Denmark participation: A given in Danish culture. In S. Joss and S. Bellucci (Eds). *Participatory technology assessment: European perspectives* (pp. 75–91). London: Centre for the Study of Democracy (CSD) at University of Westminster in association with TA Swiss.
Knight, J. L., Guiliano, T. A., and Sanchez-Ross, M. G. (2001). Famous or infamous? The influence of celebrity status and race on perceptions of responsibility for rape. *Basic and Applied Social Psychology*, 23, 183–190.
Kobayashi, C., and Greenwald, A. G. (2003). Implicit-explicit differences in self-enhancement for Americans and Japanese. *Journal of Cross-Cultural Psychology*, 34, 522–541.
Kobayashi, T. (2004). *Dare ga kagaku gijutsu ni tsuite kangaeru no ka: Konsensasu kaigi to iu jikken* (Who thinks about scientific techniques?: The experiment of consensus conferences). Nagoya: Nagoya Daigaku Shuppan Kai.
Kōsei Rōdō Shō (Ministry of Health, Labour and Welfare) (2004). *Kajō rōdō/mentaru herusu taisaku no arikata ni kakawaru kentōkai: Hōkokusho* (Committee for Investigations Relating to the State of Overwork and Mental Health Policies: A report). *http://www.mhlw.go.jp/houdou/2004/08/h0818-1.html*.
Kovel, J. (1970). *White racism: A psychohistory*. New York: Pantheon.
Kramer, R. M., and Tyler, T. R. (1996). *Trust in organizations*. Thousand Oaks, California: SAGE Publications.
Kramer, R. M., Shah, P. P., and Woerner, S. (1995). Why ultimatums fail: Social identity and moralistic aggression in coercive bargaining. In R. M. Kramer and D. M. Messick (Eds). *Negotiation as a social process* (pp. 285–308). Beverly Hills, California: Sage.
Kudo, E., and Numazaki, M. (2003). Explicit and direct self-serving bias in Japan: Reexamination of self-serving bias for success and failure. *Journal of Cross-Cultural Psychology*, 34, 511–521.
Kumagai, T., and Ohbuchi, K. (2001). The effect of collective self-esteem and group membership on aggression of 'third-party victims.' *Tohoku Psychologica Folia*, 60, 35–44.
——— (2003). The effect of mortality salience and collaborative experience on aggression of 'third-party victims.' *Tohoku Psychologica Folia*, 62, 109–119.

———— (2004). Effects of group membership and uncertainty on third party aggression. *Tohoku Psychologica Folia*, 63, 8–14.

Kurman, J. (2003). Why is self-enhancement low in certain collectivist cultures? An investigation of two competing explanations. *Journal of Cross-Cultural Psychology*, 34, 496–510.

Laszlo, T. (1998). *Burajiru-jin to iu dake de* (Just for being Brazilian). http://www.issho.gol.com/writings/herculano72098.html (accessed 13 November 2005).

Leary, M. R., and Baumeister, R.F. (2000). The nature and function of self-esteem: Sociometer theory. In M. P. Zanna (Ed.). *Advances in experimental social psychology* (Vol. 32, pp. 1–62). San Diego, California: Academic Press.

Leary, M., Springer, C., Negel, L., Ansell, E., and Evans, K. (1998). The causes, phenomenology, and consequences of hurt feeling. *Journal of Personality and Social Psychology*, 74, 1225–1237.

Lerner, M. J. (1982). The justice motive in human relations: Some thoughts on what we know and need to know about justice. In M. J. Lerner and S. C. Lerner (Eds). *The justice motive in social behavior* (pp. 11–35). New York: Plenum Press.

Leung, K. (2005). How generalizable are justice effects across cultures? In J. Greenberg and J. Colquitt (Eds). *Handbook of organizational justice* (pp. 555–587). Mahwah, New Jersey: Lawrence Erlbaum Associates, Publishers.

Leventhal, G. S. (1980). What should be done with equity theory? New approaches to the study of fairness in social relationships. In K. Gergen, M. Greenberg, and R. Willis (Eds). *Social exchange: Advances in theory and research* (pp. 27–55). New York: Plenum Press.

Leventhal, G. S., Karuza, J., and Fry, W. R. (1980). Beyond fairness: A theory of allocation preference. In G. Mikula (Ed.). *Justice and social interaction* (pp. 167–218). New York: Springer-Verlag.

Lewin, K. (1948). *Resolving social conflicts*. New York: Harper and Bros.

Lind, E. A. (2001). Thinking critical about justice judgments. *Journal of Vocational Behavior*, 58, 220–226.

Lind, E. A., and Tyler, T. R. (1988). *The social psychology of procedural justice*. New York, New York: Plenum Press.

———— (1995). *Feanesu to tetsuzuki no shakai shinrigaku* (The social psychology of fairness and procedure). I. Sugawara and K. Ohbuchi (Trans.). Tokyo: Brain Shuppan.

Lind, E. A., and Van den Bos, K. (2002). When fairness works: Toward a general theory of uncertainty management. *Research in Organizational Behavior*, 24, 181–223.

Lind, E. A., Kanfer, R., and Earley, P.C. (1990). Voice, control, and procedural justice: Instrumental and noninstrumental concerns in fairness judgments. *Journal of Personality and Social Psychology*, 59, 952–959.

Lind, E. A., Kulik, C.A., Ambrose, M., and de Vera Park, M.V. (1993). Individual and corporate dispute resolution: Using procedural fairness as a decision heuristic. *Administrative Science Quarterly*, 38, 224–251.

Lind, E. A., MacCoun, R. J., Ebener, P. A., Felstiner, W. L. F., Hensler, D. R., Resnik, J., and Tyler, T. R. (1990). In the eye of the beholder: Tort litigants' evaluations of their experiences in the civil justice system. *Law and Society Review*, 24, 953–996.

Loewenstein, G. F., Thompson, L., and Bazerman, M. H. (1989). Social utility and decision making in interpersonal contexts. *Journal of Personality and Social Psychology*, 57, 426–441.

Lynn, F. M., and Kartez, J. D. (1995). The redemption of citizen advisory committees. In O. Renn et al. (Eds). *Fairness and competence in citizen participation* (pp. 87–110). Dordrecht: Kluwer Academic Publishers.

Mabuchi, R. (2000). Fukōheikan ga takamaru shakai jōkyō wa nani ka: Kōseikan to fukōseikan no rekishi (Under what social conditions does a sense of unfairness grow?: The history of the perception of fairness and the sense of unfairness). In M. Umino (Ed.). *Nihon no kaisō shisutemu 2: Kōheikan to seiji ishiki* (Stratification system in Japan 2: A sense of fairness and political consciousness) (pp. 151–170). Tokyo: Tōkyō Daigaku Shuppan Kai.

Mackie, D., Devos, T., and Smith, E. (2000). Intergroup emotions: Explaining of offensive action tendencies in an intergroup context. *Journal of Personality and Social Psychology*, 79, 602–616.

Macrae, C. N., Bodenhausen, G. V., Milne, A. B., and Jetten, J. (1994). Out of mind but back in sight: Stereotypes on the rebound. *Journal of Personality and Social Psychology*, 67, 808–817.

Markovsky, B. (1988). Injustice and arousal. *Social Justice Research*, 2, 223–233.

Markus, H. R., and Kitayama, S. (1991). Culture and the self: Implications for cognition, emotion, and motivation. *Psychological Review*, 98, 224–253.

Marsh, H. W. (1989). Confirmatory factor analysis of multitrait-multimethod data: Many problems and few solutions. *Applied Psychological Measurement*, 13, 335–361.

Masterson, S. S., Lewis, K., Goldman, B. M., and Taylor, M. S. (2000). Integrating justice and social exchange: The differing effect of fair procedures and treatment on work relationships. *Academy of Management Journal*, 43, 738–748.

Matsuda, M. (2002). Doitsu, Kārusurūe shi no toshi sōgō kaihatsu purojekuto (A comprehensive urban development project in Karlsruhe City, Germany). *Dai-4-kai Kōchi-ken yunibāsaru dezain shinpojiumu 'Toshi saisei to sono shuhō'* (The 4th Kōchi Prefecture Universal Design Symposium: 'Urban revival and its means'). Kōchi-ken Seisaku Sōgō Kenkyūjo, pp. 22–35.

Matsuda, W., and Ishida, H. (2002). Toshi keikaku ni okeru PI purosesu no arikata ni kansuru kenkyū (A study for effective public involvement in the Ushiku city master plan process). *Doboku Keikakugaku Kenkyū Ronbun Shū* (Infrastructure Planning Review), 19(3), 129–135.

McCullough, M. E., Bellah, C. G., Kilpatrick, S. D., and Johnson, J. L. (2001). Vengefulness: Relationships with forgiveness, rumination, well-being, and the Big Five. *Personality and Social Psychology*, 27, 601–610.

McCullough, M. E., Pargament, K. I., and Thoresen, C. E. (2000). The psychology of forgiveness. In E. M. McCullough, K. I. Pargament, and C. E. Thoresen (Eds). *Forgiveness: Theory, research, and practice* (pp. 1–16). New York: Guilford Press.

McCullough, M. E., Rachal, K. C., and Worthington, E. L. J. (1997). Interpersonal forgiving in close relationships. *Journal of Personality and Social Psychology*, 73, 321–336.

McCullough, M. E., Rachal, K. C., Sandage, S. J., Worthington, E. L. J., Brown, S. W., and Hight, T. L. (1998). Interpersonal forgiving in close relationships:

Theoretical elaboration and measurement. *Journal of Personality and Social Psychology*, 75, 1586–1603.

McGuire, W. J., McGuire, C. V., and Winton, W. (1979). Effects of household sex composition on the salience of one's gender in the spontaneous self concept. *Journal of Experimental Social Psychology*, 15, 77–90.

McGuire, W. J., McGuire, C. V., Child, P., and Fujioka, T. (1978). Salience of ethnicity in the spontaneous self-concept as a function of one's ethnic distinctiveness in the social environment. *Journal of Personality and Social Psychology*, 36, 511–520.

Messick, D. M. (1993). Equality as decision heuristics. In B. A. Mellers and J. Baron (Eds). *Psychological perspectives on justice* (pp. 11–31). New York: Cambridge University Press.

Messick, D. M., and Sentis, K. P. (1993). Fairness, preference, and fairness biases. In D. M. Messick and K. S. Cook (Eds). *Equity theory: Psychological and sociological perspectives* (pp. 61–94). New York: Praeger.

Mikula, G., Petri, B., and Tanzer, N. (1990). What people regard as unjust: Types and structures of everyday experiences of injustice. *European Journal of Social Psychology*, 20, 133–149.

Miller, D. T. (2001). Disrespect and the experience of injustice. *Annual Review of Psychology*, 52, 527–553.

Mirowsky, J. (1987). The psycho-economics of feeling underpaid: Distributive justice and the earnings of husbands and wives. *American Journal of Sociology*, 92, 1404–1434.

Misumi, K. (1993). Umino no kyōyūchi jirenma moderu kōsatsu (Rethinking Umino's 'commons dilemma' model). *Riron to Hōhō* (Sociological Theory and Methods), 8, 277–285.

Miyamoto, Y., Fukui, W., Michigami, M., Kita, H., and Hinokidani, O. (2001). Mizu kankyō hozen katsudō ni taisuru jūmin sanka o sokushin suru hōhō ni kansuru kenkyū (The methodology for stimulating public participation in activity for preservation of the water environment). *Suikōgaku Ronbun Shū* (Annual Journal of Hydraulic Engineering), JSCE 45, 25–30.

Miyano, M. (2000). Kōhei rinen wa dono yō ni keisei sareru no ka: Gainen no seiri to Nihon no ichizuke (How is a philosophy of fairness formed?: A consolidation of concepts and the Japanese position). In M. Umino (Ed.). *Nihon no kaisō shisutemu 2: Kōheikan to seiji ishiki* (Stratification system in Japan 2: A sense of fairness and political consciousness) (pp. 85–102). Tokyo: Tōkyō Daigaku Shuppan Kai.

Miyano, M. (Ed.). (1996). Shakaiteki kōsei no kenkyū: Riron, jisshō, ōyō (Research on social justice: Theories, demonstrations and applications). *Kagaku kenkyūhi hojokin kenkyū seika hōkokusho* (Reports on the outcomes of research funded by scientific grants-in-aid).

———(Ed.) (1998). *Kōheikan to shakai kaisō: 1995-nen SSM chōsa shirīzu 7* (The Sense of Fairness and Social Strata: 1995 SSM Survey Series 7). SSM Chōsa Kenkyūkai Hōkokusho.

———(Ed.) (2000). *Japanese perceptions of social justice: How do they figure out what ought to be?* Tokyo: Ministry of Education, Science, Sports and Culture Grant-in-aid for Scientific Research Report (Grant number 09410050).

Miyauchi, T. (2001a). Jūmin no seikatsu senryaku to kyōdō riyō ken: Soromon Shotō no jirei kara (Residents' life strategy and common-use rights: Taking examples from the Solomon Islands). In T. Miyauchi (Ed.). *Shirīzu kankyō shakaigaku 2: Komonzu no shakaigaku* (Environmental sociology series 2: The sociology of commons) (pp. 144–164). Tokyo: Shinyōsha.

———(2001b). Komonzu no shakaigaku: Shizen kankyō no shoyū, riyō, kanri o megutte (The sociology of commons: Issues around the ownership, use and management of the natural environment). In Torigoe Hiroyuki (Ed.). *Kōza kankyō shakaigaku dai-3-kan: Shizen kankyō to kankyō bunka* (Environmental sociology course, Vol. 3: The natural environment and environmental culture) (pp. 25–46). Tokyo: Yūhikaku.

Moorman, R. H. (1991). The relationship between organizational justice and organizational citizenship behaviors: Do fairness perceptions influence employee citizenship? *Journal of Applied Psychology*, 76, 845–855.

Moorman, R. H., Blakely, G. L., and Niehoff, B. P. (1998). Does perceived organizational support mediate the relationship between procedural justice and organizational citizenship behavior? *Academy of Management Journal*, 41, 351–357.

Morrison, E. W., and Robinson, S. L. (1997). When employees feel betrayed: A model of how psychological contract violation develops. *Academy of Management Review*, 22, 226–256.

Moshman, D. (2005). Genocidal hatred: Now you see it, now you don't. In R. J. Sternberg (Ed.). *The psychology of hate* (pp. 185–210). Washington DC: American Psychological Association.

Mullet, É., and Girard, M. (2000). Developmental and Cognitive Points of View on Forgiveness. In E. M. McCullough, K. I. Pargament, and C. E. Thoresen (Eds). *Forgiveness: Theory, research, and practice* (pp. 111–132). New York: Guilford Press.

Mummendy, A., and Otten, S. (2004). Aversive discrimination. In M. B. Brewer, and M. Hewstone (Eds). *Emotion and motivation* (pp. 298–318). Malden, Massachusetts: Blackwell Publishing.

Mumpower, J. L. (1995). The Dutch study groups revisited. In O. Renn et al. (Eds). *Fairness and competence in citizen participation* (pp. 321–338). Dordrecht: Kluwer Academic Publishers.

Muramoto, Y. (2003). An indirect self-enhancement in relationship among Japanese. *Journal of Cross-Cultural Psychology*, 34, 552–566.

Muramoto, Y., and Yamaguchi, S. (1997). Mō hitotsu no self-serving bias: Nihonjin no kizoku ni okeru jiko hika/shūdan hōshi keikō no kyōson to sono imi ni tsuite (Another self-serving bias: Concerning the coexistence and significance of self-devaluation and group-serving bias in Japanese attribution). *Jikken Shakai Shinrigaku Kenkyū*, 37, 65–75.

Murata, Y., and Endō, Y. (1999). Kōei jūtaku tatekae keikaku sakutei ni okeru jūmin sanka to sōsharu sapōto ni kansuru kenkyū (A study of ways and means of participation in view of social support in the planning process of public housing renewal). *Nihon Kenchiku Gakkai Keikaku Kei Ronbun Shū* (Journal of Architecture Planning Environment Engineering), AIJ, 523, 171–178.

Murnighan, J. K., and Pillutla, M. M. (1995). Fairness versus self-interest:

Asymmetric moral imperatives in ultimatum bargaining. In R. M. Kramer and D. M. Messick (Eds). *Negotiation as social process* (pp. 240–267). Beverly Hills, California: Sage.

Murrell, A. J., Dietz-Uhler, B. L., Dovidio, J. F., Gaertner, S. L., and Drout, C. (1994). Aversive racism and resistance to affirmative action: Perceptions of justice are not necessarily colorblind. *Basic and Applied Social Psychology*, 15, 71–86.

Nagata, M., and Sugiman, T. (1993). Toshi kaihatsu o meguru konfurikuto kaiseki: Kyōto eki biru kōsōka mondai ni tsuite (Conflict analysis on urban development: On the case of Kyoto Terminal building). *Shakai Shinrigaku Kenkyū* (Research in Social Psychology), 9(1), 48–64.

Nakayachi, K., and Watabe, M. (2005). Hitojichi kyōshutsu ga shinraisei hyōka ni oyobosu eikyō: Jihatsuteki kyōshutsu to kōi jisseki no kōka (The influence of hostage-posting on estimation of trustworthiness: The effect of voluntary posting and reliable results). *Shinrigaku Kenkyū* (The Japanese Journal of Psychology), 76(3), 235–243.

Neale, M. A., and Bazerman, M. H. (1991). *Cognition and rationality in negotiation*. New York: Free Press.

Niehoff, B. P., and Moorman, R. H. (1993). Justice as a mediator of the relationship between methods of monitoring and organizational citizenship behavior. *Academy of Management Journal*, 36, 527–556.

Nihon Shakaigakkai Chōsa Iinkai (Japanese Sociological Society SSM Research Committce). (1958). *Nihon shakai no kaisōteki kōzō* (The stratum structure of Japanese society). Tokyo: Yūhikaku.

Nuttin, J. M., Jr. (1985). Narcissism beyond Gestalt and awareness: The name letter effect. *European Journal of Social Psychology*, 15, 353–361.

O'Reilly, C., and Chatman, J. (1986). Organizational commitment and psychological commitment. *Journal of Applied Psychology*, 71, 492–49.

Oda, T., and Abe, K. (2000). Fukōheikan wa dono yō ni shōjiru no ka: Seisei mekanizumu no kaimei (How does a sense of unfairness arise?: An elucidation of the formation mechanism). In M. Umino (Ed.). *Nihon no kaisō shisutemu 2: Kōheikan to seiji ishiki* (Stratification system in Japan 2: A sense of fairness and political consciousness) (pp. 103–125). Tokyo: Tōkyō Daigaku Shuppan Kai.

Ōhashi, M., and Harihara, M. (2000). Jibun o 'futsū' da to ninchi suru koto wa jiko hyōka o takameru ka? (Does perceiving oneself as being 'average' heighten one's self-evaluation?). *Nihon Shakai Shinri Gakkai dai-41-kai taikai happyō Ronbun Shū*, 20–21.

Ohbuchi, K. (1998). Conflict management in Japan. In K. Leung and D. Tjosvold (Eds). *Conflict management in the Asian Pacific* (pp. 49–72). New York: Wiley and Sons.

——— (2003). A study of justice bond theory: Justice in social policies, institutions, and organizations. *Research Report of Grant-in Aid for Scientific Research by the Japan Society for the Promotion of Science (Japanese)*. Sendai, Japan: Tohoku University.

——— (2004a). Shūdan no shakai shinrigaku to kōsei (Hō to shinri gakkai dai-4-kai taikai kōen kiroku) The social psychology of groups and fairness: Record of presentations at the 4th Conference of the Japanese Society for Law and Psychology). *Hō to Shinri* (Law and Psychology), 1, 43–53.

——— (2004b). Tasuijun no kōsei hyōka to kuni ni taisuru taido (Multistandard fairness evaluation and attitudes to the state). In K. Ohbuchi (Ed.). *Nihonjin no kōseikan: Kōsei wa kojin to shakai o musubu kizuna ka?* (Japanese perceptions of fairness: Is fairness the bond that binds individuals and society?) (pp. 127–163). Sagamihara: Gendai Tosho.

——— (2004c). Kuni ni taisuru fuhen shinnen to shakaiteki kōsei (Immutability beliefs about the state and social justice). In K. Ohbuchi (Ed.). *Nihonjin no kōseikan: Kōsei wa kojin to shakai o musubu kizuna ka?* (Japanese perceptions of fairness: Is fairness the bond that binds individuals and society?) (pp. 165–197). Sagamihara: Gendai Tosho.

——— (2004d). Minji soshō riyōsha no hannō to kōseikan (Civil litigants' reactions and perceptions of fairness). In K. Ohbuchi (Ed.). *Nihonjin no kōseikan: Kōsei wa kojin to shakai o musubu kizuna ka?* (Japanese perceptions of fairness: Is fairness the bond that binds individuals and society?) (pp. 231–264). Sagamihara: Gendai Tosho.

——— (2006a). The social bonds of justice: Theory and research. In K. Ohbuchi (Ed.). *Social justice in Japan: Concepts, theories and paradigms* (pp. 3–33). Melbourne: Trans Pacific Press.

——— (2006b). The structure of justice: Theoretical considerations. In K. Ohbuchi (Ed.). *Social justice in Japan: Concepts, theories and paradigms* (pp. 72–92). Melbourne: Trans Pacific Press.

Ohbuchi, K and Fukumo, M., (2003). Shakaiteki kōsei to kini ni taisuru taido no kizuna kasetsu: Tasuijun kōsei hyōka, bunpaiteki oyobi tetsuzukiteki kōsei (A justice-bond hypothesis on the relationship between social justice and attitudes towards the state: Multi-level evaluation of distributive and procedural fairness). *Shakai Shinigaku Kenkyū* (Japanese Journal of Social Psychology), 18, 204–212.

Ohbuchi, K., Fukuno, M., and Imazai, K. (2003). Kuni no fuhen shinnen to shakaiteki kōseikan: Demogurafikku hensū, kuni ni taisuru taido, oyobi kōgi hannō to no kankei (Immutability beliefs towards the state and perceptions of social justice: Demographic variables, attitudes towards the state, and their connection with protest responses). *Ōyō Shinrigaku Kenkyū* (Japanese Journal of Applied Psychology), 28, 112–123.

Ohbuchi, K., and Imazai, K. (1999). Kokumin ni yoru kuni ni taisuru kōseikan to komittomento oyobi sono kinō hyōka (Citizens' perceptions of fairness and commitment towards the state and their functional assessment). *Shinrigaku Kenkyū* (Japanese Journal of Psychology), 70, 310–318.

Ohbuchi, K., Kameda, M., and Agarie, N. (1989). Apology as aggression control: Its role in mediating appraisal of and response to harm. *Journal of Personality and Social Psychology*, 56, 219–227.

Ohbuchi, K., Sugawara, I., Teshigahara, K., and Imazai, K. (2005). Procedural justice and the assessment of civil justice in Japan. *Law and Society Review*, 39(4), 875–891.

Olekalns, M., Smith, P. L., and Kibby, R. (1996). Social value orientations and negotiator outcomes. *European Journal of Social Psychology*, 26, 299–313.

Olson, J. M., Roese, N. J., Meen, J., and Robertson, D. J. (1994). The reconditions and consequences of relative deprivation: Two field studies. *Journal of Applied Social Psychology*, 25, 944–964.

Oosterbreek, H., Sloof, R., and van de Kuilen, G. (2004). Cultural differences in ultimatum game experiments: Evidence from a meta-analysis. *Experimental Economics*, 7, 171–188.

Opotow, S. (1990). Moral exclusion and injustice: An introduction. *Journal of Social Issues*, 46, 1–20.

——— (2005). Hate, conflict, and moral exclusion. In R. J. Sternberg (Ed.). *The psychology of hate* (pp. 121–154). Washington DC: American Psychological Association.

O'Reilly, C., and Chatman, J. (1986) Organizational committment and psychological committment. Journal of Applioed Psychology, 71, 492–49?

Organ, D. W. (1988). *Organizational citizenship behavior.* Lexington. MA: Lexington Books.

Orth, U. (2004). Does perpetrator punishment satisfy victims' feeling of revenge? *Aggressive Behavior*, 30, 62–70.

Otten, S. (2002). I am positive and so are we: The self as determinant of favouritism toward novel ingroup. In J. P. Forgas and K. D. Williams (Eds). *The social self: Cognitive, interpersonal, and intergroup perspectives* (pp. 273–292). New York: Psychology Press.

Oyserman, D. O., Coon, H. M., and Kemmelmeier, M. (2002). Rethinking individualism and collectivism: Evaluation of theoretical assumptions and meta-analysis. *Psychological Bulletin*, 128, 3–72.

Perloff, L. S. (1987). Social comparison and illusions of invulnerability to negative life events. In C. R. Snyder and C. Ford (Eds). *Coping with negative life events: Clinical and social psychological perspectives* (pp. 217–242). New York: Plenum.

Petts, J. (2001). Evaluating the effectiveness of deliberative processes: Waste management case-studies. *Journal of Environmental Planning and Management*, 44, 207–226.

Petty, R. E., and Cacioppo, J. T. (1986). The elaboration likelihood model of persuasion. In L. Berkowitz (Ed.). *Advances in experimental social psychology* (Vol. 19, pp. 123–205). New York: Academic Press.

Postmes, T., Spears, R., Sakhel, K., and de Groot, D. (1999). Social influence in computer-mediated communication: The effects of anonymity on group behavior. *Personality and Social Psychology Bulletin*, 27, 1243–1254.

Prichard, D., Dunnette, M. D., and Jorgenson, D. O. (1972). Effects of perceptions of equity and inequity on worker performance and satisfaction. *Journal of Applied Psychology*, 56, 75–94.

Rabbie, J. M., and Horwitz, M. (1969). Arousal of ingroup-outgroup bias by a chance win or loss. *Journal of Personality and Social Psychology*, 13, 269–277.

Rawls, J. (1971). *A theory of justice.* Cambridge, Massachusetts: Harvard University Press.

Renn, O., Webler, T., and Wiedemann, P. (1995). The pursuit of fair and competent citizen participation. In O. Renn et al. (Eds). *Fairness and competence in citizen participation* (pp. 339–368). Dordrecht: Kluwer Academic Publishers.

Renn, O., Webler, T., Rakel, H., Dienel, P., and Johnson, B. (1993). Public participation in decision making: A three-step procedure. *Policy Sciences*, 26, 189–214.

Robinson, R. V., and W. Bell (1978). Equality, success, and social justice in England and the United States. *American Sociological Review*, 43, 125–143.

Rose, A. J., and Asher, S. R. (1999). Children's goals and strategies in response to conflicts within a friendship. *Developmental Psychology*, 35, 69–79.

Rosenbaum, M. E., Moore, D. L., Cotton, J. L., Cook, M. S., Hieser, R. A., Shover, M. N., and Gray, M. J. (1980). Group productivity and process: Pure and mixed reward structures and task interdependence. *Journal of Personality and Social Psychology*, 39, 626–642.

Rosenberg, M. (1965). *Society and adolescent self image*. Princeton, New Jersey: Princeton University Press.

Ross, L., Greene, D., and House, P. (1977). The 'false consensus effect': An egocentric bias in social perception and attribution processes. *Journal of Experimental Social Psychology*, 13, 279–301.

Roth, A. E. (1995). Bargaining experiments. In J. H. Kagel and A. E. Roth (Eds). *The handbook of experimental economics* (pp. 253–348). Princeton, New Jersey: Princeton University Press.

Roth, A. E., Pransnikar, V., Okuno-Fujiwara, M., and Zamir, S. (1991). Bargaining and market behavior in Jerusalem, Ljubljana, Pittsburgh, and Tokyo: An experimental study. *American Economic Review*, 81, 1068–1095.

Rousseau, J.-J. (1985). *Du contrat social; Discours sur l'origine et les fondements de l'inegalité parmi les hommes*. Paris: Gallimard.

——— (1991). *Shakai keiyaku ron, ningen fubyōdō kigen ron* (On social contract theory and discourse on the origin of human inequality), K. Sakuta and Y. Hara (Trans.). Tokyo: Hakusuisha.

Rubin, J. Z., Pruitt, D. G., and Kim, S. H. (1994). *Social Conflict: Escalation stalemate and settlement*. 2nd Ed., New York: McGraw-Hill.

Rubinstein, A. (1982). Perfect equilibrium in a bargaining model. *Econometrica*, 50(1), 97–109.

Rupp, D., and Cropanzano, R. (2002). The mediating effects of social exchange relationships in predicting workplace outcomes from multifoci organizational justice. *Organizational Behavior and Human Decision Processes*, 89, 925–946.

Saitō, Y. (1994). Kaisō ishiki kenkyū ni okeru kōhei no mondai (Fairness issues in stratum consciousness studies). *Riron to Hōhō* (Sociological Theory and Methods), 16, 143–156.

——— (1998). Jasutisu no shakaigaku: Seisakuron no keifu (The sociology of justice: The genealogy of policy theory). In K. Kosaka and Y. Kōtō (Eds). *Kōza shakaigaku 1: Riron to hōhō* (Sociology course 1: Theory and methodology) (pp. 165–198). Tokyo: Tōkyō Daigaku Shuppan Kai.

Saitō, Y., and Yamagishi, T. (2000). Nihonjin no fukōheikan wa tokushu ka: Hikaku shakaironteki shiten de (Is the Japanese sense of unfairness unique?: From the perspective of comparative social theory). In M. Umino (Ed.). *Nihon no kaisō shisutemu 2: Kōheikan to seiji ishiki* (Stratification system in Japan 2: A sense of fairness and political consciousness) (pp. 127–149). Tokyo: Tōkyō Daigaku Shuppan Kai.

Sakakibara, H., Isobe, W., Okada, N., and Tatano, H. (2001). Fukanbi jōhōka de no purojekuto sentaku o meguru konfurikuto no chōsei mekanizumu ni kansuru kenkyū (A study on the coordination mechanism for conflict over project selection with incomplete information: The case of two players and two projects). *Doboku Gakkai Ronbun Shū* (Journal of Infrastructure Planning and Management), JSCE, 674 (IV–51), 3–15.

Sakamoto, Y. (2005). Nihonjin no kokuminsei 50-nen no kiseki: 'Nihonjin no kokuminsei chōsa' no hanseiki (The 50-year trajectory of the Japanese national character: A half-century of the 'Survey of the Japanese National Character'). *Tōkei Sūri* (Procedings of the Institute of Statistical Mathematics), 53(1), 3–33.

Sakuta, K. (1985). Kachi taikei no senzen to sengo (Value system before and after the World War). *Rīdingusu Nihon no shakaigaku 12: Bunka to shakai ishiki* (Readings for sociology in Japan 12: Culture and social attitudes) (pp. 190–205). Tokyo: Tōkyō Daigaku Shuppan Kai.

Sanders, G. S. (1982). Social comparison and perceptions of health and illness. In G. S. Sanders and J. Suls (Eds). *Social psychology of health and illness* (pp. 129–157). Hillsdale, New Jersey: Lawrence Erlbaum Associates.

Sani, F. (2005). When subgroups secede: Extending and refining the social psychological model of schism in groups. *Personality and Social Psychology Bulletin*, 31, 1074–1086.

Saris, E. S., and Aalberts, C. (2003). Different explanations for correlated disturbance terms in MTMM studies. *Structural Equation Modeling*, 10, 193–213.

Schelling, T. (1960). *The strategy of conflict*. Cambridge, Massachusetts: Harvard University Press.

Schmitt, M., Gollwitzer, M., Forster, N., and Montada, L. (2004). Effects of objective and subjective account components on forgiving. *Journal of Social Psychology*, 144, 465–485.

Schneider, F., Oppermann, B., and Renn, O. (1998). Implementing structured participation for regional level waste management planning. *Risk: Health, Safety and Environment*, 9, 379–395.

Schoeneman, T. (1981). Reports of the sources of self-knowledge. *Journal of Personality*, 49, 284–294.

Schwartz, S. H. (1992). Universals in the content and structure of values: Theoretical advances and empirical tests in 20 countries. In M. P. Zanna (Ed.). *Advances in experimental social psychology* (Vol. 25, pp. 1–65). New York: Academic Press.

Schwartz, S. H., and Huismans, S. (1995). Value priorities and religiosity in four Western religions. *Social Psychology Quarterly*, 58, 88–107.

Schwarz, J. M., and Smith, W. P. (1976). Social comparison and the influence of ability difference. *Journal of Personality and Social Psychology*, 58, 878–891.

Sedikides, C. (1993). Assessment, enhancement, and verification determinants of the self-evaluation process. *Journal of Personality and Social Psychology*, 65, 317–338.

Seiyama, K., and Umino, M. (Eds). (1991). *Chitsujo mondai to shakaiteki jirenma* (Problems of order and social dilemmas). Tokyo: Hābesuto Sha.

Sekiguchi, T., and Hayashi, Y. (2003). Feanesu 'kōheisei' jinji no susumekata: Soshiki no kōhai o bōshi shi, shinrai o kaifuku saseru (Methods for implementation of 'fairness'-oriented human resources: Preventing organisational deterioration and restoring trust). *Jinji Manējimento* (Human resources management), 153, 8–23.

Sen, A. (1985). *Commodities and capabilities*. Amsterdam: North-Holland.

Sherif, M., Harvey, O. J., White, B. J., Hood, W. R., and Sherif, C. W. (1961). *Intergroup cooperation and competition: The robber's cave experiment*. Norman, Oklahoma: University of Oklahoma.

Shihō seido kaikaku shingikai (Justice System Reform Council) (2001). *Minji soshō riyōsha chōsa: Hōkokusho (Survey report of civil litigants)*. Tokyo: Survey Research Center.

Shinohara, H. (2004). *Shimin no seijigaku* (Politics of citizenry). Iwanami Shinsho.

Shinotō, A. (2005). Purānunkusutēre kara mita 'shimin tōronkai' no igi (The significance of 'citizens' forums' from the perspective of the Planungszelle). *Chiiki Shakai Kenkyū* (Regional studies), 11, 22–31.

Shklar, J. (1990). *The faces of injustice*. New Haven, Connecticut: Yale University Press.

Singelis, T. M., Triandis, H. C., Bhawuk, D. P. S., and Gelfand, M. J. (1995). Horizontal and vertical dimensions of individualism and collectivism: A theoretical and measurement refinement. *Cross-Cultural Research*, 29, 240–275.

Singer, J. (1980). Social comparison: The process of self-evaluation. In L. Festinger (Ed.). *Retrospections on social psychology* (pp. 158–179). New York: Oxford University Press.

Smith, E. R. (1993). Social identity and social emotions: Toward new conceptualizations of prejudice. In D. M. Mackie and D. L. Hamilton (Eds). *Affect, cognition, and stereotyping: Interactive processes in group perception* (pp. 297–315). San Diego, California: Psychology Press.

———(1999). Affective and cognitive implications of a group becoming part of the self: New models of prejudice and of the self-concept. In D. Abrams and M. A. Hogg (Eds). *Social identity and social cognition* (pp. 183–196). Oxford, England: Blackwell.

——— (2002). Overlapping mental representations of self and group: Evidence and implications. In J. P. Forgas and K. D. Williams (Eds). *The social self: Cognitive, interpersonal, and intergroup perspectives* (pp. 21–36). New York: Psychology Press.

Smith, E. R., and Henry, S. (1996). An in-group becomes part of the self: Response time evidence. *Personality and Social Psychology Bulletin*, 22, 635–642.

Smith, G. (2003). *Deliberative democracy and the environment*. London: Routledge.

Smith, G., and Wales, C. (1999). The theory and practice of citizens' juries, *Policy and Politics*, 27, 295–308.

Snibbe, A. C., Kitayama, S., Markus, H. R., and Suzuki, T. (2003). They saw a game: A Japanese and American (football) field study. *Journal of Cross-Cultural Psychology*, 34, 581–595.

Snow D. A., Rochford, E. B., Jr., Worden, S. K., and Benford, R. D. (1986). Framing alignment process, mobilization, and movement participation. *American Sociological Review*, 51, 464–81.

Snyder, C. R., and Fromkin, H. L. (1980). *Uniqueness: The human pursuit of difference*. New York: Plenum.

Sommer, K. L., and Baumeister, R. F. (1997). Making someone feel guilty: Causes, strategies, and consequences. In R. M. Kowalski (Ed.). *Aversive interpersonal behaviors* (pp. 31–55). New York: Plenum Press.

Staub, E. (1990). Moral exclusion, personal goal theory, and extreme destructiveness. *Journal of Social Issues*, 46, 47–64.

Straub, P. G., and Murnighan, J. K. (1995). An experimental investigation of ultimatum games: Information, fairness, expectations, and lowest acceptable offers. *Journal of Economic Behavior and Organization*, 27, 345–364.

Strube, M. J., and Roemmele, L. A. (1985). Self-enhancement, self-assessment, and self-evaluative task choice. *Journal of Personality and Social Psychology*, 49, 981–993.

Suls, J., Wan, C. K., and Sanders, G. S. (1988). False consensus and false uniqueness in estimating the prevalence of health-protective behaviors. *Journal of Applied Social Psychology*, 18, 66–79.

Suzuki, Y., and Aoki, T. (2004). Isawa damu kaihatsu ni okeru gōi no kōzu (The structure of consensus-building in Isawa Dam construction). *Doboku Gakkai Tōhoku Shibu Gijutsu Kenkyū Kōen Gaiyō* (Proceedings of annual conference of JSCE in Tohoku), 484–485.

Swann, W. B., Kwan, V. S. Y., Polzer, J. T., and Milton, L. P. (2003). Fostering group identification and creativity in diverse groups: The role of individuation and self-verification. *Personality and Social Psychology Bulletin*, 29, 1396–1406.

Tafrodi, R.W., and Swan, W. B. (1995). Self-liking and self-competence as dimensions of global self-esteem: Initial validation of a measure. *Journal of Personality Assessment*, 65, 322–342.

Tajfel, H., and Turner, J. C. (1979). An integrative theory of intergroup conflict. In W. G. Austin and S. Worchel (Eds). *The social psychology of intergroup relations* (pp. 33–47). Monterey, California: Brooks-Cole.

——— (1986). The social identity theory of intergroup behavior. In S. Worchel, and W. Austin (Eds). *Psychology of intergroup relations* (pp. 7–24). Chicago: Nelson-Hall.

Tajfel, H., Flament, C., Billig, M. G., and Bundy, R. P. (1971). Social categorization and intergroup behaviour. *European Journal of Social Psychology*, 1, 149–178.

Takada, N., and Ohbuchi, K. (2003). Forgiveness in interpersonal conflict resolution: An association between resolution strategies and interpersonal relationship. *Proceeding of the 66th Annual Meeting of Japanese Association of Psychology*, 1605.

——— (2004). Why do we forgive offenders? Egocentric, altruistic, and normative motives for interpersonal forgiveness. *Tohoku Psychologia Folia*, 63, 95–102.

——— (2006). Forgiveness and the role of audience in conflict resolution. Poster presented at the International Symposium, 'Management of Social Problems and Justice in Group Contexts,' Sendai, Japan.

Takagi, J. (1999). *Shimin kagakusha toshite ikiru* (Living as citizen-scientists). Tokyo: Iwanami Shoten.

Takahashi, K. (1998). Kigyō nai kōseisei no rironteki mondai (Theoretical issues in intra-corporate fairness). *Nihon rōdō kenkyū kikō zasshi* (Japanese Journal of Labour Studies), 460, 49–58.

Takaku, S. (2001). The effect of apology and perspective taking on interpersonal forgiveness: A dissonance–attribution model of interpersonal forgiveness. *The Journal of Social Psychology*, 141, 494–508.

Takaku, S., Weiner, B., and Ohbuchi, K. (2001). A cross-cultural examination of the effects of apology and perspective taking on forgiveness. *Journal of Language and Social Psychology*, 20, 144–166.

Takao, K. (2002). Perceived procedural fairness and the evaluation of authorities: A case of an urban development project. *Shakai Shinrigaku Kenkyū* (Japanese Journal of Social Psychology), 17(3), 136–140.

Takata, T. (1981). Taijin kyōfu to shakaiteki hikaku (Social phobia and social comparison). *Nenpō Shakai Shinrigaku* (The Japanese Journal of Experimental Social Psychology), 22, 201–218.

——— (1987). Shakaiteki hikaku ni yoru jiko hyōka ni okeru jiko hikateki keikō (Self-devaluative tendencies in self-evaluation by social comparison). *Jikken Shakai Shinrigaku Kenkyū* (The Japanese Journal of Experimental Social Psychology), 27, 27–36.

——— (1993). Seinen no jiko gainen keisei to shakaiteki hikaku: Nihonjin daigakusei ni mirareru tokuchō (The formation of self-concept among youth and social comparison: Characteristics seen in Japanese university students). *Kyōiku Shinrigaku Kenkyū* (The Japanese Journal of Experimental Social Psychology), 41, 339–348.

——— (1995). Jiko ninshiki hōto toshite no shakaiteki hikaku no ichi: Nihonjin daigakusei ni mirareru tokuchō (The position of social comparison as a method of self-awareness: Characteristics seen in Japanese university students). *Nara Daigaku Kiyō* (Journal of Nara University), 23, 259–270.

——— (1998). Kenkō to byōki no shakaiteki hikaku: Bunkenteki kōsatsu (The social comparison of health and sickness: A cultural consideration. *Nara Daigaku Kiyō* (Journal of Nara University), 26, 71–91.

——— (2000). Nihonjin no 'hi-jiko-kōyō/jiko-hihan keikō' saikō: sono kitei jōken to kanjō taiken no jikkenteki kentō (Re-thinking Japanese 'non-self-enhancement/ self-critical tendencies': An experimental investigation of their rules [and] conditions and emotional experiences. *Nihon Shinri Gakkai Dai-64-kai Taikai Happyō Ronbun Shū* (Collected Papers from the 64th conference of the Japanese Psychological Association), 162.

——— (2001). Self-enhancement and self-criticism in Japanese culture: An experimental analysis. Paper presented at the 4th Annual Conference of Asian Association of Social Psychology, Melbourne, Australia.

——— (2003). Self-enhancement and self-criticism in Japanese culture: An experimental analysis. *Journal of Cross-Cultural Psychology*, 34, 542–551.

——— (2004). *'Nihonjin rashisa' no hattatsu shakai shinrigaku: Jiko, shakaiteki hikaku, bunka* (Developmental social psychology on 'typical Japanese': Self, social comparison, and culture). Kyoto: Nakanishiya Shuppan.

Takata, T., and Hayashi, H. (1981). Availability of objective information and social comparison behavior. *Japanese Psychological Research*, 23, 88–100.

Tamura, T., and Ohbuchi, K. (2006). Hiningenteki raberingu ga kōgeki kōdō ni oyobosu kōka: Kakutō TV gēmu o mochiita jikkenteki kentō (An experimental study of the effects of dehumanising labels on aggressive behaviour in a fighting-type video game situation). *Japanese Journal of Social Psychology*, 22 (2), 165–171.

Tanaka, M. (Ed.). (1978). *Sekai no meicho 6, 7: Puraton* (World classics 6, 7: Plato), Tokyo: Chūō Kōron Sha.

Taylor, D. M., and Moghaddam, F. M., (1994). *Theories of intergroup relations: International social psychological perspectives* (2nd Ed.) New York: Preager Publishers.

Taylor, S.E. (1982). Social cognition and health. *Personality and Social Psychology Bulletin*, 8, 549–562.
Taylor, S. E., Buunk, B. P., and Aspinwall, L. G. (1990). Social comparison, stress, and coping. *Personality and Social Psychology Bulletin,* 16, 74–89.
Tekleab, A. G., Takeuchi, R., and Taylor, M. S. (2005). Extending the chain of relationships among organizational justice, social exchange, and employee reactions: The role of contract violations. *Academy of Management Journal*, 48, 146–157.
Tepper, B. J. (2001). Health consequences of organizational injustice: Test of main and interactive effects. *Organizational Behavior and Human Decision Processes*, 86, 197–215.
Terabe, S., Yai, T., and Seki, K. (1999). Chōki kōtsū keikaku sakutei ni taisuru shimin sanka ishiki no bunseki (An analysis of public attitude towards involvement in long-range transportation planning processes). *Doboku Keikakugaku Kenkyū Ronbun Shū* (Infrastructure Planning Review), 16, 161–167.
Thaler, R. H. (1988). Anomalies: The ultimatum game. *Journal of Economic Perspectives*, 2, 195–206.
Theorell, T., and Karasek, R. A. (1996). Current issues relating to psychological job strain and cardiovascular disease research. *Journal of Occupational Health Psychology*, 1, 9–26.
Thibaut, J., and Kelly, H. H. (1959). *The social psychology of groups.* New York: Wiley.
Thibaut, J., and Walker, L. (1975). *Procedural justice: A psychological analysis.* Hillsdale, New Jersey: Lawrence Erlbaum.
Tice, D. M. (1992). Self-concept change and self-presentation: The looking glass self is also a magnifying glass. *Journal of Personality and Social Psychology*, 63, 435–451.
Toda, K. (1994). *Kankyōteki kōsei o motomete: Kankyō hakai no kōzō to erīto shugi* (Seeking environmental justice: The structure of environmental destruction and elitism). Tokyo: Shin'yō Sha.
Tominaga, K. (Ed.). (1979). *Nihon no kaisō kōzō* (The stratification structure of Japan). Tokyo: Tōkyō Daigaku Shuppan Kai.
Torigoe, H. (1997). *Kankyō shakaigaku no riron to jissen: Seikatsu kankyō shugi no tachiba kara* (The theory and practice of environmental sociology: From the standpoint of life-environmentalism). Tokyo: Yūhikaku.
——— (2004). *Kankyō shakaigaku: Seikatsusha no tachiba kara kangaeru* (Environmental sociology: Considering from the standpoint of people living their lives). Tokyo: Tōkyō Daigaku Shuppan Kai.
Triandis, H. (1995). *Individualism and collectivism.* Boulder, Colorado: Westview.
Tripp, T. M., Sondak, H., and Bies, R. J. (1995). Justice as rationality: A relational perspective on fairness in negotiations. In R. J. Bies, R. J. Lewicki, and B. H. Sheppard (Eds). *Research on negotiation in organizations* (Vol. 5, pp. 45–64). Greenwich, Connecticut: JAI.
Turner, J. C., Hogg, M.A., Oakes, P.J., Reicher, S.D., and Wetherell, M. (1987). *Rediscovering the social group: A self-categorisation theory.* Oxford, UK: Blackwell.
Tversky, A., and Kahneman, D. (1981). The framing of decisions and the psychology of choice. *Science*, 40, 453–463.

Tyler, T. R. (1988). What is procedural justice?: Criteria used by citizens to assess the fairness of legal procedures. *Law and Society Review*, 22, 301–355.
——— (1989). The psychology of procedural justice: A test of the group value model. *Journal of Personality and Social Psychology*, 57, 850–863.
——— (1990). *Why people obey the law: Procedural justice, legitimacy, and compliance*. New Haven, Connecticut: Yale University Press.
Tyler, T. R., and Bies, R. J. (1990). Interpersonal aspects of procedural justice. In J. S. Carroll (Ed.). *Applied social psychology in business settings*. Hillsdale, New Jersey: Lawrence Erlbaum.
Tyler, T. R., and Blader, S. L. (2000). *Cooperation in groups: Procedural justice, social identity, and behavioral engagement*. Philadelphia, Pennsylvania: Psychology Press/Taylor and Francis.
——— (2002). Autonomous versus comparative status: Must we be better than others to feel good about ourselves? *Organizational Behavior and Human Decision Processes*, 89, 813–838.
Tyler, T. R., Boeckman, R. J., Smith, H. J. and Huo, Y. J. (1997). *Social justice in a diverse society*. Boulder, Colorado: Westview Press.
Tyler, T. R., and Caine, A. (1981). The role of distributional and procedural fairness in the endorsement of formal leaders. *Journal of Personality and Social Psychology*, 41, 642–655.
Tyler, T. R., and Degoey, P. (1995). Collective restraint in social dilemmas: Procedural justice and identification effects on support for authorities. *Journal of Personality and Social Psychology*, 69, 482–497.
Tyler, T. R., Degoey, P., and Smith, H. J. (1996). Understanding why the justice of group procedures matters. *Journal of Personality and Social Psychology*, 70, 913–930.
Tyler, T. R., and Griffin, E. (1991). The influence of decision makers' goals on their concerns about procedural justice. *Journal of Applied Social Psychology*, 21, 1629–1658.
Tyler, T. R., and Lind, E. A. (1992). A relational model of authority in groups. In M. P. Zanna (Ed.). *Advances in experimental social psychology* (Vol. 25, pp. 115–191). New York: Academic Press.
Tyler, T. R., Rasinski, K., and Spodick, N. (1985). The influence of voice on satisfaction with leaders: Exploring the meaning of process control. *Journal of Personality and Social Psychology*, 48, 72–81.
Tyler, T. R., and Smith, H. J. (1999). Justice, social identity, and group processes. In T. R. Tyler, R. M. Kramer, and O. P. John (Eds). *The psychology of the social self* (pp. 223–264). Mahwah, New Jersey: Lawrence Erlbaum Associates, Inc.
Umino, M. (1988). Gendai shakai no hyōka – fukōheikan no dansō (The evaluation of contemporary society – the tomography of perceptions of unfairness). In Tōhoku Daigaku Bungakubu Tōhoku Bunka Kenkyū Kai (Eds). *Kyōiku to shakai ni taisuru kōkōsei no ishiki dai-ichiji chōsa hōkokusho* (Upper secondary school students' awareness about education and society: Report on the second survey) (pp. 23–38). Sendai: Tōhoku Daigaku Bungakubu Kyōiku Bunka Kenkyū Kai.
——— (2000b). Yutakasa no tsuikyū kara kōhei shakai no kikyū e: Kaisō ishiki no kōzō to hen'yō (From the pursuit of affluence to the desire for a just society: The structure and transformation of stratum consciousness). In M. Umino (Ed.). *Nihon no kaisō shisutemu 2: Kōheikan to seiji*

ishiki (Stratification system in Japan 2: A sense of fairness and political consciousness) (pp. 3–36). Tokyo: Tōkyō Daigaku Shuppan Kai.

──────── (2003). Fukōheikan wa dono yō ni shōjiru no ka: Keiryō bunseki no hōhō (How does a sense of unfairness arise?: Quantitative analysis methodology). In K. Hara (Ed.). *Jinbun shakai kagaku no shin seiki* (The new century of humanities and social sciences) (pp. 183–189). Sendai: Tōhoku Daigaku Shuppan Kai.

──────── (2005). Chichioya no fukōheikan wa naze hikui no ka: Sendai toshiken ni okeru kōkōsei chōsa dēta no tōkei bunseki (Why is fathers' sense of unfairness low?: A statistical analysis of senior high school student survey data in the Sendai metropolitan area). *Tōhoku Bunka Kenkyūshitsu Kiyō* (Bulletin of Tohoku Culture Research Room), 46, 1–15.

Umino, M. (Ed.). (2000a) *Nihon no kaisō shisutemu, 2: Kōheikan to seiji ishiki* (Stratification system in Japan, 2: A sense of fairness and political consciousness). Tokyo: Tōkyō Daigaku Shuppan Kai.

Umino, M., and Saitō, Y. (1990). Kōheikan to manzokukan – shakai hyōka no kōzō to shakaiteki chii (Senses of fairness and satisfaction: The structure of social evaluation and social position). In J. Hara (Ed.). *Gendai Nihon no kaisō kōzō 2: Kaisō ishiki no dōtai* (The strata structure of contemporary Japan, 2: The dynamics of stratum consciousness). Tokyo: Tōkyō Daigaku Shuppan Kai.

Van Den Bos, K., Lind, E. A., and Wilke, H. A. M. (2001). The psychology of procedural and distributive justice viewed from the perspectives of fairness heuristic theory. In R. Cropanzano (Ed.). *Justice in the workplace: From theory to practice* (Vol. 2, pp. 49–66). Mahwah, New Jersey: Lawrence Erlbaum Associates.

Van den Bos, K., Vermunt, R., and Wilke, H. A. M. (1997). Procedural and distributive justice: What is fair depends more on what comes first than on what comes next. *Journal of Personality and Social Psychology*, 72, 95–104.

Van den Bos, K., Wilke, H. A. M., and Lind, E. A. (1998). When do we need procedural fairness?: The role of trust in authority. *Journal of Personality and Social Psychology*, 75, 1449–1458.

Van Lange, P. A. M. (1999). The pursuit of joint outcomes and equality in outcomes: An integrative model of social value orientation. *Journal of Personality and Social Psychology*, 77, 337–349.

Vangelisti, A., and Sprague, R. (1998). Guilt and hurt: Similarities, distinctions, and conversational strategies. In P. Anderson and L. Guerrero (Eds). *Handbook of communication and emotion: Research, theory, application, and contexts* (pp. 123–154). New York: Academic Press.

Vermunt, R., and Steensma, H. (2001). Stress and justice in organization: An explanation into justice processes with the aim to find mechanisms to reduce stress. In R. Cropanzano (Ed.). *Justice in the workplace: From theory to practice* (Vol. 2, pp. 27–48). Mahwah, New Jersey: Lawrence Erlbaum Associates.

Vidmar, N. (1974). Retributive and utilitarian motives and other correlates of Canadian attitudes toward the death penalty. *Canadian Psychologist*, 15, 337–356.

Vidmar, N., and Ellsworth, P. (1974). Public opinion and the death penalty. *Stanford Law Review*, 26, 1245.

Vidmar, N., and Miller, D. T. (1980). Social psychological processes underlying attitudes toward legal punishment. *Law and Society Review*, 14, 401–438.

Wakamatsu, Y. (1999). Gōi keisei e no shimin sanka: Igi to hōhō (Citizen participation aimed towards consensus-building: Significance and methodology). *Heisei 11-nendo kagaku gijutsu shinkō chōseihi chōsa hōkokusho: 'Seimei rinri ni kakawaru shomondai ni kansuru kenkyū kaihatsu dōkō oyobi shakaiteki gōi keisei ni kansuru chōsa'* (Survey report: 'Survey on social consensus-building and trends in research and development relating to various issues concerning life ethics,' supported by Coordination Funds for the Promotion of Science and Technology, 2000–01), pp. 222–244.

———(2003). 'Sanbanze no mirai o kangaeru shinario wākushoppu' shakai jikken hōkoku (Social experiment report on the 'Scenario workshop to consider the future of Sanbanze'). *Kagaku gijutsuron gakkai dai-2-kai nenji kenkyū taikai yokōshū* (Collected papers from the 2nd annual conference of the Japanese Society for Science and Technology Studies), pp. 121–122.

Walzer, M. (1983). *Spheres of justice: A defence of pluralism and equality*. New York: Basic Books.

Watanabe, N. (2002). Keiei soshiki no rinshō shinrigaku (The clinical psychology of management organisations). In H. Shimoyama and Y. Tanno (Eds). *Kōza rinshō shinrigaku (6) Shakai rinshō shinrigaku* (A course in clinical psychology (6) Social clinical psychology) (pp. 269–292). Tokyo: Tokyo Daigaku Shuppan.

Webler, T. (1995). Right discourse in citizen participation: An evaluative yardstick. In O. Renn et al. (Eds). *Fairness and competence in citizen participation* (pp. 35–77), Dordrecht: Kluwer Academic Publishers.

Wegner, D. M., and Schneider, D. J. (1989). Mental control: The war of the ghost in the machine. In J. S. Uleman and J. A. Bargh (Eds). *Unintended thought* (pp. 287–305). New York: Guilford Press.

Wegner, D. M., Schneider, D. J., Carter, S. R., and White, T. L. (1987). Paradoxical effects of thought suppression. *Journal of Personality and Social Psychology*, 53, 5–13.

Weiner, B., Graham, S., Peter, O., and Zmuidinas, M. (1991). Public confession and forgiveness. *Journal of Personality*, 59, 281–312.

Weinstein, N. D. (1980). Unrealistic optimism about future life events. *Journal of Personality and Social Psychology*, 39, 806–820.

———(1987). Unrealistic optimism about susceptibility to health problems: Conclusions from a community-wide sample. *Journal of Behavioral Medicine*, 10, 481–500.

Weiss, H. M., Suckow, K., and Cropanzano, R. (1999). Effects of justice conditions on discrete emotions. *Journal of Applied Psychology*, 84, 786–794.

West, M. A. (1990). The social psychology of innovation in groups. In M. A. West and J. L. Farr (Eds). *Innovation and creativity at work: Psychological and organizational strategies* (pp. 4–36). Chichester: Wiley.

Wheeler, L., Martin, R., and Suls, J. (1997). The proxy model of social comparison for self-assessment of ability. *Personality and Social Psychology Review*, 1, 54–61.

Williamson, W. E. (1991). Interpersonal trust and attitudes toward human nature. In J. P. Robinson, P. R. Shaver, and L. S. Wrightsman (Eds). *Measures*

of personality and social psychological attitudes (pp. 373–412). New York: Academic Press.
Wills, T. A. (1981). Downward comparison principles in social psychology. *Psychological Bulletin*, 90, 245–271.
——— (1987). Downward comparison as a coping mechanism. In C.R. Snyder and C. Ford (Eds). *Coping with negative life events: Clinical and social-psychological perspectives* (pp. 158–179). New York: Plenum.
Wilson, S. R., and Benner, L. A. (1971). The effects of self-esteem and situation upon comparison choices during ability evaluation. *Sociometry*, 34, 381–397.
Wood, J. V. (1996). What is social comparison and how should we study it? *Personality and Social Psychology Bulletin*, 22, 520–537.
Worchel, S., and Andreoli, V. (1978). Facilitation of social interaction through deindividuation of the target. *Journal of Personality and Social Psychology*, 36, 549–556.
Worthington, E. L. J. (2003). Forgiving the devil: Coming to terms with damaged relationships. *Journal of Marital and Family Therapy*, 29, 429–430.
Wright, S. C., Aron, A., and Tropp, L. R. (2002). Including others (and groups) in the self: Self-expansion and intergroup relations. In J. P. Forgas and K. D. Williams (Eds). *The social self: Cognitive, interpersonal, and intergroup perspectives* (pp. 343–364). New York: Psychology Press.
Wyer, N. A., Sherman, J. W., and Stroessner, S. J. (2000). The roles of motivation and ability in controlling the consequences of stereotype suppression. *Personality and Social Psychology Bulletin*, 26, 13–25.
Yai, T., Terabe, S., and Seki, K. (2000). Kōiki kōtsū keikaku ni okeru paburikku inborubumento no hōhō ni kansuru kenkyū (A study on methods for involving the public in wide-area transportation planning). *Doboku Gakkai Ronbun Shū* (Journal of Infrastructure Planning and Management), JSCE, 653(IV–48), 105–115.
Yamada, A. (Ed.). (1968). *Sekai no meicho 14: Augusutinus* (World classics 14: St. Augustine). Tokyo: Chūō Kōron Sha.
Yamada, K. (1994). Shakaiteki sogai ishiki to seiji kōdō (Consciousness of social alienation and political behaviour). In A. Hiroshi (Ed.). *Seiji kōdō no shakai shinrigaku* (The social psychology of political behaviour) (pp. 128–154). Tokyo: Tōkyō Daigaku Shuppan Kai.
Yamagishi, T. (1998). *Shinrai no kōzō: Kokoro to shakai no shinka gēmu* (The structure of trust: The evolutionary games of mind and society). Tokyo: Tōkyō Daigaku Shuppan Kai.
Yamaguchi, S. (2003). Amae (Dependence). In S. Yamaguchi (Ed.). *Shakai shinrigaku: Ajia kara no apurōchi* (Social psychology: From Asian perspectives) (pp. 147–161). Tokyo: Nihon Hōsō Shuppan Kyōkai.
Yamamoto, R. (1989). 'Jiko' no nimensei ni kansuru ichi kenkyū: Seinenki kara seijinki ni kakete no hattatsu (One study on the dual nature of 'self': Development from adolescence towards adulthood). *Kyōiku Shinrigaku Kenkyū* (Japan Journal of Educational Psychology), 37, 302–311.
Yamaoka, S., Fujita, M., and Matsui, H. (2000). Chiku kōtsū seibi jigyō no shinchoku dankai to jūmin sanka no ishiki kōzō ni kansuru kenkyū (Analysis on the consciousness structure of residents' participation in microarea transportation planning, considering the progress stages of the project). *Toshi Keikaku Ronbun Shū* (Papers on City Planning), 35, 433–438.

Yasuda, S. (1971). *Shakai idō no kenkyū* (Studies in social mobility). Tokyo: Tōkyō Daigaku Shuppan Kai.
——— (1973). *Gendai Nihon no kaikyū ishiki* (Class consciousness in contemporary Japan). Tokyo: Yūhikaku.
Yatomi, N. (1999). Sutoresu no sokutei: Soshiki sutoresu (The measurement of stress: organisational stress). In N. Watanabe and H. Noguchi (Eds). *Soshiki shinri sokutei ron: Kōmoku hannō riron no furontia* (Organisational psychometric theory: The frontiers of item-response theory) (pp. 155–178). Tokyo: Hakutō Shobō.
Yoshida, A. (2003). Jiko hikateki komyunikēshon ga tekiō ni oyobosu eikyō no kentō: Bunkateki kihan no naizaika no shiten kara (An examination of the influence of self-comparative communication on adjustment: From the viewpoint of internalization of cultural norms) (Unpublished doctoral dissertation). Hiroshima University Graduate School of Biological Science.
Yoshida, A., and Ura, M. (2003). Jiko teiji kihan no naizaika keikō ni kansuru tansakuteki kenkyū (An exploratory study on the tendency to internalise self-presentation norms). *Jiko Shinrigaku Kenkyū*, 1, 27–39.
Yoshida, A., Ura, M., and Kurokawa, M. (2004). Nichijōteki na sōgo sayō bunmyaku ni okeru jiko hika teiji no tamenteki rikai (A multi-faceted understanding of self-devaluative presentation in contexts of mundane interaction). *Shakai Shinrigaku Kenkyū*. 20, 144–151.
Young, H. P. (1994). *Equity: In theory and practice.* Princeton: Princeton Academic Press.
Yuki, M. (2003). Intergroup comparison versus intragroup relationships: A cross-cultural examination of social identity theory in North American and East Asian cultural contexts. *Social Psychology Quarterly*, 66, 166–183.
Zaidan hōjin shakai keizai seisansei honbu mentaru herusu kenkyūjo (Mental Health Research Institute of the Japan Productivity Centre for Socio-Economic Development (JPC-SED) (2005). 'Rōdō kumiai no mentaru herusu no torikumi' ni kansuru ankēto chōsa kekka (Results of a questionnaire survey relating to 'Labour union efforts for mental health'). http://www.js-mental.org/images/03/kekka.pdf.
Zechmeister, J. S., and Romeo, C. (2003). Victim and offender accounts of interpersonal conflict: Autobiographical narratives of forgiveness and unforgiveness. *Journal of Personality and Social Psychology*, 82(4), 675–686.
Zeisel, H. (1985). *Say it with figures.* 6th Ed., New York: Harper and Row.
Zimbardo, P. G. (1970). The human choice: Individuation, reason, and order versus deindividuation, impulse, and chaos. *Nebraska Symposium on Motivation*, 17, 237–307.
Zohar, D. (1995). The justice perspective of job stress. *Journal of Organizational Behavior*, 16, 487–495.

AIJ: Architectural Institute of Japan.
JSCE: Japan Society of Civil Engineers.

Index

Abelson, J. 276
Adams, J. S. 172, 194, 293
advantage 25, 49, 58, 69, 82, 93–6, 98, 100–4, 109, 111, 117, 137, 240, 242, 246–7, 250, 279, 292
  area 94, 96
  of forgiveness 114–16
Alicke, M. D. 109
allocation 11, 15, 33–5, 41, 51, 52, 55–6, 58, 59, 61, 67–9, 85, 88, 93–104, 108, 129, 171, 173, 187, 192, 194, 292
allocation principle 35, 41, 51, 93
alternating offer game 97
Aoki, S. xvi, xx, 239, 248, 256, 293, 294
Aoki, T. xv–xvi, xx, 211–12, 216–20, 224–6, 233, 236
apology 111, 117, 121–2
attraction
  group 178–9, 181–2, 188, 191
authority 6–9, 14, 19, 33, 61, 67, 79, 82, 108, 139, 173–6, 186, 189, 195, 198, 276

Baba, K. 218, 276
Bandura, A. 138–9, 141–2, 144, 146
bargaining set 96
Batson, C. D. 120–1
bidding value 100–3
Blount, S. 55, 65
Brewer, M. B. 129, 178–9
Brickman, P. 161–3, 214, 225

Brockner, J. 197, 207
Brown, R. 111, 155, 158, 178

capability 93–4
centre as benefit zone 247
Christianity 76, 82
citizens' forum 272, 279, 282, 285, 289
citizens' panel conference 265, 267–8, 270–5, 277–9, 281, 282, 284–5
civic referendum 268, 270, 275, 282, 284
civil proceedings 23–5
Cloke, K. 112–14
collective identity 256, 261
Colquitt, J. A. 192, 195, 198, 203
commitment hypothesis 43
commons theory 241, 261–2
compatibility of justice and forgiveness 119
conference
  citizens' panel 265, 267–8, 270–5, 277–9, 281–2, 284–5
  stakeholder 265–6, 268, 271–5, 277, 279, 285
  hybrid participatory 268
conflict resolution 6, 24, 90–1, 110, 125–6, 190, 201
consensus-building 264, 280–1
  legitimacy of 277, 280, 282–3, 287
cooperative behaviour 179
corporate 28–9, 31, 172
costs of forgiveness 117, 126

covariance structure analysis 145

dehumanisation 140–3
dehumanising label 141–6
democracy 80, 88, 127, 241, 245–6
deservedness 85–90
Deutsch, M. 55, 85, 87, 172
De Cremer, D. 7, 176, 184, 190
De Dreu, C. K. W. 70
Dienel, P. C. 266–7, 271, 279
disinhibition
 moral 138
distributive justice 3, 9, 10, 18–19, 32–3, 34, 93, 107, 194–5, 198, 199, 240, 243–4, 246, 262
Doi, T. 153, 156
Dovidio, J. F. 129, 133–6
dual group identification 183–4

educational background 34, 42–5, 48–50, 198
effort principle 52–3
egalitarian 93–8, 100, 104, 128, 131, 133–4, 137, 292
empathy 33, 111–12, 137–8, 259
enlightenment effect hypothesis 49
Enright, R. D 115–18
environmental justice 239–42, 244–7, 261–3
 as distributive justice 241
 in the community 241, 262
 participatory democracy-oriented 245–6
 utilitarian 241–2
environmental planning 264–5, 268, 288, 290
environmental racism 240

environmental sociology 239–42, 244–6, 262–3
equilibrium 94, 101–3, 109, 111
equity theory 172, 194, 293
equivalent allocation 98
expert 274
 forum 274

fairness
 distributive 55, 59–60, 64, 66–8, 84, 172
 heuristic theory 194
 interactional 55, 61, 63, 66–7, 108
 management 207
 procedural 7, 33, 55, 59, 61, 66, 68–9, 72, 85, 172–7, 183–91, 265, 269, 276, 282–5, 287–290
 restoration 4
 subjective 90–1
fair process effect 206
Falk, A. 59, 64, 68
favourableness of outcome 9, 27
feasible 94, 96
Fehr, E. 59–60, 64, 69
Festinger, L. 161–2, 166–7
Folger, R. 61, 173–4, 195, 206, 214, 217, 225
forgiveness 107, 110–12, 114–26
 advantages of 114–16
 compatibility with justice 119
 costs of 117, 126
 hollow 112
 motivations for 115
 true 112
formal procedure 55, 61–2
framing 248, 254, 256, 261, 292
Frijda, N. 108
Fujii, S. 212, 216–7

Fujikawa, Y. 75–7, 79–80
Fukuno, M. xi–xii, xix, 18, 21, 55, 58, 61–2, 65, 67, 70–1, 217–18
functional evaluation 15–16

Gaertner, S. L. 129, 133–6
general public 264–9, 273, 276, 279, 282–6, 288
Gong, L. 154–5
Greenwald, A. G. 154
group-oriented behaviour 5, 7, 9–12, 19, 29, 31
group attraction 178–9, 181–2, 188, 191
group identification 5, 171, 177–91
  dual 183–4
group membership 85, 87, 89, 177
group process 175
group value model 174–5, 183, 189
group values 7
guilt 113, 117, 121, 123–4, 141
Güth, W. 58

Hara, J. 35, 39, 291
Heine, S. J. 149–52, 155–6, 158–9, 167, 169
Hirose, Y. xvii, xx, 264, 269, 271, 283, 286, 289
Hobbes, T. 78–9
Hoffman, E. 62
Honda, H. 263
hybrid participatory conference 268

Ikeda, K. 240–2, 244–5
image of society 37
immutability beliefs 19, 21

information
  disclosure of 265
  provision of 265, 276–9, 282, 285, 287, 289
informational justice 198–201
instrumental model 5–6
intentionality 64, 65, 66, 68, 69
interpersonal justice 30, 33, 198–203
interpersonal relationship 111–13, 116, 126, 193

Jackson, J. W. 135, 178, 181–2
job satisfaction 11
judicial system 25, 26, 27
justice 4–11, 13–19, 22, 25–34, 69, 72, 74–84, 88–92, 107–9, 117–26, 133, 140–1, 192–207, 239–48, 256–65, 291
  compatibility with forgiveness 119
  environmental 239–47, 261–3
  informational 198–201
  interpersonal 30, 33, 198–203
  moral 120, 121, 123, 126
  restoration of 110, 118, 122, 125
  transcendent 77
  universal 242, 261
  workplace 192
justice bond 4–5, 10–13, 19, 27, 30–1
justice elite 77
justice violation 108
justification 4, 67, 76–7, 95–8, 104, 123, 135, 142, 240, 292
Just World Belief (JWB) 4

Kahneman, D. 56, 292

Index

Kajita, T. 243
Karlsruhe 264–5, 268–84, 287–9
Karlsruhe participatory project 268, 277
Karremans, J. C. 111, 119–20
Kellen, R. C. 122
Kidder, L. H. ix, 91
Kitayama, S. 149–50, 152, 156–7, 168, 170
Kramer, R. M. 63–4, 179, 213, 217
Kumagai, T. xiv, xix, 171, 185
Kurman, J. 153–4

lack of autonomy 193
legitimacy 74, 77, 82, 88, 182, 240, 256–61, 276–7, 280–3, 287
legitimacy of consensus-building 277, 280–3, 287
Leventhal, G. S. 6, 61, 218, 276
life-environmentalism 241, 246, 261–2
Lind, E. A. 6, 24, 28, 61, 66, 174–6, 179, 191, 194, 213, 217–19, 224, 265, 276, 283
Loewenstein, G. S. 55, 67

Mabuchi, R. 37, 42
Macrae, C. N. 129–31
macro-level 17–19
Markus, H. R. 149, 152, 156, 170
mathematical induction 102–3
Matsuda, M. 222, 270
McCullough, M. E. 109–12, 114
mental health 192, 196
Mikula, G. 87
Miyano, M. 41, 53,

Miyauchi, T. 241
Moorman, R. H. 5, 11, 30, 61, 197
mental health 192, 196
moral disinhibition 138
moral justice 120–3, 126
movement frame 248, 251, 254, 256, 259
Muller, S. ix, 91
multi-stage auction game 100–4
Mummendey, A. 137

Nakayachi, K. 216
Nash 95–6, 98, 101–2, 292
natural right 78, 80, 82, 257
need to belong 176, 184
negative resource 87

occupational 17–19, 34–5, 38, 40, 45, 199
Ohbuchi, K. ix–x, xii–xiii, xv, xviii–xix, 3, 5, 14–29, 31–2, 62, 65, 67, 70–2, 91, 107, 110–12, 114, 120, 124, 126, 144, 148, 185, 217–18
Opotow, S. 138–40, 144
orientation
  competitive 55, 69–70
  individualistic 69–70
  social value 69–70

participative climate 197, 199, 203, 205–6
participatory conference model 276, 287
  procedural fairness of 269, 276
participatory democracy-oriented environmental justice 245–6

passive environmental injustice 241, 244, 246
Patristic philosophy 76–7
perceived organisational support 199
performance 12, 29, 82, 86–7, 199–201
Perloff, L. S. 164
perpetrator–victim structure theories 246
plan effectiveness 286–7
planning cells 264, 266, 271, 275, 278, 279, 281
Plato 75–7, 82–3
polis 75
political establishment 45
position of victim 117
prerequisites for procedural fairness 276, 278
pride 5, 7, 12–16, 28, 29
primary goods 93–4
principle
 social 74, 83, 87–9, 120–1
pro-group attitudes 5– 9, 19, 28–30
procedural fairness
 of participatory conference 269, 276
 prerequisites for 276, 278
procedural justice 3, 5–9, 15–19, 24–34, 108, 171, 194–5, 198–9, 202, 207, 264, 276, 283, 287
protest 21–2, 29, 248–54, 257, 259, 262–3, 294
prototype 177, 181–2
provision of information 265, 276, 278–9, 282, 285, 287, 289
psychological debt 122–3
public-opinion poll 36–7

public acceptance 264–5, 269, 283, 286–9
public participation 264, 269–71, 275, 277–90
public recruitment 267, 277

qualification 84–5, 89

racism
 environmental 240
random selection 267, 277, 281
Rawls, J. 77, 80–3, 93–4, 239, 243–4, 262
realistic group conflict 173
rebound effect 129, 131–2
reciprocity 109, 116
regional 17–19, 75, 247, 250, 262–3, 294
reinforcement 86
relational factors 6, 7, 9, 26, 30, 33, 67
relational model of authority 175–6
representativeness 265, 276, 277, 281–9
resource allocation 10, 32–3, 35, 55, 58–9, 85, 88–9, 93, 95, 98, 101
respect 7, 9, 18, 29, 33, 67, 73, 91, 94, 128, 175, 179, 183, 190, 199
restoration of justice 110, 118, 122, 125
retribution 107, 109–11, 117–18, 120–6, 139, 174, 184–5
Rosenbaum, M. E. 180
Rousseau, J-J. 78–81, 83
Rubinstein, A. 97

St Augustine 76, 83
St Augustine 76, 83

Saitō, Y. 44–5, 47, 52–3, 239, 291, 293
scenario experiments 60, 176
Schmitt, M. 121
Schwartz, S. H. 119, 154
self-definition 182–3
self-evaluation 174, 176
self-interest 4–6, 24–8, 32, 55–7, 61, 67, 70–1, 80, 112, 117
self-justification hypothesis 50
self-regarding 95
Sen, A. xii, 93–4
sense of unfairness
  due to a specific attribute 40–4, 48, 51
  in general 40–5, 51
shifting the environmental burden outside 247
Shklar, J. 244–5, 262
sincerity 120
Smith, G. 3, 7, 58, 62, 70, 110, 120, 135, 150, 175–9, 181–2, 185, 213, 219, 224, 264, 266–7, 276
social comparison 32
social consciousness 34–5, 39
social contract theory 77–9
social decision 5, 74
social dilemma theory 242–3
social evaluation 35–41
social exchange theory 173
social harmony 89, 91, 108, 121, 126
social identity theory 11, 174, 177–8, 183
social injustice 21–2, 251–2, 256–7, 262–3
social order 24, 76, 79, 88, 89
social principle 74, 83, 87, 88–9, 120–1

social resources 33–5, 48, 50–1, 86, 89, 117, 122, 125, 128
social stratification xviii, 34–5
SSM Survey 38–43, 46, 51, 53, 291
stakeholder 265–6, 268, 271–9, 285
stakeholder conference 265–8, 271–9, 285
state 3–4, 12, 14–19, 21–2, 28–31, 33, 75–83, 85, 89, 110, 136, 190, 194, 206, 245, 249–52, 254–6, 258–9, 261–3, 272, 284–5, 287
Straub, P. G. 60
stress 192–7, 199, 203, 205–7
stressor 193–5
St Augustine 76
sub-game perfect equilibrium 97, 101–4
Suls, J. 165–6
Survey of Civil Litigants 25

Takada, N. xiii–xix, 107, 110, 112, 114, 124, 126
Takata, T. xiv, xix, 149–50, 156–63, 166, 168
Thibaut, J. 3–10, 12, 16, 18, 24, 28–9, 32–3, 58, 61, 66, 172–6, 179, 190, 194, 213, 217–19, 224, 265, 276, 283
third party 23, 96, 185
Tominaga, K. xi, 34, 38, 40, 42
treatment 5–10, 14, 21, 28–9, 32–3, 36, 59, 61, 63, 66, 68, 73, 76, 83–8, 108–9, 119, 128, 134, 171, 176, 179, 183, 188, 195, 207, 242, 291, 293
Triandis, H. ix, 13, 150, 153
trust 6, 8–10, 21, 23, 27, 78, 88, 91, 175, 197, 199, 200, 203

turnover 192
Tyler, T. R. 3–10, 12, 16, 18, 24, 28–9, 32–3, 58, 61, 66, 172–6, 179, 190, 213, 217–19, 224, 265, 276, 283

ultimatum bargaining 55–70, 292
Umino, M. ix, xi, xix, 34, 36, 41–5, 47,53, 242–3, 291, 293
uncertainty management 194
unfairness 3, 6, 34–50, 53, 59, 61, 68, 73, 82, 91, 107, 135, 187, 190, 194, 240, 243, 245–6, 248, 251, 291
  due to education 48–50
universal justice 242, 261
urban planning 272, 279
utilitarian 4, 8, 10–17, 25, 28, 31, 239, 241–3
  environmental justice 241–2
utilitarianism 93
utility function 93, 96
utility set 94

Van den Bos, K. 194, 217
veil-of-ignorance 81
vengeance 108–10, 117, 119–20, 124
Vidmer, N. 108

Walzer, M. 241
Wegner, D. M. 130, 131
well-being 23, 110, 179–80, 192, 242
Western thought 74–5, 82, 84
Wheeler, L. 166–7
work motivation 192
Worchel, S. 144
workplace justice 192

Yai, T. 222
Yasuda, S. 39